Moving Words

The explosive growth of dance studies over the past decade has led to controversies on a host of fundamental issues, from how dance is to be analyzed and interpreted to dance's place in culture and history. The contributors in *Moving Words* take up these issues, their diverse views reflecting the conceptual clashes of a field in dynamic transition. At the same time, the authors examine the broader questions of gender, class, ethnicity, nationalism, and cultural exchange within the context of bodily practice.

Essays address topics such as the representation of the black male body on the concert stage, gender performativity and subversion in Mark Morris's dances, race and gender in Martha Graham's *American Document*, and historical revisions of the "oriental" dance. Throughout the book, contributors consider ethnographic, feminist, cultural, and literary theory in relationship to penetrating analyses of the body in motion. *Moving Words* gives historians, critics, and students of cultural and performance studies essential insights into the key issues of dance and society, while at the same time documenting critical thought in the making.

Gay Morris is a dance and art critic whose work has appeared in numerous journals and periodicals, including *Dance Chronicle*, *ArtNews*, and *Art in America*. She teaches dance history at Sonoma State University, California.

Moving Words

Re-writing Dance

Edited by
Gay Morris

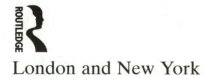

London and New York

First published in 1996
by Routledge
11 New Fetter Lane, London EC4P 4EE

Simultaneously published in the USA and Canada
by Routledge
29 West 35th Street, New York, NY 10001

Routledge is an International Thomson Publishing company I(T)P

Typeset in Times by
Keystroke, Jacaranda Lodge, Wolverhampton

Printed and bound in Great Britain by
Biddles Ltd, Guildford and King's Lynn

British Library Cataloguing in Publication Data
A catalogue record for this book is available from the British Library

Library of Congress Cataloguing in Publication Data
Moving words : re-writing dance / edited by Gay Morris.
     p.   cm.
   Includes bibliographical references and index.
   1. Dance criticism. 2. Dance—Philosophy. 3. Dance—History.
 4. Dance—Social aspects. I. Morris, Gay, 1940– .
 GV1600.M68   1996
 792.8—dc20   95-39924
                                                        CIP

ISBN 0–415–12542–1 (hbk)
ISBN 0–415–12543–X (pbk)

To my mother, Eileen Overhulse Dufur
and to my husband, Gordon Gamsu

Contents

Figures

Contributors

Gwen Bergner teaches American literature and women's studies at Middleburg College. Her work has appeared in *PMLA* and *Discourse*.

Judy Burns writes about social and cultural histories of dance and music in the United States. She has taught at Brooklyn College and New York University. She is an editor of *Women and Performance: A Journal of Feminist Theory*.

Thomas DeFrantz is on the faculty of the Music and Theater Arts Department of Massachusetts Institute of Technology. His writing has appeared in the *Encyclopedia of African-American Culture and History* and the *Village Voice*. He earned his Ph.D. from New York University's Department of Performance Studies.

Joan L. Erdman is professor of anthropology and humanities at Columbia College, Chicago, and a research associate on the Committee on Southern Asian Studies at the University of Chicago. Her book *Patrons and Performers in India: The Subtle Tradition* was published in 1985.

Mark Franko is associate professor of dance history and performance studies at the University of California, Santa Cruz. Founder and director of the dance company Novantiqua, his choreography has recently been shown in Berlin, New York, and Los Angeles. His latest book is *Dancing Modernism/Performing Politics* (1995).

Constance Valis Hill is a choreographer and dance historian who coordinates the dance history program at the Alvin Ailey School of American Dance. Her writing has appeared in *Dance Magazine*, *Dance Research Journal*, and the *Encyclopedia of African-American Culture and History*.

Stephanie Jordan is professor of dance studies at Roehampton Institute London. Her books include *Striding Out: Aspects of Contemporary and New Dance in Britain* and *Parallel Lines: Media Representations of Dance* (co-edited with Dave Allen). She is currently writing a book on music and ballet, supported by a research grant from the Radcliffe Trust.

Amy Koritz is an assistant professor of English and co-director of the Program in Cultural Studies at Tulane University. Her work has appeared in numerous journals including *Theatre Journal, Genre*, and *Modern Drama*. Her book *Gendering Bodies/Performing Art: Dance and Literature in Early Twentieth-Century British Culture* was published in 1995.

Susan Manning is an associate professor of English and Theater at Northwestern University. Her book, *Ecstasy and the Demon: Feminism and Nationalism in the Dances of Mary Wigman*, won the 1994 De la Torre Bueno Prize. She is currently researching the staging of race and gender in American modern dance.

Carol Martin is an assistant professor of drama at New York University. She is the author of *Dance Marathons: Performing American Culture in the 1920s and 1930s*, which was awarded the De la Torre Bueno honorable citation in 1995.

Gay Morris is a critic and historian whose work has appeared in numerous journals and publications, including *Dance Chronicle, Art in America*, and *ArtNews*. She teaches dance history at Sonoma State University.

Miwa Nagura is a dancer, writer, and a native of Japan. Her dance reviews have appeared in the *Village Voice*. She currently works in television in New York.

Sally Ann Ness is an associate professor of dance at the University of California, Riverside. Her recent book, *Body, Movement, and Culture: Kinesthetic and Visual Symbolism in a Philippine Community*, won the 1993 De la Torre Bueno prize for the year's most distinguished work of dance scholarship.

Nicole Plett has worked as a dance critic and arts writer since 1979. She is the editor of the 1988 illustrated anthology, *Eleanor King: Sixty Years in American Dance*. In 1991 she joined the research staff of the Program in Women's Studies at Princeton University.

Leslie Satin teaches at New York University and the State University of New York/Empire State College. She is a member of the editorial board of *Women and Performance: A Journal of Feminist Theory*. She is also a choreographer and dancer.

Marcia B. Siegel is a dance critic and a member of the resident faculty of the Department of Performance Studies, Tisch School of the Arts, New York University. Her books include *Days on Earth: The Dance of Doris Humphrey, The Shapes of Change: Images of American Dance*, and three collections of dance writings.

Helen Thomas is senior lecturer in sociology at Goldsmiths' College, University of London. She is editor of and contributor to *Dance, Gender* *and Culture* (Macmillan 1993) and author of *Dance, Modernity and Culture* (Routledge 1995). At present, she is the project director of *Unequal Pay for Equal Parts*, a survey of actors/actresses in the theater and the media. She is also editing a new collection entitled *Dance in the City*.

June Adler Vail is associate professor and chair of the Department of Theater and Dance at Bowdoin College. Her work has appeared in numerous publications, including *Dance Research Journal*. She also publishes extensively in Swedish magazines and journals and is author of *Cultural Choreographies: Dance in Sweden Today*.

Acknowledgments

The creation of a book always involves many people, but an anthology multiplies those numbers many times over. Above all, I want to thank the authors of *Moving Words*, who not only contributed superb essays but who also generously gave advice and assistance on many parts of the project. I also thank Routledge editor Julia Hall, her assistant Alison Foyle and desk editor Claire Chandler who handled everything from routine queries to catastrophes with calm efficiency. In addition, I would like to thank Ann Daly, Ann Murphy, Lynn Garafola, Jacqueline Shea Murphy, Peter E. Romo, Jr, Heather Zwicker, and David Vaughan for their help and advice. Also Barbara Fougier and John Bennett, for essential technical support, and Pamela Romo, for holding the fort.

The editor and publishers are grateful to the following photographers, dance companies, and institutions for permission to reproduce photographs and diagrams: New York Public Library for the Performing Arts, Dance Collection; New York Public Library for the Performing Arts, Theater Collection; the Willard and Barbara Morgan Archives; University of Chicago Press; the Fine Arts Museums of San Francisco and the Nijinska Archives; Johan Elbers; Beatriz Schiller; Jack Mitchell; David Vail; James Klosty; Tom Brazil; Arthur Elgort; Jane Comfort and Company; and the Mark Morris Dance Group.

The editor and publishers also thank the following authors and publishers for permission to reproduce written material: Miyabi Ichikawa, to reprint material from his books and articles; the Cunningham Dance Foundation, Inc. to reprint material by Merce Cunningham; *The New Republic*, to reprint material by Roger Copeland; and Routledge, to reprint material by Judith Butler. Grateful thanks also go to Karen Gerald Wheaton for permission to publish an excerpt from personal correspondence to Bill T. Jones. The extract from "The Nonsense of an Ending: Closure in Haydn's String Quartets" in *Musical Quarterly* by George Edwards, 1991, is reproduced by permission of Oxford University Press. The extract from *Reading Dancing: Bodies and Subjects in Contemporary American Dance* by Susan Leigh Foster, Copyright © 1986 The Regents of the University of California, is reproduced by permission of University of California Press.

Extracts from *Modern Dance Forms in Relation to the Other Modern Arts* by Louis Horst and Carroll Russell, 1961, and *The Modern Dance* by John Martin, 1993, are reproduced by permission of Princeton Book Co. An extract is reprinted by permission of the publishers from *Philosophy in a New Key: A Study in the Symbolism of Reason, Rite, and Art* by Susanne K. Langer, Cambridge, Mass.: Harvard University Press, Copyright © 1942, 1951, 1957 by the President and Fellows of Harvard College; renewed in 1970, 1979 by Susanne Knauth Langer; 1985 by Leonard C. R. Langer. Extracts are also reprinted with permission of Simon & Schuster, Inc. from the Macmillan College text *Feeling and Form* by Susanne K. Langer, Copyright 1953 Charles Schribner's Sons; copyright renewed © 1981 Susanne K. Langer.

1 Introduction

Gay Morris

Shifting ground seems best dealt with by movement.

Susan Suleiman

Dance scholarship is developing at a pace never experienced before, its energy and creativity recalling the choreographic outpouring of the 1960s and 1970s "dance boom" years. A decade ago we could expect little more than a handful of forward-thinking work each year. This has expanded into a flood of books, articles, conferences and symposia on dance history, criticism, and theory. Nor has growth meant simply an increase in the flow of material being produced. Ann Daly remarked in 1991 that dance scholarship had both the potential to enrich what we already know of dance "as an aesthetic, cultural, and political phenomenon," and to lead it "into a more prominent place in the humanities and social sciences" (1991: 50). The potential Daly saw a few short years ago is being realized in a host of studies that puts the dancing body at the center of research cutting across a multitude of disciplinary lines. This new dance scholarship is flourishing on both sides of the Atlantic, as witnessed by such recent conferences as "Written on the Body," sponsored by the American Dance Guild in 1994 at Denison University in Ohio; a multi-disciplinary conference devoted to the work of Sir Frederick Ashton entitled "Following in Sir Fred's Footsteps" at the Roehampton Institute, London in 1994; "Engendering Dance: Engendering Knowledge: Dance, Gender and Interdisciplinary Dialogues in the Arts," presented by the Congress on Research in Dance (CORD) at Texas Women's University in 1994; and "Border Tensions," held at the University of Surrey in 1995, which explored the changing character of discourse in dance.

This book, in part, is a response to the current work in dance studies and the interest it has occasioned. At the same time the collection comes to grips with many of the issues that inevitably arise in a field in dynamic transition. At the moment virtually every aspect of dance is being tested and debated. Basic questions are being asked, including how is dance to be defined? What should our methodology be? Are there dangers in taking on concepts from other fields, or will new thinking spark insights and set dance more firmly in the intellectual mainstream? Where should dance research be focused – on enlarging the foundation of the field where many areas have hardly been touched, or on placing dance within the wider context of culture? Does dance need to establish its own turf, with a strong disciplinary bent? And if it doesn't, will more established disciplines colonize what until recently has been a marginalized terrain, and use it opportunistically? What is dance's relationship to language and is it possible to deconstruct the dichotomy between body and mind that has worked to dance's disadvantage for so long? Some of these questions reflect more general shifts in the arts and humanities as modernist methods and concepts have given way to postmodern ones. But others are peculiar to dance itself, where for much of this century history was anecdotal, theory underdeveloped, and criticism rudimentary. For dance, then, the situation is not only one in which the field is being rethought, but where it is sometimes being conceptualized in detail for the first time.

One of the persistent questions within dance studies concerns the boundaries of dance itself. In a paper presented at the 1992 conference "Choreographing History" at the University of California, Riverside, art historian and theorist Norman Bryson advocated as inclusive a definition as possible.

> Opening the viewfinder to maximum and moving the definition of dance from "ballet" to "socially structured human movement" may be vertiginous as an opening move, but it has heuristic advantages in showing how local and limited our sense of dance tends to be. Furthermore, the maximally capacious definition is typically found to lose its amorphous character the moment it is actually put into practice, and the potentially infinite space of analysis it opens up (the study of *any* human movement?) fills with remarkably finite objects.
>
> (1992)

Bryson goes on to say, echoing Roland Barthes, that what would seem to be wide-open definition is actually bound by the conventions and institutions that authorize fields of meaning so that in practice only a small part of the arena of possibilities is activated.

Although dance research has long been devoted to more than "ballet," recent studies in movement ranging from parades and pageants to wedding rituals and strip shows suggest that dance scholars are pushing far beyond traditional western definitions of theater dance. Wherever the borders of dance are drawn, they must be open and flexible rather than rigid and closed in order to cope with the "shifting ground" of a postmodern world. Under the circumstances it would seem wise to keep in mind the defining assumptions – one's own and those of the dance being studied – when considering any dance form, even the most familiar. Carol Martin's essay in this book, "High Critics/Low Arts," deals with problems that arise when differing notions of what constitutes dance are not acknowledged. In this case, a modernist model of autonomous art clashes with another set of expectations. Martin examines Arlene Croce's written condemnation of Bill T. Jones's *Still/Here*, a work that focuses on people with life-threatening illnesses. Croce confronts the piece from a modernist perspective, where movement is the essential element of dance. Martin says, however, that *Still/Here* is not meant to be looked at solely in terms of movement. Movement is simply one element of a larger whole that characterizes much postmodern performance. Within the parameters of postmodernism, dance may include images of people with real illnesses, it may include overt politicization and it may be utilitarian as well as aesthetic in aim. Certainly, differing concepts of what dance can or ought to be contributed to Croce's attack on Jones's work. In quite a different vein, Sally Ann Ness considers definition in her essay, "Observing the Evidence Fail: Difference Arising from Objectification in Cross-Cultural Studies of Dance." She examines the work of several anthropologists who attempted, unsuccessfully, to create objective models that would bridge cultural boundaries to account for differing ways of identifying dance. Despite the creation of some extremely elaborate systems, these researchers were frustrated by cultural assumptions at odds with the dance they were studying.

If scholars are reassessing ways in which dance may be defined, they are heatedly debating how dance can best be analyzed and interpreted. This latter issue has emerged as one of the most prominent in current dance studies. As in most fields, dance scholarship has tended to move in an inter-disciplinary direction, which has included the use of theory from a variety of sources, as well as an approach that embeds dance within culture (Novack 1990, Daly 1991, Banes 1994). However, while many dance scholars may be looking to analytical and interpretive models outside the field, others contend that dance must have its own methodology. Jane Desmond makes a persuasive argument for such a need:

> If we are to talk about dancing in anything other than the broadest terms, we must be able to do close analysis of dance forms, just as we might of literary texts. While most scholars have spent years developing analytic skills for reading and understanding verbal forms of communication, rarely have we worked equally hard to develop an ability to analyze visual, rhythmic, or gestural forms. As cultural critics, we must become movement literate.
>
> (1993–4: 58)

Desmond suggests systems such as Laban Movement Analysis as a starting point. In particular, she points to the analytical work of Irmgard Bartenieff as being a possible model for cross-cultural comparisons of movement lexicons. In the 1960s and 1970s Bartenieff used Laban Movement Analysis as a basis to describe and compare movement patterns in particular communities.

Although Desmond is specifically speaking of cross-cultural analysis in her appeal for a dance methodology, Marcia B. Siegel uses Movement Analysis as a lexical foundation for analysis of many different kinds of dance, including western modern dance. Her essay in this book, "Visible Secrets: Style Analysis and Dance Literacy" is an example of how she employs this methodology. Siegel examines Paul Taylor's *Speaking in Tongues* by observing the structure of the work and of individual dances, and by looking at the piece in the context of Taylor's previous work and the quotations he makes from other choreographers, in particular Martha Graham. She also notes the literary devices such as puns, metaphors, double entendre, and irony, which he translates into movement. Throughout her analysis, Siegel takes a formalist approach, depending primarily on movement as a way of creating meaning. "Almost everything [I do]," she says, "comes from the dance itself, not from what the artist or anyone else says about it" (1995). She is not primarily interested in looking at the way Taylor's work functions within the purview of culture, nor is she concerned with bringing concepts from other disciplines to bear on dance. She has argued for this position on the basis of the dearth of material that exists on dance compared to other disciplines. She believes it is only by closely examining the dance itself that we can form a foundation for further scholarship.

Stephanie Jordan also counts her project as formalist in her essay "Musical/Choreographic Discourse: Method, Music Theory, and Meaning." In noting dance scholarship's move toward interdisciplinarity and away from structural analysis, she contends that a separation between the two is not necessary. Her essay attempts to integrate dance and cultural theory, and to open a dialogue between them. "Indeed," she says, "in-depth analysis of structure is seen to make its own special contribution to an understanding of the 'broader picture.'" She points out that music scholars, like many dance scholars, worry that the individual work will disappear if it is too deeply lodged in social and cultural theory, and she documents ways in which music has solved the problem with a balance of formal analysis and social thesis. She then outlines her own method for analyzing dance through a combination of analysis derived from dance (beginning with music visualization as theorized by Ruth St. Denis and Doris Humphrey and including Bartenieff) to which she has added musical concepts. She then goes on to analyze several works by Ashton, Balanchine, and Humphrey, showing in each case how the structure of the dance can reveal elements of social meaning.

Although the use of cultural theory in the analysis and interpretation of dance has already made a considerable impact, there is doubt in some quarters about the efficacy of so cerebral an element being interposed between the dance and spectator. Siegel speaks about the experience of observing dance as "fundamentally intuitive, visceral, and preverbal. Only later do we bring words, categories, systems to rationalize what we've experienced. If a dance doesn't suggest meaning by its performance, no amount of intellectualizing can put meaning into it" (1992: 30). Mark Franko takes a different view, looking at theory not only as a tool that can productively open up and expand interpretive possibilities but which also can come to grips with dance expression, key to the visceral, intuitive aspects of the viewing experience of which Siegel speaks (Franko 1995: 75–92). In his essay "Five Theses on *Laughter After All*" Franko touches on the point of communication between work and viewer through Paul Sanasardo and Donya Feuer's 1960 dance, *Laughter After All*. Drawing on the post-Marxian theory of Georg Lukács, Franko suggests that only when experience is mediated, that is, attached to "the net of social relations," is it given life. Immediate (unmediated) experience is reified or abstract because it is disconnected from interpretation. Franko finds a useful contradiction in Lukács's theory, which he sees played out in Sanasardo and Feuer's dance. Franko structures his essay around a written "re-eventing" of *Laughter After All* gained through memory, interviews with the choreographer and dancers, visual material such as photographs, and his own experience as a dancer in Sanasardo's company (although he did not perform in *Laughter After All*). He alternates this reconstruction with his commentary, which deals with a number of issues including, provocatively, the possibility of a performable critical theory.

Franko is a choreographer and scholar who, like dancer/theorist Susan Foster, has long been interested in dance's relationship to language. In 1986 Foster published *Reading Dancing: Bodies and Subjects in Contemporary American Dance*, a pioneering work that drew on semiological models to create a theory of dance analysis. That same year Franko's first book, *The Dancing Body in Renaissance Choreography* appeared, which employed semiology as a means of analyzing Renaissance dance forms. Franko (1995) and Foster (1995) were among the first to dissolve the destructive polarization between dance and the word, and they continue to play a leading role in scholarship in this area.

Leslie Satin is another choreographer/scholar who works toward a closer connection between language and dance. She applies both literary and feminist theory to the notion of autobiography in Meredith Monk's *Education of the Girlchild*. Her essay is a kind of written choreography that moves in and through the various manifestations of *Girlchild*, engaging the work in a manner at once highly personal and analytically rigorous. Using concepts ranging from Nancy Chodorow's psychoanalytic theory of individuation to Wayne Koestenbaum's erotics of opera, she traces what she sees as Monk's alternative form of autobiography, one which is based within community and that can "question, rethink, or displace individualistic models of selfhood." At the same time, Satin points up ways in which she, as a spectator, interacts with the work, creating parts of another auto-biography in the process.

If Mark Franko believes theory is so basic to dance it can become an integral part of it, Helen Thomas, in her essay "Do You Want to Join the Dance?: Postmodernism/Poststructuralism, the Body, and Dance," warns of an uncritical application of theory by dance scholars. Looking closely at the methodology of several writers, she critiques their use of feminist theory, in particular Laura Mulvey's theory of the male gaze. Some scholars, she writes, have failed to contextualize Mulvey's work within the framework of Lacanian psychoanalysis and thus have collapsed the psychic subject into the social subject. At the same time, Thomas acknowledges the appeal of poststructural, postmodern, and feminist theory for dance scholars (including herself) since it brings new attention to the body and to culture, "which, in turn, offers dance . . . the possibility of a new found [academic] legitimacy, an authorial voice that it had not achieved hitherto." Her plea is for a rigorous use of these new tools.

Susan Manning, while also warning of the dangers of flattening out and oversimplifying gaze theory, has spoken of the great value feminist theory in general holds for dance scholarship. In a paper on feminism and dance she wrote,

> feminist theory addresses a range of issues relevant to dance historians – the social construction of gender and sexuality, the dynamics of specta-torship, the cultural coding of the female body – feminist theory provides dance historians a myriad of perspectives from which to think through these issues in relation to the dancing body.
>
> (1994: 331)

Although Manning points out that the larger goal of her own research is not necessarily to apply feminist theory to dance history, but to write dance history into cultural history, feminist theory nonetheless plays an important role in her work. In her essay for this collection, "*American Document* and American Minstrelsy," she is concerned with both race and gender in Martha Graham's 1938 work. She brings a feminist perspective to a number of aspects of the dance, including Graham's introduction of a male performer into her hitherto all-female company. Manning notes that the women in *American Document* generally stood for universal humankind until Erick Hawkins appeared onstage, at which the women reverted to the particular and he became the universal.

A number of essays in this volume similarly profit from feminist analysis. Gwen Bergner and Nicole Plett turn to the nineteenth century in their essay, "'Uncanny Women and Anxious Masters': Reading *Coppélia* Against Freud." In one of the best-loved ballets in the classical repertory, they locate a number of male cultural anxieties, including the fear of female deception and agency. To elucidate their argument they look closely at E. T. A. Hoffmann's story "The Sandman" on which *Coppélia* is based, and at Freud's essay "The Uncanny," in which he analyzes Hoffmann's tale. The authors' aim, they say, is "to show that the similarity between the horrific literary story and the comedic ballet resides in gender issues rather than atmosphere." They then argue against Freud's exclusion of the figure of woman as the basis of male anxiety in the story, countering with the contention that both in "The Sandman" and *Coppélia*, woman is at the heart of male fear.

Judy Burns also turns a feminist eye on the nineteenth century, in this case nineteenth-century middle-class America. In her essay "The Culture of Nobility/The Nobility of Self-Cultivation" Burns looks at Delsartism, including women's adoption of Delsarte principles and practice both to reinforce their status and to gain a small degree of freedom. At the same time, these women attempted to remake their bodies to conform to an impossible ideal modeled on classical Greek sculpture, a phenomenon not vastly different from women today attempting to emulate the bone-thin, computer-manipulated images of young models in fashion magazines.

One complaint often heard among dance historians is that with so much emphasis placed on broader issues, not enough attention is being given to basic research within the field. Unlike long-established disciplines, dance history is filled with gaps and thin areas where we know very little. Yet focusing solely on dance may further ghettoize and disempower it. Further-more, as Janet Adshead-Lansdale has remarked, "the old idea, that history discovers the 'truth,' has to be replaced by a multiplicity of accounts, constructed in the present" (1994: 20). Certainly dance historians and critics are in a more complicated position than scholars in fields where a thorough-going canon exists which can be supported or criticized. A canon does exist in western theater dance, a primarily modernist one, but it is far from thorough. So the challenge for dance scholars today is to strike a balance among several, sometimes conflicting, needs.

Dance scholars also labor under the supposed stigma of an ephemeral form, one that lacks a complete text. However, part of the perception of dance's ephemerality may be due to the fact that less work has been done in the field than, for example, in literature or architecture. With the current stream of new research, dance may begin to look richer and less mysterious. As for not possessing a complete text, no performance medium does. Susan Manning's comments on the pros and cons of scholarly work in a performance form are instructive:

> An event bound in space and time, a performance can be read only through its traces – on the page, in memory, on film, in the archive. Each of these traces marks, indeed distorts, the event of performance, and so the scholar pursues what remains elusive as if moving through an endless series of distorting reflections. But this pursuit leaves its own sort of illumination, and that illumination is what the scholar records, in effect penning a journal of the process of inquiry.
>
> (1993: 12)

This evocative description of the illumination to be found in inquiring after an elusive art form sounds anything but unrewarding. And in its elusiveness, its very instability, dance would seem to be an exemplary field for scholars working amidst the indeterminacy of the postmodern age.

If dance is elusive, it is also, as Manning says, clearly "bound by space and time." The impetus to place dance within the larger framework of culture has been going on since the 1970s (Kendell 1979, Shelton 1981, Souritz [1979] 1990), but for a number of years this trend moved against a tide of formalist-dominated critical and historical writing in which it was believed the vast majority of meaning resided in movement alone. As recently as 1989, when Lynn Garafola's pathbreaking *Diaghilev's Ballets Russes* appeared, it was attacked in the pages of *The New Yorker*, where dance criticism is strongly formalist based. Garafola viewed one of the most thoroughly canonized eras in western dance history through a prism of feminist and ideological theory, placing the *Ballets Russes* within a social, political, and economic framework that moved far beyond the theater footlights.

If Garafola met resistance to a dance research that was culturally based, others encountered simply indifference. Helen Thomas, in her essay in this volume, documents her attempts as a sociologist in Britain in the early 1980s to merge sociological methodology and theory with dance. When she began, she says, there was very little to go on and no visible support for such a project. Today, of course, the situation has changed markedly and the social sciences play an important role in dance research. Dance ethnologists, in particular, were among the first to question the origins and history of dance promulgated by well-known dance writers like Agnes de Mille, Walter Sorell, and John Martin (Williams 1977, Kealiinohomoku 1983 [1970]) and by sanctioned authorities such as Curt Sachs (Youngerman 1974). Ethnographic theory from Clifford Geertz to James Clifford and Renato Rosaldo has proved particularly valuable to dance scholars, who have benefited from recent concepts of societies as dynamic, flexible, and unpredictable, and of social analysis as processual.

The concept of the researcher as a participant/observer has been particularly helpful to dance scholars. Many researchers are dancers themselves, and how to deal with the scholar's own dancing body is often a subtext of their work. The stigma of performance, prevalent in much of the academic world, is a problem that dancer/scholars work out in a number of ways. Cynthia Novack, an anthropologist, was an active participant in the research for her book *Sharing the Dance: Contact Improvisation and American Culture*. Susan Foster reads academic papers and dances at the same time, probably to the surprise of some of the more staid members of the academic community. Mark Franko directs his own company, Novantiqua, choreographing his ideas of danced theory within a historical context, often of Renaissance and Baroque dance. June Adler Vail was a member of the dance group Borovčani, which is the basis of her essay "Balkan Tradition, American Alternative: Dance, Community and the People of the Pines." As a participant/observer using a processual approach to research, she asks how dance created culture for a group of Americans who formed a Balkan dance troupe in Maine in the late 1970s. For this collection of enthusiasts, the dance defined a sense of intimacy and inclusivity as well as group structure at a particular moment in time.

Sally Ness takes a more theoretical approach to anthropology in her essay, "Observing the Evidence Fail," in which she examines four well-known cross-cultural studies on dance ethnography, to find that none is successful at creating an "objective" method for describing dance of a different culture. She does not consider this distressing; rather she concludes that cross-cultural differences can only be fully appreciated "when the limits of their translation are defined through interactive failures." If western observers fail to objectively describe dances of other cultures, Miwa Nagura argues that the same failure occurs traveling in the opposite direction. In this volume, she makes the first translations from Japanese into English of the work of critic Miyabi Ichikawa, who devoted much time to writing on the choreography of Merce Cunningham in the 1970s. Nagura describes the difficulties Ichikawa faced in writing across the boundaries of language as well as those of society and culture. Both Ness and Nagura ask questions about how dance is analyzed and interpreted, not simply to critique methodologies but to productively gain insights into how cultures function.

Joan Erdman defines a host of issues facing dance scholars in her essay "Dance Discourses: Rethinking the History of the 'Oriental Dance.'" Tracing the interweavings of Indian and western "oriental" dance in this century, she goes on to ask how scholars in both the East and West can proceed in the twenty-first century. Edward Said's *Orientalism* has clearly had a profound effect on thinking on all sides. For Indian scholars, Erdman asserts, the challenge lies in rewriting their own history with the knowledge that the dance they have received is not as purely ancient as once thought. For western scholars, the question is how to present and maintain the increasingly intricate dialogue between East and West. Erdman warns against using only current theoretical trends to reconstruct the past, which, she says, may produce structures as mythical as those scholars attempt to critique. She pleads for contextualization, for considering the connections between events in their own times, which will give a fairer picture of the past and greater freedom for dance's development in the future.

Embedding dance in culture makes it possible for scholars to address a number of issues that in a more formalist-dominated era would be of little interest. Among these are questions of gender, race, class, and the body, all of which now loom large in dance research. A number of the essays here confront issues of gender, from the feminist informed work of Burns, Satin, Manning, Bergner and Plett, to Thomas DeFrantz's study of the ways African-American men have depicted themselves on the concert stage and my own analysis of gender in Mark Morris's *Dido and Aeneas* and *The Hard Nut*.

Four of the essays deal specifically with racial issues. Constance Valis Hill examines ways in which white choreographers in Paris in the 1920s responded to jazz music and dance, arguing that the work of black artists was a defining element in the development of dance modernism. DeFrantz revisits the dances of several black male twentieth-century choreographers, particularly Alvin Ailey, in "Simmering Passivity: The Black Male Body in Concert Dance." He finds that many African-American men created images of themselves on stage that both reinscribed and subtly shifted long-standing stereotypes of the black body. Amy Koritz, like Manning, examines race in Martha Graham's work, although her project is quite different. She views several of Graham's dances in conjunction with Eugene O'Neill's plays to determine how race acts as an element in the definition of a national subjectivity. This inquiry serves as a means of illustrating the kind of intertextual project that is possible when a scholar is working within the framework of cultural or performance studies. Race and class are implicitly linked in the work of DeFrantz, Hill, Koritz and Manning, however Judy Burns turns specifically to issues of class in her essay on Delsarte. She finds that Delsartism helped define prevailing bourgeois attitudes towards a number of social concerns, including the increased presence of immigrants and worries over the physical weakening of the dominant class through excessive "brain work."

Dance research always deals in some way with the body, but one of the challenges now is how to mend the dichotomy between mind and body that has marginalized dance for too long. In *Sharing the Dance*, Cynthia Novack writes of the dangers of continuing to separate mind and body in dance research.

> Researchers who wish to redress the imbalance of mind over body may react by positing the body and movement as the primary reality. . . . They maintain the dichotomy between mind and body by emphasizing the body alone. Some researchers tend to look only 'at the movement itself' ('just describe what you see,' they say) as if the body, movement, and mind were independent entities, scarcely connected to social and cultural ideas, interactions, and institutions.
>
> (1990: 7)

Certainly much of the impetus for reconciling dance and language, as well as for investigating dance's relationship to society, comes from an attempt to deconstruct the mind/body dichotomy. *Moving Words* contains numerous examples of work that supports this viewpoint, from essays by Satin and Franko to DeFrantz and Vail.

With so much intertextual, interdisciplinary work going on, the question arises once again of boundaries. Is there a danger that dance will be lost, that it will simply dissolve into a broad-based cultural studies or be consumed by scholars in established fields? Amy Koritz tackles these questions in "Re/Moving Boundaries: From Dance History to Cultural Studies." Koritz, viewing the issues from the standpoint of an English professor whose research is in dance, argues that dance will grow stronger from associations within a larger framework of cultural or performance studies. The question, as she sees it, is whether it is more dangerous to insist on a narrow purview for dance with the chance of continued marginalization or to move out and meet competition head on.

Related to this question is another, equally important one. As dance scholars roam far afield in their research methods and subject matter, do they, themselves, risk losing the "dance" in dance studies? Linda Hutcheon writes in *A Poetics of Postmodernism*, "what I want to call postmodernism is fundamentally contradictory, resolutely historical, and inescapably political" (Hutcheon 1988: 4). Since dance scholarship is flowering in a postmodern era, it is unlikely to reverse itself and settle into comfortable modernist formulas where boundaries are fixed and forms pure. Yet as Hutcheon and others have pointed out, postmodernism is not modernism's opposite, postmodernism works from within the system it critiques. This may be why so many dance scholars show no great enthusiasm for evicting formal analysis as an outmoded artifact of modernism. Marcia Siegel's plea not to forget dance in the rush to embrace theory does not fall on deaf ears for the excellent reason that formalism is what pried dance scholarship out of the mire of anecdote and myth in the first place. On the contrary, the issue is more how to develop ways of doing research that, as Stephanie Jordan suggests, can accommodate both formal analysis and social thesis in innovative and satisfying ways. At the same time, scholars must heal the damaging dichotomies that have cut dance off from intellectual discourse, as if the mind were not somehow engaged in dance, nor the brain a part of the body. This is a kind of nostalgic primitivizing that will no longer do.

The fractiousness of current dance studies is not solely the result of modern–postmodern tensions. It also comes from another source: the exuberant creativity of the field. Dance studies is growing but has not yet been fully defined; the drag of institutionalization lies in the future. What you read here emerges from a laboratory of experiment where questions are being asked but answers are still up in the air and rich with possibility. The essays in *Moving Words* both contribute to and celebrate this important moment in dance.

BIBLIOGRAPHY

Adshead-Lansdale, J. (1994) "Border Tensions in the Discipline of Dance History," in *Proceedings of the Society of Dance History Scholars*, (February 10–13) Brigham Young University, Provo, UT.

Banes, S. (1994) "Criticism as Ethnography," in *Writing Dancing in the Age of Postmodernism*, Hanover, NH: Wesleyan University Press.

Bryson, N. (1992) "Dance History and Cultural Studies," *Choreographing History*, conference held at the University of California, Riverside, February 16 and 17.

Daly, A. (1991) "'What Revolution?' The New Dance Scholarship in America," *Ballett International* (January): 49–50.

Desmond, J. (1993–4) "Embodying Difference: Issues in Dance and Cultural Studies, *Cultural Critique* (Winter): 33–63.

Foster, S. (1986) *Reading Dancing: Bodies and Subjects in Contemporary American Dance*, Berkeley: University of California Press.

—— (1995) *Choreographing History*, Bloomington: Indiana University Press.

Franko, M. (1986) *The Dancing Body in Renaissance Choreography*, Birmingham, AL: Summa Publications.

—— (1995) *Dancing Modernism/Performing Politics*, Bloomington: Indiana University Press.

Garafola, L. (1989) *Diaghilev's Ballets Russes*, New York, Oxford: Oxford University Press.

Hutcheon, L. (1988) *A Poetics of Postmodernism: History, Theory, Fiction*, London: Routledge.

Kealiinohomoku, J. ([1970] 1983) "An Anthropologist Looks at Ballet As a Form of Ethnic Dance," in Roger Copeland and Marshall Cohen (eds) *What is Dance? Readings in Theory and Criticism*, Oxford: Oxford University Press.

Kendall, E. (1979) *Where She Danced*, New York: Alfred A. Knopf.

Manning, S. (1993) *Ecstasy and the Demon: Feminism and Nationalism in the Dances of Mary Wigman*, Berkeley: University of California Press.

—— (1994) "Borrowing from Feminist Theory," in *Proceedings of the Society of Dance History Scholars*, (February 10–13) Brigham Young University, Provo, UT.

Novack, C. J. (1990) *Sharing the Dance: Contact Improvisation and American Culture*, Madison: University of Wisconsin Press.

Shelton, S. (1981) *Divine Dancer: A Biography of Ruth St. Denis*, Garden City: Doubleday & Company, Inc.

Siegel, M. B. (1992) "The Truth About Apples and Oranges," *The Drama Review* 32, 4: 24–30.

—— (1995) Unpublished notes on methodology.

Souritz, E. ([1979] 1990) *Soviet Choreographers in the 1920s*, Sally Banes (ed.), Durham, NC: Duke University Press.

Suleiman, S. (1992) *Subversive Intent: Gender Politics and the Avant Garde*, Cambridge: Cambridge University Press.

Williams, D. (1977) "The Nature of Dance. An Anthropological Perspective," *Dance Research Journal* 9, 1: 42–4.

Youngerman, S. (1974) "Curt Sachs and His Heritage: A Critical Review of World History of Dance with a Survey of Recent Studies That Perpetuate His Ideas," *CORD News* 6, 2: 6–17.

Part I

Strategies, Analytical and Interpretive

2 Musical/Choreographic Discourse
Method, Music Theory, and Meaning

Stephanie Jordan

For excellent reasons, dance academe today is eager to site dance within an interdisciplinary framework, to raise the level of dance scholarship itself by drawing on academic traditions of longer standing, and, by engaging with what is valuable to dance from other disciplines, to lessen the risk of reinventing the wheel. The major thrust of this interdisciplinarity has been towards contextual studies of dance, using models from literary criticism and the social sciences, in a direct response to the key raging academic debates of our times. In recognizing their responsibility to take part in such debates, dance scholars have tended to distance themselves from the analysis of movement structures, those formalist aspects that some would say are special to dance. This essay suggests that this separation does not necessarily have to happen: it attempts to integrate these apparently oppositional perspectives, dance theory and broad cultural theory, and to open a dialogue between them. Indeed, in-depth analysis of structure is seen to make its own special contribution to an understanding of the "broader picture." I also suggest that the discipline of musicology provides one very useful methodological model for this formalist area of analysis. There is the proviso that one cannot apply every musical idea unreservedly to dance. Nevertheless, in the analysis of dances, especially those without plot, music provides obvious parallels for thinking, or, at least, appropriate starting points for argument. Its theories also relate directly to my focus of study, musical/choreographic relationships, a study that draws together my two areas of specialist training.

A secondary subject of this essay is an outline of my analytical method devised for examining relationships between music and dance. The nature of the method is discussed, the limitations as well as potential of music theory in relation to it, and also the process of development and refinement of the method through application, in other words, the dialogue between the method and the material to which it is applied.

First, however, it is useful to consider the recent upheavals within the discipline of musicology itself. In the 1970s, musicology was still embedded in its positivist phase, at a time when this way of thinking was long outmoded in the humanities and social sciences. Musical works were regarded as autonomous, unified entities, aching for strictly abstract, non-contextualized formal analysis. I refer to western musicology – ethnomusicology was a different matter.

There were major changes in musicology during the 1980s, and anthropological/ethnomusicological thinking was by this time proving highly influential. There was the admission of the centrality of the beholder's share, the subject's role in relation to text, and an insistence on music's capacity to mean and to move. "Emotion and meaning are coming out of the musicological closet," wrote Rose Subotnik (1988: 88), and the seminal book *Music and Society* (1987) edited by Richard Leppert and Susan McClary countered the ideology of autonomy to propose a musicology that was socially informed. Today music is once again discussed in terms of its expressive qualities and semiotic conventions, but, even in its most "abstract" forms, music has become both narrative and socially circumscribed discourse. Thus music, like dance (both are latecomers), has entered the broader cultural debates of our times.

All this happened after the work of Heinrich Schenker (1935), whose theory dominated the 1950s and 1960s, and who proclaimed the values of unity, wholeness and goal-oriented construction, all as a foregone conclusion. Then there was the important work of Leonard B. Meyer (1956, 1973), Eugene Narmour (1977) and David Epstein (1979), who, countering Schenker, gave weight to implications in musical structure, which may only be partially realized, and thus to ambiguity rather than certainty. As for the issue of pure form becoming narrative, this is a concept common to other "representational" arts. In novels, paintings, theater and television, conventions and stylistic devices are seen to have narrative meaning, as much as the level of character and story. Janet Wolff maintains that meaning is constructed at a variety of levels and that the ideology of the arts is contained in their devices and stylistic aspects as well as in their "stories" (1987: 11–12). Indeed, it is for this reason that Raymond Williams insists on the need for analysis of form in literature, for instance, of the soliloquy form in English Renaissance drama, it too being a social practice (1981: 142).

An interesting adjunct to these changes in musicology is the new self-awareness of musicologists. They see that not only the music itself but the theory and theorists attached to it, as well as performance practice, are a product of context and period. Acontextualization itself can now be seen as a contextualized phenomenon.

Not surprisingly, the new musicology has been strongly criticized from some quarters. It has been pointed out that the individual work is in danger of disappearing in this move towards viewing music entirely in social or narrative terms. There is also the possibility of over-simplification. Margaret Murata provides the amusing example of connecting chromatic half-steps with the Thirty Years War (1988: 84). Yet, whether choosing to undertake it or not, the new wave of musicologists does not deny the value of formal analysis – there are many statements to this effect – provided, that is, that it is now kept in dialogue with meaning. McClary herself integrates analysis of a Bach Brandenburg Concerto and Cantata with her consideration of Bach within social politics (1987). The two instrumental forces in the Concerto metaphorically enact the interactions between individual and society. The Cantata evokes an imaginary compatibility between orthodox and pietist religious positions.

In his provocative article, "The Nonsense of an Ending: Closure in Haydn's String Quartets," (1991) George Edwards provides a far more detailed consideration of formal issues than McClary, while at the same time exposing Haydn to the dialogic, polyphonic models of Bakhtin's Menippean satire and carnivalization. He calls for a dialogue between the two positions of purely musical analysis and social thesis: "The only thing more deadening than formalism's attempt to treat music as a closed, self-referential system would be the attempt to understand music in entirely social and narrative terms" (1991: 250).

Then, Subotnik undertakes an analysis of the tonal schemes of Mozart's last three symphonies and finds the composer highly critical of conventional eighteenth-century syntax (1991: 98–111). She proposes that, while Mozart had not relinquished his optimistic belief in Enlightenment rationality, his belief was troubled, and he opened the way to a new world view which challenged this interpretation of rationality, and even challenged the ultimate rationality of reality. There are a number of musicologists now working against the old model of closed, unified systems, focusing on what is disjunctive and dissonant. Edwards's Haydn, for instance, is a master of collage, even a post-modernist. In his critique of recent Brahms research, Kevin Korsyn insists on the ideological motivations that are behind our making exaggerated claims for unity, which, he says, is a direct reflection of the consoling, comfortable unity and stability that we want for ourselves (1993). He illustrates how Brahms's work can be seen as open and ambiguous, creating a more fragmented sense of self. Yet, all these writers draw on the means of formalist analysis to unmask its claims.

My main point now is that music has this formalist tradition of analysis to be used or unmasked: theories of climax, mobility/closure, thematic analysis, studies of the individual parameters of rhythm, harmony, and melody. It has a major analytical history to be self-conscious about. That, I believe, is a particular power of musicology for dance scholars. Some fine formalist analysis of dance has been undertaken: like, for instance, the examination of Doris Humphrey's *Water Study* by Martha Davis and Claire Schmais (1967), using the principles of Labananalysis through which to locate the structural outlines of the piece; the choreutic (spatial) analysis of dances by Valerie Preston-Dunlop, again developing from Laban's theory (1981); and, using Labanotation scores, the comparative study of the "syntactical" styles of Balanchine and Tudor by Muriel Topaz (1988). Other valuable work is referred to later in this paper. However, dance scholars do not yet have an analytical tradition to compare with that of music. I believe that dance analysis can often be greatly enriched by formalist musicological models, leading to an enriched network of inter-pretations, other, no less important, connections between dance forms, their narrative value and social/artistic context.

In this spirit, integrating ideas from the "new" musicology as well as from formalist music theory, I will give an outline of my analytical method first, devised to examine relationships between music and dance, and then provide examples of my findings and of further questions that the method poses.

The analytical method was devised as part of my doctoral research into the work of Doris Humphrey (Jordan 1986) (her series of "music dances," from the early music visualizations to her final work, *Brandenburg Concerto* – first movement, 1959), but this method has now been tested in application to the work of ballet choreographers such as Balanchine and Ashton. The method continues to develop, but it has immediately proved relevant beyond Humphrey's work.

Departure points were established music visualization theory, taken from an article by Ruth St. Denis (1925), and Humphrey's own theory, documented in a variety of written sources stemming from the middle and late periods of her career (the main source is Humphrey, 1959). Visualiz-ation theory suggests close relationships between dance and music in terms of, for instance, rhythm, movement level and pitch, dynamics, and legato and staccato. Humphrey suggests more varied structural relationships between music and dance than music visualization, including oppositional, contrapuntal relationships. However, in order to reveal the complexity of the works analyzed, it was necessary to reorganize and expand from these theoretical beginnings. What evolved was a method that derived from two strands, visualization and rhythmic counterpoint. The augmentation of rhythmic concepts was crucial, and it is here that I am especially indebted to music theory.

A list of categories was drawn up within which rhythmic organization could be analyzed and then the respective organizations of music and dance were compared. Existing dance rhythmic theory was incorporated, beyond that of St. Denis and Humphrey. Margaret H'Doubler's *Movement and its Rhythmic Structure* (1946), together with Humphrey's own account of rhythm, was the most thorough examination to date of rhythmic structure in dance. Also considered was anthropological research which involves establishing a basic unit of duration for dance and, following that, a strati-fication/hierarchical structure for dance (Kaeppler 1972, the International Folk Music Council Study Group for Folk Dance Terminology 1974, Giurchescu 1984, and Bartenieff *et al.* 1984). However, many of the dance categories were borrowed from music theory, which has developed a much more thorough detailing of rhythmic theory concepts and of their interrelation. Music theory has also considered the expressive capacities of rhythmic structure: its capacity to build and defeat expectations, to contribute to mobility and closure, tension, and relaxation.

The rhythmic categories were divided into four strands:

1 Categories related to duration and frequency of incident: event (the term coined here for the basic unit of duration in music and dance), beat, rubato/breath rhythm, speed.
2 Categories related to stress (relative accentuation of incident).
3 Categories related to the grouping of sounds or movements, the inter-action of 1 and 2.
4 Energy pattern, the pattern of tensions and relaxation, of climaxes and releases, in a piece.

In relation to the manifestation of the basic unit of duration and of dynamics, fundamental differences between music and dance had to be established. The question of the rhythmic organization of the unit that expressed duration, for instance, is more problematic in dance than in music. Music is built from discrete units. Units of sound and units of duration concur: sound impulses begin both. This is not the case in dance, where impulses often do not occur at the beginning of a movement. Impulses can occur at the onset of motion after stillness, but they can also occur within a continuum of motion (for example, within a swing) or at the end of a continuum of motion. However, it is the impulses still that determine our grasp of duration in dance. We perceive time in dance as divided into units (events) that begin with an impulse or onset of stillness, regardless of the beginning of a movement. This conclusion is reflected in the conventions used in notating dance rhythm. For example, in the Labanotation of steps, a step symbol does not begin with the initial leg gesture, but rather with the moment when the foot first touches the ground (Hutchinson 1977: 491), an approximation of the moment of perceived impulse.

Now, other concepts will be discussed in connection with actual dance examples. These are all concepts relating to grouping, or the linking of movements, notes, or beats into units.

Metrical hierarchy and hypermeter are established concepts in music theory related to metrical grouping, the grouping of beats (Cone 1968: 79–80). If the fundamental metrical unit is the bar (measure), which groups beats into twos, threes, fours, and so forth, with a metrical accent at the beginning of each group, similar grouping and accenting can be seen to occur at sub-bar and broader levels, the hierarchy extending from the length of the smallest note or movement values. Thus, a bar of 6/8, which is a grouping of two beats (dotted quarter-notes), contains two sub-bar groupings of three eighth-notes. Then, several 6/8 bars may group together into hypermeasures, each bar lasting one hyperbeat. Metrical accents become stronger the broader the level in the hierarchy; in other words, they are strongest at the hypermetrical level.

Hypermeter does not always exist in music and dance, but when it does, it is usually regular and perceived either as a result of regular events every two or more bars or successive groups of events, each group of equal length (two bars or more), most strongly when dance and musical material repeats, exactly, or with an element of variation. Hypermeasures can sometimes indicate units that we might call phrases. In dance, the concept already has a direct parallel: the counts that dancers use in rehearsal often demonstrate the grouping of bars into a hypermetrical structure, and those counts are sometimes marked in dance scores.

A first example is Balanchine's *Valse Fantaisie* (1969), in which hypermetrical play, here, counterpoint between music and dance, might be said to provide the main substance and liveliness. Glinka's hypermeter is already a little wayward for waltz music, as he builds generally in three-bar as opposed to the more normal four-bar hypermeasures, thus creating larger phrases of either twelve bars (3+3+3+3) or eight bars (3+3+2). There are many passages in which Balanchine takes the rhythmic mobility a stage further, setting two-, four-, and occasionally five-bar hypermeasures against the music. An example is the opening step for the small corps, which, at its first appearance, not only keeps to the three-bar hypermeasure of the music but also visualizes pitch contour with a développé, tombé, and temps levé in attitude. That especially close relationship between music and dance established, Balanchine sets out to loosen it. After a transition, the opening musical theme returns (bar 52) and the soloists enter, now with a five-bar variation on the opening three-bar step, incorporating a lift. The Labanotation score counts out the five-beat hypermeasure. But, throughout *Valse Fantaisie*, the rhythmic lines of dance and music are in flux, meeting occasionally, only to set up their independent lines again. The effect here is of a constant blurring of structural seams, of music and dance playfully swimming through each other. In harder, biting-pulse Balanchine, like the last movement of *Stravinsky Violin Concerto* (1972), hypermetrical incongruence suggests rather the effect of a brittle, polyphonic machine at work.

Then, where there is incongruence at a lower level, the metrical level, the more rapid succession of crossing accents can create the effect of two voices racing or chasing each other. There is a simple example in the woman's solo in Balanchine's *Tchaikovsky pas de deux* (1960). The music remains in 2/4 time, but a repeated dance combination introduces a passage of 3/4 time against the music: piqué, close in fifth position, entrechat trois, the passage lasting for six bars of music. The step seems to aerate the solo, freshening it after a series of square, regular rhythms.

In Humphrey's *Passacaglia and Fugue in C minor* (1938), counterpoint, together with concurrence (music visualization), between music and dance is seen to contribute to the broad energy pattern of the work. Humphrey uses Leopold Stokowski's flamboyant orchestration of this work. There is one passage of hypermetrical incongruence: in the Passacaglia, the repeating Processional step establishes a three-bar hypermeasure, riding over the standard eight-bar unit of each Passacaglia Variation: the Processional consists of three steps forwards, a slow extension to the side, like a large breath, ending in a second position plié (the exhalation), lower arms crossed one above the other in front of the chest (the familiar position photographed as the frontispiece of Humphrey's *The Art of Making Dances* [1959]). There are several passages in which meters are incongruent (4/4 or 9/8 in the dance against 3/4 continuing in the music) or where the choreography disregards the musical meter. These passages create the maximum rhythmic tension in the work and become more frequent as the work progresses: two passages in the Passacaglia, five in the Fugue. To return to the point about energy pattern, rhythmic tension is a contributing factor to energy growth while music visualization is also a significant feature reinforcing passages of high energy or climax. Together, the extremes of concurrence and independence also generate excitement through contrast. They alternate at the final, major climaxes of Passacaglia and Fugue. Reinforcing the musical climax, already so exaggerated in the Stokowski orchestration, confirms the idealistic and "vitalist" nature of Humphrey's statement.

The next example is concerned with the concept of grouping in terms of events (notes or moves) rather than beats, drawing from the psychological principle that we group elements together in terms of their proximity and similarity and perceive rest, contrast, and repetition as factors of separation between groups. Here again, dance can borrow from music in terms of factors that determine grouping, but some factors are special to dance: dance has some of its own ways of establishing mobility and closure. Recent important research by Anita Donaldson into the choreutic parameter of dance suggests, for instance, that the vertical dimension has stronger closural implications in many styles than the other two dimensions (1993: 187).

It is important also to consider the concepts of downbeat and upbeat grouping. Concerned with the relationship between notes/moves and meter, these are groupings that begin at or before the bar-line respectively.

In the following Ashton example, the effect can be seen of shifting relationships between dance steps and the bar-line and overlapping groupings of music and dance. This is Ashton's Sarabande solo created in 1968 for the Prince in *The Sleeping Beauty* (inserted before he sees Aurora in the vision scene). The interaction between grouping and meter is a rhythmic feature often discussed by music analysts – meter shapes the group dynamically – and it is an extremely subtle and important feature of this dance. Dance steps recur here, but most often in a new dialogue with the music: that changes and inflects differently what we see for a second time. The dance opens with a développé posé fondu in arabesque followed by a step back. The high point is the strong, downbeat of the bar, and the step back occurs on the second beat of the bar – this is downbeat grouping in both music and dance. The moment is soon repeated, but this time, the posé fondu occurs on the third, final beat of the bar, and the step back meets the downbeat of the next bar. This is upbeat grouping in both music and dance.

There are many other examples of steps that shift in rhythmic and dynamic tone in this way, the pas de bourrée, fouetté sequence that follows soon afterwards, for instance. Then, there is Ashton's delayed response to the return of the opening musical theme at the halfway point. That downbeat beginning in the music is the final reverberation of the previous dance phrase. Ashton's new phrase then begins a beat later than that of the music, like an afterthought reawakening after a slight indulgence in time.

There are also constant shifts in speed and energy in this solo, which are not suggested by the music, sharpnesses in steps, brisk switches of the arms, little stuttering jumps and, after the slow opening, a broad, sweeping, galloping step that begins the last section of the dance and which takes the Prince in a big circle round to the back of the stage. The pressure against the structure and dynamic implications of the music only heightens the sense of change.

Now, considering the effect of these devices, we come to a point about meaning, how constantly shifting musical/choreographic relationships contribute greatly to the instability of mood and ambiguity in this short solo: impetuosity, uncertainty, searching, gentleness, nobility, thoughtfulness. The effect is of continuous change, process rather than finished, stabilized statement. This seems to be very much a twentieth-century expressiveness, although I am not ready to claim that my analysis here demonstrates any direct, literal link between dance and social context or ideology.

There are similar dynamic discrepancies produced by different means in Ashton's *The Dream* pas de deux (1964), sharpnesses, as in the sissonnes into arabesque near the end, which create a dangerous restlessness against musical resistance. Here, too, these sharpnesses are in character, suggesting the willfulness and impetuous power of Oberon and Titania.

Turning to the issue of establishing a style, my method proved revealing about the various aspects of a choreographer's musical/choreographic style. In the case of Humphrey, it revealed an evolving style. Across her career, Humphrey continued to develop more independent musical and dance structures, including, for instance, different kinds of metrical incongruence. Yet, contrary to her comments about ridding herself of music visualization techniques, Humphrey referred to such techniques throughout her series of music dances. Then, looking broadly across whole movements or works, as an example of a stylistic feature, similar patterns of concurrence and counterpoint between music and dance were found to occur in the two works analyzed from Humphrey's middle and late career: the *Passacaglia* and *Brandenburg Concerto*. The method also readily proved itself capable of highlighting difference between choreographers. For instance, Balanchine's work is much more pulse- and meter-driven than that of Ashton, who, in turn, develops a counterpoint in dynamic terms, the energy of dance accents and phrases often pulling in a different direction from that of the music. The method was also capable of revealing subtleties, for instance, that it is nonsense to say simply that Balanchine's work visualizes the music. It does, but often it does not. However, the method demonstrated at the same time that the choreographers selected for analysis were all part of an age of complex and dissonant rhythms, at least in the terms of western high art. Furthermore, it also demonstrated the importance of musical/choreographic style *per se*, in providing patterns of change through a work, in contributing to the statement as a whole, the complete picture. Musical/choreographic style is a source of meaning.

The analytical method was first tested out on Humphrey's *Passacaglia*, as a complex work with large proportions. But developing and applying the method was then, and continues to be, seen as a two-way process. In other words, while use of the method can be revealing about a work, application of it can also lead to its own refinement. *Passacaglia* itself suggested further ideas about the method, for instance that dance might simply reflect musical continuity, broken or continuous, rather than precisely duplicate the musical rhythm; or that similar rhythmic patterns in dance and music might not occur simultaneously, but might be separated by a gap in time. Humphrey's *Air for the G String* (1928) proposed that analysis should relate the body to two parts of the musical texture, the upper body to the breathing melody line, the stepping feet to the pulsating accompaniment. The coda of Balanchine's *Agon* (1957) suggested another dimension to the concept of speed in dance: speed in terms of shifting the viewer's eye across the stage, which contributes to climax here, the moment of the most manic machine vitality of the work (Jordan 1993).

There are a couple of other points to make about the circularity of procedure in the development and application of analytical method. First, seeing and hearing have generated methodological concepts, which in turn have generated seeing and hearing more and more distinctively, and more differently. Thus, the method continues to develop. Second, the method has its logical base, focusing on rhythm, a principle of organization common to music and dance, and drawing from the experience of the choreographers themselves (their theoretical statements). It also acknowledges that choreographers work with concepts and devices that are shared by our broader culture and through which we understand artistic experience: across the temporal arts, for instance, patterns of climax and dénouement, the hierarchy of structural units (phrases, periods, paragraphs, and so on), concepts of return as a method of closure (as in ABA musical form). But these points only emphasize the circularity: that the method is a product of its context, time, and ultimately, of myself.

As hinted at in the discussion of Ashton and Balanchine examples, I am now particularly interested in the "narrative" implications of formal devices. There was the reference to Edwards's paper, which proposes that Haydn constantly questions the attainability of closure, and to Subotnik's analysis of Mozart. And it is interesting that Ashton's Sarabande ends "open" and questioning, with an unsupported stretching into arabesque on demi-pointe as we hear the last note of the music. But there is also the particular form of closure that comes with return, repetition after a break, a sense of coming-home stability, resting the perceptions. Sonata form in music provides a useful example, with the exposition of contrasting material and tonalities, followed by a development section, followed by a recapitulation (more or less a return of the exposition, but with changed tonal organization), and a coda.

Dealing with sonata form structure, choreographers can choose to provide the most powerful sense of return, implied completion, by repeating the familiar steps and formations of the exposition with the music, from the point of recapitulation onwards; or at a later point in the recapitulation, by introducing merely some kind of variation on the familiar steps; or by making no clear reference at all to the steps that we saw in the exposition. It is all a matter of degree, and the choice can have a decisive effect upon our experience of closure.

Balanchine clearly saw some sonata form structures as more open for him than others (reference here is to the structure of a single movement within a multi-movement work). In *Ballet Imperial* (1941), Balanchine's treatment of Tchaikovsky's first movement does anything but reinforce its tripartite musical form with recapitulation, at least in the Royal Ballet version of the piece (Jordan 1993/4). This is a long movement, about twenty minutes in duration, quite difficult in terms of long-term legibility, in other words, of remembering back across the large span of the movement.

The exposition contains three theme groups (Figure 2.1): the curtain rises with the second theme, so there is no chance of recapitulating the dance at the moment of musical recapitulation. The development contains two cadenzas, one the entry of the main female soloist, the other a duet for her and her partner. When the musical recapitulation occurs, the corps simply continue with a step in the familiar diamond formation that has characterized the development, in other words, emphasizing continuity from this section. Then, crossing both second and third theme groups, there is a very long trio for the second female soloist and two men. The trio is like a new discrete entity, beginning in a new, quiet, strange mood for this ballerina, with two "new" solo men plucked from the corps. Finally, there is a short coda which rapidly reassembles some of the steps that we have seen before, but it seems inconclusive, a rushed ending, bringing back the full corps, but, of the soloists, the first ballerina alone.

My reading is that Balanchine was exploring the tension between the over-arching narrative, which is about the changing relationship between the first ballerina and her partner, and the three distinct frames (three musical movements) in *Imperial*, and he went on exploring this tension, at various times cutting the mime elements in the second movement and the *Imperial* decor. Certainly he keeps dance material compartmentalized

	EXPOSITION (200 bars)			DEVELOPMENT (302 bars)				RECAPITULATION (126 bars)			‖ CODA (40 bars)
MUSIC	1st theme	2nd theme	3rd theme	Piano cadenza I	Orchestra 2nd theme (first cut, Balanchine, 11 bars)	Orchestra 1st theme (var.) (second cut, Siloti, 24 bars)	Piano cadenza II (third cut, Balanchine, 20–22 bars)	1st theme	2nd theme	3rd theme	
DANCE	Curtain down Corps: 8 couples. 8 more women arrive.		2nd woman soloist and corps *	Corps circles. Men leave. 16 women < >	1st women soloist * 16 women < >	16 women < > 2nd woman soloist + 2 female sub-soloists, and 16 women. *	Duet: 1st woman soloist and partner. *	16 women < >	2nd woman soloist + 2 men *		Full corps (24). 1st woman soloist joins. *

Figure 2.1 *Ballet Imperial*: first movement. Diagram of movement and dance. The musical diagram shows the original Tchaikovsky structure: cuts by the arranger Alexander Siloti are indicated by a diamond formation (< >) on stage. * indicates passage for soloist(s)

© Stephanie Jordan 1993

within single movements. To this extent, he goes along with the three-frame principle. But my main point is that how he relates to the large musical structure, particularly with regard to return, is crucial to the relative effect of mobility or closure, and thus to narrative. In this respect, he seems determined to keep the first frame relatively open, to maintain a sense of evolution, of becoming. Not only this, but one might say that the late, emphatic weighting towards the second ballerina in the first movement leaves an effect of "dissonance" unmatched in the music: she is very much the "other," dressed too in black in Eugene Berman's designs for the Royal Ballet. There is another dissonance late in the recapitulation of the third movement, an athletic solo for the man, rather like an afterthought. Critics seem to have concentrated on the "positive" aspects of Balanchine's references to Petipa in *Ballet Imperial*: they have not alluded to these underside, deconstructive, aspects of the ballet. My point can be seen to relate closely to Korsyn's view of Brahms and Brahms research, which is referred to earlier in this essay: we have tended to seek the comfort of unified, closed forms.

Similarly, in *Serenade* (1934), there is the tendency to mask the straight emphatic return, dance with music, in favor of evolution and openness, even more emphatically expressed in this piece, which epitomizes the romantic sense of becoming.

We might contrast Balanchine's use of Bizet in *Symphony in C* (1948), of Mozart in *Symphonie Concertante* (1947), and of Bach in *Concerto Barocco* (1941). All these choreographies respect the convention of musical return and closure with far more regularity than *Imperial* or *Serenade*. In them, there is far more long-distance repetition of dance with music. But there is also a far greater tonal imperative for closure in baroque and classical music, and generally a greater period respect for convention (Bizet is, of course, looking back to the classical period here).

Can we rationalize these differences in Balanchine's approach? I have often heard the explanation that Balanchine repeated dance material because he was short of time or because he liked what he had made and wanted to see it again. Could we also suggest that Balanchine's choreography negotiates a relationship with the different sensibilities of different musical choices, as exemplified in their structures, mediated of course through his own understanding, and the performance practices that he experienced in Russia and later in the West?

This raises a final point, about the narrative of musical performance practice and its implications for dance. I am indebted here to Richard Taruskin's critique of the ideology of the Early Music movement (1988), its "authentic" ideals, which he places squarely in the nexus of modernist thinking, particularly the contemporary, anti-romantic Stravinskyian aesthetic. Thus Bach performance becomes increasingly dry, inelastic, and geometrical through the twentieth century, Taruskin's example being a series of recordings of the Fifth Brandenburg Concerto. This provoked my observation that *Concerto Barocco* (1941) and the Balanchine of *Barocco* are poised precariously on the border between the old vitalist and new modernist aesthetics. In the outer movements at least, Balanchine seems to have heard the dawnings of the new Bach and a new machine age for choreography. Listen to what Denby saw: "sure pulse . . . powerful onward drive . . . syncopated fun and sportive jigging . . . its coolness and its simplicity are not [yet] in the current fashion" (1986: 177, 201, 322). Most powerfully of all, he singles out the work as an especially good example of percussive, beat-emphatic choreography. He all but uses the word "jazz." Others since have certainly done so. This is the new, sewing-machine Bach with the neat, mathematical, metrical hierarchy of beat, hyperbeat and mini-beat. These are the terms of twentieth century rather than baroque music theory. Dancers map out different rates of beat simultaneously or at different times. It is significant that Balanchine replaced costumes with modernist practice clothes by 1951.

The Tchaikovsky and Bach examples discussed exemplify a number of the issues touched upon in this essay. Their scores can be seen to be mediated through 1930–40 dancers and musicians and through a choreographer. They are also subject to new cultural debates such as those in current musicology as it rethinks its past. And there is also the analytical method designed to examine structural relationships between music and dance, and which is open to development as it acts in dialogue with the very text to which it is applied. It remains for these perspectives to be integrated with others that may have nothing to do with music. Yet, this paper makes a case for the contribution of music, for examination of this one aspect in detail before looking again at the whole picture. The role of music is highly pertinent in certain kinds of dance work. Music offers theories of form and of the narrative of form that are invaluable to dance scholars, as well as a layer within the dance event itself that is an important and subtle source of meaning.

BIBLIOGRAPHY

Bartenieff, I., Hackney, P., Jones, B. T., Van Zile, J., and Wolz, C. (1984) "The Potential of Movement Analysis As a Research Tool: A Preliminary Analysis," *Dance Research Journal* 16, 1: 3–26.

Cone, E. (1968) *Musical Form and Musical Performance*, New York: W. W. Norton.

Davis, M. and Schmais, C. (1967) "An Analysis of the Style and Composition of *Water Study*," *Dance Research Annual* 1: 105–13.

Denby, E. (1986) *Dance Writings*, London: Dance Books.

Donaldson, A. (1993) "The Choreutic Parameter: A Key Determinant of Choreographic Structural Style," unpublished Ph.D. dissertation, Laban Centre for Movement and Dance, London.

Edwards, G. (1991) "The Nonsense of an Ending: Closure in Haydn's String Quartets," *Musical Quarterly* 75, 3: 227–54.

Epstein, D. (1979) *Beyond Orpheus*, Cambridge, MA: MIT Press.

Giurchescu, A. (1984) "European Perspectives in Structural Analysis of Dance," Report on the Third Study of Dance Conference, University of Surrey: "Dance, A Multicultural Perspective," 33–48.

H'Doubler, M. (1946) *Movement and Its Rhythmic Structure*, Madison, WI: Kramer Business Service.

Humphrey, D. (1959) *The Art of Making Dances*, New York and Toronto: Rinehart.

Hutchinson, A. (1977) *Labanotation*, London: Oxford University Press.

International Folk Music Council Study Group for Folk Dance Terminology, trans. W. C. Reynolds (1974) "Foundations for the Analysis of the Structure and Form of Folk Dance: A Syllabus," *Yearbook of the International Folk Music Council* 6: 115–35.

Jordan, S. (1986) "Music As a Structural Basis in the Choreography of Doris Humphrey," unpublished Ph.D. dissertation, University of London, Goldsmiths' College.

—— (1993) "*Agon*: A Musical/Choreographic Analysis," *Dance Research Journal* 25, 2: 1–12.

—— (1993/4) "*Ballet Imperial*," *Dance Now* 2, 4: 28–37.

Kaeppler, A. (1972) "Method and Theory in Analyzing Dance Structure with an Analysis of Tongan Dance," *Ethnomusicology* 16, 2: 173–217.

Korsyn, K. (1993) "Brahms Research and Aesthetic Ideology," *Music Analysis* 12, 1: 89–103.

Leppert, R. and McClary, S. (eds) (1987) *Music and Society: The Politics of Composition, Performance and Reception*, Cambridge: Cambridge University Press.

McClary, S. (1987) "The Blasphemy of Talking Politics in Bach Year," in R. Leppert and S. McClary (eds) *Music and Society: The Politics of Composition, Performance and Reception*, Cambridge: Cambridge University Press.

Meyer, L. (1956) *Emotion and Meaning in Music*, Chicago: Chicago University Press.

—— (1973) *Explaining Music*, Berkeley: University of California Press.

Murata, M. (1988) "Scylla and Charybdis, or Steering Between Form and Social Context in the Seventeenth Century," in E. Narmour and R. Solie (eds) *Explorations in Music, the Arts, and Ideas: Essays in Honor of Leonard B. Meyer*, Stuyvesant, NY: Pendragon Press.

Narmour, E. (1977) *Beyond Schenkerism*, Chicago: University of Chicago Press.

Preston-Dunlop, V. (1981) "The Nature of the Embodiment of Choreutic Units in Contemporary Choreography," unpublished Ph.D. dissertation, Laban Centre for Movement and Dance, London.

St. Denis, R. (1925) "Music Visualization," *The Denishawn Magazine* 1, 3: 1–7.

Schenker, H. ([1935] trans. E. Oster, 1979) *Der Freie Satz*, New York and London: Longman.

Subotnik, R. (1988) "Toward a Deconstruction of Structural Listening: A Critique of Schoenberg, Adorno, and Stravinsky," in E. Narmour and R. Solie (eds) *Explorations in Music, the Arts, and Ideas: Essays in Honor of Leonard B. Meyer*, Stuyvesant, NY: Pendragon Press.

—— (1991) *Developing Variations*, Minneapolis: University of Minnesota Press.

Taruskin, R. (1988) "The Pastness of the Present and the Presence of the Past," in N. Kenyon (ed.) *Authenticity and Early Music*, Oxford: Oxford University Press.

Topaz, M. (1988) "Specifics of Style in the Works of Balanchine and Tudor," *Choreography and Dance* 1, 1: 3–36.

Williams, R. (1981) *The Sociology of Culture*, New York: Schocken Books.

Wolff, J. (1987) "The Ideology of Autonomous Art," in R. Leppert and S. McClary (eds) *Music and Society: The Politics of Composition, Performance and Reception*, Cambridge: Cambridge University Press.

3 Visible Secrets
Style Analysis and Dance Literacy

Marcia B. Siegel

At the end of the twentieth century, the fields of dance history and dance criticism remain curiously stunted. While dance itself has made many original contributions to cultural life, the study and analysis of those contributions have been rudimentary. "History" is synonymous with the survey course, an endless recycling of a constructed lineage from the Greeks – or the Egyptians, or the cavemen – to ballet and modern dance. Criticism consists of the stereotypically despised yet sought-after judgment of individuals assumed to have power they don't really want and don't actually have. Thus narrowly defined, history and criticism for the most part make no real contribution to dance performance, nor do they significantly inform or complement each other. There is no intellectual infrastructure within the dance field, and – more shocking – no felt need for one.

Here's how mega-role-model Mikhail Baryshnikov reinscribed dance's alienation from the rationalizing process in a 1994 interview:

> I was never very interested in documenting or even recording my life as a dancer. I've made a few light entertainment programs: TV and video productions of classical pieces and Balanchine choreographies. That's all. I live in the present and don't think about the past or the afterlife. It doesn't bother me whether people remember me or my performances; it was never my aim to preserve my works. Neither is it possible; TV for instance is never able to give a truthful rendering of a production. . . .
>
> I don't like talking about my work. Either you've seen me dance or you haven't. You either liked it or you didn't. I don't believe that people would like to know why and how I dance a piece, or why I work with this or that choreographer. Dance is an ephemeral, a fleeting art. To describe this momentum, every movement on stage, in words is virtually impossible. I don't know myself every time, why a performance is good. I only sense that it is. This isn't false modesty, but I've never considered that it could be interesting to package dance in words.
>
> It's much more difficult to write about dance than about music or poetry. Neither rhyme nor style, rhythm nor score set the parameters. Dance is the most extraordinary of all art forms; whether we record it

on video, in words or in notation we can never pin it down. We can only
be witnesses; share the experience of dance when dance happens. This
unique moment when the eyes meet a movement in space, these seconds
when the eyeball reflects the images and they are flooded with feelings
. . . you just can't explain that . . .

(Baryshnikov in Christen 1994: 11)

As long as the dance profession is content to exist from day to newly
choreographed day, grounded in nothing more solid than glamorous
myths and unexamined pseudo-histories, the public won't have any reason
to share its self-regard as a primary component of culture.[1] What I want
to argue here, in building a critical history for one work by one choreographer, is that dance has an intellectual life as well as a temporal life.
Choreographers go to great lengths to conceal this aspect of creativity,
as if any suspicion of it would spoil the viewer's experience or somehow
render the dance invalid. The reasons why they do this are another great
unexplored dance mystery.

Paul Taylor has cultivated a persona as a faux-naif so as not to appear to
"know" very much about what he's doing. He has made many remarks like
those of Baryshnikov quoted above.[2] But in fact, his literary alter ego has
produced a splendid autobiography–satire and several other writings.
Under the name of George Tacet (Tacet is a term used in a musical score
directing an instrument to be silent) this persistent thinker and talker has
designed costumes and sets for Taylor, and has jousted with him about the
moral issues in dance-making. Tacet usually doesn't get credit, but Taylor
listens to his ideas. In fact, Tacet is one of the characters in a long-running
representation of Paul Taylor – a self-portrait devised with literary cunning
to allow the artist to vent his personal perversities and digressions without
quite owning up to them.

Contrary to his aw-shucks air, Taylor is perhaps the most literary choreographer of our time. He's certainly not bookish in the sense that Martha
Graham was. He seldom makes a dance based on an existing text, and
doesn't often admit to being inspired by myths or poems. Although he is
extremely musical, he has been known to change from one score to another
after choreographing a dance. In the act of choreographing, though, Taylor
translates literary devices into movement imagery. His works are full of
visual puns and analogies, ironic references, double entendre, metaphor,
and action that identifies a theme or a character, like a leit-motif in music.
Over the years he has built up a vocabulary of group patterns, phrases,
body shapes, and gestures that recur in different contexts, and not only
convey an immediate idea but sometimes echo scenes in other dances.
He recasts his current preoccupations in terms of his dance company as it
evolves, and his dancers frequently play similar roles, as if they were
members of a family. He even seems to favor role-replacements when he
hires new dancers. On the stage we are looking not only at a Taylor dance

but at a community with a history, a set of customs and rituals, and a shared language developed out of its common experiences.

Speaking in Tongues was choreographed in 1988–9 and filmed for public television's *Dance in America* in 1991 with nearly all the original cast. After its stage premiere at City Center in New York, critics agreed that it was one of Taylor's darkest dances. Laura Shapiro thought "he illuminates the scary underside of America's most cherished definition of itself: one nation under God" (1989: 72). Dale Harris, not one of Taylor's admirers, saw "the presence of evil just beneath the surface of daily life" (1989: A21). The action is dancelike throughout, with only a few "readable" episodes of more literal action: for instance, a girl is attracted to a young man; her mother pulls her away. Although the characters have descriptive titles (a Man of the Cloth, Townsmen and Women, etc.) they don't act out a story that is accessible to the casual viewer. As noted in an unsigned *New Yorker* comment on the video version, it "conveys the illusion that its sections are linked by a narrative that is nowhere specified but everywhere understood."[3]

The TV version, which is the basis of my discussion since I was only able to see the dance onstage once or twice, was reconceived by Taylor, designer Santo Loquasto, and television director/former dancer Matthew Diamond.[4] Several changes were made in the staging of the dance for the television cameras, and the result was an unusually compelling translation that kept, or even enhanced, the original choreography's identity but made satisfying viewing on the home screen.

Videographer Diamond jettisoned the orthodox, straight-on proscenium view that captures a minimal record of a dance. So many abuses had been committed by over-eager filmmakers trying to document dances – treacherous closeups, disorienting cuts to different parts of the stage or camera locations, shots that concentrated on one dancer and eliminated the others – that in the early days of *Dance in America* and its companion PBS series, *Live from Lincoln Center* and *Great Performances*, it was felt best to use a basic, conservative overall shot, simulating the audience's view of the dance in the theater. But this has disadvantages, too. It reduces the dancers to lilliputian size and compresses the action as well. *Dance in America*'s directors over the years have tried variations that would bring the screen to life without killing the dance. For *Speaking in Tongues* they let go of the idea of making a strict documentation, returning with great success to the very devices that had been detrimental to an all-encompassing, stagelike record.

Not only did Diamond approach Taylor's dance from different camera angles, the original proscenium set was redesigned so that the dance could take place in a filmic environment. The stage set, which remained in place for the whole dance and changed only with the play of lighting, consisted of a proscenium-height backdrop painted to look like horizontal wooden slats. The entire surface was covered with faded words and phrases that had a vaguely scriptural import but seemed to have long since lost their

clarity. This bulwark of forgotten dogma represented the spiritual core of
the dance. The people who depended on its shelter were also hemmed in
by it; they had nowhere else to go.

In the video, large and small enclosures are marked off by fences and
walls built of unpainted wooden boards, some of them still scrawled with
dire warnings. We never see the whole layout of these slatted spaces, but the
camera looks into them, angles around corners, peeps through the cracks.
The dance space becomes a series of rooms, indoor and outdoor areas, even
a barnyard. The action can take place in one or more of these spaces at
a time, and can shift without transition from one to another. We have at
least the illusion that we're seeing the dance from all sides. The effect of
this fluid use of space is to increase the dance's narrative possibilities, and to
give visual form to Taylor's predominating theme of community. The set
simulates a village, where the inhabitants lead separate but connected lives,
where public and private deeds are inextricably tangled together.

The idea of community has dominated Taylor's dances throughout his
career. He is far more interested in how individuals interact, how they
influence each other, and how they assume responsibility for each other,
than he is in exploiting their separate personalities. There are often
featured performers in his work, but they emerge from and are defined by
a group of their peers. In both narrative and non-narrative dances, multiple
featured roles and a shifting discursive center diffuse the power that any
individual can have over the work. Asymmetrical or serial structures
also shift the audience's attention from one dancer or situation to another.
In *Speaking in Tongues* the form is episodic; the encounters between
characters are fragmentary, and one feels they become a community
only when ritual or survival depends on it. Even his visually tight endings
read as collective decisions that could break up or mutate further after
a moment's cohesion. So even though we develop a passing interest in
individuals, the real throughline of a Taylor dance is the life of the group,
however tenuous or transitional that organism might be.

Speaking in Tongues depicts a religious community, troubled, as Taylor's
communities often are, but ultimately saved by its faith. In a series of scenes,
the characters wrestle with their inhibitions, doubts, and terrors. Taylor
may have been influenced by the scandals involving popular evangelists
Jimmy Swaggart and Jim Bakker that were going on at the time he made the
dance, and it is Swaggart's voice we hear fading in and out of Matthew
Patton's taped score, telling of tumultuous conversions and revelation.

But the question of religious faith and hypocrisy is only one of many
dualities Taylor finds in the human condition. In *Speaking in Tongues* he
explores the two sides of spiritual extremism, the tension between public and
private life, the consequences of liberated versus repressed sexuality, and
the play of insider/outsider roles. All of these can be seen as symptomatic
of a group of people in submission to a leader who entices them with a
mixture of faith, fear, and magic. Metaphorically, Taylor has proposed the

same structure of relationships in a family, and in a modern dance company. I would suggest that the three layers, of community/family/dance company, are present in nearly all his work, one or another of them shadowing even seemingly abstract movement patterns with expressive potential.

It seems to be in the nature of modern dance to generate close familial units, and for those communities to share not only a practical arrangement for working but a way of thinking about dance and society. Modern dance is by nature utopian, in the sense that it seeks alternatives to dance forms it considers decadent and/or conservative. It is a persistently marginal activity in the culture, and sacrifice has always been an accepted condition of a modern dancer's life. In return, he or she molds body and soul to the aims of the company, ideals that are often political as well as aesthetic. Paul Taylor's predecessors in the first generation of modern dancers were even more dedicated, their mission more strongly pursued, and their familial connections more constricting. He has referred to his ancestral obligations often in his dances, overtly identifying the multiple nature of the relationships they required.

His danse-noir version of *Le Sacre du Printemps* stitches a cops-and-robbers scenario, very loosely based on Nijinsky's 1913 tribal dance of sacrifice, into the rehearsal of a dance company led by a dictatorial female director. Elsewhere he borrows from other choreographers to enrich his own text. In *Speaking in Tongues*, an outsider tries to enter the group and is excluded. One girl is attracted to him and is pulled away by her mother. Later the stranger is ritually beaten by the group. All of this occurs in Doris Humphrey's 1936 dance about a community that turns into a mob, *With My Red Fires*. Taylor's stranger is later accepted by the mother, but the girl grows up with severe sexual problems. His dance ends with another image that recalls Humphrey. His characters, having gone through an orgiastic revival meeting, lie down and fold their camp chairs over their bodies. Humphrey signified the end of one generation in *Day on Earth* (1947) by having the adults lie down and pull a cloth over them, while the child sits above them symbolizing the future.

The difference between Taylor and Humphrey – and all the other early dance utopians – is his pessimism. Taylor, a product of the post-World War II generation, is fundamentally an anti-utopian. He's not merely a choreographer with an acrid sense of humor or a somber view of life. Virtually every one of Taylor's dances, from the dramatic to the lyrical, offers some vision of heaven and then snatches it away or turns it sideways to expose its dingy corners. In the rare cases where he seems to propose utopia untainted, as in the idyllic dance of lovers, *Roses* (1985), he offsets it with pure hell, as in the violent, obsessive and self-destructive *Last Look*, made in the same year.

Although Martha Graham was hardly a social utopian, her dance had the character of a crusade, a cult, from its inception. She had been the first stellar dancer to cross Taylor's path, and his years in her company (1955–61) had a lasting effect on his work, although he sometimes reciprocates with satire. His statement after her death is probably quite sincere: "The tradition that's passed from one generation to another in modern dance – a real family – has helped me very much. . . . I'm her rightful son" (Mazo 1991: 45).

Taylor's movement style can be seen as a softened, more rhythmic and harmonious edition of Graham's vocabulary, with frequent inversions of grotesqueness. In his dance, as in hers, the body enacts its emotional states. Neurotic characters are tense, jittery, misshapen. Lighthearted ones dance in released big spirals and jumps. People who are in accord with one another move in unison; those who disagree are asynchronous. This kind of expressive movement lies at the core of modern dance. Narrative is constructed by nonrealistic, expressively appropriate movement, as well as by the more obvious devices of gesture and realistic acting.

Not only does Taylor reflect Graham's movement style, he often seizes on iconic or metaphoric possibilities in a similar way. Although his musicality and architectonic use of space show Taylor to be an heir of Humphrey, he hasn't used large group forms as inventively as Humphrey did. With any more than five or six dancers on stage, he reverts to circles and lineups, a simple solution more characteristic of Graham. She framed the recitative-like musings of her heroic characters with ritualistic action – processional lines, monolithic groupings and couplings that sculpted the ensemble into a timeless backdrop for the central characters' struggle.

Taylor's lineups do more than frame a bigger story or create an element of design. For him, the lineup is a versatile and expressive trope. At times he uses it for ritualistic reasons, such as the endless marchers crossing the front and back of the stage in *Runes*, where, like sentries, they solemnize and partly conceal ceremonies of mysterious importance. In more playful dances, like *Esplanade*, *Cloven Kingdom*, and *Aureole*, lineups produce follow-the-leader games, celebratory explosions of jumping, panoramic backdrops for the passage of eccentric comrades. The lineup often suggests the parade, one of several American festive rituals that are dear to Taylor's heart. In *Speaking in Tongues*, the lineup means conformity, and, for the tight-minded community of this dance, snobbery or bigotry toward those who don't conform.

Above all, for Taylor, lineups signify the illusory security of being with other people like oneself, people who know what is right and how to behave, and who understand each other completely. For the time being, the individual gives up a certain amount of autonomy to gain social protection. I would suggest that for Taylor this very meaningful configuration refers directly back to his days in Graham's class. Daily class is at the center of every dancer's life, a ritual of communal enactments that invoke personal discovery. As Martha Graham remarks, with the dancers prancing and soaring across the floor in her 1957 film *A Dancer's World*:

It is here in the studio that the dancer learns his craft. . . . The dancer is realistic. His craft teaches him to be. Either the foot is pointed or it is not. No amount of dreaming will point it for you. This requires discipline. Not drill, not something imposed from without. But discipline imposed by you upon yourself. Your goal is freedom, but freedom may only be achieved through discipline. In the studio you learn to conform, to submit yourself to the demands of your craft so that you may finally *be* free.[5]

Taylor pays his homage to the power of classroom decorum most explicitly near the end of *Speaking in Tongues*, when a benevolent character enters in the midst of a wild sexual debauch and calms everyone down with her serene, smooth movements. One by one she takes the fevered celebrants aside and gentles them; then gradually they gather around her in a semi-circular lineup and she leads them through a trace of a dance class. It's not only her soothing manner but the dance process itself, a ritual completed by following the teacher's example, that redeems them.

All the performers in *Speaking in Tongues* have names, which gives another layer of meaning to the dance. This peacemaking figure is His Better Half, a double-entendre, or perhaps a triple-entendre. She represents the wife of the flawed Man of the Cloth who looms over the community, and is indeed the better spirit of the two. She may be his alter ego, the soft, female half, who has none of his doubts about faith, sexuality, or authority. This character is also a distillation of several imperturbable earth-mother types in Graham, particularly the Pioneer Woman in *Appalachian Spring*, who reassures the jittery bride and pronounces benedictions to counteract the hellfire sermons of the Revivalist.

Appalachian Spring is one of at least three Graham shadow-texts for *Speaking in Tongues*. Graham's Revivalist, like Taylor's Man of the Cloth, has taken the sins of his congregation upon himself, and is tormented not only by that burden but by a lacerating self-doubt. They both dance solos of twisted anger and guilt. Although both of them have taken responsibility for their community, neither has much direct contact with his parishioners. They're aloof; Graham's preacher seems a bit disdainful, Taylor's is often menacing. The Revivalist gets a certain cheerless gratification from four adoring followers; the Man of the Cloth is almost an outsider to his flock, becoming one of them only when drawn into the light created by His Better Half. Physically both characters are stiff and straight, unbending, and when they get worked up they twist themselves off balance, topple to the ground, writhe in fury.

Taylor knows these strangulated prophets and demigods of Graham's, having danced or accompanied many of them as a Graham dancer during her High Greek period. The other male type in Graham, the hero, is equally stultified – pompous and solemnly macho. Taylor mocks him in a farcical duet added to *Speaking in Tongues* for the video version, the same year Graham died. To a section of music called "Barnyard Reflections," a Hayseed (Christopher Gillis) pays court to a Woman with Airs (Denise Roberts). Taylor has often portrayed himself as a country boy, a hayseed.[6] On one level this duet could be about Taylor's relationship with Graham during the 1955 Asian tour when he had just joined the company. He's described this encounter with the imperious Graham in his autobiography (1987: 65–75). More obviously, though, this dance parodies the courtship duet between Oedipus and Jocasta in *Night Journey*, which was filmed in 1961 with Bertram Ross and Graham as the doomed couple, and Taylor as the prophet Tiresias.

Accompanied by squawking roosters, twittering birds, satisfied piggy grunts, and an ominous repeated figure on a keyboard, Gillis awakes from a nap in the hay, limbers up by shaking out his hands while everything else remains stiff, then notices Roberts poised fetchingly on a box. Curious, then excited, Gillis approaches her and clamors for her attention. She pretends to ignore him but remains available. After a two-minute courtship, they begin to boogie together. The more bumptious he gets, the more he looks like Bertram Ross preening and making phallic gestures at the demurely seductive Graham. Taylor is ridiculing not only Graham's characters but the solemnity and aestheticized eroticism with which she deployed her dance–drama. Even the score alludes to similar pretensions in Graham's musical collaborators.

Although we live in an age of the sendup, modern dancers are not supposed to parody or borrow from one another. If suspected, the appropriation is usually ignored. Taylor quotes his predecessors frequently. Often he simply lifts material as a source of movement and a layer of meaning in the textual web he's weaving. He takes Graham's language and her philosophy as subjects for endless meditation and re-examining. You could say her dances are in his artistic genes, his personality, as the traits of any parent are embedded in any offspring. Paul Taylor was born in Allegheny City, Pennsylvania, near Graham's birthplace, Pittsburgh. As a believer in spirits, he must feel that this too is a significant coincidence.

While Graham's characterizations have been the target of some of Taylor's funniest satire, they have also provided him with another choreographic model, the archetype. In the fictional community that his repertory of dances represents, his own archetypal family makes continual reappearances. The central character in *Speaking in Tongues*, the Man of the Cloth, is one of these recurring types, the father-figure with a shady side. It is danced on tape by Elie Chaib, who alternated in the stage role with Christopher Gillis. Chaib arrived in 1974 and inherited the choreographer's mantle – and many of his roles – as the Big Man in the Company. 1974 was the year Taylor stopped dancing, after he collapsed on stage in a disastrous big Bible/Americana epic he called *American Genesis* (Taylor 1987: 334–53). In this three-part saga, Taylor, called Lucifer, played the Angel of

Light, the Puritan Father, and Captain Noah, who was pictured as an evangelistic bigot.

The Man of the Cloth is only one of the incarnations of this character that Taylor has choreographed since *Genesis*. In less complex form, he goes back almost to the beginnings of Taylor's career. Sometimes he has been thoroughly corruptible, like the all-American father in *Big Bertha* (1971), and sometimes he's a benign paterfamilias, as in *Kith and Kin* (1987). Other Taylor archetypes include the monster–mother, originated by Bettie de Jong, perhaps as early as her bored and haggard Statue of Liberty in *From Sea to Shining Sea* (1965). As Big Bertha, the gaudy band machine that comes to life and takes possession of a supposedly innocent family, and as the militaristic dance director in *Le Sacre du Printemps*, she brings weaker characters under her domination and scales off all their manners to expose their raw instincts. Karla Wolfangle took over these roles when de Jong stopped dancing, and it's she who plays the repressive Mother in *Speaking in Tongues*.

The little girl or little sister character was probably originated by Elizabeth Walton as the playful center of the female trio in *Aureole* (1962). Taylor seems to reserve this role (the Unwanted Daughter in *Speaking in Tongues*) for the smallest, quickest dancer in the company at any time. She has been played in different dances by Janet Aaron, Carolyn Adams, Lila York, Kate Johnson, and most recently Mary Cochran. There are others in the Taylor canon – the juvenile hero, the lustful virgin, the beast – but this nuclear family (dubious father, monster–mother, and little girl) is the most frequently depicted.

The establishment of clear character types allows for the possibility that characters can have two sides or two aspects. This is another Graham device that Taylor has developed for his own dramatic purposes. I have mentioned the creation of antagonistic or complementary roles, the Man of the Cloth and His Better Half in *Speaking in Tongues*, for instance. Taylor also extends the dimension of narrative time through alternative personas signifying memory and prophecy. The Man of the Cloth has a double, Himself, As He Recollects, a more innocent man who dances a tender duet with His Better Half. We see the (Unwanted) Daughter Grown Up in terrified flight from Her Husband, as her mother and her younger self look on from the corner of the bedroom.

The two-sidedness of personality is almost taken for granted by Taylor, whether the character has an actual double to show how he or she has been traumatized by life, or whether the same character engages in contradictory behavior. Very early in his career, Taylor played a two-faced Sun God, wearing benign and satanic masks on the front and back of his head, in a cosmological allegory called *Orbs* (1966). And in one of several transformations in *Runes*, Chaib conjured Monica Morris, brought her under his spell, and ultimately fused with her body to create an astonishing hermaphrodite image. Most often this split nature shows up in Taylor as a confused, hampered, or overactive sexuality. His characters occupy a middle ground between the lurid, disguised excesses of Graham and the nearly impersonal promiscuity of nineties dance. He accepts the complexities of need and desire, not only as motivations for dance expression but as springboards for narrative and theatrical imagery.

Like Graham, Taylor uses symbolic objects and effects. In *Speaking in Tongues*, holy water serves as a conduit for deeper meanings. A bowl of water is first seen, with a reflection of the moon in it, held by the Mother, about midway through the dance. The preacher takes a handful of water. The group of women gathered around him look at his extended palm. A red spot has appeared. He then pours the water back and leaves. He seems to have consecrated it in preparation for a ritual of some kind. Attended by the Mother, the Unwanted Daughter and the Daughter Grown Up dance a quiet duet, one shadowing the other. This seems to be a dance of initiation, a menstrual rite perhaps, recalling a similar scene in Martha Graham's *Dark Meadow*. After this, the camera peers down through a hole in the roof at the preacher, who has retreated into another room. The same white bowl is on the floor. The camera descends to watch him take a handful of water, look into it, then let it flow through his fingers.

During the tortured solo that follows, he returns to the water and again scoops up a handful and gazes at it. As if repelled by what he sees, he throws it back. At the end of this soliloquy of grief, rage, and panic, he deliberately puts his head in the bowl, face down, a simultaneous baptism and drowning. In these two sequences, the preacher is symbolically martyred. The stigmata, the holy water, and a bright light in the form of a cross blazing behind him during his solo all suggest he bears a supernatural power or burden. The parishioners recognize it and assemble outside the room where he's undergoing his trial.

The preacher may be accepting a Christlike responsibility for his flock, but he is also a man driven by anger and guilt of his own, and he is forced to confront himself when he looks into the water. One of the ongoing symbols Taylor has adopted to expand the idea of sexuality and sexual awareness is the mirror. His dances are full of actual mirrors, mirror gestures, and reflecting surfaces. In his comic-book farce version of *Snow White*, the Evil Queen, Elie Chaib, gazes into her mirror to discover the fairest one of all, but Snow White's innocent beauty conquers the queen, who then turns into a handsome prince, also played by Chaib. In the grisly *Last Look*, the pathologically repressed characters confront themselves in a set made of mirrored panels and lit with uncertain glare so that neither we nor they can tell where the edges are.

Although there are no actual mirrors in *Speaking in Tongues*, Taylor makes frequent use of mirroring in movement to show us the relationship between his characters. For example, the duet between the preacher's remembered self and His Better Half begins with a mirror dance and continues almost entirely in either mirroring or side-by-side movements.

When this woman returns to absolve the whole community, her dance could be made of softened phrases from the preacher's guilty solos.

In the scene immediately following the preacher's martyrdom, we see the first of *Speaking in Tongues'* several uninhibited sexual encounters. A Party Girl (Sandra Stone) teases and arouses three men, one of whom is the preacher's younger self (Jeff Wadlington). Suddenly Chaib appears and almost violently seizes her and carries her off. Wadlington crawls away after them. Stone and the three men reprise their revels later. Throughout the dance we have been half-hearing voices fading in and out, like a radio playing in the next house, and at the end of this episode we can make out the words "his holy feet have nails in them." The preacher's guilt comes from his own sins, then, as well as from those he's assumed for his flock. For Taylor – or at least for many of Taylor's characters – sex seems to be a sin that weighs down the personality forevermore with guilt. This may seem old-fashioned today, but it's not inconsistent with Taylor's generation and with the example Graham set for him. The magnetic appeal that today's fundamentalist and cult leaders have for their followers may be rooted in a similar sexual guilt, lingering into the age of permissiveness and still seeking chastisement.

But along with the guilt, desire persists. In some ways the most interesting character in *Speaking in Tongues* is the Odd Man Out (Thomas Patrick). After his rejection by the group there is a prolonged, ritualistic scourging that seems to be presided over by Chaib. Having been beaten, kicked, and stepped on by the other men and women, Patrick kneels before the preacher and is blessed. The preacher's frozen gesture of sanction throughout the beating, and his absolution of the stranger by placing both hands on the sides of Patrick's head are echoes of St. Michael guarding and eventually canonizing the martyred St. Joan in Graham's *Seraphic Dialogue*. It seems Taylor's outsider is compelled to endure this wanton cruelty in order to be accepted. Immediately after the blessing, the picture cuts to a sunlit shot of the preacher with his arm around Patrick. Together they lead the group in a playful romp over the rooftops and later a solemn procession after the absolution. This stranger seems to be a third alter ego of the preacher, perhaps the one that will never conform or suppress his instincts, nor feel guilty for them.

The video has a formal opening and closing scene: a happy and innocent party with all the characters dancing – cut apart by an editor's freeze-frame to make room for an hour's worth of memories. When the party continues in the post-flashback segment, the participants work themselves into violent ecstatic states. Writhing in the grip of unknown spirits, they fall to the floor one by one. Then the dance ends formally with the appearance of the preacher and the funereal folding of the chairs.

During the excitement of the party, the Odd Man Out spins and somersaults along the floor. Suddenly I saw him as another Taylor archetype, the mischievous demon. This character hasn't been much in evidence since

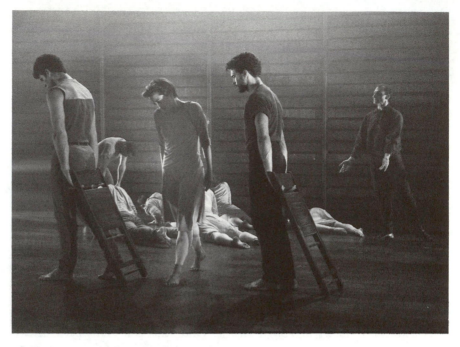

Figure 3.1 Speaking in Tongues: humble transgressors. Left to right: Christopher Gillis, Francie Huber, Thomas Patrick, Elie Chaib, and members of the Paul Taylor Dance Company. (Photo: © Johan Elbers 1995)

the departure from the Taylor company of Danny Williams [Grossman], who scrabbled and leered as Pan in *Agathe's Tale* (1967), where the not-so-innocent heroine was beset by three suitors, a unicorn, a satyr, and a big burly knight. In *Speaking in Tongues* this little demon may represent the survival of libido – and adventurous spirit – in the Man of the Cloth.

As I studied and wrote about this dance over the course of a year, its meaning kept changing. I finally came to see it as a much more coherent narrative than at first reading. I decided that what Taylor was doing was exploring the personality of the Man of the Cloth through a series of recollections. Perhaps the whole story is taking place at the moment of his death (another favorite device of Martha Graham). He watches over his flock and sees them as initially childlike, then becoming more and more uncontrolled as they are drawn into the physicality of their dance. He means to be kindly, but his gaze is menacing, and their pleasure congeals until they grow tense and finally spastic. His Better Half calms them momentarily, spinning in ecstatic circles in their midst.

The preacher remembers himself as a young man, encountering this woman. He may once have been the Odd Man Out, arriving in the community, being rejected for reasons he doesn't understand. Although they finally accept him, he may still carry some resentment for this, some sense that he is alien to them although they have entrusted him with their souls. He certainly feels unworthy; he has sinned as much as they. Only His Better Half can redeem them all.

Speaking in Tongues is a dramatization of Paul Taylor's anti-utopianism, of a hope deeply infected by skepticism. In order to be disillusioned, one must first have entertained illusions, and heaven always flickers somewhere around the edges of Taylor's universe – his America. Martha Graham sought absolution through her dance for a guilt fixed squarely on the shoulders of her heroines: Jocasta, Medea, Phaedra, Clytemnestra. Taylor sees guilt – and hope too – as a collective responsibility, even a contagious one. Since there is no sure or conclusive way to hold on to the individual's better nature, collective vision is the only way, tortured though it may be, to avoid destruction.

I think of Taylor among the great, dark American storytellers, especially William Faulkner. *Speaking in Tongues* lays out the territory more explicitly than some of Taylor's other dances, but they all could call Yoknapatawpha County home. Taylor's town is a tight community where everyone knows everyone's secrets, but won't talk about them. Coarse, shoddy types as well as gentry look out from behind the shutters and accept their neighbors. There's a sense of secrets, madness, awful mistakes committed in the past, latent irrationalities inherited from unwise escapades, and a capacity for sudden violence and injustice. An old geezer's offstage raucous laughter tells us not to take any of it too seriously. Graham's dance might be said to be a protest or a struggle against fate. Taylor's is an acceptance.

Faulkner could almost have been describing Taylor when he wrote about the spinster–recluse, Miss Emily, whose lover disappeared one day and was discovered years later in her attic, embalmed and resting in a bed where she'd slept beside him till her own death: "Thus she passed from generation to generation – dear, inescapable, impervious, tranquil, and perverse" (1977: 442). When Taylor's congregants lie down in death at the end, they may be re-enacting the mass suicide in Jonestown or predicting the Branch Davidians in Waco. These grisly episodes flash through my mind, yet Taylor's conclusion is as tranquil as it is chilling. I'm still not sure whether they're going to their damnation or their heavenly reward.[7]

NOTES

1 An unsigned editorial in the same publication blissfully re-interprets Baryshnikov's words: " . . . dancers such as Baryshnikov demonstrate that the understanding of dance, of virtuosity, has altered: a starting point for another way of dealing with *dance as the premier twentieth-century cultural form.*" [Italics mine] *Ballett International/Tanz Aktuell* (May, 1994: 3).

2 Asked to say how he would choreograph a dance on a given theme for Selma Jeanne Cohen's *The Modern Dance: Seven Statements of Belief*, he wrote: "One

idea that I would start with and attempt to achieve, no matter how ruthlessly, is the idea that the stage should become a magic place and unbelievably beautiful in a curious new way that cannot be described, but would cause the viewer to say Yes, uh-huh, yes!" (Taylor in Cohen, 1966: 102).

3   *The New Yorker* (October 28, 1991: 6).

4   *Speaking in Tongues* was released in 1992 by Judy Kinberg for Great Performances/Thirteen WNET. Electra Nonesuch Dance Collection.

5   Martha Graham in the film *A Dancer's World* (1957), produced by Nathan Kroll. Peter Glushanok, director and filmmaker.

6   In a hilarious Sunday piece for the *New York Times Magazine* he described a visit two of his dancers paid him at his country house: "Look here, son . . . what did you expect, a couple of rhinestone-collared wolfhounds? Just because a person is well known doesn't mean he can't keep a pig." (Taylor 1992: 30)

7   This essay was given in a slightly different form at the 1994 annual conference of the Society of Dance History Scholars at Provo, Utah.

BIBLIOGRAPHY

Christen, R. (1994) "This Unique Moment . . . Mikhail Baryshnikov in Conversation with Regina Christen," *Ballett International/Tanz Aktuell* (May): 10–11.

Cohen, S. J. (1966) *The Modern Dance: Seven Statements of Belief*, Middletown, CT: Wesleyan University Press.

Faulkner, W. (1977) "A Rose for Emily," *The Portable Faulkner*, Malcolm Cowley (ed.), New York: Penguin Books.

Harris, D. (1989) *The Wall Street Journal* (April 25): A21.

Mazo, J. H. (1991) "Martha Remembered: Interviews Introduced by Joseph H. Mazo," *Dance Magazine* (July): 34–45.

Shapiro, L. (1989) *Newsweek* (May 1): 72, 75.

Taylor, P. (1987) *Private Domain*, New York: Alfred A. Knopf.

—— (1992) "About Men," *New York Times Magazine* (October 25): 30.

4 Five Theses on *Laughter After All*

Mark Franko

February 1, 1964: my surprise on entering the theater. An exposed space, the stage literally denuded. No "wings" either, only "fire walls" of striated, burned, discolored brick. Hunter Playhouse in New York City as a sinister cavern. The stage lights, pipes and all, are dropped practically to the ground where they cast small, intense specks of light. Some stools and chairs scattered about at random. Behind the rows of low-hanging lights, a higher pipe to which an unkempt mass of painted canvas is attached, looking shredded and bloodied. A devastated curtain.

Audience find seats while women move about on stage at unexpected intervals. As if in a backstage area or insignificant place, a dancer with a pair of high-heeled shoes in one hand sits on a chair to slip them on. Another unselfconsciously dons a kimono, talks to someone invisible, checks a corner of the stage, disappears. City sounds filter dully through the theater. One dancer at the left downstage corner pauses to stretch in a somewhat stylized reach of both arms to her right side and up to her shoulder level and above. A personal moment, but theatrically pronounced. Boat whistles. The women who come and go on the stage pull their kimonos tightly around them, hugging themselves at the waist (Figure 4.1). Is it cold? Is it morning? Weirdly slowed-down recording of a woman's laughter. Between each drawn-out peal, a gasp for air. Hardly recognizable sounds. Moaning? The lights dim over this continuous distorted laughter.

These words to reconstitute a 1964 performance of *Laughter After All* choreographed by Paul Sanasardo and Donya Feuer in 1960.[1] I exchange dormant memories with re-eventing, and add a commentary whose post-Marxian theses orient the work's impact, but can't "explain" it.

The performance's eventfulness was memorable precisely because of its mediated character. "Mediation" is a term literary critic Georg Lukács used to oppose abstraction's *immediacy*.[2] Being blind to the net of social relations isolates us in an abstract immediacy with regard to things that appear and events that happen. To perceive things or events as abstract or "immediate" is to accept their inevitability, to be seduced by the vivid presence of their now. Thus is their "immediacy" constituted, but so also their abstraction because they remain disconnected from interpretation:

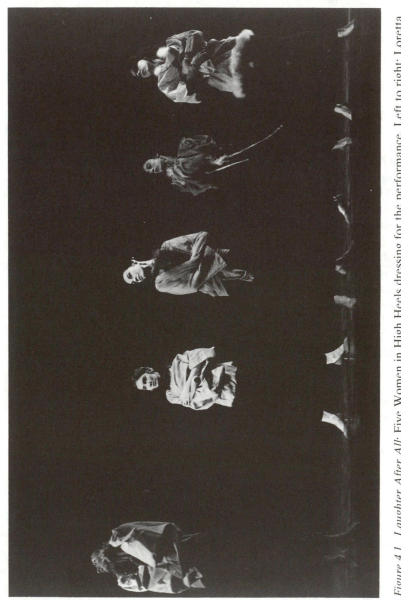

Figure 4.1 Laughter After All: Five Women in High Heels dressing for the performance. Left to right: Loretta A'bbott, Sally Bowden, Barbara Dolgin, Rena Raskin, Regina Axelrod. (Photo: Keith Brian Staulcup)

unmediated or im-mediate. The immediacy and facticity of appearances paradoxically dehumanizes our relation to them.

There is a productive contradiction in the idea that immediacy is reifying, or that mediation, to the contrary, is enlivening. Or that critical theory is performable. The reified laughter in *Laughter After All* evokes that contradiction. It is all hysterical abandon, until we hear the end of its breathed cycle, and perceive its mechanical program of self-repetition. What at first sounded abandoned, now sounds manufactured. What appeared direct is now indirect, in need of mediation. Nonetheless, *Laughter* was among the most direct, and unrelenting of dances. What follows is as much an interpretive sketch as an attempt to reconstruct the eventing of this contradiction.[3] The lights dim for . . .

Act One: "Fall on Your Face." The front curtain falls, removing from view the Women in High Heels. Almost immediately, however, it lifts again.[4] Fire alarms sound. The dropped light apparatus is gradually lifted from the ground, as the lights spread their pinpoints into broadening pools and then disappear aloft. The violated curtain unfurls at back and flattens into a canvas splashed with erratic shapes. As do other of Robert Natkin's works of the late 1950s and early 1960s, this backdrop has a theatrical quality in its vertical dimensions, sensuous color, and hieroglyphic-like notations (Fuller 1981). Curtain wings fly down from above. These changes, occurring in overlapping moments, are stealthy and noiseless.

"Five Women in High Heels," like the theater itself, are now "dressed": flimsy kimonos and boa stoles over the leotards and ankle-length tights of modern dance. The kimonos lined with feathers at the neck; only one has feathers along the lower hem. The women stand in line on a low platform before the unfurled backdrop. Will this now become a performance?

The Five Women in High Heels are suggestive of burlesque performers. Sanasardo identified the impetus for *Laughter*'s burlesque imagery in a Detroit burlesque act whose star executed Graham-esque contractions.[5] Yet the Women are also (especially in the second act) a modern dance "chorus." We cannot ignore the lean, stylized, trained bodies of modern dancers in the early 1960s. The reference to burlesque is complex because it draws on both a sexualized spectacle implicating modern striptease and the historical burlesque of the mid-nineteenth century in which the female performer demonstrated a threatening "awarishness," a "directness of address and complicity in her own sexual objectification" (Allen 1991: 129).[6] The Five Women in High Heels embody neither the epic presence of historical modern dance nor fully realistically transgressive evocations of burlesque theatrics. Their effect, instead, is to blur modern dance's use value with burlesque's exchange value.[7] Modern dancers as burlesque performers; burlesque performers as modern dancers. A sharp distinction between these two identities is never stabilized. Much like the Detroit performer, they fetishize use value (modern dance), and humanize exchange value (burlesque).

The women face the audience and "vamp" (Figure 4.2). Gun shots ring out, as in a shooting gallery. With each shot, one of them is "hit": a leg flies up, a back is turned, a robe falls off a shoulder. Other responses. The robes eventually drop to the floor. The boa stoles are now tied through a leg and around a hip. Typewriters tapping and cash registers ringing. The women file down off the platform and march toward the audience, stamp their legs in a wide "second position," and balance there while rotating their heads back and crying out "me-ow."

Sanasardo refers to these characters as "the whores." Their poses and gaze are aggressive and menacing. The image of vamping that is so prevalent in the choreography for Five Women in High Heels – "standing erect, chin up, hand on hip, and right foot advanced forward, patting the floor" – suggests what Robert Allen has called the "feminization of the [American] burlesque in the 1860s." (1991: 134, 107). But this feminization is not to be entirely confused with sexualization. What is overemphasized is their *appearance* (not what they look like, but the fact that they are there to be seen), as if to say theater is the market, it is "the part [of the system] which constantly *appears*" (Hall, 1986: 35). The theatricality of the Women performs the fascination of commodities.

Coming forward, they remove their shoes and hold them down toward the floor, each shoe in one hand, as they stamp in a straddled balance on their toes, dropping their head backwards and screaming. Much of the choreography for this part of the work has the women in lines or minstrel-show Walk Arounds. These patterns, however, are never uniform. Invariably, the women do different things at different times.

American modern dance has presented itself historically as unalienated labor. No objectification (reification) of the dancer's body is thinkable because modern dance itself cannot be considered a product separable from the human body that dances.[8] Unalienated, its use value can be contaminated only by imagined or thematically repressed exchange values. Movement, process, and relation do not lend themselves to fixity, abstraction, or objectivity.

"Commodity fetishism" suggests a sexual fascination that commodities derive by comparison with sexed human bodies, but which in turn can be redeployed across the living human body of the prostitute, the human body as sexual commodity. The commodity is an object, properly speaking; the worker's body is a commodity in that s/he sells her labor. The working body of the prostitute takes this commodity situation one step further, dramatizing how the worker's labor is also a commodity, "inseparable from his physical existence" (Lukács 1971: 166). As Christine Buci-Glucksmann pointed out apropos of Walter Benjamin, the prostitute is "the allegory of the allegory of commodities" (1984: 120). So are The Five Women in High Heels.

They dance with one shoe in hand, limping on the other high heel. They beat the pointed shoe heel rhythmically against the other palm. They meow,

Figure 4.2   Laughter After All: vamping in the shooting gallery. Left to right:
Barbara Dolgin, Rena Raskin, Loretta Abbott, Regina Axelrod, Sally Bowden.
(Photo: Keith Brian Staulcup)

hiss, and scream to the sounds of beating jackhammers. The sounds they make, although violent, also presuppose a physical assurance, an ease with mediating voice and movement. Since the screams are not of shock or frozen horror, they call forth something beyond sexual objectification. They are shocks which liberate the body from its mere use as a commodity. The Women walk closer and closer to the ground where they ultimately sit to beat the heels into the floor (Figure 4.3).

The prostitute in *Laughter* is not involved in a narrative premise: there is no assignation, no striptease. She is a commodity threat whose exaggeration unleashes other thoughts or possibilities about the relation of bodies to commodities, i.e., commodified sexual relations. The Five Women in High Heels form a modern dance chorus mediating a logic of commodity fetishism: they act out a movement between immediate abstraction and mediated concreteness, a movement toward realization. This occurs most remarkably in the historical hybridity of *Laughter*'s burlesque evocations. The Five Women have voices and use them. This is characteristic of the historical burlesque. As Allen attests, striptease did not dominate burlesque until the mid-1920s. He calls striptease "the form [that] focused . . . on female sexual spectacle, causing the burlesque performer to lose her 'voice' and much of her transgressive power" (1991: 198).[9] The Five Women in High Heels wield transgressive power. They have voices. Their violence consists in wrenching the human commodity they ostensibly evoke from its equivocal appearance as themselves. There is a real contradiction in their vamping: a strength and a weakness, a power and a loss.

Fire alarms. (Alarms demarcate the work's different sections.) Varese's "Octandre." A quartet for "Two Men" and "Two Women." Their movements are lithe and animal-like. The men serve, however, largely as props for the women. These figures break through the claustrophobia of the work's beginning. A "Celebrity" saunters through: very young, flaming red hair, white spangled and bejeweled leotard, white net tights, white high heels. She is like the Women in High Heels, but as a surplus rather than exchange value. She emits blood-curdling screams, but appears otherwise blasé, and tends to drop her head straight backwards and hug herself at the waist. Looking at the audience, her eyes participate in the scream's intensity, but also mask that intensity by projecting it at the audience. High glamour, but at the same time, a certain built-in critique. Carrying a whip, she appears at other moments supercilious and self-satisfied.

Later, she enters holding a white porcelain chain at the end of which a bare-chested male dancer ("Her Pet") leaps. Each time she screams, she tugs on the chain and her pet falls to the floor. Close to the floor, he hops beside her, puppy-like, looking up adoringly. She smiles smugly at him as well as at the audience. Her performance is a demonstration of self-conscious control. As they exit, others enter: "A Young Man" and "A Girl" perform an isolated duet across the quartet still in progress. Their painted costumes resemble the patterns painted on the curtain, but against

Figure 4.3 Laughter After All: descending toward the floor. Left to right: Regina Axelrod, Rena Raskin, Sally Bowden, Barbara Dolgin, Loretta Abbott. (Photo: Keith Brian Staulcup)

white rather than black or red. Like refugees from another world, these lone romantic figures move tentatively through the work, as if wrapped in the blind cocoon of their dance. They are the unalienated, alienated from alienation.

First thesis: *Laughter After All* relativizes the myth of modern dance as unalienated labor. This was, it seems to me, one of the common tasks of 1960s modern dance, that is, not to commodify the body, but to displace its myth of use value, often by appropriating technology.[10] The task was to cease presenting movement as a fulfillment of need, as what the dancer "needed" to do in some psychological or symptomatic way. Use value's invasion of modern dance had characterized 1930s activist performance, but led as well to theatrical representations of hysteria in the 1940s. By the 1950s, it had led to a generalized emotionalism becoming habitually associated with modern dance. Sanasardo and Feuer introduced an alienated modern dance body without "avant-garde" reference to technology. Their work reinscribed emotion within a social frame where its very uses became dislocated. They preserved emotion intact as a history of need: madness, cruelty, or physicality and emotion caught in the circuitry of production and consumption. Its historicity derives from its divorce from immediacy: it is not wholly explicable in/as a present. This history of need montages high culture (Graham) with low (the Detroit burlesque act) at various historical conjunctures, and expressionism with realism. It is a performance of social and aesthetic contradictions.

"Density 21.5" (solo flute): a solo dance for "One Man," Sanasardo in brown leotard and tights, wearing a gorilla wig and other different wigs tied to his knees. He is "inward" (eyes almost closed) but also maniacal. Typically, he lifts one leg in toward the other, foot pressing against his inner thigh, one arm reaching above his head. Fetal, tense, dangerous; but also suffering and shaping. Sensitive and poetic, there is a fury as well as an art to this figure: he can be brutal and unpredictable. His solo blends into a duet with "One Woman," who wears a tan leotard and tights, with blond wigs tied to her knees. She runs to him, he lifts her and throws her backwards over his head. He repeatedly throws her to the ground. Repeatedly she rises and returns to him. This is a competitive, challenging, and physically dangerous relationship. There is no sensitivity, sensuality, or tactile exchange. In its mutual involvement, however, there is some residue of sexuality. He is abusive, she is passionate, energetic, and unsubmissive. The recorded laughter returns at high speed. The duet ends with One Woman on his shoulders. Totem-like, they depart in this shape.

Although sado-masochistic couples were a familiar feature of American popular entertainments, abusive relationships were not on the conscious cultural agenda of the early 1960s as they presently are in the 1990s. One critic said the work lacked universality whereas today its universality might be all too clear. Yet, One Woman is not directly presented as a victim. Abuse itself seems to reproduce, to regenerate their relationship. Another critic, wrote: "The Man directed his passion for physical mishandling against One Woman who, flattened consistently by blows that would have made a professional boxer reel, managed to drag herself gallantly erect repeatedly" (Maskey 1964: 64).[11]

Second thesis: Abuse, or "cruelty and madness" becomes a way to think about productive negativity, and it should be conceptualized as negativity in that it exposes false organic harmony. Indirectly negated is what Herbert Marcuse called "affirmative culture," the autonomy of "bourgeois subjectivity" in a separate and invariably private sphere of inwardness where there is also creative freedom. This is traditionally the sphere of art that cannot be touched by, but also reciprocally cannot affect, social processes. In other words, art is a traditionally autonomous sphere to which the private soul repairs as recompense for an unredeemably exploited social existence. Cruelty and abuse, however, render such a closed world of emotions and subjectivity inescapably social, for they force that world into the outside, turning it into a social disturbance. Negativity is an explosion of the private into the public, of the subjective into the social, of the personal into the cruel. Negativity is critique without a utopian proposition.

Unsubmissive, One Woman's energy is expended in bonding with One Man after every assault. Although it might have a psychological explanation, the relationship in its very physical terms is uncanny. In the 1960 version of *Laughter* **there were three characters: The Man, His Companion, and One Woman Alone. His Companion (Donya Feuer) was passionate whereas One Woman Alone (Chifra Holt) was more passive.[12] In the 1964 version, one dancer (Diane Germaine) embodied both of these qualities, which increased the psychological complexity of the figure and of the relationship.[13]**

Affirmative culture is by definition set apart from the "material reproduction of life" (Marcuse 1988: 129). Marcuse defines it as a refuge from life in art. In this sense, art can affirm life by standing apart from its material realities. Yet, what *Laughter* produces is materiality of relationships as performance, that is, as modern dance. And, perhaps, cruelty and madness (expressed as abuse) are the only paths, short of pornography, on which human relationships can be exposed in their materiality. Before it is considered as itself, cruelty instantiates a functional distance from the stock conventions of sexual difference. The uncanny pliancy of One Woman points to an impossible reciprocity, a mythical hallmark of heterosexual relations. The characters and relationships presented without parody or irony in *Laughter After All* are in themselves illusions, and therefore, critiques of affirmative culture.

Act Two: "For God's Sake." The curtain rises, but the separation of house and stage is purely formal. Most of the cast (except the Celebrity) sit on chairs and stools in a wide semicircle oriented toward the audience. In its quality of waiting, the scene suggests a rehearsal. Everyone knows everyone. The Women in High Heels no longer have high heels. One

dancer slumped in a chair pares an apple with a knife, detaching the skin in one long spiraled strip. An element of task work within an overall dramatic context, it takes her the whole scene to complete. The others also have something in hand to eat. But primarily they watch. With a particularly malevolent expression, One Man stares at One Woman who is standing and walking toward the audience when the curtain opens. She appears to be leaving when One Man pounds his foot against the floor. She stops in response to the aggressivity of this pounding but does not turn. She walks again, he pounds again: she stops. He rises and goes to her. The onlookers begin to exit. An extended duet ensues. There is something fascinating about this duet in that it does not depict abuse. Abuse emerges in dancing terms, that is, from the very movements performed. A lift, for example, becomes a throw, or an intricate interlacing of bodies, a stranglehold. Differences between dance and violence are not dramatically marked in the performance (Figure 4.4).

Third thesis: The heterosexual relation in *Laughter* does not stand as an autonomous and natural given outside of history any more than, for Marx, does production. This is Marx's starting point in *Grundrisse* where production and consumption are reframed in performative terms: "one appears," writes Marx, "for the other, mediated by the other" (1973: 93). Marx's view of political economy is performative: performances are products because they are completed (produced) by their own dissolution, which is also their consumption by onlookers. The consumption of violence is voyeurism.

A transitional scene: Five Women on chairs and stools (without high heels) reaching toward the light, which comes in a narrow beam from one corner. They pull away and hide their faces. They reach again. They are not threatening and taunting characters here, but contemplative, and they allow the audience a space for reflection. Here they function subtly as chorus, the conscience of the work, redirecting its negativity. "This is the portentous power of the negative; it is the energy of thought" (Hegel 1967: 93–4). The couple of innocents crawl onto the stage and roll over one another. The Women watch them with nostalgia.[14] In this most peaceful scene of the work, the Women's voyeurism serves introspection.

Sanasardo explained that their desire was entirely determined by feeling, was not fetishized.[15]

The Celebrity's last scene: She is dressed in a black-sequined bodice. The Women in High Heels are now dressed as men: pants, shirts, brimmed caps, and street shoes. They appear only in profile or back view; standing threateningly near the down stage wings and moving slowly in toward the center with a sudden broad transfer of weight, and a dragging of the foot behind (Figure 4.5). The Celebrity approaches them, bravely haughty. She lifts one leg and places it over the back of a chair provocatively; they push the chair out from under her leg, but take a "wait and see" attitude. She goes to the chair and sits. They come closer; one reaches out to touch her

Figure 4.4   Laughter After All: Paul Sanasardo and Donya
Feuer in the second act, 1960 performance. (Photo: Mary-Alice
McAlpin)

face or caress her hair. She looks up terrified, lonely, and abused. The chair is suddenly pulled out from under her. She tries to hold onto it, but collapses to the floor. Total loss of composure. On her stomach, she stretches out her arms, catches the two rear legs of the chair, lifts it in the air, and pounds it down in front of her as far as her arms will allow. She then drags and twists her body again close to the chair. With impotent fury but enormous theatrical strength, she lifts and pounds the chair and crawls after it, her red hair flying in every direction, wriggling painstakingly out of view.

When The Celebrity reappears in the second act, she is accosted by a group of "men" easily recognizable as the Five Women in High Heels cross-dressed. This scene of women playing men and women touches upon the historical character of the American burlesque which, until the mid-1920s, was cross-dressing rather than striptease. Burlesque featured vocal, verbal women impersonating males without "intention to deceive the spectator or to suppress their femininity" (Allen 1991: 134). "Horrible prettiness" was at once the exposure of female sexuality in the guise of trouser roles, the possibility that this sexuality was coded as homosexual, and the added fact that the male audience might, through some un-explained process, be in fact viewing this spectacle as one of male homo-sexuality. The cross-dressed Women in High Heels are, in other terms, the allegory of the allegory of male homosexuality.

The Celebrity's last scene is at once her violation through heterosexual scopic consumption become highly tangible (the "men" transform the stage into a back alley in which they encounter The Celebrity), a lesbian gang rape, and if one extends the transgressiveness of the burlesque to male homosexual fantasy, a scene of male homosexual panic. It is all three interchangeably because of the ambiguous readings one can give the cross-dressed figures and because, by extension, the role of The Celebrity itself as a figure of surplus value can, although clearly played by a young girl, be read symbolically as a male transvestite. In fact, the performer's very youth supports the baroque quality of this reading by indicating a daring transferal. In this way, and perhaps with a more precise set of concerns than Allen is able to attribute to burlesque's "political paradox," *Laughter* reproduces what Allen calls the "irreducible complexity of the burlesque" (1991: 283). (One of the only ways to get at that complexity, in my opinion, would be to recover, or to speculate on, the kind of laughter early burlesque audiences produced.)

Lying on a hospital cart, A Young Man and A Girl are rolled out onto the stage. Both nearly naked in flesh-colored trunks and rubber hospital caps, he lies on his back and she is draped over him face down. About seven people grouped around and on boxes and chairs observe this scene as a show (Figure 4.6). One Man lifts the couple's limp bodies from the cart, sets them in standing positions with arms extended to the side, jumps madly up and down in anticipation, winds up like a pitcher to the sound of

Figure 4.5 *Laughter After All*: The Celebrity's final assignation. Judith
Blackstone and cast. (Photo: Keith Brian Staulcup)

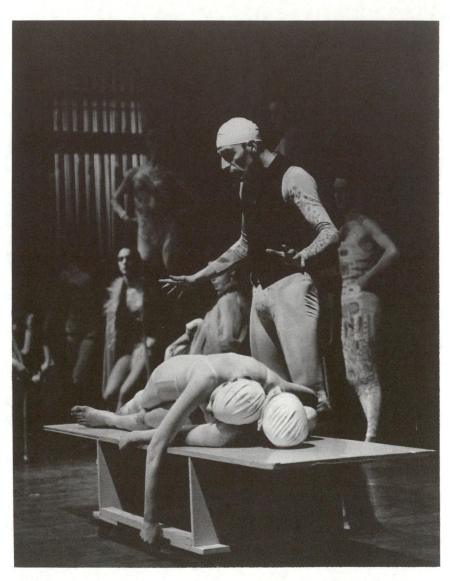

Figure 4.6   Laughter After All: Sanasardo, anticipating the torment to come, as his audience looks on. On the table: Manuel Alum and Willa Kahn. (Photo: Keith Brian Staulcup)

Figure 4.7 Laughter After All: a high point of hilarity over One Man's cruel stunts, 1960 performance. Center: Paul Sanasardo; behind him, Milagro Llauger and Edward Sutton; in shadow, Donya Feuer. (Photo: Mary-Alice McAlpin)

a drum roll and punches them one by one. Each blow is punctuated by a crash of symbols. One Woman hovers around him as an accomplice in this macabre exercise. The innocents appear to be anaesthetized. Placed on their feet, they stand by themselves but remain otherwise immobile with eyes closed, as if drugged. There is something clinical about this scene, but also patently absurd. When One Man hits an arm, the other flies up. The onlookers laugh at these reflexes. At each stunt, One Man laughs maniacally but voicelessly, holding his head in his hands while hopping on one leg (Figure 4.7).

In a similar manner, the final scene of the work in which the madman brutalizes the practically naked bodies of the innocent couple also constitutes a consumption of their earlier romantic duet. Performing for the other members of the cast, One Man inverts their first act duet by replaying it as a duet between corpses, set in motion (quite literally) by the choreographer. The work ends by consuming itself from within (from its own creative source), reproducing itself as internal consumption of its own process, stereotypes, and theatrical scenes.

Fourth thesis: The physiological activity of laughter, its expulsion of air and sound via energetic rejection from the oral cavity, has a highly ambiguous negativity. Exploring this negativity is part of the strategy behind recorded "fun house" laughter replayed at different speeds. Laughter must be the last "organic" metaphor available to the unalienated modern dance body, since it contains the seed of alienation, confronting the organic with its own mechanism.

The woman's recorded mechanical laughter returns for the first time at normal speed. After different experiments with both figures, One Man hits them both in the back, kicks them in the back of their legs and hauls their collapsed bodies back onto the cart. They are then wheeled offstage. One Man and One Woman perform a short and uncharacteristically tender duet, after which she steps aside. She leaves. He throws himself repeatedly to the floor, pitching his upper body in a dive to the ground from a standing position. His audience leaves; some of the Women dig their heels into his back as they go (Figure 4.8). **We are left with a final image of One Man frozen in a diving posture from his knees to the floor, head covered by his hands, pointed foot in the air as the others desert him.**

In *Laughter*'s final scenes, the work's cruellest protagonists, The Celebrity and One Man, achieve thematic totality. The Celebrity is the "exceptional" being who is demystified (whose surplus value is reduced to subjectivity) and One Man ("One" indicating he is representative of many) is the "unexceptional" being become mediatized as a mad doctor in a chamber of horrors. The abuse practiced by One Man on the innocents (by the choreographer on his dancers) is, in The Celebrity's experience, a spectating abuse visited upon her by her audience. One Man's scene of madness turns the two unalienated subjects of the work – A Young Man

Figure 4.8 Laughter After All: the Women, Regina Axelrod and Sally Bowden, and One Man, Paul Sanasardo, in the final moments of the work. (Photo: Keith Brian Staulcup)

and A Girl – into objects. Production is cruelty (performance); consumption is voyeurism (spectatorship). One Man performs for spectators who laugh but ultimately abandon him in disgust.

Final thesis: From the 1930s through the 1960s, modern dance was modernist in the way it sought organic "solutions" to the reification of modern industrial society.[16] Novel "solutions" become choreographic/pedagogic "styles" whose signatures are Graham's contraction, Cunningham's use of chance, Rainer's pedestrian task, etc. Each stylistic signature is an "organic" metaphor, by which I mean only that it can be theatrically embodied, and the degree to which each creator can distinguish her/himself from a choreographic predecessor is the degree to which s/he can successfully deploy a new metaphor, a new aesthetic-ethical solution, a new performance of use value. Each solution implicitly proposes a new social space as style, a different training. Thus both the need for and the enormous difficulty of innovation.

Laughter thwarted this modernist challenge by taking it up in a distinctly negative direction. Laughter itself has been an overwhelmingly powerful metaphor for use value in western culture. Rabelais identified it as the physical-behavioral trait that uniquely defined humanity as such.[17] But, *Laughter*'s laughter is reified, alienated, mechanized, and manipulated from beginning to end. It is a sign of unalienable human identity, but "after all," that is, revisited ambiguously as consuming rather than producing humanity. It is this in-organic metaphor, the last embodiment derived from bodiliness, that links exchange value (the Five Women in High Heels) and surplus value (The Celebrity) to a critique of the "natural" (the heterosexuality of One Man and One Woman). *Laughter* not only explored abuse in sexual relationships much ahead of its time, but issues of gender and sexuality as well, issues that had barely reached the left cultural surface in 1960.

How can this work be re-evaluated in the context of 1960s dance? Certainly, *Laughter After All* is not a "reflection of society," as I have tried to show with the help of post-Marxian theory. But neither did Feuer and Sanasardo "shape the very form and style of political and cultural protest in the later Sixties" (Banes 1993: 9). How can Feuer and Sanasardo be situated with reference to a 1960s American avant-garde which, in the historiography of Sally Banes, does not include them, and certainly excludes others as well. Feuer and Sanasardo did not work in Greenwich Village, that mythical locus of radicalism, but in studios on 19th and 21st streets just east of Sixth Avenue, in the heart of New York City's garment district. Does this matter? More importantly, is the issue of "style" and "form" the key issue in the relation of art to politics in decades such as the 1930s, the 1960s, and even the 1990s? Is productive rather than reflective art an art that presages styles of protest alone, or also content? These are perhaps questions to reconsider in plumbing the unknown continent of 1960s dance.

NOTES

1 *Laughter After All* was premiered on June 18, 1960, performed again on December 4, 1960, and in a "revised" version on February 1, 1964 at Hunter Playhouse in New York City. Sounds were taped and arranged by Jan Syrjala. The music was by Edgard Varese ("Density 21.5," "Ionization," "Octandre," "Integrales," and "Poème Electronique"). Varese also provided further taped sounds. Set and costumes were by visual artist Robert Natkin, and lighting was designed by Nicola Cernovich. *Laughter* was to be the last in a series of evening-length collaborations between Feuer and Sanasardo that included *In View of God* (1959), *Excursion for Miracles* (1961), and *Pictures in Our House* (1961). Their choreographic collaboration lasted from 1958 until 1963 and included shorter works as well. Subsequent shorter works by Sanasardo embroidered on aspects of *Laughter*, notably: *Cut Flowers* (1966), *Pain* (1969), and *Consort for Dancers* (1975). Although condensed reworkings of *Excursions* and *Pictures* were revived in the 1960s, *Laughter After All* was not performed again after 1964.

2 What follows is a brief resume of Lukács's philosophical argument in "Reification and Class Consciousness." See also, Eugene Lunn, *Marxism and Modernism: An Historical Study of Lukács, Brecht, Benjamin and Adorno*, Berkeley: University of California Press, 1982: 97–8.

3 I wish to thank Paul Sanasardo, Judith Blackstone, Diane Germaine, Sally Bowden, Regina Axelrod, and Robert Natkin for remembering many details of the work in the process of this verbal reconstruction. My description is structured on my own visual memory as enhanced by the accounts of the choreographer and the performers in recent interviews.

4 The effect here is to place performance outside of its traditional (representational) theatrical sphere, since what the curtain opens onto is what we already know or have just seen. But this move is as much toward an expressionism as toward a realism, since what we have seen and will see is just as likely to be on the far side of implausibility.

5 Personal communication with Paul Sanasardo, January 3, 1995.

6 Allen's study points to the difficulties of interpreting the historical burlesque, citing a contemporary report that, "Though they were not like men, [they] were in most things as unlike women, and seemed creatures of a kind of alien sex, parodying both. It was certainly a shocking thing to look at them with their horrible prettiness, their archness in which was no charm, their grace which put to shame" (1991: 134–5). The menacing demeanor of the Five Women in High Heels contradicts their more modern reference to a burlesque sexuality, and brings *Laughter* in line with burlesque's historical complexity. Allen's position is that burlesque performance was initially erotic, amusing, and disturbing, but he is unable to specify the concerns of its transgressiveness.

7 Exchange value induces us to evaluate everything in relation to a market. The market, by definition, has isolated things from their sources and abstracted them from their destinations. As commodities, they are fetishistic, that is, fascinating in their insular and autonomous appeal to our needs. Use value, on the other hand, refers to things only inasmuch as they intrinsically address and satisfy our needs as well as reflect our subjectivity and the subject positions in which they originate. This is what Baudrillard refers to as the theocracy of use value: "But value in the case of use value is enveloped in total mystery, for it is grounded anthropologically in the (self-) 'evidence' of a naturalness, in an unsurpassable original reference." Jean Baudrillard, *For a Critique of the Political Economy of the Sign* (trans. Charles Levin), St. Louis, MO: Telos, 1981: 139.

8 Although this was not at all unheard of in German modern dance. See, in particular, the work of Valeska Gert in the 1920s and early 1930s, or more

recently the work of Pina Bausch. It is perhaps significant that Bausch worked with Sanasardo and Feuer on the original version of *Laughter After All*.

9   As Allen shows, burlesque only becomes associated with striptease in the 1920s.

10 Sally Banes has remarked: "Like the Soviet avant-garde of the 1920s, the early Sixties artists were both interested in and historically capable of truly acknowledging the sophisticated mass culture they were part of – and the fact that they were part of it. They used computers and television, collaborated with engineers, and brought mass media techniques into the art gallery" (1993: 7).

11 This was the only positive review of the work I have been able to find. Although there is not space here to examine the difficulties of Sanasardo's critical reception in the 1960s, it should be noted that dance critics almost unanimously praised the development of his company over that decade (Feuer relocated to Sweden in 1963), and the quality of the dancing, but almost universally disparaged its emotional directness. As a company member between 1965 and 1970, I was considerably influenced by this approach.

12 This triangle was developed from an earlier work for Sanasardo, Feuer, and Bausch entitled *Three Phases of Madness*. Personal communication with Paul Sanasardo, January 3, 1995. The 1960 version of *Laughter* had only three Women in High Heels, and no Celebrity and Her Pet. The subtitle of the first version was "An Unspoken Drama Revealing the Cruelty and Madness of One Man and His Companion."

13 Due to an injury, Germaine did not actually perform the 1964 version. Replacing her, Loretta Abbott played both a Woman in High Heels and One Woman.

14 "Although melancholy always contains the moment of nostalgia, nostalgia is not necessarily melancholic. Nostalgia is often the ideological and feeling aspect of a new choice of values and tasks." Agnes Heller, *A Theory of Feelings*, Assen: Van Gorcum, 1979: 187.

15 Personal communication with Paul Sanasardo, February 9, 1995.

16 See Mark Franko, *Dancing Modernism/Performing Politics*, Bloomington: Indiana University Press, 1995.

17 "Rire est le propre de l'homme" ("Laughter is man's most distinguishing feature"). Rabelais, *Oeuvres complètes*, Paris: Gallimard, 1955: 2.

BIBLIOGRAPHY

Allen, R. C. (1991) *Horrible Prettiness: Burlesque and American Culture*, Chapel Hill: University of North Carolina Press.

Banes, S. (1993) *Greenwich Village 1963: Avant-Garde Performance and the Effervescent Body*, Durham, NC: Duke University Press.

Baudrillard, J. (1981) *For a Critique of the Political Economy of the Sign*, St. Louis, MO: Telos.

Buci-Glucksmann, C. (1984) *La Raison baroque: De Baudelaire à Benjamin*, Paris: Galilée.

Fuller, P. (1981) *Robert Natkin*, New York: Harry N. Abrams.

Hall, S. (1986) "The Problem of Ideology – Marxism Without Guarantees," *The Journal of Communication Inquiry* 10, 2: 28–43.

Hegel, G. W. F. (1967) *The Phenomenology of Mind*, New York: Harper & Row.

Lukács, G. (1971) "Reification and the Consciousness of the Proletariat," in *History and Class Consciousness: Studies in Marxist Dialectics*, Cambridge, MA: Massachusetts Institute of Technology Press.

Marcuse, H. (1988) "The Affirmative Character of Culture," in *Negations: Essays in Critical Theory*, London: Free Association Books.

Marx, K. (1973) *Grundrisse, Foundations of the Critique of Political Economy*, New York: Vintage.

Maskey, J. (1964) review in *Dance Magazine* (March): 64.

5 Do You Want to Join the Dance?

Postmodernism/Poststructuralism, the Body, and Dance

Helen Thomas

This paper focuses on a consideration of certain aspects of developments in dance research that have taken place over the past several years that bear witness to a shift of interests towards the social, cultural sciences, and humanities. The aim is to assess the value and/or the problems that arise from the growing predilection in what might be called "new" dance studies[1] (evidence of which is readily available in this collection) to graft discourses stemming from literary and/or cultural studies, particularly those informed by poststructuralism and postmodernism, onto the analysis of dance. In the course of this, the paper will also consider what it is about these discourses that makes them so appealing to dance writers. This will entail some lengthy diversions away from dance towards a discussion of certain points of reference that seem to underpin the discourses. The paper will center on writing that addresses western theatrical dance, although the aforementioned discourses have also had an impact on dance analyses that are not centered on performance (see, for example, Cowan 1990, Novack 1990, Sklar 1991).[2]

However, I am not going to discuss the shift towards a theorization of "culture" in dance scholarship as some disinterested observer. Rather, the intention is not only to locate these changes with reference to particular aspects of the work of writers like Foster (1986), Dempster (1988), Cooper Albright (1990), Daly (1991a,b), Adair (1992), Copeland (1993), but also through the lenses of the evolution of my writing on dance over this time span. Indeed, it is from the latter perspective that I wish to begin this inquiry. This is not for reasons of mere self-indulgence, although, in truth, there may an element of that involved. More importantly, it relates to a commitment to the practice of self-reflexivity, to situate the discourses that ground my voice in relation to those of others with and of whom I speak.

One of the valuable things sociology teaches is that those very issues and concerns which we think of as personal and individual, for the most part, are much more common, shared and/or structural than we imagine and therefore, can also be said to reside within the bounds of the sociological imagination.[3] The individual is situated in and articulated through a complex web of social relations, discourses, and practices. There is a constant interchange between the writing self/selves (in this case the particular–woman–academic) and others (texts, authors, discourses), and that interrelationship is worthy of exploration. So it is from this point that I wish to begin: from a space that is already enmeshed in a range of discourses and practices to the engagement with the others (texts, authors, discourses) I encounter(ed) through the journey into the dance research maze.

In the early part of the 1980s when I began to direct serious attention towards formulating a sociological framework[4] for analyzing dance, in this case American modern dance, the concern was to generate an approach that, on the one hand, would attend to the specificity of performance dance as a reflexive practice with movement at its center and on the other, to demonstrate the social facticity of dance, which would make it a legitimate topic of sociological inquiry. In the late 1970s and early 1980s, there was little systematic interest in focusing on the social issues surrounding dance, either from the "mainstream"[5] of dance scholarship or from the social and cultural sciences.[6] However, there were certain small but observable pockets of interest and dissent in, for example, the anthropology of dance, where there had been developing a small but growing "systematic" interest in theorizing the structure and functions of dance (see Kaeppler 1991 and Grau 1993 on these developments in the U.S. and Europe respectively). Despite the differences between anthropology and sociology (Thomas 1995), the anthropology of dance is instructive for a sociology of dance, not least because it invites us to turn the telescope round and look at our own culture as if it were "anthropologically strange" (Garfinkel 1984). It was also from this site that what appeared to be the first assault on the theoretical "evolutionist" grounds of "mainstream" dance history, dance ethnology, and dance criticism was mounted (see Youngerman 1974, Williams 1977).

Within dance history in the U.S. there was also an emergent interest in situating theatrical dance within the context of the wider cultural formation (Kendall 1979, Shelton 1981, Sorell 1981). While these texts were clearly "culturally" informed, they were virtually silent on the issue of theory and/or method of approach. Thus, the issue of historiography was not problematized.

The place where social questions surrounding dance were being raised in dance writing in the late 1970s and early 1980s in the U.K. was between the covers of *New Dance*. The assault on mainstream performance dance and dance criticism in *New Dance* was influenced by Marxist rhetoric, particularly the cultural Marxism of Antonio Gramsci (Hoare and Smith 1971).[7] Gramsci's concept of "hegemony," it seemed, could be heard coming through every pore of the magazine. The influence of early second-wave feminist analysis, particularly the critique of patriarchy, and the idea of consciousness raising, also informed the discourse. Although the discussions and criticisms in *New Dance* were lively and often challenging in terms of rocking the boat of "orthodox" criticism, it was also the case that the borrowed terms and concepts were often used in a somewhat simplistic and unrigorous manner.

Thus, there were very few places in dance scholarship for a budding sociologist of dance to go to directly to draw inspiration for theorizing the relations between dance and culture. My attention was directed to just about everywhere apart from current dance research in order to set out the basis for the methodology, except perhaps dance anthropology and certain aspects of the phenomenology of dance. Ultimately, I found my direction through two main avenues: first, the idea of the text, image, etc. being more than the sum of the parts that comprise it, that was gaining credibility in the sociology of art and culture through the increasingly pervasive influence of structuralism and semiotics in Anglo-American academic circles; second, the contention that the body is a symbol of society that stemmed from the Durkheimian tradition of thought (see Polhemus 1975, Thomas 1995) which situated the body firmly in the domain of culture and as a site for sociological inquiry.

When I was invited to rework this material in 1992, I was confronted with a rather different scenario. It became apparent that significant theoretical and methodological shifts in dance scholarship had begun to be set into motion from the latter half of the 1980s.[8] The new trends have centered around a concern to explicate the relations between dance and culture and to analyze dance as a mode of representation. In many respects these shifts echoed changes that had reverberated through the social sciences and the humanities during the 1980s which were characterized by "a series of crises of representation," whereby:

> older modes of defining, appropriating and recomposing the objects of artistic, philosophical, literary and social scientific languages are no longer credible and in which one common aspect is the dissolution of the very boundary between language and its object, this in turn being related to the acceptance of the inevitability of a plurality of perspectives and the dissolution of various older polarities (popular/elite forms, subject/object) and boundaries (for instance between disciplines such as philosophy, sociology, history and psychoanalysis).
>
> (Boyne and Rattansi 1990: 12)

The "crises in representation" in the various discourses, in part, can be characterized by the challenges to the dominant cultural hegemony of modernity posed by postmodernist, poststructuralist, and feminist analyses. It would have been almost impossible for anyone engaged in the sociology of culture in the 1980s not to have been affected by the way in which the influential "linguistic turn" of semiotics was itself being turned upon by deconstructionism. Similarly, the concepts of postmodernism/modernism and postmodernity/modernity and the related issues they engendered became highly contested areas (Featherstone 1988). What Stuart Hall once referred to as the "'steamroller' of structuralism" moving over cultural studies and the social sciences in the late 1970s[9] could be used equally to point to the impact of postmodernism and poststructuralism in the 1980s.

When I began working in the area, "culture" was seen as a rather marginal (and somewhat unworthy) topic of sociological analyses, in comparison to the more established areas of class, power, and social structure that emanated from the classical tradition. Sociologists of culture did not draw on other "aesthetically" oriented frameworks like art history, literary criticism, and philosophical aesthetics, but were more concerned with the extrinsic factors of social class, biography, taste, and so on. As I have pointed out elsewhere, "the relaxing of traditional disciplinary boundaries in sociology has been accompanied by a shift towards the theorization of culture" (Thomas 1995). Cultural issues have been pushed to the center of sociological discourse, so much so that it sometimes appears we are in danger of losing sight of the fact that issues of class, race, etc. are embedded in the discourses of taste and style of consumer capitalism (Bourdieu 1984). Although this shift was given impetus through other discourses such as Marxism, semiotics and feminism, poststructuralism and postmodernism have accelerated the drift. The theorization of culture constitutes a common strand that runs across the chain of meanings that shelter under the umbrella of postmodernism and poststructuralism (Featherstone 1988). My approach to the sociology of dance began to develop and shift its ground through the processes of my intellectual and institutional engagement with the changing discourses of the sociology of culture and cultural studies in the early 1980s. The subsequent confrontations with postmodernism, poststructuralism, and feminism in the late 1980s had implications for the re-writing of the aforementioned work, which was completed in the first half of the 1980s, and for re-positioning or re-writing myself in relation to it. It was not enough to add these onto an already given frame in order to provide a fuller picture. That would be similar to the idea of adding *her*story to *his*tory so as to achieve a more accurate picture of historical processes, a view that beleaguered early feminist analysis in the 1970s. Rather, it entailed a re-working of and through the text and to a certain extent, the undoing of it, particularly in relation to the discussions of modernism in the arts and dance, and the body in society and dance. Modernism, for example, can now only be seen by me, and I suspect by others also, through the lenses of the modernism/postmodernism debate.

In the introduction to the second edition of *Terpsichore in Sneakers* in 1987 Sally Banes indicated with some relief that, at that point, dance scholarship had not fallen prey to these intellectual fads which Boyne and Rattansi (1990) considered contributed to the above named "crises in representation." These fads which were founded on the "linguistic turn," for Banes, perhaps echoing what Lyotard (1984) has called the "post-modern condition," constituted a response to a crisis for meaning in the arts and contemporary culture:

The recent intellectual infatuation with structuralism and poststructuralism, symptomatic of our present rage for meaning and order, is in turn perhaps a symptom of our national, indeed global, sense of insecurity and doom. Scholars in every field turn to linguistic analysis and the jargon of new literary criticism and French psychoanalysis in attempts to make tidy sense of the messiness of experience. . . .

While the critical community in dance has not rushed to embrace semiotics and post-structuralism with the fervor found in other fields, choreographers (though not necessarily motivated by deeply theoretical concerns) have been exploring the implications of this perspective.

(Banes 1987: xxiii–xxiv)

Banes, however, almost spoke too soon. The recent burgeoning interest in the interrelation between dance and culture within dance scholarship also carries the marks of the influence of semiotics, postmodernism, poststructuralism, and feminism, all tied up with a cultural studies bow. The work of such scholars as Susan Foster (1986), Marianne Goldberg (1987/8), Ann Cooper Albright (1990), Cynthia Novack (1990), Ann Daly (1991a), Roger Copeland (1992), despite his cries to the contrary, and Susan Manning (1993) in the U.S., and Christy Adair (1992), Ana Sanchez-Colberg (1993), Valerie Rimmer (1993), and, to some extent, Jordan and Thomas (1994) in the U.K. bears witness to this.[10] Although cultural studies started out in Britain in the late 1960s, it was taken up in the United States in the 1980s and much of what now counts as "critical" cultural studies emerges from the U.S. Cultural studies embraced postmodernism and poststructuralism like a new lover. The eclecticism in theory and method which lay at the very roots of the formation of cultural studies lent itself well to the adaptation and incorporation of the issues which these discourses brought to the fore.

Clearly, terms like feminism, postmodernism, and poststructuralism are highly contentious, involving a variety of approaches and political stances, and it goes beyond the scope of this paper to draw these out in any systematic or detailed manner. Rather, I am going to look at some of the issues that poststructuralism and postmodernism have generated and see how these have found their way into some recent dance writing, particularly texts concerned with generating a feminist perspective. Despite differences between the proponents of postmodernism, there are a number of commonalities. There is general agreement that the postmodern represents a cultural break or shift in sensibilities, practices, and discourses that has taken place in western cultural formations since the end of World War II. Postmodernism stresses the collapsing of the boundaries between high art and popular culture, between art and life, and a celebration of eclecticism through a mixing and matching of styles and genres. As the prefix suggests, *post*modernism (as with *post*structuralism) is a relative term. In order to understand the otherness of postmodernism, "the move beyond/away" from modernism and its "links" with modernism (Kaplan 1989), we have to reconstruct the image that it has of modernism itself. And that image, according to Andreas Huyssen (1986), has been a changing one that requires articulation.

Huyssen (1986) considers postmodernism's critique of modernism to have been founded initially on a specific image of modernism represented by "high modernism" as formulated by the American critic Clement Greenberg in the 1950s. Like Sally Banes (1987) in her re-assessment of the development of "post-modern" dance, Huyssen (1986) maintains that there is an historical distinction between the postmodernism of the 1960s, 1970s and the 1980s. There is no concern in Huyssen, however, as there is in the discussions between Susan Manning (1988, 1989) and Banes (1989) in the pages of *The Drama Review*, to demarcate "real" postmodernist choreography from other choreography. That would be a contradiction in terms, because postmodernism's and poststructuralism's otherness as they have developed, to a large extent, has centered on a critique of the real, the authentic truth or logic in the western rationalist tradition as a "fiction" that operates in the guise of truth. Those thinkers who celebrate postmodernism because it opens up ironies, intertextualities, differences and so on, view attempts to set out a conclusive version or a model of postmodernism as impaired attempts to totalize or theorize (Featherstone 1988). The advocates of cultural postmodernism reject traditional grand or meta-narratives as authoritarian because they offer a single unitary view of the world. The very act of asking "the real postmodernism to stand up" is itself operating within the canons of modernism, postmodernism's berated other. Manning, in effect, offers an inclusive view of postmodern dance from the perspective of cultural postmodernism as it has developed in the 1980s, while Banes maintains that she is concerned with *post-modern* dance as an exclusive historical description of the work of certain choreographers. Banes takes as given the descriptive term that dancers give to their work while Manning's focus is on dance texts. This reflects their respective positions of analytical modernism and postmodernism. At the same time, however, Manning proposes that her definition of *dance modernism* is better than that of Banes who, she maintains, is really operating in terms of Greenberg's framework of high modernism or, to use Manning's term, "modernist dogma." Thus Manning, through her concerns to take the moral high ground by proposing more accurate and therefore more authentic definitions, is also to a certain extent operating within the canons of modernism, despite her attempts to open up the discourse.

This debate is useful because it enables us to point to a set of prevalent contested meanings surrounding the term postmodernism and its other, modernism, within the area of dance (see also Daly 1992a). Moreover, it resonates with the debate within a wider cultural sense in which modernism is seen as the *culture* of modernity and postmodernism as the *emergent culture* of postmodernity (Featherstone 1988).

If the emergence of postmodernism, as Huyssen (1986) argues, has to be seen against the backdrop of American culture in the 1960s, then the rise of poststructuralism needs to be seen as a response to the failure of the political left in Europe after 1968 (Eagleton 1983). Although there are differences in approaches and perspectives between those thinkers who have been labeled poststructuralist, there are here, too, certain common-alities to be found. Central to these is the critique of the cogito, the concept of the individual as a formally free, rational thinking, acting, unified self, which has been the cornerstone of western humanist rationalist tradition of thought since the Enlightenment. Poststructuralism rejects the idea of a fixed subjectivity "in favor of a dislocated, fragmented subjectivity which is not fixed but is constituted through language on each and every occasion on which we speak. The subject, in poststructuralist theory, contrary to the western humanist tradition is constructed in and through language" (Thomas 1985: 15), as I shall go on to elaborate in relation to Lacanian psychoanalysis.

The challenges to the modernity that are inscribed in the anti-humanist stance of poststructuralism are also visible in the modernism/postmod-ernism debate, as are other key ideas such as "intertextuality, difference, plurality and reflexivity" (Thomas 1995: 16). It is hardly surprising, then, that postmodernism is often used as an extended term to include the impact of the work of poststructuralists like Jacques Derrida in literary theory, Jacques Lacan in psychoanalysis, Michel Foucault in history, and Richard Rorty in philosophy. A number of writers have warned of the dangers of collapsing poststructuralism into postmodernism because, not only are there variations within each but also across their divide (see Huyssen 1986: 179–221, Kaplan 1989: 1–9, Boyne and Rattansi 1990: 1–43, McNay 1992: 116–56). Nevertheless, given that the extension has to a great extent taken place, as Boyne and Rattansi argue, "it is legitimate to use the term [postmodernism] broadly to include discussions of, especially, post-structuralism in literary theory, philosophy and historical and social analysis as the kind inspired by Foucault and Derrida" (1990: 11). However, they go on to stress that this should be done with "the recognition of the fundamental difficulties of such an assimilation" (ibid.). But what makes this extension even more credible is that postmodernism and poststructuralism are also characterized by the aforementioned "crisis in representation" (ibid.: 12).

I want to turn back to dance now and consider the kinds of theories and issues that have drawn the interest of writers who are concerned with examining the relation between dance and feminism, largely because I think there is some very interesting work in this area. As before, the discussion will seek to address the theories that seem to underpin these interests.

The "new wave" of dance scholars, for the most part, have not turned to the more "traditional" divergent approaches of "liberal," "radical," or "socialist feminism" (Jaggar 1983) for inspiration. Rather they have drawn on feminist analyses of representational systems that have been passed on

through the route of critical cultural studies[11] and which point to the influences of psychoanalysis, semiotics, poststructuralism, and postmodernism.
Laura Mulvey's (1989b) concept of the "male gaze," for example, which has
had a considerable impact on feminist film theory and on feminist cultural
analyses of representations of women since it was first published in 1975,
has also been used by the new generation of dance writers like Marianne
Goldberg (1987/8), Elizabeth Dempster (1988), Ann Cooper Albright
(1990) and Ann Daly (1991a), to criticize the notion of the "to-be-looked-
at-ness" of the appearing female body in performance, sometimes, as I hope
to demonstrate, rather uncritically.[12] And it is for that reason that I think
it is important at least to contextualize the frameworks that are cited or
invoked. There are a number of occasions, for example, where writers are
cited one after the other to support or advance a discussion without
acknowledging the fact that the citations are drawn from competing or contrary theoretical positions. I am thinking here of the all-too-easy running
together of quotes from poststructuralist French feminists such as Luce
Irigaray, Hélène Cixous, and Julia Kristeva, without pointing to their tense
relationship with Lacanian theory or to each other (Cooper Albright 1990,
Daly 1991a, Adair 1992, Copeland 1993). It may be argued that this does
not matter because, in the endless play of signifiers within postmodernism,
it is quite legitimate to mix and match and quote from different perspectives. However, and perhaps I betray my "creeping rationalism" here,
I think it is important to be clear about the ways in which other writers are
invoked so as not to do violence to their ideas, or the manner in which they
are being interpreted, despite the fact that those ideas may be read/written
in a variety of ways. Thus, I hope readers will forgive my frequent sorties
into the realm of theory that dance writers draw from before I discuss the
dance texts themselves.

The incorporation of psychoanalytic semiotics in film theory and cultural
analyses owes much to the formidable influence of Jacques Lacan (1977)
and his re-reading of Freud. Before discussing Mulvey's analysis of the
male gaze and then going on to consider how it has been used by dance
writers, I want to give a brief if somewhat "ideal typical" description of the
Lacanian problematic which seems to inform much of the work and
debates in feminist film theory.

Lacanian psychoanalysis attempts to draw together the Freudian
problematic of the structuring of gender subjectivity with the Saussurian
paradigm of structural linguistics, in order to provide a corrective for
absences and problems in both theories (Fraser 1992: 181–2). Freud was
concerned with revealing the construction of gender identity through
a complex process of psycho-sexual development. To a certain extent
Freud's theory of the psycho-sexual development of the subject challenges
theories of innate biologically determined sexual identity because it insists
that the structures of psycho-sexual development form the basis of
social organization. However, by claiming universal status for the theory,

psychoanalysis can be criticized for reducing gender to the outcome of a set of pre-ordered psycho-sexual processes and thus for shutting off the issue of gender differences from historical processes.

In his "return" to Freud, Lacan stresses the link between sexuality and the unconscious (Rose 1982). In formulating his account of sexual desire, Lacan returns to Freud's central controversial concept of the castration complex, i.e. "the presence or absence of the phallus and *nothing else* that marked the distinction between the sexes" (Mitchell 1982: 7), which had split the psychoanalytic community in the 1920s. The subject for Lacan, however, is constituted through language, and the unconscious is structured like a language. The loss of the *imaginary* and the entry of the subject into the *symbolic* has a correspondence with the child's entry into language: "The mirror stage represents the moment when the subject is located in an order outside itself to which it will henceforth refer. The subject is the subject *of* speech (Lacan's parle-être), and subject *to* that order" (Rose 1982: 31).

Lacan draws on Saussure's theory of language but rejects the "correspondence between words and things" (Lacan 1977: 151) that is implied in Saussure's concept of the arbitrary relation between the signifier and the signified, in favor of the idea of language as a chain of signifiers whose meanings are fixed temporarily in relation to their differences from one another. However, the process of signification for Lacan, unlike Derrida's deconstructionist model, for example, is not that of an endless free play of signifiers whose meanings are constantly in the process of being deferred. Lacan inverts Saussure's model of the linguistic sign and gives primacy to the determinacy of the signifier over the signified to produce certain meanings in relation to the production of the subject within the symbolic system.

In Lacan's model, as Nancy Fraser (1992) notes, the speaking subject, which is absent in the Saussurian paradigm, appears to be given a voice through the introduction of the Freudian problematic, and in so doing seems to open up a space for raising the vexing questions of identity, speech, and social practice which Saussurian linguistics cannot address. At the same time, the notion that gender subjectivity is socially produced through the child's entry into the symbolic order which is structured and sanctioned by the rules of language, appears to offer the possibility of remedying the charges of biological reductionism directed at Freud.

Meaning and the symbolic order, for Lacan (Weedon 1987: 53–4), is fixed in relation to the primary signifier of sexual difference, the phallus. "For it is essential to his [Lacan's] argument that sexual difference is a legislative divide which creates and produces its categories" (Rose 1982: 41). And it is the phallus that guarantees the patriarchal structure of the social order. The phallus, as the privileged signifier, signifies power and control through authority over the satisfaction of desire. Women's relation to language in this framework is always negative. Woman, in Lacanian theory, signifies a lack or an absence. Men occupy a central position in relation to power in the symbolic order – they have access to it by virtue of the fact that they possess a penis. Women, however, cannot aspire to power and control by virtue of the fact that they lack a penis – their difference, their identity, is defined in terms of what they are not. They constitute the "Other" to language, power, and control. In Lacan's framework:

> Sexual difference is [then] assigned according to whether individual sub-jects do or do not possess the phallus, which means not that anatomical difference *is* sexual difference . . . but that anatomical difference comes to *figure* sexual difference, that is, it becomes the sole representative of what difference is allowed to be.

> (Rose 1982: 42)

Thus, Lacan claims to describe the mechanisms through which people achieve subjectivity through their entry as young children into an already phallocentric symbolic order. The structure of the symbolic order which is patriarchal determines the attributes of individual subjectivity. At the same time, however, the framework affirms that the symbolic order has to be phallocentric because the achievement of subjectivity can only be reached through the submission to the "rule of the father." This circularity in the theory leads to an iron cage from which there can be no escape. As Fraser (1992: 182) argues, Lacan's various stages of development are coated in a theoretical frame of necessity and inevitability. There seems to be no way out of the patriarchal symbolic order, at least through social practice, which has been the driving force of feminism. Like Fraser, I have always been somewhat skeptical about this framework which has come to have such a powerful influence on feminist cultural analyses in recent years. Despite some persuasive arguments put forward in its defense (see Mitchell and Rose 1982, Kaplan 1983: 23–35, Phelan 1993), I appear unable to get over the fact that Lacanian theory, despite its claims to point to the "fictive" character of the power of the phallus in the symbolic order (Rose 1982: 38–41), is already implicated in sustaining its privileged position as the universal signifier. There seems to be no space for women; whenever or wherever they appear, they are always in masquerade. And it is precisely this spacelessness that has sent poststructuralist psychoanalytic feminists like Irigaray, Cixous, and Kristeva scurrying in different but related direc-tions to find a possible space from which the voice(s) of the feminine can be raised (Rose 1982). That space, they argue, albeit from different positions in the poststructuralist continuum, is locatable in the body: the female libido in Irigaray's case; the feminine of the pre-Oedipal phase for Cixous; the semiotic (imaginary) but non-sex specific phase for Kristeva, and thus, their concern with "writing the body" (Weedon 1987: 63–73).

Despite my reservations about Lacanian psychoanalytic semiotics, I think Toril Moi (1985) is correct when she says that the importance of psychoanalysis lies in its challenge to discourses that assume a unified self, a rational, free-thinking subject which can be entirely known. Psychoanalysis proposes that our unconscious desires and drives continuously exert pressures on our conscious thoughts and actions, as do other material and ideological factors of which we are unaware. The human subject for psycho-analysis is a complex network of intersecting structures and processes, and the conscious aspect forms only a small part. If this stance is pushed to its logical conclusion, it becomes infeasible to maintain that our conscious actions and thoughts emerge from a unified, stable subject, as the humanist tradition of thought would maintain, because we cannot know the many possible converging unconscious processes that come to impinge upon our conscious actions and thoughts. "It is this highly complex network of conflicting structures," according to psychoanalysis, "that produces the subject and its experiences, rather than the other way around" (Moi 1985: 10). Thus, it challenges the very idea of the "self" which is the central tenet of the humanist tradition, and it demands that any analysis of the "real" world must take account of these other determinants of which conscious thought is but one part. Thus, it points to the fact that any analysis can only be partial.

In her psychoanalytic semiotic approach to "Visual Pleasure and Narrative Cinema," Laura Mulvey (1989b: 14–26) argues that the pleasure in looking at narrative Hollywood cinema comes from and replicates the structure of male looking. The woman in the film is the object of the "male gaze" and the viewer is invited to see the film through the male look. Hence the female becomes objectified and this, in turn, replicates the unequal structure of power between the sexes. Feminist cinema, according to Mulvey, must disrupt the pleasure of the gaze. Mulvey's idea of the gaze is grounded in psychoanalytic theory and as such, it is difficult to move out of the way in which the individual (sexed) psyche is structured in an undifferentiated universal manner. In Mulvey's framework, as with Lacan, woman stands for what she is not, the phallus. The presence of women as an obsessive image is linked to male castration anxiety and its resolution. The body of the woman, the "other," is frightening for men. She signals the loss of "active" phallic power. In order to deal with castration anxiety, men turn women into fetishized objects and thus "women in representation can signify castration and activate the voyeuristic or fetishistic mechanisms to circumvent threat" (ibid.: 21).

Mulvey's analysis of the "male gaze" was important to feminist analysis because it offered a theoretical framework for understanding the association of the objectification of women through their bodies and their lack of cultural power within the discourse of patriarchy which had been implicit in earlier "second wave" analysis (Gamman and Makinen 1994). However, it also incurred certain criticisms; the analysis proposes that "all" gaze is male and heterosexual, and that men, unlike women, are not objectified through the look (see Gamman and Marshment 1988). It does not take account of difference (except along the lines of the Lacanian binary divide) or change over time, and thus, its approach can be criticized for being monolithic and static.

Mulvey is not unaware of some of these criticisms and in a later paper she attempts to address the problematic issue of the "male only gaze." She maintains that the "actual" sex of the spectator was not an issue for her at the time of writing. Rather, her "interest lay in the relationship between the image of woman on the screen and the 'masculinization' of the spectator position" (1989a: 29). In the later discussion, Mulvey extends her analysis of spectatorship to take account of some of the deficiencies in the earlier piece. She sees that the identification of the woman in the audience with the "active" male gaze could speak to the rediscovery of the lost aspect of her sexual identity; i.e. the loss of the "active" or phallic phase and thus the female spectator "oscillates" between the active/male and passive/female subject positions. The consequence of this, however, is that the possibility of bringing women to the position of an active knowing subject depends not on *her* identity and difference, but, rather, on what she is not or what she lacks.[13] She is constantly deferred or is deferring to the power of the privileged signifier, the marker and measure of her difference. Mulvey does argue, however, that when the female protagonist occupies center stage in the narrative structure, revealing that "she is unable to achieve a stable sexual identity" (ibid.: 30), a discursive shift is produced and she no longer represents sexuality, but, rather the narrative becomes about sexuality.

Despite Mulvey's attempts to correct some of the problems inherent in the first piece, the fact remains that her model of the gaze is underpinned by psychoanalysis and thus neglects considerations of historical change. This is because it ultimately locates explanations of representations and looking in the presumed trans-historical (dare I say essential) occurrence of male castration anxiety. This model, as Gamman and Makinen (1994: 182) argue, cannot adequately address postmodernist aesthetic moves – "kitsch, camp, pastiche and parody" – which have come to pervade many of the representations we see on the billboards, the cinema, and our TV screens (or in some dance performances). "Nor is it able to explain the way gay, lesbian, bisexual as well as heterosexual women (rather than men) get pleasure from erotic spectacle in their own right, without recourse to what Mulvey calls psychic transvestism" (ibid.).

Given these various dilemmas, I want to look at the ways in which some dance scholars have invoked the "male gaze" (usually, although not exclusively, without elucidating its psychoanalytic grounding) and ask why they considered it (and its various revisions and developments) a useful concept to apply to dance in the first instance. The discussion will follow the routes taken by Ann Cooper Albright (1990), Ann Daly (1991a), and Christy Adair (1992), and will also draw attention to further problems in relation to psychoanalytic theory.

In her book, *Women and Dance: Sylphs and Sirens* (1992), Adair devotes a chapter to the ways in which women have been viewed in dance. In the preceding chapter Adair warns the reader to beware of the trap of essentialism *vis-à-vis* certain theories on sexual difference (she is discussing Irigaray and Cixous at this point), and wishes to stress the social construction of the (female) body in dance and culture. Drawing on Mulvey's concept of representation of women, dragging in the psychoanalytic constructs of voyeurism and desire, Adair sees that the importance of the bodily "look" of the (female) dancer in the western theatrical dance tradition emphasizes the "to be looked-at-ness." "The audience is in the role of the voyeur in relationship to the dancer. The voyeur has power over the looked at, so that the dancer is traditionally displayed to gratify the audience's desire" (1992: 72).

Adair suggests that some "dance work resists mainstream dance practices," implying a disordering of the gaze (as Mulvey, too, suggests that the task of feminist film making is to disrupt the gaze), by emphasizing the "processes and performers' experiences and subjectivities" (ibid.: 74). Like Susan Foster (1986) and Cooper Albright (1990), Adair sees that these "advanced" subject positions are taken up by particular contemporary (postmodern?) choreographers. So the hierarchy Auslander (1989) argues is inherent in Foster's work in particular, is also visible in Adair's discussion, that is, the idea of a "postmodernism of resistance" as a yardstick by which to measure other dance practices.

Adair cites Pina Bausch's *Rite of Spring* (1975) as an exemplar of dance work that resists mainstream practices ensnared in patriarchal discourse. Quoting from one of her own collaborative papers, Adair sees that in Bausch's work, "women's experience of the world is expressed in . . . [the] many grounded, inward, focused, womb-like movements; there's not the extension and exposure of the body that we are used to seeing in many other dance works. The woman is subject" (1992: 74). Thus, although Adair argues against essentialist views of women, she too becomes caught up in them. There is more than a suggestion, here, that women experience themselves through their wombs (biology is destiny?) and that "womb-like movements" express the "real" of woman as subject as opposed to "extension and exposure of the body," which, presumably, Adair views in terms of the fetishization of woman as object enmeshed in the male gaze.

Part of the problem is to be found, I think, in the sociologizing of psychoanalytically grounded constructs of spectatorship without theorizing the oppositions between the social subject as agent, actor, etc., and the subject of psychoanalysis as defined above. As Mary Anne Doane points out, traditionally the problematic of spectatorship in film theory stems from a "psychoanalytically informed linguistics, not from a sociologically based analysis" (1987: 8). Feminist theory, according to Doane, has set itself on course to show that this spectator "has been constantly posited and delineated as masculine" (ibid.). In so doing, argues Doane, feminist theory "necessarily introduces the question of the social subject, but, unfortunately, it frequently and overhastily collapses the opposition between social subjects and psychic subjects, closing the gap prematurely" (ibid.).

Although this is a problem in Adair's work, it is not in Foster's (1986) text where, following Barthes, she purposely outlines her approach to "the subject" through the poststructuralist notion that it comes into being through participation in a range of discursive practices. Although Foster recognizes the influence of Lacan and Freud on Barthes' treatment of the subject and the body, she opts for the semiotic/structural side of the Barthes formula in which the body is seen as a "locus of mindful articulations," rather than "a sign for the structure of the unconscious" (Foster 1986: 237).

Adair also discusses key psychoanalytic concepts such as "desire" and "pleasure" in looking, and it is here that she topicalizes psychoanalysis as a useful resource for feminism because "it has attempted to extricate meanings from its cultural surroundings" (1992: 79). However, Adair does not elaborate on what this might mean and the notions of desire and pleasure that she discusses, once more, tend to collapse the psychoanalytic into the sociological frame. A further problem might also lie in the all-too-easy transfer from film spectatorship to that of performance. According to Adair:

> Dance provides an ideal opportunity for the voyeur. Sitting in the dark of the auditorium the spectator is offered the body endlessly displayed to gratify the desire of the looker. The woman is not as remote as she might appear to be in the screen. She is there in the flesh, constantly exposed.
>
> (ibid.)

Thus, for Adair, performance and film spectatorship have much in common, but there is something of an excess in performance. The presence of the real, live body, Adair seems to suggest, makes the (female) body more available and vulnerable to the gaze. But is there in fact such an unproblematic "goodness of fit" between film and performance, and need the possibility of the excess be viewed as more repressive? According to Peggy Phelan (drawing on psychoanalysis and feminist theories of representation), the import of performance in the ontological sense of the word, in contrast to film for example, lies in its non-reproducibility – "Performance implicates the real through the presence of living bodies" (1993: 148). Spectatorship involves consumption of performance as it appears and disappears into the memory. Phelan argues that unlike other arts involved in the system of mechanical reproduction, performance does not become enmeshed in the circulation of capital, "it resists balanced circulations of finance. It saves nothing; it only spends"(ibid.). This excessive pouring out, she maintains, makes performance susceptible to "charges of valuelessness and emptiness" (ibid.). In turn, however, this gives rise to the possibility of performance "revaluing that emptiness, which "gives performance art its distinctive oppositional edge"(ibid.).

Ann Daly, in her discussion on dance and feminist analysis, points out that contemporary feminist analysis focuses on the "the entire *process* of representation" rather than a consideration of the image in itself, and that this includes "the spectator and his/her process of interpretation" (1991a: 2). Although Daly sees Mulvey's nomenclature *vis-à-vis* spectatorship as "tiresome" (although she does not elaborate on this), she states, nevertheless, that the "male gaze" remains "a fundamental concept" which reveals the gendered positions inherent in the unequal structure of looking (active/male) and being looked at (passive/female) in contemporary western culture in which the spectator is the consumer of the image, "regardless of his/her actual sex" (ibid.). In the preceding paragraph, where she discusses the idea of woman as "other" in western culture, Daly implicitly invokes psychoanalytic theory when she adds that this otherness has been defined according to "the *fantasies* [my emphasis] and power structures of men" (ibid.). However, as with Adair's (1992) discussion, the psychic subject which resides in the realm of the symbolic crosses over into the realm of the social subject, despite the fact that she indicates once more that the actual sex of the spectator is not an issue: "The spectator is in the position of power: a traditionally male position. Thus, the term, 'male gaze'" (Daly 1991a: 2).

Like Adair (1992), Daly sees that the theory of the male gaze has much to offer dance and vice versa: "How can women represent themselves on stage without being co-opted by the conventions of the male gaze? Is it possible for women to reconstruct their own standards of beauty that need not depend on becoming the object of the male desire?" (1991a: 3) Once again, the overriding message is that all gaze is male and heterosexual.

However, in a slightly later paper, Daly does call into question the "monolithic" male gaze and problematizes the all-too-easy transference of concepts from film theory to that of dance. She proposes that "a new theory of representation is required: one that includes within its very structure the capacity for change" (1992b: 244). Daly recognizes that other cultural analysts have attempted to move beyond a simplistic notion of representation, such as Teresa de Lauretis with her view of "space-off" or "elsewhere"(discussed below), Jessica Benjamin's (1986) concept of "intersubjective space" to which Cooper Albright (1990) also alludes, and Mulvey's (1989a) revised analysis of "Visual Pleasure . . . " (discussed above).

The theory of representation that Daly finds illuminating, however, is that of the French psychoanalytic feminist, Julia Kristeva. But just what kind of change does Kristeva offer? Daly sees that what Kristeva offers in *Revolution in Poetic Language* (1984) is "really a semiotics of art, that provides an excellent framework within which to analyze the cultural significance of Isadora Duncan's work" (1992b: 244). Kristeva's model in this earlier work takes on and challenges Lacan's framework. Although she utilizes the concept of the symbolic order and the construction of the subject in Lacanian theory (Weedon 1987: 69–70), Kristeva rejects Lacan's all-encompassing view of the symbolic order (the iron cage) and the subject is more fluid and multiple. Kristeva proposes a rupture between two modes of language, the semiotic which is rooted in the pre-Oedipal, maternal body, and the symbolic which is constituted through the rules of language. Like Lacan, Kristeva sees that the feminine, whose meanings are to be found outside language and sexuality, is repressed by the phallocentric symbolic order. Because it cannot be contained by the rational structure of phallo-centrism, the semiotic or feminine signification is pushed to the margins of the symbolic (Moi 1985: 11–13). The feminine (used in a deconstructionist sense not in terms of the biological female), is located in the semiotic dimension of language and it is from this site that the potential arises to disrupt, contest, break through or displace, the symbolic order. The repressed feminine, according to Kristeva, finds a voice in the marginal discourses of the literary avant-garde, such as in the writings of modernists like Mallarmé or Joyce. It is in such writings that "the rhythms of the body and the unconscious have managed to break through the strict rational defenses of conventional social meanings" (ibid.: 11). These social meanings shore up the symbolic order and in challenging them, argues Kristeva, modernist poetics can be seen as equivalent to or pre-figuring social revolution. These poetic practices are comparable to sexual and political transformation and point to the fact that the symbolic order can be transformed from within.

Although Daly (1992b) stresses what Fraser (1992: 185) has termed the "pragmatic dimension" of Kristeva's framework, which is the analysis of language as a social practice in a social context, both Fraser and Judith Butler (1990), from a Gramscian and Foucaultian framework respectively, have argued that despite Kristeva's attempts to transcend the limits of Lacanian theory, nevertheless, she ends up by privileging the hegemony of the symbolic and subsuming the semiotic, thus once more locking us into the law of the father.

> Despite her critique of Lacan, however, Kristeva's strategy of subversion proves doubtful. Her theory appears to depend upon the stability and reproduction of precisely the paternal law that she seeks to displace. Although she effectively exposes the limits of Lacan's efforts to universalize the paternal law in language, she nevertheless concedes that the semiotic is invariably subordinate to the Symbolic, that it assumes its specificity within the terms of a hierarchy immune to challenge. If the semiotic promotes the possibility of subversion, displacement, or disruption of the paternal law, what meanings can those terms have if the Symbolic always reasserts its hegemony?
>
> (Butler 1990: 80)

In Kristeva's analysis the modernist avant-garde is celebrated because it embodies feminine signification. Modernism, however, as Huyssen (1986:

45–62) has demonstrated, stands in opposition to mass culture, and woman in modernism represents the mass to modernism's high culture. Huyssen considers that the recouping of gender typifications of mass culture with femininity could "have some bearing on the current debate about the alleged femininity of modernist/avant-gardist writing" (ibid.: 48). The documenting of the fact that the modernism/mass culture opposition has been gendered since the middle of the nineteenth century as male/female, according to Huyssen, seems to call into question analyses like that of Kristeva, which posit modernist avant-garde writing as feminine. One of the dangers, here, is that the tradition of "real" women writing (making dances) which could also embrace non-modernist aesthetics, would get ignored. Moreover, given Kristeva's deconstructionist version of the feminine, Duncan's artistic ruptures, which Daly (1992b) discusses, could have had little to do with her experiences as a woman. If we push this further, it means that men can speak (write, dance) for and on behalf of the feminine subject, thus once more ignoring "real" women and the misogynist character of patriarchal society (Huyssen 1986: 49).

One of the most interesting dialogues with psychoanalytic film theory that I have encountered is in Yvonne Rainer's film *The Man Who Envied Women*, as, indeed, the title's inversion of the Freudian problematic suggests. Rainer takes Mulvey's theory of the male gaze and pushes it to its logical conclusion, asking what happens when the object of the male gaze, the female protagonist, is not represented through her bodily image.

Trisha, Rainer's protagonist, is sight unseen throughout the film. She is "off screen," like the viewer, with whom at times she seems to share a space as a spectator in her own story. Trisha marks her presence in the film by a voice, not her body – the mark of what she is not in Lacanian theory – and thus Rainer, as Phelan argues, "implicitly challenges the nature of filmic presence" (1993: 72).

Rainer's challenge to the conventions of film and film theory resonates with challenges to visualism in other fields. Postmodern anthropologists like James Clifford (Clifford and Marcus 1986), for example, argue that ethnography has traditionally privileged sight and that the paradigm of visualism has been a key device in the domination and surveillance of non-western "others." Clifford (ibid.) calls for a postmodern anthropology which shifts away from the ethnographic gaze towards a more discursive paradigm that enables a multiplicity of "voices" to be heard, in which the anthropologist is simply one voice among many others. Listening is treated as potentially more equalitarian than seeing. However, as Foucault states in his discussion of the confessional: "the agency of domination does not reside in the one who speaks (for it is he who is constrained), but in the one who listens and says nothing; not in the one who knows and answers, but in the one who questions and is not supposed to know" (1984: 62). Foucault is discussing the confessional in relation to Catholicism prior to the Reformation, but he goes on to point out that although confession lost its local and ritual context, confession has come to be employed in a variety of relations, including the analyst/patient relation in psychoanalysis.

Returning to Rainer's film for a moment, it is interesting to note that the other character in the film who, like Trisha, is not seen, is the male protagonist's psychiatrist. But the psychiatrist is not heard either. The film begins with the protagonist Jack Deller, the husband Trisha walked out on four years before, "on the couch" talking to the silent analyst. The latter's authorial (Lacanian) subject position, as Phelan's (1993: 75–7) discussion shows, is much more secure than that of the speaking but unseen Trisha who aligns herself with the spectator.

Rainer's erasure of the body of the female protagonist in the film is the starting point for Ann Cooper Albright's (1990) interesting discussion which centers on "spectacle, moving subjects and feminist theory." Cooper Albright (ibid.: 32) asks, rightly I think, if Rainer's strategy of erasure is the "ultimate route for feminists to take." This seems especially pertinent in relation to the tradition of western theater dance where the body is the primary instrument of expression, with the female body as the dominant representational choreographed site (sight). How is it possible to create a space to represent the unrepresentable (female psychic subject) and the unrepresented (female social subject), and thereby challenge the dominant (male centered) gendered discourses?

Following Teresa de Lauretis's (1987: 26) concept of "space off" or a view from "elsewhere" ("the space not visible in the frame but inferable from what the frame makes visible"), Cooper Albright (1990: 33) sees that by "using Trisha's disembodied voice to fracture the conventions of the filmic gaze, Rainer envelopes her audience in this elsewhere." De Lauretis's analysis of spectatorship attempts to go beyond Mulvey's view of the female spectator as "oscillating" between male/active passive/female positions by positing the idea that there is a simultaneous movement between two kinds of space, the "represented space" and the "space off, the elsewhere," which "coexist concurrently and in opposition" (de Lauretis 1987: 26). For de Lauretis, "the subject of feminism is en-gendered" in the elsewhere (ibid.). Thus, in the final analysis, for de Lauretis, Rainer's film is also en-gendered.

Cooper Albright (1990: 33) suggests that contemporary dancing "finds ways to rupture traditional representations which objectify the human body" and jolt the gaze of the spectator by shifting the discourse to another space or "elsewhere."

> Slipping in and out of their culturally determined frames, the ebullient bodies in these [specific contemporary] dances elude a traditional gaze and defy the powerful pleasure of spectacle – that of looking at some-thing to-be-looked-at, the audience, in turn, can be pushed out of its conventional consumption of these bodies.
>
> (ibid.)

This opens up the possibility for a different kind of spectatorship, one which looks at the "physical experience of the dancer – her moving, her motion – her subjectivity" (ibid.).

Although Cooper Albright recognizes that dance performances are not "'the imaging machines' in quite the same way that cameras are," nevertheless, she argues, they do reveal "a certain politics of imagery" that raises questions about "'woman': woman as a spectacle, as an object to be admired, as a vision of beauty, and as a site of pleasure" (ibid.: 34). Dancers in ballet or the musical stage are often seen as embodying "some kind of eternal or essential woman" (ibid.). However, the image of ideal-typical dancer, according to Cooper Albright, does not speak of or to the subjectivity of the dancer in question, but, rather, "[of] her role in the lives and the fantasies of *male* directors, choreographers and audience members" (ibid.: 33). Once again, the psychic subject and the social subject are collapsed. Despite the fact that Cooper Albright places the term "male gaze" in inverted commas, that gaze is still a monolithic one. The result of this is that, like de Lauretis and Mulvey, the male spectator is theorized as pure while the female spectator at some level is achieved through recourse to bisexuality – "transvestism" in Mulvey's case and "double identification" in de Lauretis's work (Doane 1987: 9).

Cooper Albright's analysis, somewhat like Foster's (1986), implies a dance hierarchy: forms that reflexively disrupt the dominant canons of representation are politically more advanced and these are most likely to be found within postmodern or new dance. Like Foster, Cooper Albright sees that while some contemporary dances might have the appearance of being more politically advanced than others, they are not because they still operate within the dominant conventions of representation. While, for example Molissa Fenley makes "fast dances that require that she and her dancers train rigorously for stamina and strength," her dances, nevertheless, "fail to challenge a traditionally static 'male gaze' because they continue to accept the classic split between the audience and the performer" (Cooper Albright 1990: 34). Fenley seems more interested in displaying the body than in the pleasure of moving. Cooper Albright feels that Fenley cannot jolt the perception of the audience into "an awareness of the physical experience of those moving bodies" (ibid.), because she remains within the bounds of conventional representation.

The problem with this view, however, is that it is somewhat at odds with the postmodernist/poststructuralist rhetoric that the paper seems to celebrate, in that it assumes it is through the relation of the creator/ performer to the spectacle that the single reading the audience is allowed/ enabled to see is fixed. Postmodernism and poststructuralism, however, emphasize the "death of the author" (the traditional privileged speaking subject), the unfixing of the text (that had been fixed by the arbitrary relation of the signifier and the signified in semiotics), and the shift towards the readers/viewers as writing/choreographing the text/dance and combining the ingredients in any way they choose. This intertextuality calls into question traditional (logocentric) notions of "true" "real" "fixed" meanings, and that goes for the audiences/spectators as well as texts/performances and authors/choreographers. In this view, there are potentially a multiplicity of voices/eyes at work in any discursive practice, the task for analysis is to hear/see and deconstruct them. Cooper Albright seems to get caught up unwittingly in a paradigm she wants to rupture, the monolithic pure male "look." She thinks audiences "could be trained to see" the dancers experiencing themselves as subjects, thus implying that they cannot possibly see it now unless they are forced or instructed to "look elsewhere" (1990: 39).

And certain dancers do create works that shift the focus to the "space off," according to Cooper Albright, such as Pooh Kaye, Ann Carlson, Marie Chouinard, and Jennifer Monson, and in so doing "often expose the problematic dynamic of a conventional performer/audience relationship" (1990: 40). These dancers/dances, although different from each other, are exemplars of the top rung in the hierarchy of dance from a feminist perspective, "it is in this space – this new frontier – that women dancers can begin to claim their subjectivity" (ibid.) and presumably teach others (the audience) to "see" difference. Thus, Cooper Albright ends by privileging author over audience, "art" over "life," and by implication, art over popular culture, which, ironically, is the very antithesis of cultural postmodernism.

This implied privileging of certain postmodern dancers/dances is also to be found more explicitly in Dempster's (1988) analysis of women "writing the body" in dance, which draws heavily from poststructuralist literary theory, Daly's (1987) critical appraisal of the representation of women in Balanchine's work, and Foster's (1986) analysis of postmodern dance. Through a discussion of the ways in which "the body is being written in dance and the ways in which dance, within the Western theatrical tradition, has defined and redefined bodies, particularly women's bodies," Dempster (1988: 31) posits a three-tier dance hierarchy with ballet at the bottom, modern dance in the middle, and postmodern dance at the top. Rather like Bourdieu's concept of "habitus" (see Jenkins 1992), Dempster (1988: 37) sees that "the dancer's body is not merely a written-upon page," that is, it is not like a set of clothes that can be put on and taken off at will (although clothes are also extraordinarily meaningful). Rather, ideologies are constructed upon and inscribed onto the "anatomical plane" of the dancer's body. The female body in ballet is a colonized body through the patriarchal discourse that inscribes it; the "natural" body is defined, redefined and transformed into a distant idealized passive icon of femininity and "the specificity of the female body is obscured . . . difference is reduced to sameness" (ibid.: 50).

The early modern dance sought to lay the dancing body bare in order to reveal the expressive potential of the "natural" body inherent in the "presymbolic human subject" (Dempster 1988: 44). However, as modern dance became more codified into a set of techniques, so the specificity of the natural female body was erased and it became "vulnerable to colonization" (ibid.: 51). "Although modern dance's representation of the feminine stands in contrast to that of ballet, it has become in its own way as prescriptive of the system that it originally sought to challenge" (ibid.).

By contrast, postmodern dance, according to Dempster, does not constitute a "newly defined dance language" but is rather an "interrogation of that language itself" (ibid.: 51) and herein lies its potential to intervene in and subvert the conventions of patriarchal discourse. The postmodern body is not fixed, but is constantly in flux, adapting and transforming itself through its engagement with the world. The "writing" of the body in postmodern dance (as in cultural postmodernism) is partial, conditional, temporal; as it is being written, so it is erased. This means that the body in postmodern dance (again like cultural postmodernism) and by extension, the "feminine," "is unstable, fleeting, flickering, transient – a subject of multiple representations" (ibid.: 49).

While I think Dempster and Daly (1987) offer an all too unitary view of ballet (see Jordan and Thomas 1994 on Daly 1987), the point behind the analysis is important. That is, the concern is to demonstrate that the body in dance is situated in and through a range of discursive practices, thus calling into question the very idea of a "natural" body that constructs and underpins theories of sexual difference. Dempster places the natural in inverted commas and unlike Adair (1992) for example, she manages to steer clear of the essentialist trap that could implicate her in a compliant relationship with the ideology of sexual difference as natural. Similarly, despite the queries I have raised with regard to the use of the male gaze, a particular mode of psychoanalytic feminism and the unproblematic collapsing of the psychic subject into the social subject in the writing under discussion here, the theoretical intention behind the work is important; that is, to show that the ways in which we look at dance are not quite as neutral or as individual as we might think but are inscribed in a chain of cultural codes and practices in and through which our bodies, our subjectivities, are situated and implicated.

This paper began by asking what it is about the discourses of postmodernism and poststructuralism that make them so appealing to dance writers. In postmodernism and poststructuralism, the central issues of "language and meaning and subjectivity" (Weedon 1987) are articulated in terms of a discourse of the body, and these are themes that are constantly being addressed in recent dance scholarship. In the light of the preceding discussion, I think that the key to understanding the sway of these discourses is to be found in the manner in which they have precipitated the elevation of culture into the academic arena and their re-positioning of the body to the center of the discourse, which, in turn, offers dance (particularly western theatrical dance) the possibility of a new-found (academic) legitimacy, an authorial voice that it had not achieved hitherto.

NOTES

1 Ann Daly (1991b), in an article entitled *"What Revolution?: The New Dance Scholarship in America*, gives a brief overview of what she sees as new dance scholarship in the United States. Here she points out the weaknesses (and some of the strengths) of "old" dance scholarship and the emergence of "new" dance analysis in which culture is a central concern. Daly explains that what was once called "dance history" has expanded in terms of its "approach, subjects and methodology" into what might be more appropriately termed "dance studies." The use of this term is significant because it follows the pattern of other multi-disciplinary based programs of study like cultural studies, literary studies, film studies. Although graduate courses at the Laban Centre in London were given the name Dance Studies at the beginning of the 1980s to indicate that dance analyses involved a range of disciplines, the particular disciplines that were taught, apart from the sociology of dance, did not particularly engage or draw on the other related areas, as perhaps they now do.

2 This is not to imply a hierarchy of forms of dance or the types of analyses involved. I think that one of the merits of postmodernism, although I must admit that I am not a convert, is that it points out that such divisions are spurious and that their retention speaks more about the "hyperinstitutionalization" of the "high" arts in western culture than anything else (Willis *et al.* 1990).

3 See C. Wright Mills (1970) for an illuminating discussion of what he saw as the promise of the "sociological imagination" that emerged through the work of the classical tradition of sociology.

4 The *a* is important, here, because it points to the notion of one possible approach among many, rather than the definitive version.

5 I use the word "mainstream" advisedly, here, because dance studies or dance scholarship at that time was a relatively young and marginal area of study in comparison with the other arts and the more established academic disciplines. Although dance scholars like Daly (1991b) and Grau (1993) have pointed to the growth and diversity in dance scholarship over the past several years, it is still the case that the more established academic disciplines hardly give dance scholarship or indeed dance itself, more than a second look (Thomas 1995). Cultural studies is also a relatively new area of research in comparison with older disciplines such as anthropology or sociology, but its ascendancy into the "mainstream" of academia was striking from the 1970s and the 1980s, initially in the U.K. where it originated, and more recently in Australia and the U.S.

6 This is not to imply that dance history did not provide a valuable resource in terms of data, nor dance aesthetics/criticism in terms of focusing the activity of dancing and moving, because they did (for example, Banes 1987, Cohen 1982, Siegel 1979) and still do so. This discussion, however, is primarily concerned with the articulation of the relations between dance and culture.

7 The rise of the "New Left" in the social sciences in the U.K. in the 1970s led to a burgeoning interest in exploring a variety of approaches within the tradition of western Marxism, such as that of Antonio Gramsci, Georg Lukács, the Frankfurt School, and Louis Althusser.

8 I first noticed these new rumblings of revolt in American dance scholarship in 1988 at the *Beyond Performance: Dance Scholarship Today* conference in Essen, Germany.

9 I recall Stuart Hall saying this in a lecture he delivered at the British

Sociological Association Conference in Brighton in the U.K. in 1978. The conference theme was "culture" and the air was thick with the new orthodoxy of "signifying practices" which combined French structuralist Marxism, semiotics, and psychoanalytic theory. Rosalind Coward and John Ellis's book *Language and Materialism* (1977) exemplified this viewpoint.

10 These names should be treated as examples, rather than the sum-total of the field.

11 I am using critical cultural studies, here, in a somewhat broader sense to include texts such as Laura Mulvey's (1989b) "Visual Pleasure and Narrative Cinema" that might more correctly come under the heading of "film theory." As recently established areas of study like cultural studies and film studies, which are in themselves interdisciplinary, interact with each other, the boundaries between them become increasingly blurred. See, for example, de Lauretis (1986).

12 To a certain extent I have to include myself in this category because I have used a quotation from Mulvey's work, albeit with a proviso, to discuss an association between the active and the appearing body in the talk of some of the young women dancers I had been studying. See Thomas (1993: 83).

13 I want to make it clear that I am not positing a "real" essential woman here, in place of a monolithic "pure" male spectator.

BIBLIOGRAPHY

Adair, C. (1992) *Women and Dance: Sylphs and Sirens*, London: Macmillan.

Auslander, P. (1989) "Embodiment: The Politics of Postmodern Dance" (Review of Susan Leigh Foster's *Reading Dancing*), *The Drama Review* (Winter) 32, 4: 7–23.

Banes, S. (1987) *Terpsichore in Sneakers: Post-Modern Dance*, New York: Houghton Mifflin.

—— (1989) "Terpsichore in Combat Boots," *The Drama Review* (Spring) 33, 1: 13–16.

Bourdieu, P. (1984) *Distinction: A Social Critique of the Judgement of Taste*, trans. R. Nice (ed.), London: Routledge & Kegan Paul.

Boyne, R. and Rattansi, A. (eds) (1990) *Postmodernism and Society*, London: Macmillan.

Butler, J. (1990) *Gender Trouble*, London: Routledge.

Clifford, J. (1986) "Introduction: Partial Truths," in J. Clifford and G. E. Marcus (eds) *Writing Culture: The Poetics and Politics of Ethnography*, Berkeley: University of California Press.

Clifford, J. and Marcus, G. E. (eds) (1986) *Writing Culture: The Poetics and Politics of Ethnography*, Berkeley: University of California Press.

Cohen, S. J. (1982) *Next Week, Swan Lake: Reflections On Dance and Dancers*, Middletown, CT: Wesleyan University Press.

Cooper Albright, A. (1990) "Mining the Dance Field: Spectacle, Moving Subjects, and Feminist Theory," *Contact Quarterly*, (Spring/Summer) 15, 2: 32–41.

Copeland, R. (1992) "The Black Swan and the Dervishes," *Dance Theatre Journal* (Summer) 9, 4: 10–13, 41–3.

—— (1993) "Dance, Feminism and the Critique of the Visual," in H. Thomas (ed.) *Dance, Gender and Culture*, Basingstoke: Macmillan.

Cowan, J. (1990) *Dance and the Body Politic in Northern Greece*, Princeton, NJ: Princeton University Press.

Coward, R. and Ellis, J. (1977) *Language and Materialism: Developments in Semiology and the Theory of the Subject*, London: Routledge & Kegan Paul.

Daly, A. (1987) "The Balanchine Woman: Of Hummingbirds and Channel Swimmers," *The Drama Review* (Spring) 31, 1: 8–21.

—— (1991a) "Unlimited Partnership: Dance and Feminist Analysis," *Dance Research Journal* (Spring) 23, 1: 2–3.

—— (1991b) "What Revolution?: The New Dance Scholarship in America," *Ballett International* (January) 14, 1: 48–53.

—— (1992a) "What Has Become of Postmodern Dance?" *The Drama Review* (Spring) 36, 1: 48–69.

—— (1992b) "Dance History and Feminist Theory: Isadora Duncan and the Male Gaze," in L. Senelick (ed.) *Gender in Performance*, Hanover, NH: Tufts University Press.

Dempster, E. (1988) "Women Writing the Body: Let's Watch a Little How She Dances," in S. Sheridan (ed.) *Grafts: Feminist Cultural Criticism*, London: Verso.

Doane, M. A. (1987) *The Desire to Desire: The Woman's Film of the 1940s*, London: Macmillan.

Eagleton, T. (1983) *Literary Theory: An Introduction*, Oxford: Basil Blackwell.

Featherstone, M. (1988) "In Pursuit of the Postmodern: An Introduction," *Theory, Culture and Society* 5, 2–3: 195–216.

Foster, S. L. (1986) *Reading Dancing: Bodies and Subjects in Contemporary American Dance*, Berkeley: University of California Press.

Foucault, M. (1984) *The History of Sexuality, Vol. 1: An Introduction*, Harmondsworth: Peregrine Books.

Fraser, N. (1992) "The Uses and Abuses of French Discourse Theories of Feminist Politics," in N. Fraser and S. L. Bartky (eds) *Revaluing French Feminism: Critical Essays on Difference, Agency, & Culture*, Bloomington: Indiana University Press.

Gamman, L. and Makinen, M. (1994) *Female Fetishism: A New Look*, London: Lawrence & Wishart.

Gamman, L. and Marshment, M. (eds) (1988) *The Female Gaze: Women As Viewers of Popular Culture*, London: The Women's Press.

Garfinkel, H. (1984) *Studies in Ethnomethodology*, Cambridge: Polity Press.

Goldberg, M. (1987/8) "Ballerinas and Ball Passing," *Women & Performance* 3, 2: 7–31.

Grau, A. (1993) "John Blacking and the Development of Dance Anthropology in the UK," *Dance Research Journal* (Fall) 25, 2: 21–32.

Hoare, Q. and Smith, G. N. (eds) (1971) *Selections from the Prison Notebooks of Antonio Gramsci*, London: Lawrence & Wishart.

Huyssen, A. (1986) *After the Great Divide: Modernism, Mass Culture, Postmodernism*, London: Macmillan.

Jaggar, A. (1983) *Feminist Politics and Human Nature*, Brighton: Harvester Press.

Jenkins, R. (1992) *Pierre Bourdieu*, London: Routledge.

Jordan, S. and Thomas, S. (1994) "Dance and Gender: Formalism and Semiotics Reconsidered," *Dance Research* (Autumn) 12, 2: 3–14.

Kaeppler, A. (1991) "American Approaches to the Study of Dance," *Yearbook of Traditional Music* 23: 11–21.

Kaplan, A. E. (1983) *Women and Film: Both Sides of the Camera*, London: Methuen.

—— (ed.) (1989) *Postmodernism and Its Discontents*, London: Verso.

Kendall, E. (1979) *Where She Danced*, New York: Alfred A. Knopf.

Kristeva, J. (1984) *Revolution in Poetic Language*, trans. M. Waller, London: Methuen.

Lacan, J. (1977) *Écrits: A Selection*, translated from the French by Ann Sheridan (ed.), London: Tavistock.

de Lauretis, T. (1986) *Feminist Studies/Critical Studies*, Basingstoke: Macmillan.

—— (1987) *Technologies of Gender*, Bloomington: Indiana University Press.

Lyotard, J. F. (1984) *The Postmodern Condition*, Manchester: Manchester University Press.

McNay, L. (1992) *Foucault and Feminism*, Oxford: Polity Press.

Manning, S. A. (1988) "Modernist Dogma and Post-modern Rhetoric," *The Drama Review* (Winter) 32, 4: 32–9.

—— (1989) "Terpsichore in Combat Boots," *The Drama Review* (Spring) 33, 1: 17–18.

—— (1993) *Ecstasy and the Demon: Feminism and Nationalism in the Dances of Mary Wigman*, Berkeley: University of California Press.

Mitchell, J. (1982) "Introduction 1," in J. Mitchell and J. Rose (eds) *Feminine Sexuality: Jacques Lacan & the École Freudienne*, London: Macmillan.

Mitchell, J. and Rose, J. (eds) (1982) *Feminine Sexuality: Jacques Lacan & the École Freudienne*, London: Macmillan.

Moi, T. (1985) *Sexual/Textual Politics*, London: Methuen.

Mulvey, L. (1989a) "Afterthoughts on 'Visual Pleasure and Narrative Cinema' inspired by King Vidor's 'Duel in the Sun'," in L. Mulvey (ed.) *Visual and Other Pleasures*, Basingstoke: Macmillan.

—— (1989b) "Visual Pleasure and Narrative Cinema," in L. Mulvey (ed.) *Visual and Other Pleasures*, Basingstoke: Macmillan.

Novack, C. (1990) *Sharing the Dance: Contact Improvisation and American Culture*, Madison: University of Wisconsin Press.

Parker, R. and Pollock, G. (eds) (1987) *Framing Feminism*, London: Pandora.

Phelan, P. (1993) *Unmarked: The Politics of Performance*, London: Routledge.

Polhemus, T. (1975) "Social Bodies," in J. Benthall and T. Polhemus (eds) *The Body As a Medium of Expression*, London: Allen Lane.

Rimmer, V. (1993) "The Anxiety of Dance Performance," in H. Thomas (ed.) *Dance, Gender and Culture*, Basingstoke: Macmillan.

Rose, J. (1982) "Introduction 2," in J. Mitchell and J. Rose (eds) *Feminine Sexuality: Jacques Lacan & the École Freudienne*, London: Macmillan.

Sanchez-Colberg, A. (1993) "'You put your left foot in, then you shake it all about . . .': Excursions and Incursions into Feminism and Bausch's Tanztheater," in H. Thomas (ed.) *Dance, Gender and Culture*, Basingstoke: Macmillan.

Shelton, S. (1981) *Divine Dancer: Biography of Ruth St. Denis*, Austin: University of Texas Press.

Siegel, M .B. (1979) *The Shapes of Change*, Boston: Houghton Mifflin.

Sklar, D. (1991) "On Dance Ethnography," *Dance Research Journal* 23, 1: 6–10.

Sorell, W. (1981) *Dance in Its Time: The Emergence of an Art Form*, Garden City, NY: Anchor Press/Doubleday.

Thomas, H. (1993) "An-Other Voice: Young Women Dancing and Talking," in H. Thomas (ed.) *Dance, Gender and Culture*, Basingstoke: Macmillan.

—— (1995) *Dance, Modernity and Culture: Explorations in the Sociology of Dance*, London: Routledge.

Weedon, C. (1987) *Feminist Practice & Poststructuralist Theory*, Oxford: Polity Press.

Williams, D. (1977) "The Nature of Dance: An Anthropological Perspective," *Dance Research Journal* 9, 1: 42–4.

Willis, P., with Jones, S., Canaan, J., and Hurd, G. (1990) *Common Culture*, Milton Keynes: Open University Press.

Wright Mills, C. (1970) *The Sociological Imagination*, Harmondsworth: Penguin Books.

Youngerman, S. (1974) "Curt Sachs and His Heritage: a Critical Review of World History of Dance with a Survey of Recent Studies That Perpetuate His Ideas," *CORD News* 6, 2: 6–17.

6 Re/Moving Boundaries
From Dance History to Cultural Studies

Amy Koritz

This essay will be primarily devoted to a metacritical discussion of the relation of dance history to a larger, inter- or post-disciplinary movement within academia known as cultural studies.[1] I will begin by framing the discussion as a choice between pursuing dance history as an autonomous discipline and seeking its greater integration into other intellectual and institutional sites. Although such binaries never do justice to the actual range of choices available, they do serve to demarcate the territory of an important debate within the field of dance history today. If, as I believe, something closer to the integration model is desirable, the role of dance in potentially receptive fields such as cultural studies should be examined. The second section of the essay offers an example of a research project that engages dance history in a way that refuses to acknowledge its autonomy as a field of study and that might be classified as "cultural studies" or perhaps "performance studies" in some versions of how those projects are currently understood. Those readers worried about the subordination of dance to other, nondance, intellectual agendas will probably find their fears confirmed at this point. The essay therefore ends with a consideration of this issue, approaching it through Jill Dolan's recent critique of performance studies. My goal is not to insist on one correct relationship that dance historians ought to establish with interdisciplinary projects such as cultural studies, but to articulate issues raised by the possibility of such an engagement that seem important to current debates in dance history.

By training and employment I am an English professor; I came to do work in dance history through my commitments to feminist criticism and women's studies. In the 1980s women's studies scholars engaged in a debate over whether they ought to pursue primarily the integration of women's work and perspectives into mainstream course offerings and scholarship, or rather concentrate on building strong autonomous curricula and scholarly journals devoted to women. The answer, to simplify a complex and diverse range of positions, was, of course, both. The existence of a strong women's studies program would increase the legitimacy of feminist scholarship and help educate faculty about women's perspectives and accomplishments, which would in turn increase the likelihood of their incorporation into traditional, discipline-based course offerings. The problems facing dance history are in important ways not analogous to those addressed by the integration/autonomy debates in women's studies. Both the constituency for dance history scholarship within other disciplines and the potential for mobilizing the resources necessary to establish and sustain any large number of autonomous programs are considerably more limited.[2] Nevertheless, the decision to pursue a disciplinary model of dance history, or to de-emphasize that project in favor of locating and arguing for the importance of dance within larger interdisciplinary frameworks such as cultural studies, is one of "integration" or "autonomy."

The easy answer is, again, that we should be doing both. Until recently it was impossible to earn a doctorate in dance history in the United States, and the work of dance scholars such as Susan Foster, Susan Manning, Mark Franko, and Cynthia Novack has by necessity been influenced by the disciplines in which they were trained. These scholars' interdisciplinary approaches to dance research have helped bring dance closer to the intellectual mainstream. It is also true, however, that work on dance is largely considered marginal within other disciplines. This persistent marginality contributes to a desire for an autonomous place in which dance scholarship (as opposed to performance) is the central concern. On another level, the "integration" or "autonomy" question in dance history can be understood as a tension between commitments to the conceptual tools of other disciplines that have enabled creative scholarship in dance history and the specificity of dance as a unique form of human activity that seems to demand its own analytic tools. My own belief is that dance historians should develop and capitalize on an ability to speak more than one disciplinary language in order to argue for the centrality of dance to any number of cultural formations, while at the same time expanding existing critical vocabularies to encompass dance or movement-specific terminology. This goal would de-emphasize the need for entirely distinct conceptual frameworks for dance scholarship. One might argue, in fact, that the age of consensus on such frameworks in any discipline (at least in the humanities) is over, and that scholars now ordinarily find it necessary to have familiarity with, if not fluency in, more than one disciplinary language.

Dance historians of all persuasions would benefit from an ability to understand and to position themselves in relation to the larger intellectual communities of scholarship in the arts and humanities, and for this reason alone it is important to think through the possible relationship of dance history to cultural studies. This project has already been begun by Jane Desmond in her essay, "Embodying Difference: Issues in Dance and Cultural Studies." Desmond notes that work in cultural studies remains "text-based or object-based, with literary texts still predominating, followed by studies of film texts and art historical objects" (1994: 34). She attributes the omission of dance to several factors, including the history of divisions of knowledge within the academy and a long-standing disavowal of the relevance of the material body to the pursuit of knowledge. The lack of serious attention directed toward dance within the academy signals, according to Desmond, the "continuing rhetorical association of bodily expressivity with nondominant groups" (ibid.: 35). Cultural studies in its inception and practice has made the world of the "nondominant" its special purview. Thus, if Desmond is right about the reasons for the devaluation of dance in western culture, cultural studies scholars *ought* to be attending to dance. What they have rather attended to is "the body."

Why, given at least ten years' worth of engaged, intelligent scholarship on the body, is dance – the cultural form most inescapably embodied – still a poor relation in cultural studies? Desmond observes that "the body" in such scholarship more often deals with "representations of the body and/or its discursive policing than with its actions/movements as a 'text' themselves" (ibid.: 34). This is true, but the two areas of concern are not mutually exclusive. Dance is a form of representation, and certainly any codified dance structure or technique can be conceptualized as a semiotic or "discursive" policing of the body. In other words, there is no methodological reason why criticism focused on "representation" and "discursive policing" should not give rise to studies of dance in culture. The fact that this has not (or seldom) occurred suggests that something beyond methodological exclusion may be at stake. Perhaps if dance scholars did a better job of teaching others how to analyze movement they would be more willing to address dance in their research. Again, however, one might note that the lack of this skill need not prevent the study of textual records of dance performances.

It is unfortunate, but true, that many scholars define their projects in ways delimited by their existing expertise rather than responding to the reach of a problem or issue by extending their intellectual repertoire, and few feel competent to deal with dance. Scholars will take on challenges of this kind, however, when developments within their fields make the incorporation of new knowledge crucial, as happened when "theory" entered into literary studies. With theory, and particularly feminist theory, came the renewed interest in the body among literary scholars. Was lack of formal training the only reason why this interest in the body failed to extend to an interest in dance?

Teresa Ebert has criticized the deployment of the body, particularly in feminist theory, as if it were the opposite of abstraction. To the contrary, she points out, "the body" functions as a concept, that is as an abstraction, in the very gesture of denying it that status (1993: 26). Fredric Jameson suggests that "as a form of philosophical hygiene" we avoid the word altogether in our intellectual work for the next ten years. "Nothing," he writes, "is more disembodied than such references to the body ... [for] materialism is scarcely achieved by the corporeal litany" (1993: 44). If the motive behind invocations of the body is a desire for the grounding of intellectual work in the "real world" grit of the material, such invocations are bound to fail. In such contexts, as Ebert notes, the body is always placed in binary opposition to concept, language, abstraction, etc. – that is to the very tools that make intellectual work possible. As a material anchor for intellectual analysis, the body is problematic. This is especially so in cultural studies and women's studies, because each seeks to give voice to the silenced, to reconnect the realm of representation with lived experience, and to understand the ways in which popular culture, mass media, elite art, and everyday life have political meaning and become sites for political action. In some sense, in this discourse, attention to the body is supposed to authorize intellectual work by guaranteeing its relevance to the material "real world." Jameson suggests rather that the current fascination with aspects of intense physicality (torture, violence, pornography) be seen as a sign of a loss of the immediacy of the body and "the longing for the impossibly concrete" (ibid.), not as evidence for its successful integration into intellectual work.

This analysis suggests that dance would appear uninteresting to cultural studies scholars in search of materialism because dance uses bodies to transmit and represent complex cultural codes in a manner that explicitly distinguishes them from the lived experience of the nondancing body. That is, the obvious distance codified dance interposes between the dancing body and the ordinary body-in-pain or body-in-pleasure makes it less useful to those who want to find in bodily life either those material conditions that, according to Marx, give rise to ideology, or, in a more utopian vein, a place free from the abstractions of ideology altogether. On the other hand, surely twenty years of poststructuralism ought to have taught us the impossibility of accessing unencoded experience of any sort. The obsession with the body to the exclusion of dance is perhaps symptomatic of a failure to think beyond the binary opposition between body and mind that seems to hold out the body as the realm where the problems of the mind take on a concrete form that removes from them the stigma of scholarly abstraction. The pervasive absence of dance from cultural studies may well reflect dance's inability to provide the sorts of bodies cultural studies scholars find most engaging. But this, far from being a disadvantage, suggests the importance of what cultural studies has to learn from dance scholarship. Dance scholars' tools for analyzing and communicating about bodies might help feminists and those working in cultural studies clarify and understand cultural uses of bodies in a variety of contexts. Dance historians from this perspective have much to contribute to the worthwhile goal of keeping cultural studies honest in its invocations of the body.

The training and deployment of bodies in dance is culturally significant, perhaps most especially in what it can tell us about the range of allowable representations of the body in motion and the policing of bodily form in a specific time and place. Historicized studies of dance that attempt to locate the theory, practice, and reception of codified bodily movement in the context of problems, events, and ideologies of significance beyond the realm of dance alone may have a great deal to teach us about how "social relations are both enacted and produced through the body" (Desmond 1994: 38). Let me emphasize, however, that individual dancing bodies are not the only category of analysis relevant to the cultural meaning of dance. The next section of this essay treats dance, along with theater, as an important location for the symbolic enactment of larger ideological issues facing a society. Dance here encompasses not only movement style but critical reception and aesthetic motivation. My purpose is to explore the ways in which dance and theater participated in the work of creating and policing a national identity in the United States. Specifically, I look at the strategies of Martha Graham and Eugene O'Neill in constructing an implied or explicit narrative of the embodied self in relation to an "authentic" American identity.

SELF/NATION/PERFORMANCE:
MARTHA GRAHAM AND EUGENE O'NEILL

Our two forms of indigenous dance, the Negro and the Indian, are as dramatically contrasted rhythmically as the land in which they root. The Negro dance is a dance toward freedom, a dance to forgetfulness, often Dionysiac in its abandon and the raw splendor of its rhythm – a rhythm of disintegration. The Indian dance, however, is not for freedom, or forgetfulness, or escape, but for awareness of life, complete relationship with that world in which he finds himself; it is a dance for power, a rhythm of integration.

(Graham 1932: 5–6)

In *Marco Millions* all the people of the East should be masked. . . . For anyone who has been in the East, or has read Eastern philosophy, the reason for this is obvious. It is an exact dramatic expression of the West confronted by the East. Moreover, it is the only possible way to project this contrast truthfully in the theater, for Western actors cannot convey Eastern character realistically, and their only chance to suggest it convincingly is with the help of masks.

(O'Neill 1961: 119)

What is the relationship between the constitution of the Negro as an "indigenous" American – like the Indian to be used as a foundational gesture in the creation of a truly American dance by a white woman – and the constitution of the East as the unrepresentable Other inhabitable by Westerners only via the subterfuge of the mask? This question leads toward a consideration of how, to quote Eric Lott, "representations of national racial difference often provide displaced maps for international ones," and of how, therefore, "the domination of international others has depended upon mastering the other at home" (1993: 476). What Lott neglects to mention is that the representation of international racial others not only depends upon the representation of national racial difference, but that the converse relation also holds: that the representation of national racial difference cannot do without an international racial other, since the contradiction between *nation* and *other* can be resolved only by the displacing of that otherness outside of the nation. The juxtaposition of O'Neill's observation on masks and the East with Martha Graham's on the indigenous roots of American dance presents two sides of a single process.

The set of problems I want to sketch out in this paper also concern some of the issues recently raised by Paul Gilroy in *The Black Atlantic*, specifically the need to question what he calls "ethnic absolutism," that is, the assumption of a racial purity and authenticity or essence able to be read off of cultural products and practices and closely aligned with definitions of national subjectivities and cultural forms. Gilroy argues that race and nation cannot be so aligned, and that further, the facts of national culture (as opposed to the imaginary, invented nationness that supports the myth of national homogeneity) can only be specified in their articulation with "supra-national and imperial" relations (1993: 11).

Gilroy's position implies that it is not only these external referents that contribute fundamentally to a nation's culture and force a disavowal of its exclusivity, but relations of antagonistic heterogeneity within the borders of a nation. Racial difference is of course one of the central forms of such antagonistic heterogeneity in the U.S. Gilroy's persuasive critique of ethnic absolutism and the conception of a national subject it engenders throws into question the clarity of borders between native and foreign. It also forces a re-reading of how white American artists represent racially marked subjects. Such representations indeed constitute attempts to manage and exclude that heterogeneity from an implied national subjectivity, even while, in that very act, such a subject is constituted through its articulation with that heterogeneity. Any narrative that represents, assumes, or implies a specifically national subject is in this view necessarily a product of both external contamination and internal heterogeneity.

In the plays of O'Neill both sides of the process I have been outlining are evident. The international other is frequently present in the early O'Neill: from the cannibalistic West Indian mulatto in *Thirst* (1913) and the West Indian Negresses who bring rum and anarchy onto the Glencairn in *The Moon of the Caribbees* (1917) to the murderous Jimmy Kanaka, who makes his entrance dressed like Tarzan, wearing only a loincloth and sheath-knife, in *Gold* (1920), and the mysterious Islander, Avahanni, of *Mourning Becomes Electra* (1931), who never appears onstage but is the sign and object of Lavinia's awakened sexuality. O'Neill's best known non-white characters, Brutus Jones (*The Emperor Jones*) and Jim Harris (*All God's Chillun Got Wings*), on the other hand, pose the problem of representing an internal racial other. Looked at in this context, the setting of *The Emperor Jones* in a soon-to-be-colonized West Indian Island becomes essential to a reading of American racial politics in the play.

In the case of Graham the same issues surface, although in very different ways. Graham began her career as a Denishawn dancer. Ruth St. Denis and Ted Shawn were famous for their exotic spectacles – Martha Graham's first roles included that of an Aztec princess, and her own early choreography showed the influence of Denishawn's orientalism, as can be seen in such dances as "The Flute of Krishna"(1926) and "Three Poems of the East" (1927). The international other was thus in a sense what had to be exorcised in order for Graham to become an American modern dancer. This imperative was exacerbated by the tendency of journalists to describe Graham's own appearance as Oriental. Graham's response was to reject "foreign" movement styles, announcing in 1927 that "[o]ne cannot hope to reproduce a dance that is of another country or another age" (Kemp 1927: 19). In her search for a distinctively American artistic identity, "disintegrative" Negro movement is absent or displaced by motifs derived from African art, although the influence of the minstrel show on *American Document* has been noted (see Susan Manning's essay in this volume). Most obvious in Graham's subject matter and style is her attraction to the American Indians. After a visit to New Mexico in 1930, Graham composed one of her most successful early dances, *Primitive Mysteries*, which was rooted in the Indian adaptation of Catholic ritual she experienced in the desert. In 1932 she was awarded a Guggenheim Fellowship, which she used to travel to Mexico to study Indian culture.

Even when any explicit contrast between Indian and Negro dance is absent from Graham's critical writings, the adjectives used to describe the essential quality of each often remains. "Integration" remains a positive quality, while language implying escape, abandon, or the loss of emotional or physical control remains negative. The proper attitude toward dance, Graham wrote in "A Modern Dancer's Primer for Action," is one of "affirmation, not of escape" (1941: 184). Of course a quick comparison with Zora Neale Hurston's description of the qualities of African-American dance in "Characteristics of Negro Expression" illustrates how problematic such characterizations of racial movement are. Every quality Graham privileges – restraint, angularity, asymmetry, the rejection of realism – is claimed by Hurston to illustrate the superiority of Negro to white dance.

The task at this point would be to analyze precisely how O'Neill and Graham deploy racial otherness and how these representations of otherness function in the task of delimiting an American art and an American artist. But first, it is important to set out a second range of issues which, I want to argue, must be considered in conjunction with that of racial or indeed other signs of internal heterogeneity in the definition of a national culture. Although Graham was more willing than O'Neill to talk about herself as a distinctly American artist, both maintain a strong universalist tendency in their aesthetics. The cosmopolitanism of modernism mitigated against the celebration of regional specificities and the evident desire of both artists to position themselves above the commercial values of popular American performance forms – from vaudeville to Broadway – led to claims of

universal human or spiritual significance with which we are all familiar from
other artists of this period.

Any analysis of race as an element in the definition of a national
subjectivity in these two artists must also be considered in the context of
an aesthetic that rejected national boundaries as delimiting the potential
relevance and value of a work of art. Consider, for example, O'Neill's
defense of *All God's Chillun Got Wings*. In the first place, O'Neill explains
to a reporter from the *New York Times*, he is simply interested in the
"progress of humanity toward Humanity" (1990: 44). The interracial
marriage of Jim Harris and Ella Downey does not represent O'Neill's
advocacy of miscegenation, to the contrary, says O'Neill, "I admit that
there is prejudice against the intermarriage of whites and blacks, but what
has that to do with my play? I don't advocate intermarriage in it. I am
never the advocate of anything in any play – *except* humanity toward
Humanity" (ibid.: 45). Further, these two characters are not to be seen as
the representatives of their respective races, but as "special cases [that]
represent no one but themselves" (ibid.: 46). Clearly these characters
cannot be both "no one but themselves" and expressions of a universal
struggle of the human toward Humanity. And the fact that the mayor of
New York denied permits for the child actors called for in the first scene
of the play in an effort to stymie its production and that the FBI apparently
saw the controversy over the play as reason to start a file on the playwright
indicate quite clearly that one could not produce a play in the United
States in 1924 with an interracial marriage in it and have it *not* become
a play *about* (or even *advocating*) interracial marriage. In such a cultural
context, racially marked representations always become representative
of "race." But my larger point is that the aesthetic values O'Neill proposes
in this interview are not consonant with an explicit project of cultural
nationalism.

This does not mean that O'Neill was not participating in such a project
– the purpose of the Provincetown Players (the group of semi-amateur
writers and actors who discovered him) was precisely one of cultural
nationalism. Further, his use of African American, West Indian and other
racially, ethnically or even class-marked characters (that is, even Robert
Smith – better known as Yank – in *The Hairy Ape*) work through the
possibility or impossibility of various ways of enacting a specifically
American subjectivity. *The Emperor Jones* provides a very clear example
of what can happen when a racially marked American comes up against
Lott's international others in the context of a high modernist aesthetic.
Simply stated, the play represents the simultaneous necessity and impossibility of Brutus Jones's national character (black Americanness). Jones's
ideology of leadership, the proper exercise of power, and the function
of the state are all direct products of America. It was, after all, the white
passengers he served as a Pullman porter who taught him his disdain for
the rule of law and the importance of "de big stealin":

Ain't I de Emperor? De laws don't go for him. . . . You heah what I tells you Smithers. Dere's little stealin' like you does, and dere's big stealin' like I does. For de little stealin' dey gits you in jail soon or late. For de big stealin' dey makes you Emperor and puts you in de Hall o' Fame when you croaks. . . . If dey's one thing I learns in ten years on de Pullman ca's listenin to de white quality talk, its dat same fact.

(O'Neill 1988: 1035)

The narrative into which the play inserts him, meanwhile, represents his Americanness as a series of incidental experiences on his way towards the final recognition and acknowledgment of his real community with the "low-flung, bush niggers" of Africa. The figurative expulsion of Brutus Jones from the "imagined community" of the United States through the construction of an alternative, un-American tradition which usurps the specificity of his national character in favor of a non-national racial character also permits the sanitation of Americanness of its racial hetero-geneity. The crucial attribute of *The Emperor Jones* as an *American* play (in the sense of one doing the cultural work of constituting an American subjectivity) is this combination of a typically modernist gesture towards a transcendent aesthetic universalism with a narrative grounding in the incommensurability of American and African American narratives of national belonging.

Martha Graham's 1929 dance, *Heretic*, depends for its effect on a sharp contrast between dark and light, individual and mass, percussive and lyrical movement. As would be the case in *Primitive Mysteries*, Graham costumed herself in white, her group in black wool jersey dresses. Her dance aesthetic at this time insisted on a particularly spare use of movement in order to avoid movements and postures she considered to be merely graceful or pretty, emphasizing instead "the virile gestures that are evocative of the only true beauty" (qtd. in Roberts 1928). Thus, for example, the dancers' hands are held cupped or with clenched fists, and often kept close to the body. *Heretic* is characterized by a strict economy of gesture, a rigidity and structural unity in the group's movements, and a repetitiveness of move-ment motifs reinforced by the music – an Old Breton song repeated exactly for each section of the dance. The unison movements of the group create a menacing frame for Graham, who frequently kneels, crouches, or even lies prone while the group remains standing or lunges over her. The dance ends with the Graham character defeated, lying flat on the stage with the group standing in a rigid semi-circle behind her. *Heretic* is generally interpreted as a cry for individual freedom from the oppression of mass society, and Graham's discussion of the dance in her autobiography concurs: "I was the heretic desperately trying to force myself free of the darkness of my oppressors" (1991: 114). In fact, according to her recollection, this dance was profoundly autobiographical, for Graham at this time felt herself to be a heretic:

I was outside the realm of women. I did not dance the way that people danced. I had what I called a contraction and a release. I used the floor. I used the flexed foot, I showed effort. My foot was bare. In many ways I showed onstage what most people came to the theater to avoid.

(ibid.)

This complexly gendered summary of Graham's aesthetic principles must be considered in the context of her statements on American dance that describe it in terms of specifically masculine qualities. In "Seeking an American Art of the Dance," Graham asserts that "America is cradling an art that is destined to be a ruler, in that its urge is masculine and creative, rather than imitative" (1930: 249). In "The Dance in America" she explains that "America's great gift to the arts is rhythm; rich, full, unabashed, virile" (1932: 5). Given such an aesthetic, she could not help being "outside the realm of women" – it was the very condition of her being an artist. It was as well the very condition of her being an *American* artist. In such a context, aesthetic universalism becomes an empowering ideology, since it enables the elision of those qualities which might tend to devalue the work of women artists in a male-dominated society. But this only occurs at the price of adopting the mask of masculinity and of acceding to a conception of the national subject of America as essentially a masculine subject. At this point the quotation from O'Neill with which I began becomes relevant to Graham in an unexpected way – just as a western actor can only represent the East by putting on a mask, so too the American woman can only represent the American artist by putting on a mask. The assumption of inaccessibility under any other terms is the same.

The dynamics of a simultaneous articulation and exclusion of race and nationality seen in O'Neill are thus complicated in Graham by the fact of her being a woman. Nonetheless, in her definition of herself as an American artist, she disassociates herself not only from womanhood, but also from anything African-American.[3] The vibrant and powerful impact of African-American dance on American popular culture of the twenties – from the shimmy to the charleston – left no trace on Graham's dancing. No doubt a number of factors contributed to this exclusion. The legitimacy of dance as an elite art was still uncertain, and any association of concert dance with low status dance forms would have threatened this goal. The perceived sensuality of African-American movement also would have given a suspicious public reason to dismiss the seriousness of women dancers who used such movements in work they wished to define as art. From this point of view, the language of a cosmopolitan modernism that privileged formal abstraction enabled the elision of African-American movement vocabulary from modern dance and thus also from the constitution of an American subjectivity as represented in that dance.

The reason, then, for considering Martha Graham and Eugene O'Neill together is not the analogies to be drawn between them in terms of aesthetic principles and techniques – although I believe these exist. Rather the project begun here has to do with the aesthetic articulation of modernist, American forms of national subjectivity. To the extent that the maintenance of such subjectivities entails disciplines of the body – of gesture, of the holding and inhabiting of space – and of the insertion of bodies into narrative contexts, their representation through the performed arts is a crucial location for understanding the strategies of exclusion and constitutive dependence of an American national subject on its others.

INTELLECTUALS AND THEIR INSTITUTIONS

The above project is organized around an issue that cannot itself be conceptualized as relevant only to a single discipline. An exploration of the relations among self, nation, and artistic representation would be pertinent to any art form. The choice of such a problem is an attempt to force an integration of dance into scholarly contexts that so far have done quite well without acknowledging its existence. Further, I have located dance within a category of performed art that includes theater, without much attention to generic distinctions that in other contexts might be crucial. Clearly these are not approaches that would be shared by all dance historians.[4] Why, one might ask, insert dance into a discourse developed to address something else (history, literature, film, or even theater)? Won't dance history thereby lose its specificity? The answer to this question is yes, dance history will lose specificity (if what is meant by that is "autonomy") if this is the only kind of work scholars writing about dance ever do – but 1) so will every other art form so treated and 2) what it loses in "specificity" it will gain in relevance to a far-reaching and vital intellectual conversation. It is, after all, an open secret in the academy that the disciplinary division of knowledge we currently operate within is a product of historical circumstance rather than the nature of the human mind or behavior. The way one divides up a field is a function of the questions one asks and the training one has received; history does not naturally occur in disciplinary segments. To my mind, then, to decide to locate one's scholarship in "dance history" rather than "cultural studies" is to make a series of decisions about what limits one's field of study that would tend to exclude the kind of project outlined in the previous section of this essay. Of course there is another way of looking at such a choice: one might attempt to attach the name of dance history to work that transgresses the traditional boundaries of that field in order to effect a change in those boundaries. This, what might be called a Trojan Horse strategy, is a covert way of presenting one's rejection of a discipline's way of organizing knowledge. Although this latter strategy may be motivated by a desire to educate or convert more traditional practitioners of a discipline, it may also indicate a fear of rejection unless one's work conforms at least superficially to disciplinary expectations.

My work might be classified as cultural studies rather than dance history, or at the very least as interdisciplinary, due to its uneasiness with the ways in which disciplinary fields of knowledge have excluded particular kinds of questions or approaches.[5] Interdisciplinarity is certainly nothing new in the academy and the version currently popular under the name of cultural studies is perhaps less revolutionary than its adherents would like to believe. Fredric Jameson has reflected on the constant reinvention and failure of "interdisciplinarity" in the academy, and observed that the effort nonetheless continues to be made "because the specific disciplines all repress crucial but in each case different features of the object of study they ought to be sharing" (1993: 20). From this perspective, it is less important that cultural studies be something absolutely original than that it enable insights and connections not otherwise accessible. Jameson in fact sees cultural studies as "a symptom rather than a theory" that expresses the potential for alliances between social groups, but that came into being specifically because of the felt inadequacy of existing disciplines (ibid.: 17–18).

Performance studies, like cultural studies, seems a response to precisely the same inadequacy of existing disciplinary structures. Its growth has recently provoked a defensive response from the feminist theater theorist Jill Dolan, who fears that performance studies threatens already weak or marginalized disciplines such as theater.[6] Dance has an even weaker place than theater in higher education, so dance scholars might with reason feel even more threatened. Because Dolan has articulated a strong case for resisting the absorption of a traditional discipline into an explicitly inter- or post-disciplinary field, it is worth looking at her argument more closely.

Before doing so, I would like to draw a distinction between the question of intellectual work and that of institutional politics. While the problems and ideas that engage us intellectually often exceed disciplinary contain- ment (racism, queer theory, national identity), prestige and status in the academy tend to be discipline-bound. Status is important, of course; this is how we get raises and job offers, but we ought to be careful not to confuse the pursuit of status with more properly intellectual motives. I am, that is, making what is no doubt a controversial distinction between politics and intellectuality. In doing so I am exploring ideas put forward by Frederick Pollock in his essay, "Theses on Intellectuals," published in *Representations*. Pollock argues that intellectuality is a form of intelligence which consists of "a self-perpetuating delight in thinking and learning for their own sake" (1992: 74). This is not a claim that the uses to which intellectual work is put may not be political, nor that intellectuals have access to a purity of character unavailable to ordinary mortals. Pollock's point is that while "intellectuality as a social fact is not distinct from its political or practical consequences, intellectuality as a motive is" (ibid.: 75). Practical politics, in his view, is inherently at war with intellectuality because the former is motivated by a desire for and an identification with

power, while the latter is not. If the *motives* for intellectuality and for
that use of intelligence concerned with power (e.g. status and prestige) are
distinct, then the appeals one must make to influence behavior in one
realm are different from those required by the other. Since what Pollock is
primarily interested in is the possibility of progressive political action by
intellectuals, he explains this point with specific reference to that goal:

> For an intellectual to be willing to act politically – and to act, not in denial
> of intellectuality, but as an intellectual – he or she must a) identify
> with that part of the self which is intellectual, rather than that part that
> is (however necessarily) devoted to power and status; b) perceive a
> genuine threat to intellectuality; and c) equate the future of the self with
> elimination of this threat.
>
> (ibid.: 78)

The point of this long prologue to a discussion of Jill Dolan's important
essay is that I believe she has confused precisely the issues Pollock, and
myself, would like to keep analytically distinct.

Dolan fears the recent growth in the metaphorical use of performance
and performativity could lead to theater studies being "dispersed into
metaphor" (1993: 417). The pervasive use of theatrical metaphors in other
disciplines (or "post-disciplines") without reference to theatrical performance *per se*, combined with the eagerness of theater scholars to absorb
the latest (non-theater) theory, has led to the "needlessly deprecated
position of theater studies in relation to other interdisciplinary fields"
(ibid.: 427). She notes that "cultural studies is becoming another site of
legitimation for theater scholars who would leave home" (ibid.: 422),
and argues for "a model of exchange between theater and other fields or
disciplines, rather than one in which the performative evacuates theater
studies" (ibid.: 421). The essay concludes with a discussion of the ways in
which the theater itself can become a place for exploring and experiencing
difference and for motivating spectators and participants to pursue social
change. Finally, then, she seems to be arguing that the political agenda
frequently associated with cultural studies is at least as effectively pursued
within the traditional discipline of theater studies.

The interesting question raised by Dolan's essay seems to me to be not
how can we redress the needless deprecation of theater studies, but what
is it that scholars trained in this field find so attractive, or even necessary,
about those elsewheres they seem so anxious to leave the farm in pursuit
of. If we bear Pollock's distinction in mind, two answers present themselves
immediately: first, the power (whether this means the power of prestige
and status or the power to effect social change) is greater "over there," and
second, the problems and questions those other fields enable one to engage
are intellectually more interesting or important (however one defines these
things) than the ones being asked in theater studies proper. These motivations are not commensurable with each other and cannot be addressed in

the same way. If Dolan wants to increase the power of theater studies as an autonomous field her work is institutional and political (in Pollock's sense of the term). If she wants scholars to *stop* finding intellectual pleasure and sustenance in writing about whatever it is they are writing about and instead find it in focusing on theatrical performance *per se*, then she has a completely different task ahead of her.

The problem of clarifying (or establishing) a relationship between institutional or disciplinary prestige and intellectual commitment faces dance historians working within the academy at this historical juncture. Although such issues are frequently discussed informally at conferences and among colleagues, much work remains to be done toward the sustenance of a public dialogue. For my own part, although I am not sure that Pollock's distinction between the intellectual and the political is completely sustainable, I do believe that these two categories should not be collapsed. In the first place, to do so would make the argument for the importance of dance to those working in related disciplines much more difficult – dance scholarship is hardly the road to political power, however defined. In the second place, cultural analysis of any sort seldom has the sort of immediate political effect Dolan seems to be after. The insistence that such effects must be the primary goal of intellectual work denies the importance of intellectuality as one of the motives behind our work, while tending to discount the very real contributions dance history has to make to the analysis of any culture in which people dance.

At the very least the role of institutional structures in the academy ought to be to enable intellectual work. Since intellectual problems and questions frequently are not containable within preordained disciplinary categories, institutional structures should avoid as much as possible forcing them into such categories. If a literary scholar finds herself engaged in an intellectual project that seems to entail some discussion of dance, she should not feel the need to truncate that project in order to conform to disciplinary boundaries. Of course she would have to do her homework, just as a dance scholar writing about literature would. Even though reading into a new field is not the same as receiving extended training from experts, and such training is important, dance scholarship can benefit from expanding the number of those authorized to speak about dance. No doubt some work done by those without special training in dance will be seriously lacking from the point of view of those who do have such training. On the other hand, it may have strengths unavailable to those more narrowly trained and less adventurous in their willingness to take on unfamiliar material. I view with deep suspicion the prima facie legitimacy of objections to intellectual projects because they are not "dance history," or "theater studies," or "English literature," or whatever the gatekeepers concerned conceive to be their particular turf.

The real questions for dance scholars, I would suggest, are 1) what options are realistically available for those wishing to work in this area and

2) what kind of an intellectual community would best further vital and challenging work that would attract scholars to dance as a research area. These questions cannot be answered without a clear-minded cognizance of important interdisciplinary trends in the humanities. In the United States, cultural studies has become one of these, and therefore should be seriously considered as an appropriate venue for work by dance scholars.

NOTES

1 I would like to thank Gay Morris and Joe Roach for their comments on an earlier version of this essay. While I fear I have not done justice to their suggestions, the essay has benefited from the attempt.
2 The consequences of these limitations for individuals trying to work in dance history were brought home to me when, in the course of researching this essay, I discovered that my library had recently cancelled its subscriptions to *Dance Chronicle*, *Dance Research Journal*, and *Ballet Review*.
3 The influence of African art, in contrast, is evident in Graham's work. See the discussion of primitivism in Louis Horst's *Modern Dance Forms*.
4 See, for example, Marcia Siegel's review of Susan Foster's book, *Reading Dancing*. Siegel objects strenuously to Foster's attempts to use methodologies adapted from structuralist and poststructuralist theorists such as Roman Jakobson and Roland Barthes. She argues that the idea of *reading* dance is wrongheaded from the outset, since "it gives no account of the actual process of looking at dance, which is fundamentally intuitive, visceral, and preverbal" (1988: 30). The implication of Siegel's position is that what dance scholars should be concerned with are those elements that are unique to dance, rather than those it might share with other art forms or cultural practices. Noel Carroll places this position in historical context in his survey of how dance theory and practice have responded to trends in aesthetic philosophy. Recently, he notes, "The view that art forms can be essentially demarcated has become suspect; processes such as narrative and representation are thought to cut across the boundaries of media" (1992: 326). He concludes that "our ways of talking about and making the dance have evolved in tandem with the development of new ways of conceptualizing art in general" (ibid.: 327–8).
5 For discussions of the definition and history of cultural studies see Brantlinger (1990), Grossberg, Nelson, and Treichler (1992) and Turner (1992). In the United States, cultural studies has tended to be defined quite flexibly and to be less securely grounded in a Marxist theoretical tradition than the British version arising out of the Birmingham Centre for Contemporary Cultural Studies.
6 In a more recent response to another critique of performance studies by W. B. Worthern, Dolan has softened her stance. Her focus remains, however, on issues of institutional turf and political power to the exclusion of intellectual motives.

BIBLIOGRAPHY

Brantlinger, P. (1990) *Crusoe's Footprints: Cultural Studies in Britain and America*, New York: Routledge.
Carroll, N. (1992) "Theatre, Dance, and Theory: A Philosophical Narrative," *Dance Chronicle* 15, 3: 317–31.
Desmond, J. C. (1994) "Embodying Difference: Issues in Dance and Cultural Studies," *Cultural Critique* 26: 33–63.

Dolan, J. (1993) "Geographies of Learning: Theater Studies, Performance, and the 'Performative,'" *Theatre Journal* 45, 4: 417–41.

—— (1995) "Response to W. B. Worthen's 'Disciplines of the Text/Sites of Performance,'" *The Drama Review* 39, 1: 28–35.

Ebert, T. L. (1993) "Ludic Feminism, the Body, Performance, and Labor: Bringing *Materialism* Back into Feminist Cultural Studies," *Cultural Critique* 23: 5–50.

Gilroy, P. (1993) *The Black Atlantic: Modernity and Double Consciousness*, Cambridge, MA: Harvard University Press.

Graham, M. (1930) "Seeking an American Art of the Dance," in O. M. Sayler (ed.) *Revolt in the Arts*, New York: Brentano's.

—— (1932) "The Dance in America," *Trend* 1, 1: 5–7.

—— (1941) "A Modern Dancer's Primer for Action," in F. R. Rogers (ed.) *Dance: A Basic Educational Technique*, New York: Macmillan.

—— (1991) *Blood Memory*, New York: Doubleday.

Grossberg, L., Nelson, C., and Treichler, P. (1992) *Cultural Studies*, New York: Routledge.

Horst, L. and Russell, C. (1961) *Modern Dance Forms in Relation to the Other Modern Arts*, Princeton, NJ: Princeton Book Company.

Hurston, Z. N. (1969) "Characteristics of Negro Expression," in N. Cunard (ed.) *Negro Anthology*, New York: Negro Universities Press.

Jameson, F. (1993) "On 'Cultural Studies,'" *Social Text* 34: 17–51.

Kemp, F. M. (1927) "Martha Graham: The Blessed Damozel of the Concert Stage," *The Dance* (March): 19, 54.

Lott, E. (1993) *Love and Theft: Blackface Minstrelsy and the American Working Class*, New York: Oxford University Press.

O'Neill, E. (1961) "Memoranda on Masks," in O. Cargill, N. B. Fagin, and W. J. Fisher (eds) *O'Neill and His Plays: Four Decades of Criticism*, New York: New York University Press.

—— (1988) "The Emperor Jones," in T. Bogard (ed.) *Complete Plays: 1913–1920*, New York: Library of America.

—— (1990) *Conversations with Eugene O'Neill*, M. W. Estrin (ed.), Jackson, MS: University Press of Mississippi.

Pollock, F. (1992) "Theses on Intellectuals," *Representations* 39: 71–9.

Roberts, A. W. (1928) "The Fervid Art of Martha Graham," *The Dance Magazine* (August): 13, 63.

Siegel, M. B. (1988) "The Truth About Apples and Oranges," *The Drama Review* 32,4 (T120): 24–31.

Turner, G. (1992) *British Cultural Studies: An Introduction*, New York: Routledge.

Part II
The Body and Gender

7 Simmering Passivity
The Black Male Body in Concert Dance

Thomas DeFrantz

Racial division, cultural fragmentation, and the absence of critical theory devoted to Afro-performance have contributed to the historical displacement of dance created by African-American men. This essay addresses the presence and potency of the black male body in concert dance through a consideration of: 1) strategies governing performance in the Afro-American grain, 2) critical reception of dancers and dances by mainstream press, and 3) analysis of representation as it is described by performance.

MARKED MEN IN SLAVE SOCIETY

The black man's body entered American consciousness as a powerful exotic commodity: a slave. Objectified on the auction blocks of the African gold coast and the Caribbean, his body reached American shores bearing a tangle of opposing physical imperatives. As commodity, it was to hold enormous labor capacity; while as personal property, it was to be eminently repressible, docile, passive. These contradictory demands fed not only the physical foundations of slave society; they also framed modes of stage performance later practiced by black men, including concert dance.

Slave society strictly regulated public dancing by black men before the 1800s. Uprisings, such as the South Carolina Stono Insurrection of 1739 linked the dancing body with rebellion: the resultant slave laws of 1740 prohibited any Negro from "beating drums, blowing horns or the like which might on occasion be used to arouse slaves to insurrectionary activity" (Winter 1947: 28). Drum dancing solidified connections between the slaves' varied West African cultures; to minimize these powerful affinities, slave owners legislated performance and carefully regulated dancing affairs which might provide opportunities "to exchange information and plot insurrections" (Hazzard-Gordon 1990: 33). Dancing came "under the strict governance and supervision of whites who legitimized violence as a means of controlling the slave population" (ibid.: 13). Eventually, serious dancing went underground, and dances which carried significant aesthetic information became disguised or hidden from public view.[1] For white audiences, the black man's dancing body came to carry only the information of its surface.

Black men approaching the concert stage also had to confront deeply entrenched, two-dimensional public perceptions formed by the minstrel stereotypes of the 1800s. Minstrelsy, a form of stage caricature created for white audiences, developed in response to a never-ending fascination with African retentions visible in Afro-American cultural habits. Performed by black and white men in blackface aping the plantation manners and festival dances of southern slaves,[2] the minstrel show solidified around 1840 and remained popular until the turn of the century. Its preferred format featured competitive and eccentric dances, boastful struts and cakewalks, and freakishly stylized characters, including stock types Zip Coon, Jim Crow, and Master Juba (Abrahams 1992: 145).

Built upon flamboyant exaggeration, minstrel stereotypes added a theatrical distance between white audiences and black male performers. Minstrelsy's success "placed American actors of all sorts in the position of agreeing to play black," with mannerisms grossly magnified and patently artificial (ibid.: 134). African-American William Henry Lane originated the stage persona of Master Juba c. 1840. In publicity, Master Juba, the internationally acclaimed "King of All Dancers," performed "irresistible, ludicrous, as well as scientific imitation dances . . . of all the principal Ethiopian Dancers in the United States. After which he will give an imitation of himself . . . " (Winter 1947: 33). Billed as an "imitation" performer, Lane in the persona of Master Juba buffered associations between the potent black body onstage and the preferred impotent everyday, male slave body.

Minstrelsy exploited cultural misreadings to survive as popular entertainment long after the Civil War. Although generations of black dancers learned their craft from the minstrel stages, "minstrelsy . . . fixed the tradition of the Negro as only an irresponsible, happy-go-lucky, wide-grinning, loud-laughing, shuffling, banjo-playing, singing, dancing sort of being" (Johnson 1930: 93). The stereotype of a singing and dancing "sort of [black] being" hardened, and Broadway musicals of the early 1900s typically presented black men as easy-going innocents whose dancing abilities could be fully appreciated in the simple delight they provided. Williams and Walker, the most popular blackface duo of this era, achieved their greatest fame in eccentric dances: Walker, the dandyish "Zip Coon" type, executed dynamic, high-stepping cakewalks "throwing his chest and his buttocks out in opposite directions, until he resembled a pouter pigeon more than a human being" (Emery 1988: 212); while Williams, the woeful, "Jim Crow" bumpkin, "brought down the house with a terrific Mooche or Grind – a sort of shuffle, combining rubberlegs with rotating hips" (Stearns 1968: 197). The minstrel mask defined the black man's body as eccentric, strange, physically dynamic, hysterically out of control, and naive. As minstrel historian Marian Hannah Winter wryly notes, "The word 'beautiful' was almost never used to describe minstrel dancing" (Winter 1947: 34).

Minstrel dance performance by black men amplified issues of body control, power, and physical expression embedded within the restrictions of segregated society. Racial division marked the black body in public American discourse, and mystified dance styles rarely witnessed by whites. The development of modernism and a corresponding interest in African arts suggested the potentially powerful convergence of social dance styles and Afro-American theme for African-American men involved in concert dance.

EARLY CONCERT DANCERS

Black men entered the concert dance arena in the late 1920s, and the earliest dances they performed were aligned with modernism in terms of theme, conception, and technique.[3] Hemsley Winfield organized several performance groups between 1925 and 1934, including the Negro Art Theater, and choreographed dances in the manner of Ruth St. Denis and Helen Tamiris (Perpener 1992: 68). In 1929 he caused a sensation dancing the role of Salome at the Greenwich Village Cherry Lane Theater. Filling in for an absent actress in the all-black cast, Winfield performed "dressed, as it were, in an old bead portiere and nothing else to speak [of]" (Long 1989: 24). Drag performance inevitably confronts boundaries of representation; Winfield's successful portrayal, however anomalous, focused attention on issues of masculinity, black men, and the modern.

Among Winfield's numerous concert works, "Life and Death" created for the theatrical pageant *De Promis Lan'* in May, 1930, cast sixteen men as the inexorable force of Death which overcomes the singular being of Life, danced with charismatic vigor by the choreographer himself. A version of this piece became a staple of Winfield's frequent concert presentations until his sudden death in 1933. Reviews and photographs indicate that "Life and Death" bore stylistic resemblances to Ted Shawn's playfully organized movement choirs, but Winfield's dance predated the first concerts of Shawn's all-male company. Modern dance by a large group of men which didn't trade on minstrel stereotypes stood well outside performance norms of the time. Typically, black bodies were essentialized as the material of naive, "primitive" dance.

Winfield premiered his solo, "Bronze Study," at the historic "First Negro Dance Recital in America" co-directed by Winfield and Ruth St. Denis disciple Edna Guy on April 29, 1931. Writing for the *New York Times*, John Martin dismissed the dance as "merely the exhibition of an exemplary physique." For Martin, physique, and its implicit work potential, lingered as the raw material of the dancing black body's value. But surely Winfield's posturing, however prosaic, sought to subvert the critical eye which refused to see beyond race. It is possible that "Bronze Study" replaced the simple marking of an "exemplary black body" with more complex distinctions of muscle tone, flexibility, stillness, cool stance, and most importantly, the public discourse of skin color.

Although the abatement of strict segregation throughout the 1930s allowed some black dancers to perform in integrated groups, their presence triggered deep-set racial biases in audiences and critics. In 1931 Randolph Sawyer danced the Blackamoor in the Gluck-Sandor Dance Center's *Petrouchka*. Reviewing the otherwise all-white production, Martin spoke euphemistically of Sawyer's "native talents" which "equip him to do a type of dance quite out of the range of his colleagues" (Martin 1931). Audiences still couldn't understand how that "type of dance," implicated by the mere presence of Sawyer's black body, could converse with ballet.

Other artists worked to align the black male body with social reform. Dancer Add Bates solidified his activities with the Communist Party as a member of the Worker's Dance League. Featured in Edith Segal's "Black and White Solidarity Dance," Bates and his partner are pictured on the cover of the March 1933 *Worker's Theater* (Long 1989: 23). Defiantly posed square to the camera, determined and shirtless, Bates raises his thickly muscled arm to the side, with a tightly clenched fist held at eye level. This powerful image of protest aligns the black dancer's body with subversion, tying its weighty volume to the work of social change.

Most pioneer choreographers working to develop an African-American audience for modern dance stuck close to mainstream models of male representation. Charles Williams formed the Creative Dance Group at Virginia's Hampton Institute in 1934 as an extension of that school's physical education activities. Hampton had been founded as a Reconstruction-era project of the American Missionary Association to socialize former slaves as they prepared for integrated life. Strong on concepts of work and morality, the school adhered to a conservative doctrine of conduct in which there was little place for the modern performing arts. It took a herculean effort on Williams's part to secure school support for the dance company; not surprisingly, the works he created were muted and discreet. Heavily influenced by Ted Shawn's all-male company, which visited Hampton in 1933, Williams made dances which exploited the physical dynamism of Hampton's male dancers in traditionally masculine settings. "Men of Valor" (1934) featured movements derived from track and field events, and "Dis Ole Hammer" (1935) set a labor dance to traditional work songs. Williams also created African dance suites, in collaboration with African students studying at the school, as well as dances with Afro-American themes, including a 1935 suite of *Negro Spirituals* (Perpener 1992: 155–60).

Creative Dance Group, which usually performed for African-American audiences, toured the country extensively throughout the 1930s and 1940s in a standard program that progressed from calisthenics and drills to modern dance pieces (ibid.: 159). The company functioned as a proponent of "official" culture, in this case validated by the missionary administration which founded the college. Williams's dutiful presentation of dance as an extension of physical culture which glorified an idealized black masculinity was certainly not lost on its large African-American audience, even if that representation included only athletic, laboring, or pious men. The Hampton group's performing success influenced the formation of a responsive, core African-American audience for concert dance and led directly to the founding of concert dance companies at other southern black schools including Fisk, Howard, and Spellman College (Emery 1988: 245).

New York performances by Asadata Dafora's African dance company forced issues of authenticity and the native black body for dancers and critics. Dafora staged subtly drawn adaptations of festival dances from his Sierra Leone homeland. *Kykunkor* (1934), the first of several evening-length works mounted by Dafora, drew wide praise for its complex synergy of music and movement. For many critics, the success of Dafora's work hinged upon its use of "authentic" African materials derived from first-hand knowledge of classic West African aesthetics. *Kykunkor* defined successful black concert performance as serious, ritual-based exotica, unimaginably complex and distinct from mainstream modern dance. Though Dafora confirmed the great theatrical potential of West African dance for American audiences and African-American dancers, his success set in motion a critical formula which emphasized the exotic novelty of the black body on the concert stage. From this time on, black dancers became increasingly obliged to prove themselves as "Other" to the concert mainstream.

Some dancers resisted the need to demonstrate their "blackness" in easily stereotyped settings. Growing numbers of classically trained dancers, denied participation in white companies, worked for several short-lived, all-black ballet companies. Eugene Von Grona's American Negro Ballet debuted in 1937 at Harlem's Lafayette Theater. The son of a white American mother and a German father, Von Grona formed a company designed to address "the deeper and more intellectual resources of the Negro race" (Acocella 1982: 24). Before starting performances, he spent three years giving his thirty Harlem company members training in ballet and modern dance relaxation techniques. Von Grona choreographed the group's first program to music by Duke Ellington, Igor Stravinsky, W. C. Handy, and J. S. Bach. Lukewarm critical reception and the absence of a committed audience led to the company's demise after only five months. Aubrey Hitchens's Negro Dance Theater, created in 1953, offered the novelty of an all-male repertory company. English-born Hitchens, who "ardently believed in the special dance talents of the Negro race," mixed ballet works set to Bach with dances to generic blues and jazz (Hitchens 1957: 12).

Both of these companies were formed with the express racialist purpose of proving the ability of the black body to inhabit classical ballet technique. The logic that pushed them to capitulate to stereotypical Negro themes in their repertory remains curious. Ballet locates its aesthetic power in the refinement of gesture *away* from everyday bodies and politics; if anything, a proliferation of black *danseurs* might have inspired a *decline* of color fetish among audiences and critics. It is possible that ballet could have *normalized* the black male body to the degree that the idiom *unmarked* the lingering minstrel persona. In giving their audiences familiar black stage types, however, the "get-down" ballets of these early all-black companies obscured issues of the body, black dancers, and western classicism.

Modern dance allowed for more fluid connections between the dancing body, cultural representation, and dance technique, and the post-World War II era saw a number of dancers and choreographers working to redefine the black male presence on the concert stage. West African aesthetic principles, still prominent in black social dance forms, emerged intact in the concert choreography of Talley Beatty, Louis Johnson, and Donald McKayle, signaling a shift in the political frame surrounding performance. Buoyed by the liberal optimism of the New York dance community of the post-war era, dancers explored ways to self-consciously align power and the black male body onstage.

ALVIN AILEY

Alvin Ailey's career in the late 1950s offers a paradigm of contemporary assumptions surrounding the black male body and concert performance. Ailey's choreography formed fires of black machismo in a number of roles he made for himself which literally displayed his body and cast it as the site of desire. Among his earliest works, *Blues Suite* (1958) transferred to the stage traditional assumptions concerning black male sexuality, including overt aggression, insatiability, and an overwhelming despair deflected by the [hetero]sexual act. As a dancer, Ailey created a persona which redefined popular stereotypes of the black male body on the concert stage to include the erotic.

Ailey was born January 5, 1931 into the abject poverty of rural Texas. The only child of working-class parents who separated when he was an infant, Ailey and his mother moved from town to town as she struggled to provide him with basic sustenance. Strictly segregated life in southeast Texas offered a hostile environment for African-Americans and nurtured a fear and mistrust of whites which Ailey later recalled: "Having that kind of experience as a child left a feeling of rage in me that I think pervades my work" (Ailey 1989: 9). This background also created a fierce pride in black social institutions, including the church and jook joints which figured prominently in his later work (Latham 1973: 446). In 1942 Ailey joined his mother in Los Angeles, where his interest in concert dance was sparked by high school excursions to the ballet and Katherine Dunham's 1945 *Tropical Revue*.

Ailey arrived in California shy, lonely, and particularly sensitive from his itinerant childhood. He found solace in the fantasy world of theater and the movies, and gravitated toward the Hollywood masculinity of dancer

Gene Kelly. Kelly's popularity hinged upon his "man's man" persona: "He was a 'man dancer,' one who did not wear tights. Here was a man who wore a shirt, pants, and a tie and danced like a man!" (Latham 1973: 457). Ailey turned to dance when a high school classmate introduced him to Lester Horton's flamboyantly theatrical Hollywood studio in 1949. Excited by Horton's utopian vision of a multicultural dance melting pot, Ailey poured himself into study and developed a weighty, smoldering performance style that suited both his athletic body and his concern with the representation of masculinity: "I didn't really see myself as a dancer. I mean, what would I dance? It was 1949. A man didn't just become a dancer. Especially a black man" (Gruen 1976: 419).

Ailey may have felt constricted by society at large, but he quickly learned to capitalize on the simmering, hyper-masculine persona he developed at the Horton studio. His appearance in the 1954 Broadway musical *House of Flowers* featured "a very sexy pas de deux" with partner Carmen de Lavallade designed to titillate its mostly white audience (Latham 1973: 500). Among the last-gasp attempts at exoticized, "mostly black" Broadway musicals set in foreign locales, *House of Flowers* boasted an extraordinary company of male dancers including Geoffrey Holder, Arthur Mitchell, Louis Johnson, and Walter Nicks. Truman Capote's libretto described two competing West Indian bordellos, and offered African-American actresses myriad "hooker" roles. According to Brooks Atkinson's *New York Times* review, the cast exuded a predictable exotic-primitive appeal:

> Every Negro show includes wonderful dancing. *House of Flowers* is no exception in that respect. Tall and short Negroes, adults and youngsters, torrid maidens in flashy costumes and bare-chested bucks break out into a number of wild, grotesque, animalistic dances ... [which] look and sound alike by the time of the second act.
>
> (Atkinson 1954: 11)

House of Flowers, a show that embodied the contradictions implicit in racial stereotyping on both sides of the stage lights, introduced Ailey to the New York dance scene as part of the "wildly monotonous" grotesquerie of black bodies performing for white audiences.

Ailey had few African-American mentors, and the concert dance techniques he encountered failed to engage him: "I went to watch Martha Graham, and her dance was finicky and strange. I went to Doris Humphrey and José Limón and I just hated it all. I suppose that I was looking for a technique which was similar to Lester's [Horton] and I just did not find it" (Latham 1973: 582). Between commercial appearances and sporadic dance study, he performed in the one-night seasons of Sophie Maslow, Donald McKayle, and Anna Sokolow. However, Ailey identified more with the theatrical macho of Broadway and Hollywood choreographer Jack Cole: "I was impressed by his style, by the way he danced, by his manner, by the masculinity of his projection, by his fierceness, by his animal-like qualities"

(Ailey and Bailey 1995: 80). While dancing for Cole in the Broadway musical *Jamaica*, Ailey and Ernest Parham gathered a group of dancers to fill an afternoon concert slot at the 92nd Street YM-YWHA on March 30, 1958.

Ailey danced in two of his three world premieres: *Redonda*, a curtain-raiser suite of five dances to a Latin theme, and *Ode and Homage*, a solo dedicated to the memory of Horton. His stage persona in this period, suggested in description, photographs and films, built upon an impassioned flailing of his body through dance passages steeped in fiery cool. Ailey seemed to enjoy tempting his audiences with an exotic allure delivered from the safe distance of the stage. Critics likened his style to the movements of wild animals: Doris Hering, reviewing for *Dance Magazine*, compared him to "a caged lion full of lashing power that he can contain or release at will" (Hering 1958: 27) while John Martin noted his "rich, animal quality of movement and innate sense of theatrical projection" (Martin 1958: 11). Jill Johnston, writing for the *Village Voice*, found Ailey's over-the-top histrionics perplexing: "he moves constantly, in high gear, as though in a panic, and like a synthetic composite figure of a smattering of contemporary influences" (Johnston 1961: 15). Ailey's machismo caused P. W. Manchester to quip that he presented a stage world "in which the men are men and the women are frankly delighted about it" (Manchester 1959: 7).

BLUES SUITE

Blues Suite, the third Ailey work premiered on the 1958 program, garnered instant popular and critical acclaim. Drawing on fragments of his Texas childhood, Ailey set the dance in and about a "barrelhouse," a backwoods music-hall/whorehouse for working-class African-Americans. To a musical background of standard twelve-bar blues, ballads, slowdrags, and shams, archetypal Depression-era characters conveyed the fleeting pleasures of dance buried within an evening fraught with fighting, regret, and despair. Costumed with dazzling Broadway-style flair, the suite sizzled with rage and sorrow, at once highly theatrical and pointedly dramatic.

Ailey's original program note aligned his dance with cultural roots: "The musical heritage of the southern Negro remains a profound influence on the music of the world. . . . During the dark days the blues sprang full-born from the docks and the fields, saloons and bawdy houses . . . indeed from the very souls of their creators" (Ailey 1958). The note served to validate the blues milieu for an uninitiated white audience by defining it as both personal (coming from the souls of their creators) and artful (part of a profoundly influential musical heritage). The reference to the dark days (of southern slavery) neatly telescoped cultural history into the premise for the dance: audiences were invited to view the dancing black bodies as authentic bearers of the blues. *Blues Suite* intended to map this southern musicality onto the concert dance stage.

The bawdy house setting played directly into traditional stereotyping of the black body as at once morally corrupt and titillating. As in *House of Flowers*, the women in *Blues Suite* portrayed hookers, and the men, their eager clients. But Ailey managed to locate the gender role-playing within a larger frame of African-American pathos. Here, blues dancing stood for the ephemeral release from the overwhelming social inequities suffered by African-Americans. The frame allowed Ailey to foreground harsh political realities in the creation of intensely flamboyant and entertaining blues dance styles.

Blues Suite reached its final form in the fall of 1964. Alternately titled *Jazz Piece* (1961), *Roots of the Blues* (1961) and *The Blues Roll On* (1963) in earlier formats, Ailey's revisions were largely due to shifting company personnel. An overarching narrative suggesting cyclical and inevitable despair remained common to its several versions. The dance became a classic example of the choreographer's early style and remained in the active repertory of the Alvin Ailey American Dance Theater through 1995. The reading of four sections of the dance which follows is based upon filmed performances made in the 1960s and 1970s, and live performances attended in the 1980s and 1990s.

The dance begins with two traditional calls to attention in African-American folklore: the train whistle, which suggests movement away from the repressive conditions of the South, and church bells, which toll not only for funeral services, but for the arrival of news worthy of community attention. Fast conga drums beat incessantly as the curtain rises, echoing the talking drum sound which traditionally dispersed information in sub-Saharan cultures. The curtain reveals bodies strewn across the stage in posed attitudes of fitful despair: eyes closed, energy drained. Are the figures asleep or dead? To classic strains that acknowledge the capitulation to oppressive circumstances – "Good Morning Blues, Blues How Do You Do?" – the dancers rise, shake off the inertia which held them, and begin an angry ritual of fighting each other to stake out territory. The atmosphere is heavy with stifled rage and disappointment.

Gradually, the fighting evolves into dance movements. In this casual progression Ailey suggests that his dance occupies a cultural space similar to the blues – as the transformation of social and political rage into art. The lexicon shift – from stasis, through the stylized drama of angry individuals, to a common ground represented in dance – draws the audience into concert dance without removing the markers which distinguish the characters as disenfranchised African-Americans. These blues people are black people, and the dance they do is defined by that unique political circumstance, whether it contains elements of social dance, ballet, Graham, or Horton technique.

Although the men in *Blues Suite* are largely defined by their interaction with women, the solo "I Cried" includes a striking demonstration of male public vulnerability. Backed by contrapuntal movements from the group, a single man sits, center stage, his body racked with contractions of pain and anger. As he shakes and trembles in the depths of his anguish, the group extends a hand towards him, bearing witness. He rises towards some offstage goal, his body tensely elongated and brittle. The group reaches after him, offering help; he pushes them away defiantly, wrestling one man to the ground in the process. The group members disperse to strike poses of studied indifference, their faces averted from his dance. As he works out his frustration, the group exits, leaving him alone. As his dance ends the train whistle sounds, stealing his attention, and he exits quickly after it.

The solo is accompanied by the full-throated wailing of singer Brother John Sellars, who has performed this piece with the Ailey company since 1961 both live and on its taped accompaniment. Sellars's wailing has a strident masculine grain rarely heard outside the rural South.[4] His vocal style gives an intensely personal interpretation to what is essentially a common song, without author or copyright. (The lyric, "I cried, tears rolled down my cheek/Thinking about my baby, how sweet the woman used to be" is a simple, bare-bones couplet, practically devoid of character.) Firmly rooted in the Afro-American vernacular, Sellars's aggressive sound masculinizes the connection between the expression of sorrow and the male dancer: it validates concert dance as an "authentic" mode of (heterosexual) male behavior.

The train whistle serves as the bridge to "Mean Ole Frisco," a dance for five men. Entering the space singly, each man looks towards an offstage train, imagined to pass over the audience's head. Watching the train closely, the dancers undulate in seething slow motion, sinking into asymmetrical stances with one hip thrust to the side. A swaying hip movement begins slowly and accelerates, finally matching the fast shuffle tempo of the song. The dance continues with mostly unison phrasing, with some interplay for groups of three against two dancers. The men describe powerful accents at the ends of phrases – shooting an arm into space, stopping the energy with a tightly clenched fist. They dance apart, in wide spatial formation, without ever seeing each other.

Although the dance is about the men's longing for a lover that the train has taken away (the "Frisco" of the blues lyric), sexuality is buried deeply beneath a brawny veneer. Ailey studiously avoided homoeroticism here through blockish phrasing, constant explosive movement, and a fierce abstention from physical or emotional contact by the men. The result is a strangely harsh depiction of black men as unable to relate to each other. The latent homophobia of the staging is made more strange by Ailey's own homosexuality. Ailey performed this dance in the 1960s, his heterosexual stage persona far removed from his offstage reality. In this dance, the desirous black male body is overtly heterosexual, single mindedly in pursuit of an offstage woman (Figure 7.1).

"Backwater Blues," the central pas de deux, features a man and woman in a low-down, brutal lovers' battle. Drawn in broad strokes of gender role

Figure 7.1 Blues Suite: impervious to empathy. Members of the Alvin Ailey
American Dance Theater in a posed arrangement for the "Mean Ole Frisco"
section. (Photo: © Jack Mitchell)

playing, the dance depicts several stages of a courtship ritual built from
boasts, struts, and Apache-style physical confrontation. The choreography
depends heavily upon a realistic acting approach Ailey derived from study
at the Stella Adler acting studio (de Lavallade 1995: 165). A pervasive use
of body language, stance, and gesture fills out details of emotional life
between the characters. Formal dance movements function as extensions
of the dramatic narrative, making the rare motionless position stand out in
sharp relief. In one instance, the woman, precariously balanced on the
kneeling man's shoulder, throws back her head to pound her chest in angry

defiance. The image resounds beyond this dance encounter, speaking of the emotional outrage brought about by dysfunctional circumstance – in this case, life in a southern whorehouse.

While trading on the entertainment value of the age-old battle of the sexes, Ailey was able to align black social dance styles with concert performance. Ailey used the dramatic narrative to essentialize black social dance as the site of sexual power negotiation. When markers of black dance appear, in flamboyant percussive breaks at the end of musical phrases, multiple meter elaborated by isolations of body parts, and apart phrasing palpable in layered rhythmic patterns, they are carefully embedded within a theatrically constructed tension between Man and Woman. Here, blues dance is masculinized to the degree it is construed to be (hetero)sexual.

In the brief solos of "In The Evening," which follow the duet, three men prepare for a night at the barrelhouse. Here, Ailey used formal dance vocabulary to describe three distinct personalities in movement terms. Arcing turns, interrupted by slight hesitations; swooping balances cut off by full-bodied contractions; and cool struts, stopped by percussive attacks of static poses, all visualize the music's underlying rhythmic structures in terms of breaks and ruptures. These oppositional contrasts are obvious functions of lingering West African aesthetic principles of compositional balance. Ailey fashioned the phrasing mostly in square blocks of four and eight counts, but sharp accents and strong rhythmic shifts from fast, sixteenth-note foot-tapping accents, to slow, half-note balances separate the dance from the music: the dance is conceived both "to" and "apart from" the steady musical beat.

Conceptually similar to classical ballet variations, these solos oblige the men to demonstrate mastery of dance technique. The difficult rhythmic structures also baldly expose the dancers' musicality and precision. In these pure dance variations, Ailey set a standard of concert dance proficiency accessible to black male bodies. In this case, dance technique is disguised as libidinous male posturing.

The solos end when the women reappear, beginning a long sequence of festive blues dancing by the group and two comic characters constantly out of step. The giddy playfulness of the "Sham" contradicts the anger, despair, and fierce attitude of previous sections, exploring instead the entertainment aspects of blues music. The section ends with tightly focused unison phrases, the dancers' smiling faces turned toward the audience in a gesture of communal celebration. Reminiscent of a scene from a Broadway musical, this false, happy ending is followed by the repetition of "Good Morning Blues," signaling the return to the painful everyday life of labor and oppression. Faces are averted and suddenly solemn; bodies carry an intense weightiness; speed and agility are buried within downward directed motions and angry demeanors. In this "real" ending to the piece, the characters are again solitary, sprawled across the stage, separated by forces beyond their control, apprehensive, gloom-ridden, and tormented.

The violent juxtaposition of euphoria and despair which ends *Blues Suite* aptly re/presents the professional experiences of Ailey and other black men through the post-war era of concert dance. Smiling through a fleeting triumph, they were inevitably burdened by political circumstances rife with racism, homophobia, and indifference. Forced to entertain audiences receptive only to broadly stereotyped personae, African-American men danced savage, hyper-masculine, aggressively heterosexual, and naive-primitive roles which catered to traditional assumptions about the black male body. Denied the opportunity to perform powerful dance that reflected the realities of their lives outside the theater, African-American men simmered passively for decades, awaiting the chance to define themselves in terms of movement.

NOTES

1 African art historian Robert F. Thompson describes particular dances as "key documents of aesthetic history . . . nonverbal formulations of philosophies of beauty and ethics" in traditional West African settings (Thompson 1986: 85).
2 Abrahams draws out the development of minstrelsy from slave corn-shucking festivals (1992: 131–43).
3 Perpener (1992) provides an overview of the pioneers and their techniques.
4 Murray associates the sound with itinerant folk style guitar strummers (1978).

BIBLIOGRAPHY

Abrahams, R. (1992) *Singing the Master: The Emergence of African-American Culture in the Plantation South*, New York: Penguin Books.
Acocella, J. (1982) "Van Grona and His First American Negro Ballet," *Dance Magazine* (March): 22–4, 30–2.
Ailey, A. (1958) "Alvin Ailey and Company, Ernest Parham and Company," YM-YWHA Program Notes (March 30).
—— (1989) "Alvin Ailey," in *Black Visions*, New York: Tweed Gallery.
Ailey, A. and Bailey, A. P. (1995) *Revelations: The Autobiography of Alvin Ailey*, New York: Birch Lane Press.
Atkinson, B. (1954) "Theater: Truman Capote's Musical," *New York Times* (December 31): 11.
de Lavallade, C. (1995) "Alvin Ailey," in A. Ailey and A. P. Bailey (eds) *Revelations: The Autobiography of Alvin Ailey*, New York: Birch Lane Press.
Emery, L. (1988) *Black Dance From 1619 to Today*, second revised edition, Princeton, NJ: Dance Horizons Books.
Gruen, J. (1976) "Alvin Ailey," in *The Private World of Ballet*, New York: Penguin Books.
Hazzard-Gordon, K. (1990) *Jookin': The Rise of Social Dance Formations Among African-Americans*, Philadelphia: Temple University Press.
Hering, D. (1958) "Alvin Ailey and Ernest Parham," *Dance Magazine* (May): 65–6.
Hitchens, A. (1957) "Creating the Negro Dance Theatre," *Dance and Dancers* (April): 12–13.
Johnson, J. (1930) *Black Manhattan*, New York: Alfred A. Knopf.
Johnston, J. (1961) "Mr. Ailey," *Village Voice* (December 21): 15.
Latham, J. (1973) "A Biographical Study of the Lives and Contributions of Two

Selected Contemporary Black Male Dance Artists – Arthur Mitchell and Alvin Ailey," unpublished Ph.D. dissertation, Texas Woman's University.

Long, R. (1989) *The Black Tradition in American Dance*, New York: Rizzoli Books.

Manchester, P. (1959) "The Season in Review," *Dance News* (February): 7.

Martin, J. (1931) "The Dance: A Repertory Movement; Stravinsky's 'Petrouschka' Opens The Dance Center's Season of Experiment – A Novel Theater and Production," *New York Times* (August 30): 7.

—— (1958) "The Dance: Review III," *New York Times* (July 6): 11.

Murray, A. (1978) "Blues Suite," Liner Notes to *Revelations*, New York: Dance Theater Foundation Records.

Perpener, J. (1992) "The Seminal Years of Black Concert Dance," unpublished Ph.D. dissertation, New York University, Department of Performance Studies.

Stearns, M. and Stearns, J. (1968) *Jazz Dance: The Story of American Vernacular Dance*, New York: Schirmer Books.

Thompson, R. (1986) "Dance and Culture, an Aesthetic of the Cool: West African Dance," *African Forum* (Fall) 2: 85–102.

Winter, M. (1947) "Juba and American Minstrelsy," *Dance Index* (February) VI, 2: 28–48.

8 Being Danced Again

Meredith Monk, Reclaiming the Girlchild

Leslie Satin

In 1979, I saw Meredith Monk's *Education of the Girlchild* at the Brooklyn Academy of Music. I was struck then by potent and beautiful images that I carried for years: women in white clothing, indecipherable but somehow familiar events, bowls and books and branches, and the solo trip down miles of muslin, Monk imagining herself first as an old woman and then winding back through the years of her life.

In the years since that viewing, I have seen many of Monk's works. I have also become deeply absorbed in considering the theoretical, critical, and aesthetic intersections of self-representational practice in dance. Rather than seeking to impose an autobiographical intention on choreographers' works, my interest is in seeing how the notion of autobiography, or self-representation, can elucidate performance, particularly dance. Autobiography functions as cover and discovery, closure and disclosure. Artists create autobiographical *oeuvres* via intention, accident, and semiotic accumulation. Some work reveals – or seems to – explicit, or documentary detail; in other instances, self-representation is a matter of what I see as implicit autobiography.

Sometimes the choreographic and critical paths are slippery, collision courses. And I – a dancer who writes, a writer who dances – slide over words, around steps, through spaces. One dancer told me that all of her work is autobiographical: "I don't think I've left any of my history out." She seemed, in a way, to say it all. But in fact, she lured me back to the seductive notion of autobiography as a retelling of fixed history.

This story suggests the hold of the predominant trope in the history of western autobiography: the individual, largely understood to be male and, generally, to be white, and the genre itself as what Sidonie Smith calls "the valorization of autonomous selfhood" (1987: 9). In this double-layered model, the notion of the autonomous self – spatially discrete, temporally linear – as the conceptual baseline of traditional autobiography is, logically enough, repeated in the actualizing of the form; that is, autobiography sets, in type and in time, the "real" events of the individual writer's life.[1]

In dance, of course, the notion of literally freezing anything or anyone in time is illusory, limited to a momentary choreographic maneuver. Dancers' acts of self-representation, which are and are not like written acts, create meaning in the framework of live, rather than written/read performance. I look here at Meredith Monk's choreographic telling of the self, at the self-representation which has emerged from longstanding through lines in her art. One of these is community, the collective self; the other is the poetic time-travel of the individual. Monk has created a self-representational model which foregrounds the notion of community, and she has created a powerful envisioning of the individual who emerges from within that collective.

Monk's *Education of the Girlchild*, a large-scale work choreographed in the early 1970s, portrays a small community of women whose personae are living links between cultural archetypes and the performers' private lives.[2] The piece is a particularly apt model for the intersection of the two auto-biographical tropes I have named: the collective and the individual self. It is made up of two sections, the first one for the women, the second a solo for Monk; the first depicts a group's quest, or journey, and the second is Monk's solo trip, in reverse, through the years of a/her life.

Any of Monk's works would be a potent site for an autobiographical reading, an exploration of the multiple possibilities of autobiographical practice. Individually and together, they all offer insights into her conception and performance of the self. The themes as well as the structures of *Girlchild*, however, make it an ideal case. These themes, in Monk's words, are "growth, change, life cycles, and community" (1994: 13) – the "education," or the process of growing up, alone and with a group. Monk, as has often been the case, plays the central figure, the young woman coming-of-age, becoming herself over time. Time is germane to Monk's creation of the dancing self as a choreographic strategy, a poetic metaphor, and a window through which to re/view her works.

I focus here on Monk's recent reconstruction of *Girlchild*, performed at the Joyce Theater in New York in May 1993. A reconstruction is a story about time: about evolution and aging, the mingled changes of the work, its creator, and its spectators. This was immediately evident to me in the first moments of the twenty-year-old *Girlchild*, in which the original performers revived their roles.[3] The opening image, of Monica Moseley sitting alone at a table, quietly engrossed in her book, did not so much propel me back in time as it compelled me to watch with an eye to the years between, my own and those of the players in the piece, and to see the work as taking place across the span.

> The process of reclaiming *Girlchild* was lively; filled with poignancy, humor, and irony. It became apparent that the process itself mirrored *Girlchild*'s themes of growth, change, life cycles, and community. . . . All of [the original cast] were dealing with the sense of ourselves now in relation to our past selves who had first performed together in 1973.
>
> (Monk 1994: 12–13)

Moseley and the "companions" who joined her were both familiar through memory and unfamiliar through the gaps in time, evoking a profound sense of community with no suggestion of sentiment, or of imitation of their former selves. Later, when Monk was alone onstage in the second section, I recalled the community from which she had departed and the individual and complex persona she has accumulated in work after work over many years.

Education of the Girlchild is Monk's most eloquent, and most direct, example of what Derrida calls "staging signatures."[4] Derrida's intertextual concept suggests a compelling possibility for reading the body as it moves over time. He uses the phrase within a discussion of the work of Nietzsche, who engaged in explicitly autobiographical, as well as philosophical, discourse. "To put one's name on the line . . . to stage signatures, to make an immense bio-graphical paraph out of all that one has written on life or death" is what Derrida names as the act through which Nietzsche's texts must be read (Derrida 1988: 7). For Monk, perhaps, the dances themselves are the signature rather than the "paraph"; nevertheless, given the phrase's engagement with action and activation, with metaphors of writing and the body, this notion of autobiographical practice seems especially apt for performance – particularly dance.

Derrida said, "Everything I write is terribly autobiographical." Claude Lévesque, in response, pointed to the mix of denotations and connotations of "terribly," its implications of terror and excess, and suggested that Derrida was saying that he had crossed over the line "of discourse and of knowledge" and moved "outside language, into a space that we enter only if we no longer are" (Lévesque in Derrida 1988: 72).

For Monk to repeat a dance – especially a solo – made many years before was to embark on a process of recovery: not a pursuit of lost moments, or, like Ponce de León, a quest for eternal youth, but a dance through layers of time, a search through those "space[s] we enter only if we no longer are" for a dearly remembered but not entirely articulable memory of an experience of the mind and the spirit. Indeed, *Girlchild*, like many of Monk's works – and more pointedly than most dance – clearly resides in Lévesque's and Derrida's space "outside language." Though many choreographers incorporate spoken text into their works or are inspired by literary sources, dance is primarily identified with movement, and its significance is situated in the moving body; our *readings* – including Susan Foster's explorations of the complex relationship of dance and language – respond chiefly to the visual stimulus of the body dancing through fields of representation. The significance of *Girlchild*, though, lies also in its sounds and music – the compelling ostinatos, the haunting melodies, the wide variety of vocalizations, and the songs of wordless syllables which seem both to precede and to transcend verbal communication – as well as in its physical actions and *mise en scène*.

Many choreographers join dance and music, of course, but Monk strategically and explicitly links sound, music, and language to create meaning; calling her works operas, she has made sound an integral element of her productions. The sounds, issuing from the dancers' bodies, simultaneously refuse and recall the communicational and syntactic limitations of conventional language: the absence of words and linguistic linearity are, in a sense, both the point and beside the point. Monk sees her work as "useful," offering both performer and spectator a perceptual disruption, a state of sheer presence transcending language.

> [W]e can offer . . . an experience of being able to let go, even a few minutes at a time, of the discursive thought process, which from my point of view is mostly learned thinking and habitual thinking. . . . If you can get it for a split second, it's kind of a miracle. And it's not to say that it's a goal, it really is just a process. I think that . . . hav[ing] the experience of nowness, in a very direct way, which has to do with perception, is something that artists can offer because what we work with all the time is shadings and refinements of perception. . . . And that, of course, the perceptual aspect, is one step toward the spiritual aspect.[5]

The poignancy of Monk's gesture in reconstructing *Girlchild*, the reaching back, was deepened by the subject of the solo: time and recollection, the backward flow of an imagined life. This life is Monk's, and her character's; by extension and implication, it is ours, too.

> I had to think about how . . . what as young people we know, in a sense we take for granted, and even though I've lived for twenty years since that time there was not going to be any way that I was going to reproduce that. At first . . . I was very sad about that, I felt like my carburetor had gotten grungy over the years, and how was I going to clean that carburetor off to get to the basic goodness that in a way I took for granted. I had a lot of knowledge in those days and I didn't even know how much I knew. When you know things more consciously it becomes more frightening, because you have to go through a process of letting go. You have to be more conscious to let go of consciousness, to get back to sensation, or to what I would call basic goodness.

Monk describes her experience of performing the piece again in terms of her interior journey to recover the depth and openness of the earlier performances rather than to attempt to copy what she had done, or been, before. Her journey is one taken in movement and in voice, a spiritual voyage into deeply felt sensation and experience and what she sees as universal expression.

In the first section of *Education of the Girlchild*, Monk and her companions take off on a quest of no named object. According to Teresa de Lauretis, the male hero of narrative embarks upon a quest in which he must conquer any obstacles which stand in his way (de Lauretis 1984). Unlike de

Lauretis's narrative path, in which the hero chops down thorny bushes impeding his progress toward the object of his desire – generally the conquest or possession of a princess in repose – *Girlchild*'s journey is open-ended and inclusive. The getting there, wherever "there" might be, is the "point" of the journey, and the obstacles are fields of potential interaction rather than conflict: selfhood is a matter of pleasurable interdependence.

When the piece opens, Moseley, wearing a little white cap, sits reading at a table in the downstage left corner; her posture is composed, serene. Others enter, slowly; most come alone, except for Monk and Lanny Harrison, holding hands. Each one bears an object of particular significance to her personal life, her public persona, the unfolding mysteries of the piece. Each entrance contributes to a changing tableau, as the performer introduces her "character" through her physical qualities, the particular detail of her white costume, and her actions. Moseley wears shorts and hiking boots; Blondell Cummings, elegantly casual in a light dress, sprawls when she sits; large, regal Lee Nagrin, dressed in a tunic, leans forward and gesticulates; Harrison, long and all limbs in shirt and trousers, sits, legs splayed, on a short chair. Small-framed Monk wears her dark hair hanging loose to her waist; wearing pants laced to her knees, she also sits on a low chair, then lays her head on the table.

The women rise to discover Coco Dalton nearby, curled under a heavy blanket with her legs raised, feet flexed. She is set apart from them by the bright colors she wears, her sombrero, her sloppy childlikeness, her air of displacement and curious confusion. The others stare at her for a while; she breaks the stillness, by looking and feeling around. She joins the group, and all return to the table in a staggered repetition – broken often by long pauses – of a phrase, a step-kneel-arch sequence executed differently by each person.

The "story" proceeds episodically. Things happen and images appear, sometimes repeat, sometimes not. Long pauses punctuate and interrupt movements and sequences. Periods of silence contrast with sequences of organ and piano music, and with laughs, whispers, yelps, cries, and singing. Actions take a long time to unfold; "real" time and the prolonged time-sense of dreams share the stage. Everyday events and mysterious ones occur at the same time; pedestrian acts, performed with uncommon deliberateness, become extraordinary: Monk braids her hair, eggplants are placed on a table.

In a procession going nowhere, each woman has her own soft and jaunty step, repeated over and over in place. Each holds a signature object on her head as she moves: Monk has a house, Moseley a globe, Nagrin a spray of branches, Cummings a lizard, Dalton a folded wooden chair. Harrison, in front of the others, swings a scythe. Someone sings, loudly, "Heh heh heh heh." Harrison takes up a suitcase, carries it to the front of the line, joins the singing. A driving tune is played on a keyboard.

The group at the table eats and drinks tea; an unreadable conversation of minimal gestures passes between them; a standing tableau is held for many minutes. Dalton repeats the kneeling phrase, performing it more jerkily than the others; deliberately unlovely, she both is and is not in the group, embraced by it but slightly apart.

Between sections, a man and woman, in vaguely Eastern European dress, perform *entr'actes* of low-key rhythmic softshoe dancing. These "Narrators" urge the piece along, periodically translating the proceedings or providing chronological or geographical data. At one point, the man, brandishing two canes, performs a mad dance to taped carousel music, displacing the companions' tender tableau. When he retreats, the keyboard music returns, wilder and more intense, and the women go back to their singing, dancing caravan.

Monk dances a solo of jumps, stretches, and flinging arms, both unrestrained and soft; the dance is doubled by her shadow, enormous behind her on the upstage wall. The Narrators pass in front of her, bearing a large sign announcing the next section: A Test. They return, bearing the seated "Ancestress" (Tone Blevins) whom they place on a platform.[6] A horrifying figure, she alternately groans, grimaces, and screeches wordless accusations. The dancers, wearing veils draped over their heads, approach her and pay dancing homage, sometimes kneeling, sometimes extending hands for a blessing. When Moseley finishes, she walks downstage and dances wildly, flailing – a doubling of Monk's solo of moments ago. The Ancestress rises, still screeching; she quiets, raising one arm skyward, as Nagrin dances for her. Now Nagrin's warm singing voice fills the air: a long, loud drawn-out "Aaaahhhh."

In one scene, the women are old, rather mad crones. With their hair covered in scarves, they dance gaily, shrieking gleefully. One by one, they are carried off by a blue bare-breasted Death figure, one of several weird unnamed characters who come onstage. When only Monk and Harrison are left, Monk chants the only actual words of the piece, the marvelous paean to material and immaterial possessions: "I still have my money, I still have my mind, I still have my philosophy, I still have my telephone, I still have my memory, I still have my . . . " Still singing, she is taken away.

Monk's artistic history is steeped in the poetic reordering of imagery, sound, spirit and intellect, her sense-crossing assemblages of mediums: "The movement is the singing and the singing is the movement." She has created a broad, diverse, and prolific store of productions, ranging from intimate concerts of song to large-scale theatrical events comprising choreography, music, film, and other media. Over the years, she has cumulatively created a vivid persona, a composite author/character, a distinctly recognizable individual who is central to the proceedings. This centralness extends to creation and production. She is the work's indispensable axis, functioning like the cinematic *auteur* who determines every aesthetic and technical element; every note of music, frame of film, and phrase of movement bears her signature. Nonetheless, her persona is inextricably linked to the others who people her pieces, to those who create and perform with her, to those she imagines and conjures into characters, to those she remembers.

Monk has created a growing anthology of tales embodying her notions of the collective self. In these stories, Monk expresses the connectedness of people across rooms and across eras and cultures. Her tales situate her as a member of a great assortment of communities, historic and invented, specified and mysterious, which collectively have come to suggest Monk's theatricalized conception of the "human family." In *Quarry* (1976), for example, performers in contemporary dress and biblical garb surround Monk, who lies wailing centerstage in pajamas and braids. The pain of the Holocaust, borne by her onstage relatives of the present and the long past, is seemingly transposed to her own small body. In *Paris/Venice/Milan/Chacon* (1974–6), the "Paris couple" – Monk and Ping Chong – dance quietly through the onstage streets of the four locales. First in heavy boots and peasantlike garb (and Monk in a mustache), later wearing evening clothes, they bob and flutter, and meet a clown, a painter, mysterious townspeople. They are like spouses of long standing, a snug unit, encountering others lightly. In the duet *Facing North* (1990), billows of white muslin turn the performance area into the universe as *tabula rasa*, a space of potentiality, a space preceding identity. Monk and Robert Een, at a small altar, manipulate tiny trees and mountains, making the world, narrating and becoming the myth that joins all cultures. They sing wordless tunes, lumber and bounce, come into language and movement – like infants, and like the first people on earth.

Monk's spectacles have historically stretched across both artistic and geographic boundaries, and have altered conventional scale to disrupt, or to reverse, traditional ways of seeing.[7] Scale is germane to Monk's auto-biographical practice because it reflects her positioning of the individual in the community – in her work, a microcosmic representation of the larger world. In piece after piece, the performers are a company of individuals, stand-ins for entire nations, representations of a character's stages of life, and components of a single person's subconscious, dream state, or developmental process. Simultaneously, the set is the performance space itself, a mix of unlikely venues, or a metaphorical stand-in for the messy march of history.

Monk consistently disrupts familiar perceptual processes and familiar readings of the individual and the community. Her strategies, aimed at liberating the spectator, are rooted in the enhancement of the experience of the performer. Her employment of unlikely repetitions and juxtapositions, disruption and discontinuity of actions and narratives, and fluid and frag-mented time suggest parallels between Monk's "transformative theater" and ritual; her inner-landscape imagery, drawn from dreams, imagination, and the subconscious, and her use of non-linear structures urge both performer and spectator out of mundane modes of experience.[8] *Girlchild* exemplifies Monk's thematic development of critical moments within a person's life, the rites of passage commonly celebrated in ritual. Creating the piece, in the safety of the rehearsal studio, cast members retrieved and exchanged memories, remodeled them. Later, in reconstructing, they were called upon to redevelop this connection to each other and to their personal discoveries. The company brought not only their movement material but elements of their lives to their characters; their resulting interaction was richly layered with collective idiosyncrasies.

Monk rarely highlights explicitly autobiographical details in her productions, yet she implies and embeds offstage elements of her own and other performers' lives. Her incorporation of the details or distillations of her own history and the lives of her performers is an oblique yet deeply personal slant on what Kathleen Woodward calls autobiography's "dimension of the interpretive" (1988: 99–100).[9] Monk's Eastern European Jewish heritage was important in creating *Girlchild*'s old woman, based on Monk's Polish grandmother. It underlies the Holocaust imagery of *Quarry*, and the cold ancestral homelands of *Facing North*. The characters of *Girlchild* emerged, during rehearsal, from elements of private lives and personalities, translated through the performers into specific styles of movement, a performative presence or affect, characteristic objects or pieces of clothing. They were understood as "enlargements of themselves rather than as fictitious personae" (Goldberg 1983: 20–1).

Monk began creating works in 1964, when she arrived in New York after graduating from Sarah Lawrence College. Sally Banes has noted how Monk's early work both departed from the primary ideals of the Judson Dance Theater, whose choreographic activities predominated in dance experimentation at that time, and simultaneously benefited from its efforts. For instance, Monk – "more the child of Artaud than of Cage" – plunged into the theatricality which other Judson dancers, preferring to reveal the pipes and bones of unadorned movement, eschewed. At the same time, Monk was as eager as the Judson choreographers to make dances that veered away from modern dance's philosophies, styles, and technical virtuosity (Banes 1980: 149–51, 1984: 1).

The desire for community was pervasive in the culture of the 1960s, both in the arts and in the broader late-decade counterculture. Monk's expression of community is central to her work, especially to *Girlchild*, and poignantly so to its revival. Monk idealizes community and sees it as a locus for both the expression of her belief in myths and dreams which join people across cultures, and the opportunity for the spectator to draw on the offered imagery in whatever way she finds most meaningful. She calls what she does "working mythically":

> You could take it as a metaphorical thing, that there's this phylogeny–ontogeny thing, where it can be seen that it's one person [and] it can be that it's the world. . . . It offers those two layers simultaneously. [In

Girlchild], it can be that each woman is coming in ... from another part of the world, so there's the whole world sitting at that table. Or it could be that it's different aspects of one person or it could be that each person has a different kind of quality.

The companions are a utopian vision, and, one may surmise, a feminist fantasy. In the 1960s, when Monk was beginning to create work, such an inclusive, powerful notion of community was a common cultural model. By the time she made *Girlchild*, this view was becoming somewhat less popular. Banes writes that by the 1970s, this "communal sensibility ... has a compensatory function, offering a vision of an integrated, productive, and stable society" (1984: 33). In the cynical mid-1990s, that vision is, at best, remote – at worst, absurd – for many artists and spectators. To perform the piece again is not only to reiterate a youthful ideal of social structure and personal identity, but to put oneself on the line, to make the restoration of recollected action a bravely autobiographical act, a performance of one's most vital self.

The concept of community, so crucial to *Education of the Girlchild*, is of particular interest to the study of autobiography. Monk is among the dance artists who have experimented with alternative concepts and tellings of selfhood which diverge from ideologies of individualism, and question, rethink, or displace individualistic models of selfhood.[10] The positioning of the teller within a group problematizes the autonomous base of conventional autobiography.

I do not mean to imply that the mere presence of other people in a work read as autobiography makes that work subversive. What I am saying is that the expression of the self as an entwined entity is not only a break from tradition but a political gesture: it situates identity and its representation as active and interactive, as something which emerges from relationships. As Peggy Phelan writes, "Identity is perceptible only through a relation to an other – which is to say, it is a form of both resisting and reclaiming the other, declaring the boundary where the self diverges from and merges with the other" (1993: 13).

The pervasiveness of Monk's voice across the mediums in her large-scale productions lends the theme of self-representation in her work an ironic frame: that of the overarching, determining voice traditionally associated with the public voice of men, and more specifically with the public telling of a man's life. The history of women and autobiography is the history of women's lack of access to the public forum and the multiple ways in which women have sought after and fought for that access, either through private texts or open arenas (acts of non-textual rebellion, or the making public of texts). Autobiography has been understood to be "normative" and representative of the public/male sphere and discourse, and female transgression of those boundaries has meant "enacting the scenario of male selfhood" and either clashing with notions of appropriate female behavior or being silenced by actual or feared censure (Smith 1987: 8–9).[11]

These historical definitions and conventions raise, by implication, one of the dilemmas underlying feminist inquiries into selfhood and authorship which comes head to head with postmodernism and poststructuralism. The poststructuralist position is that the self is a "process constituted by various cultural and historical circumstances" (Foster 1986: 236). Nonetheless, feminist discomfort which has arisen about the meaning for women of the proverbial "death of the author" is particularly germane to female auto-biography, when neither the life nor the author has full cultural significance. This instability is replicated in western concert dance, whose relatively recent history includes a progression of women of great power but also idealizes and romanticizes that power.

These women and their work may be thought of as trespassers onto the property of the largely male choreographic power structure. The notion of gender trespassing as situated in the overall form and production of a work rather than in a particular style or detail has been raised in another feminist rereading of dance, in Ellen Graff's observation that Martha Graham wished to appropriate the male role in her dances (Graff 1988, 1992). I do not see Monk's work as emulating or laying claim to a male voice or positioning through her work (as an artist) or within her works (as a persona). I believe, instead, that her occupation of the central role in *Girlchild* and other stories of quest and growth are a restoration of balance: of what she calls "male and female aspects," and what I see, too, as power.

For Monk, gender is about qualities shared by both men and women, qualities which are thrown out of kilter by cultural prerogatives.

> I think that each of us has male and female aspects . . . we're all in a different kind of balance, but basically, all of us have a complete male and female spectrum of aspects of our personalities and to our beings. What's interesting about *Girlchild* is that I was taking pretty much the whole cast as the female, as female human beings, but basically within that, we were exploring the worlds of male and female within female. So, in other words, you could have a complete world with female characters.

Her words point to a belief in, or a yearning for, a kind of ideal state, unmediated by culture. She sees "male and female characteristics [as] culturally determined [and] learned"; and her desire to allow both performers and spectators the full range of "the human archetypal spectrum" is a continuation of her project to elevate people's experiential and perceptual habits. Both she and many of her observers speak of her link to the universal – a seductive, but problematic, concept. Much of recent feminist scholarship has been directed toward deconstructing the notion of universality in patriarchy, revealing, in short, the cultural assignments of the male as universal, the female as "other". In the 1970s, feminists turned to psycho-analysis, using it as a tool to focus on the gendered representations of human development;[12] later work, assuming these broad cultural processes, has concentrated on material manifestations and interventions.

Monk's work and its presentation both reflect images associated in our culture with the feminine and, by extension, feminize the work and the artist. Community, for example, has gendered associations. It is especially interesting, then, that Monk calls her production company The House. Banes, in essays titled, aptly, "Homemade Metaphors," has noted the name's contribution to the aura of community associated with Monk's work (Banes 1980, 1984). I suggest that the nomenclature literally contains the work – which, ironically, is so powerful in its expansive use of material stage space and its evocations of extra-real geographical, bodily, and psychic space – within its architectural metaphor, contributing to a domesticization of her theater. This notion extends the effects of the imagery contained in the work, for example, the "furnishing" of the stage space in *Girlchild* and *Facing North*, among others, with enormous swaths of white fabric which both extend the spatial parameters into imagined, boundless realms and gather it into the familiar glossary of the home. Also, Monk has always made use of objects and images which are intimately connected to herself, other performers, or, by their widespread familiarity, the viewer; it is the theatrical recontextualizing of these objects which underlies the poetry and the transformational quality of her work; it is their very familiarity which makes them both ritually charged and representationally "safe." Monk becomes, then, by extension, the homemaker, who cares for and maintains her domain, as well as the creator who owns it.[13]

Susan Stanford Friedman and Sidonie Smith are among the feminist and literary scholars who have addressed the notion of autonomy in autobiography, contesting the convention that individualism is a cultural precondition for autobiography, and noting that it is problematic for those who see the self as differing for women and others outside of the dominant position in the culture (Friedman 1988; Smith 1987). This insistence on the individualistic model, they argue, reflects our culture's glorification of a notion of the self "that privileges individuality and separateness over connectedness" (Smith 1987: 12). This standard disregards female models of interdependent identity, acknowledging neither culturally imposed group identity nor the role of socialization in the development of gender identity. Further, it glosses over the racial or ethnic component of selfhood and autobiography – that is, the importance of collectivity as an element of identity formation and representation in the lives of non-dominant populations.

It also ignores possible differences for males and females in the individuation process itself, as uncovered in feminist rereadings of psychoanalytic models. For example, psychoanalytic theorists such as Nancy Chodorow, Dorothy Dinnerstein, and Sheila Rowbotham point out the male bias in the way we understand individuation as the desired end point of psychological development, and claim that the process of individuation differs for males and females. For Chodorow, who sees the mother/daughter as both model and cause of a girl's experience of self, one from which grows a process of "merging and separation" and a "fusion of identification and object choice," the female experience of the self is more continuous with others, the "object-world" of the female more complex than men's (Friedman 1988: 40–2).

If we are entirely "framed" by Freud's theories of identity, in which the Oedipal marks the painful moment of separation, or the Lacanian turn which adds the bite of eternally false unity of the self to that life history – both tales blatantly modeled on a central male figure – we can nonetheless be resistant to essentialist psychoanalytic theories. Chodorow, for example, says: "The basic feminine sense of self is connected to the world, the basic masculine sense of self is separate" (ibid.: 40). But a lesson of Friedman's analysis of the relation of theories of selfhood to theories of autobiography is that different models produce different texts. Monk's texts grow from her mix of models of selfhood.

To talk about individualism is to talk about the power of the unseen: "Isolate individualism is an illusion. It is also the privilege of power" (ibid.: 39). On the other side, though, women's collective identity can be a source of power, too, and of what bell hooks, recalling her segregation-era childhood, called "sweet communion: solidarity shrouding and protecting [her] growing up years" (hooks 1990: 35). Hooks cites Linell Cady, who writes, "In a community, persons retain their identity, and they also share a commitment to ... the relational life uniting them" (ibid.). *Girlchild*'s little community is just such a relational entity; each of the characters is clearly unique, yet the group operates as a unit. For Monk, the group explicitly joins the tropes of individuality and collectivity within the frame of gender.[14]

> I think that in our culture, male-bonded groups are something that is taken for granted, hero groups, Seven Samurai or the Magnificent Seven, teams of men. . . . The culture is pretty much geared to male hero teams. I thought that it was interesting to see what would happen if you had a female hero team with each person being their strong and unique personality, background, almost like six worlds unto themselves, and then meeting together. And that piece was really an affirmation of that kind of individuation, you could say, or autonomy, and the comfort of the interaction of strong people like that.

Part II of *Education of the Girlchild* reverses the conventional structure of autobiography by performing the path of a person's life in reverse. In this solo section, Monk, as an old woman – known only as One Person – dances back through time, a pure-dance inversion of the chronological conventions of traditional autobiography. By the end of the dance, she has traveled through old age and middle age and become, again, the young girl she was in Part I. The dance speaks silently through the highly nuanced performance of gestures which mark her passages through the years of a life. It emerges from the white calm of stillness, its visual analogue the yards

try to recreate a
past pert. work → turn this
into an
assignment

look up words you
don't know

p. 130 re male ♀female

ALVERNO INTERLIBRARY LOAN MATERIAL REQUEST

_____ 1/26/99 _____ JC

(Date Retrieved) (By)

NAME: Cate Deicher

Please Print

Address: _____

Status: Fac ___ Staff ✓ ___ Grad ___ Undergrad ___ Other ___

Email _____

Phone 6306 Dept. ____

LC Barcode # _____

Have you checked TOPCAT holdings for

this item? Yes ___ No ___

Book (Monograph) Request

Author Meredith Monk

Title Education of the Girlchild (VDO)

_____ : _____ _____ _____ _____

Place Publisher Date Edition

This ed. only? ___ yes ___ no

Series: _____

Periodical Request

Periodical Title _____

Do not abbreviate

Volume ___ Issue ___ Date ___ Pages ___

Author of Article _____

Title of Article _____

Source for citation above: _____

Date ___ Vol. ___ Pages ___ Need by ___

FORM NO. 347

08/61 MC

Copies: White *Requester*; Pink & Buff *ILL*.

Figure 8.1 Education of the Girlchild: Meredith Monk, 1993. (Photo: © Beatriz Schiller 1993)

of pale muslin spread in a backward L-curve along the stage floor and leading to the upstage platform where Monk has sat, unmoving, throughout the intermission.

She wears a white apron over white pants and shirt, a white wig, frameless glasses, soft black shoes.[15] Her hands are folded in her lap, her torso inclined slightly forward. She breathes deeply, turns her head slowly, waking, blinking, looking. Gazing at one hand, she extends her arm; her hand trembles as it returns. She sways, smiling slightly, as though only she hears the tinkling piano phrase repeated and embellished over and over. She performs almost-legible gestures – sewing, cooking – and begins to step. She begins to sing, her rich deep voice wrapping itself around the chanted "Dayin dayin yay wyin do" (I can't help but hear "dyin'," the ironic coincidental homonym); the pauses are filled with the tinkling piano. Her eyes closed, she is rapt, internally focused, lost in the pleasure of memory. She touches her arm, her breast, then slowly rises and turns, bouncing, in place. She performs a little sequence, a soft backward kick, one arm thrown back, then step-turns, fingertips touching. She sings again, now more eccentrically and intermittently, the sounds reduced to vowel runs. She lowers herself to the floor and then sings more erratically still, encompassing more extreme ranges, rising – sometimes sliding – to higher notes. She is lost in sound.

She poses sharply, rooted in a wide stance: one outstretched arm points up, and her face is startled, startling. Then carefully, she removes her wig, jumps off the platform, and moves to the middle phase of her life/dance. She resumes singing; this time her voice is a sweet soprano, a cascade of "nehnehnehneh." She proceeds down the muslin road, freely moving now, alternately stepping and pausing. She borrows the earlier gestures, making them more athletic – vigorous rises, falls, curls – further abstracting them; she methodically repeats an action in several facings. Her singing is louder, more assertive, more directed outward; it sounds like Yiddish now, and conversational, full of enjoyment and anger and knowing.

At the curve of the L, she removes her eyeglasses and apron, unpins and loosens her hair. Her song is soft, a young girl's sound. The familiar gestures return, fuller and more lyrical, and the sequences are extended: the early kick phrase now adds a step and a circling arm. Her hand moves from face to neck, down her body, with youthful enjoyment. She step-turns in place, arms raised, and briefly, unexpectedly, the piano stops. She slows, stops; her face is beatific. The piano resumes and she sings over it, swaying, and strikes the startled pose. Her hands circle her mouth and her song is like calling from a mountaintop. She hits the pose again, the piano gone and the air filled with her rolling open sounds; her face is excited, uninhibited, unconstrained. She freezes.

The wordplaying title of Derrida's essay "Otobiographies" gathers in a single term the life of the autobiography with the one who speaks (of) it and the one who hears (of) it. In his conception of autobiography, the ear bears multiple functions and meanings. It is the organ of reception, and it is specifically the organ that "perceives differences" (1988: 50). This ear is the eponymous Ear of the Other, which plays a primary role in the economy of exchange through which Derrida structures the movement, in time and space, of the autobiography. According to him, the signature of the auto-biography takes place posthumously, when the other hears and "comes to sign with" the teller: "[I]t is the ear of the other that signs. The ear of the other says me to me and constitutes the *autos* of my autobiography" (ibid.: 51).

For Derrida, this is the structure not only of the autobiographical economy, but of all textuality (ibid.). However, following the argument further, it becomes evident that his words can open new avenues for thinking about dance. Derrida's idea is that the ear in question does not simply "receive" the voice: "To hear and understand it, one must also produce it, because, like his voice [the writer's] signature awaits its own form, its own event" (ibid.).[16] This statement sings out its parallel to the concept of kinesthesia, which describes the spectator's completion (or, in Derrida's words, signing) of the dance not only through the experience of intellectual observation, or emotional or psychological identification, but through the somatic, neuromuscular, dialogic response with the performer and the performance.

The concept of kinesthesia, perhaps because of its seeming vagueness, makes some critical observers suspicious. But it is through this process, I believe, that much of the exchange of dance, and the experience of the dancing self of both "signers" of autobiographical performance, is conveyed. In an essay which moves toward appropriating the work of Julia Kristeva to develop a cultural theory of dance, Ann Daly suggests that much of the communication regarding dance takes place at the overlapping borders of what Kristeva calls the semiotic and the symbolic. Kristeva, she tells us, sees the self as "a process that fluctuates through space and through time," and, seeing semiotics, too, as a process rather than a formula of static elements, understands "any signifying practice . . . as consisting of two inseparable, simultaneous realms: the semiotic and the symbolic" (Daly 1992: 244). According to Daly, that which we claim not to "get" about dance, that which eludes all conventional critical and theoretical methods of knowing, we do, indeed, know perfectly well – but we "know" it at the level of communication which does not preclude preverbal knowledge (Daly 1992). Certainly this encompasses the kinesthetic response to dance which includes not only the physical response to specific movements but the more general response to the *gestalt* of a performance, comprising both the material elements of the *mise en scène*, and the ways we sense a dance "through the skin."

This way of considering dance is particularly compelling in looking at Monk's work, especially her reconstruction of the *Girlchild* solo, as autobiography. The physical quality of the dance is rather subtle, delicate, and the communicative qualities of the performance depend on the richness lying within the quiet. In repeating the work, Monk aimed not simply at doing the same movements she had done before, but at recalling – with intellect and abandon – an experience, a deeply moving physical and spiritual experience of dancing.

> I really worked hard . . . trying to incorporate my sadness and pain into the improvisation. . . . In a way it was really literally letting go of my head . . . and just trying to accept what came up in that moment. [But I had] certain words that I said to myself each time as something that I was looking for in terms of quality, like fluidity was one, continuousness, wit. . . . You see, the wit made [sure] it didn't turn into this dreamy concept of a young girl. The wit made me have to be alert.

She aimed to fill the time/space between the present moment of one performance and the moments of performances long gone – filling them with all of the moments of her life, and presenting them to the spectators for their pleasure, and their replies.

The exchange of replies (of I's and eyes and ears) extends to the sounds of *Girlchild*. When Monk dances, in her great chockfull cinematic scenes of history and fantasy and sense and intellect, and, again, when she stands alone among the shards of what she has created and the suggestions of what might become, there are sights and there are sounds, the sounds of Monk singing her songs of no words and no fixed meanings, the dialogues of histories which imply and elude. Like conventional opera, in which so much of the literal meaning of the arias, the linguistic function of describing and advancing the plot, is at best secondary – the true meaning of the song is to touch the listener at the back of the throat: Wayne Koestenbaum, who writes eloquently of the erotics of opera, locates the site of exchange, or of meshing, of selves in the throat, the "organ from which 'I' speak" (Koestenbaum 1993: 16). He says, "We drink sound through our throats: our throats are activated, brought to life, by what we hear. Listening is a reciprocation: grateful for what the ear receives, the throat responds by opening" (ibid.: 14).

It is in the space of memory, presentness, and the multiple exchanges of action (movement, song, speech) and reception that the blurry borders of life and work that Derrida speaks of reside. It is in that interweave of Kristeva's symbolic (the realm of language and law) and the semiotic, or the *chora*, which Kristeva describes as "[i]ndifferent to language, enigmatic . . . irreducible to its intelligible translation" (in Daly 1992: 245) that we can experience Monk's dance back from her imagined final days. Monk's description of her process in reconstructing the solo crystallizes her paths through memory, movement, and desire. The solo has re-formed: it has become, from a new perspective, a dance about aging, and about returning to youth.

I gave myself a lot of time, especially on my own material. I had to really work very systematically and very gently with myself to rediscover, first of all, the characters and the gestures and the movement, but then to somehow get past that sense of what felt to me like stiffness and closing off and fear that builds up over the years. . . . I worked a lot on thinking about the breathing. I think that younger people breathe quieter, they breathe lower and quieter. And when I saw tapes of myself, I saw that my breathing was very low and very quiet, and so I just would start working with that. . . .

I realized that I *loved* that material, and then I realized that I loved those characters and I realized that the form had such an organic right-ness to it. So that I could work with it very quietly and slowly and kind of work on . . . reclaiming those characters. . . . And to find the flow I realized that in those days I could really let myself be *danced* by the air and by the space and I could let myself be *sung* and it had been a lot of years since I had felt that and I had a lot of sadness about that in the last few years. . . . I went back to my journal from about two years ago and I wrote in the journal, "I really want to be danced again, I want to feel myself sung again."

NOTES

1 I will not debate in these pages what, exactly, constitutes "the real"; I direct the reader to Peggy Phelan's *Unmarked* (1993) for a provocative grappling with that concept. What I refer to here with the colloquial phrase is a generally understood notion of the empirical. I am more interested in artists' aesthetic zigzags across boundaries of self-representation than in determining what is fiction or non-fiction.

2 The original version of *Education of the Girlchild*, consisting only of the solo section, was first performed at The House Loft, 597 Broadway in New York City on April 22, 1972. The group section was first performed at Hampshire College in Amherst, Massachusetts, November 15, 1972. Following numerous performances on tour as a work-in-progress, complete versions were presented in 1973, first at Common Ground in Soho and later that year at Common Ground again and at the Cathedral of St. John the Divine. Since then, productions of *Girlchild* have been offered twice in New York City (February 7–25, 1979, May 11–16, 1993) and produced elsewhere in the United States and abroad.

   I did not see the work when it was originally performed but first saw it performed live in 1979 at the Brooklyn Academy of Music. I have, additionally, seen the piece many times over the years both on videotape and through its textual reinscription on the printed page. The 1993 reconstruction is rooted in the 1973 version (Monk 1994: 13). My observations rely primarily on the 1993 reconstruction, memories of the 1979 reconstruction, and the 1977 videotape (other tapes are dated 1973 and 1982).

3 Along with Monk and Monica Moseley, these performers included Blondell Cummings, Lanny Harrison, Lee Nagrin, and Coco Pekelis (Dalton), to whom I refer in this essay as Dalton. Other performers have periodically joined the cast. For example, the Narrators were originally played by Daniel Ira Sverdlik and Anne Clark, later by Sverdlik and Gale Turner; in 1993, the performers were Turner and Dick Shea. Margo Lee Sherman originally played the

Ancestress; Tone Blevins has played the role since 1974. In addition to these central figures and several smaller roles, the 1993 production included six younger women (Janis Brenner, Allison Easter, Dina Emerson, Katie Geissinger, Karen Ginsburg, and Maya Kanasawa), who were brought in to "open our world to women from other generations even while the companions would continue on and on" (Monk 1994: 13).

4 All references to Derrida in this essay come from two sections of his collection, *The Ear of the Other*: "Otobiographies," a lecture, and "Roundtable of Auto-biography," a discussion following the lecture. Because these pieces are interwoven, I do not distinguish between them in my citations.

5 Unless otherwise noted, all unattributed quotations are Monk's words, from my interview with her on June 8, 1993.

6 Jennifer Dunning tantalizingly suggests that the Ancestress "looks uncannily like Martha Graham" (1993).

7 In *Vessel* (1971), for example, Monk set segments in different venues, requiring spectators to travel from her loft to the Performing Garage and then to a parking lot. In *Juice* (1969), spectators went on three separate occasions to performance areas scattered around the city. Audience members spent an afternoon-into-evening on Roosevelt Island for *American Archeology* (1994), first in a sunny field, later, across the island on the grounds of a crumbling asylum. In each instance, the scale of the setting and the activities grew or diminished over time, and the audience's perception was framed by the real-time, real-space experience.

8 The term "transformative theatre" is borrowed from Marianne Goldberg's 1983 "Transformative Aspects of Meredith Monk's 'Education of the Girlchild,'" *Women and Performance* 1, 1: 19–28; this article explores the ways *Girlchild* "provok[es] a shift in the usual ways of thinking, feeling, imagining, or perceiving" (19).

9 Woodward cites Karl Weintraub, who specifies that autobiography "derives its values from rendering significant portions of the past as *interpreted past*" (Weintraub 1975: 827, in Woodward 1988: 99); see Karl Weintraub, "Autobiography and Historical Consciousness," *Critical Inquiry* (June 1975) 1, 4: 821–48.

10 The importance of dance and community was made clear at the conference entitled "Of, By, and For the People," held June 11–13, 1993 in New York City and co-sponsored by the Congress on Research in Dance and the Society of Dance History Scholars. Presentations at this conference explored the multiple meanings of community in dance history and the choreographic and social avenues through which dancemakers express their relationships to the multiple communities they inhabit.

11 As autobiography has become an increasingly compelling area of inquiry, it has drawn the attention of literary and feminist scholars seeking to unravel the history, poetics, and politics of the genre. Among the many recent works which look specifically at women's autobiography are: Shari Benstock (ed.) *The Private Self: Theory and Practice of Women's Autobiographical Writings* (Chapel Hill: University of North Carolina Press, 1988); Bella Brodzki and Celeste Schenck (eds) *Life/Lines: Theorizing Women's Autobiography* (Ithaca: Cornell University Press, 1988); Carolyn G. Heilbrun, *Writing a Woman's Life* (New York: Ballantine Books, 1988); Françoise Lionnet, *Autobiographical Voices: Race, Gender, Self-Portraiture* (Ithaca: Cornell University Press, 1989); Sidonie Smith, *A Poetics of Women's Autobiography: Marginality and the Fictions of Self-Representation* (Bloomington: Indiana University Press, 1987); Sidonie Smith and Julia Watson (eds) *De/Colonizing the Subject: The Politics of Gender in Women's Autobiography* (Minneapolis: University of Minnesota Press, 1992).

12 See, for example, Juliet Mitchell, *Psychoanalysis and Feminism* (New York: Random House, 1974).
13 I am grateful to Nicole Plett for our November 30, 1993 conversation which generated these observations about the metaphor of domesticity.
14 Monk has referred to "a female version of the Knights of the Round Table" (Goldberg 1983: 20). A review of the recent *Girlchild* reconstruction used the same image; Jennifer Dunning wrote of Monk's "continuing speculation on the legends of male groups like the Knights of the Round Table, reworked into a group of strong women" (Dunning 1993).
15 In earlier versions of the piece, Monk performed this section barefoot.
16 In the original text, "the writer" whose presence is bracketed in the quotation is Nietzsche; I made the change for the smoothness of my own argument, which proceeds from the outline of Derrida's words rather than specifically engaging with the work of Nietzsche.

BIBLIOGRAPHY

Banes, S. (1980) *Terpsichore in Sneakers*, Boston: Houghton Mifflin Press.
—— (1984) "Homemade Metaphors," *On the Next Wave* Catalogue (October): 1–6, 33.
Benstock, S. (ed.) (1988) *The Private Self: Theory and Practice of Women's Autobiographical Writings*, Chapel Hill: University of North Carolina Press.
Brodzki, B. and Schenck, C., (eds) (1988) *Life/Lines: Theorizing Women's Autobiography*, Ithaca, NY: Cornell University Press.
Cady, L. (1987) "A Feminist Christian Vision," in P. Cooley, S. Farmer, and M. E. Ross (eds) *Embodied Love*, New York: Harper & Row.
Daly, A. (1992) "Dance History and Feminist Theory: Reconsidering Isadora Duncan and the Male Gaze," in Laurence Senelick (ed.) *Gender in Performance: The Representation of Difference in the Performing Arts*, Hanover, NH: University Press of New England.
de Lauretis, T. (1984) "Desire in Narrative" in T. de Lauretis (ed.) *Alice Doesn't: Feminism, Semiotics, Cinema*, Bloomington: Indiana University Press.
Derrida, J. ([1985] 1988) *The Ear of the Other: Otobiography, Transference, Translation.* "Otobiographies: The Teaching of Nietzsche and the Politics of the Proper Name" and "Roundtable of Autobiography." English edition edited by C. V. McDonald, trans. P. Kamuf, "Otobiographies," trans. A. Ronell, Lincoln: University of Nebraska Press. Based on the French edition edited by C. Lévesque and C. V. McDonald, New York: Schocken Books.
Dunning, J. (1993) "Some Mythical Women at Their Own Round Table," *New York Times* (May 15): 11.
Foster, S. (1986) *Reading Dancing: Bodies and Subjects in Contemporary American Dance*, Berkeley: University of California Press.
Friedman, S. S. (1988) "Women's Autobiographical Selves: Theory and Practice," in S. Benstock (ed.) *The Private Self: Theory and Practice of Women's Autobiographical Writings*, Chapel Hill: University of North Carolina Press.
Goldberg, M. (1983) "Transformative Aspects of Meredith Monk's 'Education of the Girlchild,'" *Women and Performance: A Journal of Feminist Theory* (Spring/Summer) 1, 1: 19–28.
Graff, E. (1988) "Founding Mothers: A Feminist Critique of Martha Graham's Early Work," paper presented at the International Congress on Research in Dance, Toronto (July 17).
—— (1992) Personal communication.
Heilbrun, C. G. (1988) *Writing a Woman's Life*, New York: Ballantine Books.

hooks, b. (1990) *Yearning: Race, Gender, and Cultural Politics*, Boston: South End Press.

Koestenbaum, W. (1993) *The Queen's Throat: Opera, Homosexuality, and the Mystery of Desire*, New York: Vintage.

Kristeva, J. (1984) *Revolution in Poetic Language*, trans. M. Waller, New York: Columbia University Press.

Lévesque, C. ([1985] 1988) "That Incredible Terrible Thing Which Was Not," in "Roundtable of Autobiography," in J. Derrida, *The Ear of the Other: Otobiography, Transference, Translation*. English edition edited by C. V. McDonald, trans. P. Kamuf, Lincoln: University of Nebraska Press. Based on the French edition edited by C. Lévesque and C. V. McDonald, New York: Schocken Books.

Lionnet, F. (1989) *Autobiographical Voices: Race, Gender, Self-Portraiture*, Ithaca, NY: Cornell University Press.

Mitchell, J. (1974) *Psychoanalysis and Feminism*, New York: Random House.

Monk, M. (1993) Personal interview, June 8.

—— (1994) In "Ages of the Avant-Garde," *Performing Arts Journal* (January) XVI, 1: 12–55.

Phelan, P. (1993) *Unmarked: The Politics of Performance*, London and New York: Routledge.

Smith, S. (1987) "Autobiography Criticism and the Problematics of Gender," in S. Smith, *A Poetics of Women's Autobiography: Marginality and the Fiction of Self-Representation*, Bloomington: Indiana University Press.

Smith, S. and Watson, J. (eds) (1992) *De/Colonizing the Subject: The Politics of Gender in Women's Autobiography*, Minneapolis: University of Minnesota Press.

Weintraub, K. (1975) "Autobiography and Historical Consciousness," *Critical Inquiry* 1, 4: 821–48.

Woodward, K. (1988) "Simone de Beauvoir: Aging and Its Discontents," in S. Benstock (ed.) *The Private Self: Theory and Practice of Women's Autobiographical Writings*, Chapel Hill: University of North Carolina Press.

9 "Styles of the Flesh"
Gender in the Dances of Mark Morris

Gay Morris

Throughout the 1980s and early 1990s Mark Morris created a number of dances that focused on issues of gender. This decade-long investigation culminated in two major works, *Dido and Aeneas* in 1989 and *The Hard Nut*, an updated version of *Nutcracker*, choreographed in 1991. In the first, Morris performed the central female roles of Dido and the Sorceress, using his own body as a site of gender instability to examine sexual desire. In the second, he turned to his company to create a proliferation of gender identities. Morris's treatment of gender in these two works, particularly his multiplication of identities and his use of parody and hyperbole as critical tools, suggested parallels with Judith Butler's gender theory. This theory, which she describes in *Gender Trouble: Feminism and the Subversion of Identity* (1990) and expands in *Bodies that Matter: On the Discursive Limits of "Sex"* (1993) provides an illuminating instrument through which to view Morris's treatment of gender in *Dido and Aeneas* and *The Hard Nut*. Conversely, Morris's dances offer, at least in part, the kind of theatricalized critique of gender Butler envisions, while at the same time enlarging her concept through dance.

Butler's theory centers on gender as a "performative" practice. The idea that gender is constructed rather than natural goes back at least as far as Simone de Beauvoir's famous dictum, "One is not born a woman, but rather becomes one" (1973: 301). For de Beauvoir and a number of other feminist critics since, gender is culturally inscribed on a sexed body.[1] Gender then becomes a role individuals learn to play. Butler radicalizes this concept by arguing that there is no natural, prediscursive sex on which gender is inscribed. Sex is not to nature as gender is to culture. Gender is, rather, the means by which male and female sexual categories are created. It is an apparatus without agent, kept in motion through an endless repetition of norms in which all is imitation. Binary gender categories act as a means of enforcing compulsory heterosexuality. They mask a social agenda aimed at constructing and regulating sexuality along reproductive lines. However, these categories are no more than fantasies or heterosexual ideals that are never fully realized. That gender follows from sex and desire to create a coherent whole, Butler says, is a fabrication.

The construction of coherence conceals the gender discontinuities that run rampant within heterosexual, bisexual, and gay and lesbian contexts in which gender does not necessarily follow from sex, and desire, or sexuality generally, does not seem to follow from gender – indeed, where none of these dimensions of significant corporeality express or reflect one another.

(1990: 135–6)

Butler is careful to differentiate between "performativity" and "performance." Gender performativity "consists in a reiteration of norms which precede, constrain, and exceed the performer and in that sense cannot be taken as the fabrication of the performer's 'will' or 'choice.' . . . The reduction of performativity to performance would be a mistake" (1993: 234). The performer, then, cannot control gender performativity (whereas "performance" for Butler apparently connotes willful control). This is because the performer is inside or part of the gender system, and therefore cannot avoid it.[2] However, in this Foucaultian-inspired construct there is room for resistance. Butler asks, "What kinds of cultural practices produce subversive discontinuity and dissonance among sex, gender, and desire and call into question their alleged relations?" (1990: xi) She suggests drag as an effective means of subverting "the expressive model of gender and the notion of a true gender identity" (ibid.: 137).[3] Butler ignores dance. But I believe Morris's choreography will show that dance (which can incorporate drag) offers far more subtle and wide-ranging possibilities for attacking rigid gender categories than does drag alone.

Morris's concern with gender issues is already apparent in such early works as *Jr. High* (1982), in which he dealt with a young teenager's feelings of confusion and alienation at the discovery of his homosexuality, and *New Love Song Waltzes* (1982) where he showed desire as free-floating and shifting both within and across gender boundaries. Over the next decade he developed a number of strategies for calling identity categories into question. He explored role-reversal in many works, including *Championship Wrestling after Roland Barthes* (1984) and *Striptease* (1986). In *Ten Suggestions* (1981), he co-opted feminine arenas of dance, in particular the music visualizations of Ruth St. Denis and Doris Humphrey. In the solo "O Rangasayee" (1984) he focused on his own body as a locus of unstable gender, which he also did within the context of drag in *Deck of Cards* (1983). Morris did not limit his interest in gender to the stage. From the time he founded the Mark Morris Dance Group in 1980, he politicized his own homosexuality by talking openly about it in interviews (Dunning 1987: C13; Gruen 1986: 49; Hellman 1987: 19; Simpson 1992: 66). He also cultivated a persona in which gender confusion reigned and which, in important instances, spilled over into how his dances were viewed. This image depended primarily on a combination of blue-collar style beer drinking and chain smoking coupled with effeminate gestures and shoulder-length curls.

A photograph in the December 15, 1992, the *Village Voice* was typical of his provocative stance. The photo shows him nude with a cigarette draped in his hand. He is balanced on one leg with the other raised to hide all of his genitals but a bit of scrotum. His body is hairy, his curly locks fall over his shoulder; his pose, curved forward in profile, is soft and yielding.

On stage and off, then, Morris used his body and his choreography during these years to ruffle the waters of gender identity. His actions, however, were not carried out in a vacuum. The 1980s were a time when gay rights activities were accelerating throughout the country, especially after the outbreak of the AIDS epidemic. It was a period of action and of increased public awareness. At the same time, as Harry Brod writes, masculinity in general began to be treated as more specifically gendered and less universal. Perhaps for the first time, men were being seen "as fully embodied beings – not as disembodied intellects which men have often portrayed themselves as being in the Western philosophical tradition" (1995: 19).[4] Nor was Morris the only dancer dealing with gender. One thinks especially of Bill T. Jones and Arnie Zane, young artists of Morris's generation who were coming to grips with issues of homosexuality in their choreography, as well as living openly gay lives.

Morris created *Dido and Aeneas* in 1989 during his first year as director of dance at the Théâtre Royal de la Monnaie in Brussels.[5] It is set to Purcell's oratorio of 1689, which was composed, with a libretto by Nahum Tate, for a Chelsea girls' school. The work tells the tragic story of the queen of Carthage, which Virgil relates in *The Aeneid*. Dido falls in love with Aeneas, who arrives in her land at the end of the Trojan War. After a night of love Aeneas is ordered to Italy and Dido, griefstricken and shamed by his inconstancy, kills herself. Because the oratorio was to be performed by youngsters, Tate kept the words of the story circumspect despite the passion and sexual nature of the plot.

Robert Bordo's set for *Dido* consists of a simple back and floor drop painted to suggest the dappled Mediterranean and a low balustrade that runs across the back of the stage.[6] The chorus and vocal soloists are, with the orchestra, out of sight in the pit. The entire cast, except Aeneas, is costumed in long black tunics with sleeveless tops. These are worn by the men and women of the chorus as well as by Morris as Dido and the Sorceress. Perhaps because of the ancient theme (one thinks of Roman togas), these costumes read as gender neutral, despite their skirts. Morris's hair is tied back for Dido, loose for the Sorceress. The whole cast wears earrings, nail polish, and with the exception of Aeneas, bright lipstick. Aeneas (danced by Guillermo Resto) is the one character whose costume is different from the others. He is dressed in a sarong-like garment tied at the waist, leaving him bare-chested.

The work begins after Aeneas's arrival in Carthage. As the curtain rises, Aeneas is seen standing on a bench downstage center, his back to the audience, his body bathed in golden light. To the music of the overture

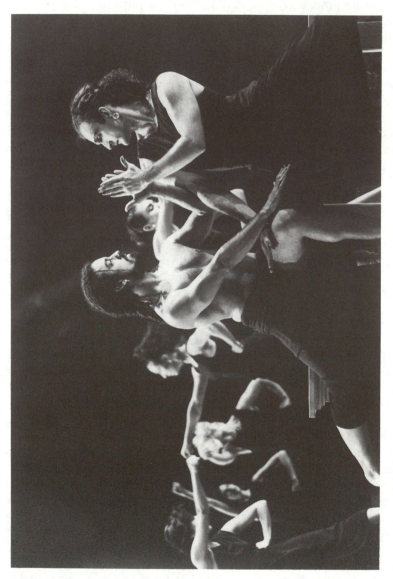

Figure 9.1 Dido and Aeneas: Guillermo Resto, Mark Morris, and members of the Mark Morris Dance Group. (Photo: Tom Brazil)

rest of the cast enters from the back, moves forward and then, with Aeneas, retreats leaving behind Dido and her confidante, Belinda, who are seen seated at each end of a bench located downstage center. Their bodies are curled over in the sorrowful poses of sculptured tomb figures, as if anticipating the tragedy ahead. In her first dance (Ah! Belinda, I am prest with torment), Dido tells Belinda of her doubts about Aeneas's intentions, to which Belinda and the chorus reassure her (Fear no danger to ensue,/The hero loves as well as you). But Dido is filled with forboding. She begins her first solo while still seated. Facing forward, she lifts her arms to the side in a majestic gesture that shifts resolutely into another, in which she turns diagonally back with one arm outstretched before her, hand in profile, thumb up, her other arm bent sharply to the back. This latter pose may have been inspired by Greek vase painting but it recalls, even more, Vaslav Nijinsky's poses from *L'Après-midi d'un faune*. In her next movement Dido faces forward again, plunging one hand downward toward her pelvis as she opens her legs into the diamond shape of a first position plié. The movements throughout the dance are dominated by such hieratic, angular steps. These change in her second dance (Whence could so much virtue spring?), in which she expresses attraction to Aeneas despite her uncertainty about him. Beginning with a series of turns in place, the dominating motif is spirals, twists of the body, and soft crouches, highlighted by two separate moments in which Dido opulently ripples her shoulders.

Butler argues for the performativity of gender by saying that if gender is not a state of being, "then gender is itself a kind of becoming or activity, and that gender ought not to be conceived as a noun or a substantial thing or a static cultural marker, but rather as an incessant and repeated action of some sort" (1990: 112). However, Butler also makes it clear that it is gender that decides the subject, not the other way round (1993: x). Morris both consciously performs or theatricalizes gender and at the same time plays on his own gender performativity. As Dido, he creates a sense of the feminine through the kind of movements he selects, which, in his second dance, are soft, rounded "feminine" shapes, as well as steps that in western theater dance fall within the domain of women, such as shoulder ripples. These are the "incessant and repeated actions" Butler contends create the illusion of gender stability. But at the same time we see Morris as a "man." Not only does he dance in a "masculine" way during his first solo, with its many flat, angular movements, but we see and read his body as masculine – large, hairy, muscular. His body, one might argue, is not an activity; it is stubbornly material. Butler, however, contends that the body, like gender, does not exist prior to discourse; rather it is shaped, its very contours created and tenuously maintained by the political forces of social regulation and control (1990: 133). Morris's body is marked by a fascinating aggregate of masculine and feminine cues. He has often been called androgynous because of the size, muscularity, and substance of his body, considered "masculine," combined with an extreme flexibility and soft, fatty quality that is read as stereotypically "feminine." Morris consciously emphasizes and uses these differing aspects of his body as an element to upset dichotomous gender categories. As Dido, Morris does this through the constant play of a double identity that confuses, overlaps, and layers masculine and feminine gender cues. As Dido, Morris reflects what Butler calls "styles of the flesh." She says: "Consider gender, for instance, as *a corporeal style*, an 'act,' as it were, which is both intentional and performative, where 'performative' suggests a dramatic and contingent construction of meaning" (ibid.: 139). Certainly as Dido, Morris combines a corporeal "act" both intentional *and* performative.

Butler asks, "what kind of gender performance will enact and reveal the performativity of gender itself in a way that destabilizes the naturalized categories of identity and desire" (ibid.). Drag is her answer. But is Dido a drag role? Joan Acocella, Morris's biographer, says no, drag is dependent on an imperfect imitation of another gender and Morris is not trying to conceal his masculinity in imitation of the feminine (1993: 94). However for Butler, drag is not an imperfect imitation of an original or prior model but an imitation of an imitation. Drag reveals the imitative structure of all gender through hyperbole and parody. Although the role of Dido is not consciously exaggerated or parodic and therefore would not qualify as drag in Butler's reckoning, I would argue that Morris's performance as Dido does embody gender discontinuities that undermine a binary structure of identity. However, rather than by parody or hyperbole, Morris accomplishes this by means of a complex mix of conflicting gender cues, movement, and the disruption of heterosexually based dance conventions. For instance, Morris co-opts feminine dance territory by invading the arena of Martha Graham through the use of myth, a monumental female figure as the central character, and the conflation of love and desire. But rather than mimicking Graham's stage through exaggeration or through what Fredric Jameson calls the pastiche of postmodernism, Morris evokes a world parallel to Graham's in which gender is magnified into an overt theme.[7]

After Dido's opening sequences, Aeneas appears and the two dance together in a few brief moments of joy (To the hills and the vales,) before exiting for a hunt. They circle the stage hand-in-hand in skipping steps, he occasionally lifting her. Again, Morris emphasizes gender discontinuities through movement and dance. Aeneas's movement is flatter than Dido's; less is going on in his body. When he raises an arm he faces directly forward. When she raises an arm she moves one shoulder slightly forward, one hip imperceptibly back, so that the whole body is in a fluid contrapposto. Morris creates great ("masculine") power in each gesture, but it is softened by a ("feminine") rounded, twist. Morris also is much bigger and taller than Resto, which sets up a minor flurry of gender disruption, since men are, according to traditional gender stereotypes, larger than women. Morris casts doubt on this stereotype while also sending conflicting cues to the audience, which is expected to see him both as a "woman" and a "man." As Dido and Aeneas dance together we are reminded that Morris is (performatively) a man playing a woman, in opposition to Resto, (performatively) a man playing a man, and that this is a romantic duet. Through these means they shatter the coherence of sex, gender, and desire, and show it to be the fabrication Butler contends it is. If one adds to this Morris's homosexuality, which he has actively publicized, the gender dissonance becomes even greater.

Dido and Aeneas deals directly with sexual desire. The formality of the Purcell music, along with the restraint of the libretto's language, temper that directness; the choreography, too, is hieratic and almost ritualized. Nevertheless Morris is explicit in portraying the sexually charged theme. Dido, in her first dance, conveys her potential relationship with Aeneas by repeatedly opening her legs and plunging her hands downward toward her pelvis. Acocella has rightly pointed out that in *Dido and Aeneas* love is equated with sex (1993: 98). But what kind of love and sex is it? Although in myth Aeneas is the embodiment of the active hero, he is here reified as a sexual object. In a disruption of what Laura Mulvey called the male gaze, Aeneas, like female film heroines, is the catalyst for action and also the sexualized object of the gaze. (It is notable that he is the one character in the dance who wears a sexy costume.) Dido, who appears to be both "male" and "female," is the actor. It is her gaze, and through her the disembodied gaze of the choreographer, that objectifies and sexualizes Aeneas, rather than the other way round. She controls the action through her persona and that of the Sorceress. For example, when Dido and Aeneas dance, he appears to dominate from time to time by taking her hand and leading her, and occasionally by lifting her or placing his arm around her. But far more often she dominates through the physical mass of her body and the baroque counter tensions of her movement set against his flat, less complicated activity. Although the music and song govern the narrative line and therefore the overall scope of Aeneas's role within the oratorio, Morris repeatedly stresses that Aeneas is acted upon. Dido accepts him knowing what will come. She allows him to approach and to touch her only when she wishes. When the moment of sexual consummation arrives, it's almost unnoticeable; Aeneas's symbolic act of male domination lasts no more than a few seconds. As we will see, the Sorceress, Dido's evil alter-ego, controls Aeneas's destiny, and when he offers to stay in Carthage and defy fate, Dido orders him to go. Here, then, Morris troubles the usual order of gender posited by feminist theorists, in which man represents the universal and woman the "other" or the particular. Aeneas becomes the particularized male, while Dido, a conflation of male and female, becomes the universal. However, Morris does not reverse the gaze, rather, he disrupts it through the characterization of Aeneas and the gender complexity of his own persona.

The second scene of *Dido* opens in a cave where the Sorceress is jubilantly plotting the Queen's downfall (The Queen of Carthage, whom we hate/As we do all in prosp'rous state/Ere sunset, shall most wretched prove/Depriv'd of fame, of life and love!). The Sorceress tells her minions she will pose as Mercury, messenger of the gods, and inform Aeneas he must go to Italy. But first she will create a storm to ruin the hunt, "and drive 'em back to court." The storm starts soon after Dido and Aeneas consummate their love. The Sorceress appears, telling Aeneas he must set sail, which he agrees to do.

Although I believe Morris's performance as Dido does not conform to Butler's definition of drag, his Sorceress does.[8] She is the epitome of hyperbole. We first meet her as she cavorts with her witches in anticipation of the ruin she is about to cause. All her movements, like those of her servants, are skewed, crooked, and often lewd. She falls back over a bench, her legs sticking up in the air, her skirt falling around her thighs; she shimmies and flops and jerks her body spasmodically. Morris, as he does with Dido, combines "masculine" and "feminine" elements within the character. Generally the Sorceress's movements are more abrupt than Dido's, and more masculine. She hikes around the stage, hitches up her skirt, throws herself onto the floor, sits like a football player on the bench, elbows resting on knees, hands hanging down between them. Yet her movements are far from exclusively masculine. She dramatically tosses back her hair, lounges about in parodies of *femme fatale* poses, and often makes florid, exaggeratedly feminine gestures. But her most "feminine" and provocative act comes in the fourth scene when she and her court are gloating over their impending victory (Destruction's our delight,/Delight our greatest sorrow!/Elissa [Dido] dies tonight,/And Carthage flames tomorrow). During this dance, the witches mime Dido's end with gestures suggesting bloody knifings. While they do this the Sorceress lies on her back and masturbates to orgasm. Not since Nijinsky's infamous orgasm in *L'Après-midi d'un faune* has masturbation provided so stunning a moment on the opera house stage, and I suspect that female masturbation has never been seen there. Nijinsky was legendarily androgynous and in life bisexual, a person whose gender was anything but stable. His ghost hovers over *Dido and Aeneas* both in the faun poses that appear intermittently throughout the choreography and in Morris's reference to the creature's notorious act. A Roman version of the Greek satyr, half-man half-goat, the faun was the embodiment of lustful sexuality. But Nijinsky's faun chose self-gratification over the nymphs he pursued in his ballet. Morris translates this act of ambivalent male sexuality into one in which a "man" sexually gratifies himself as a "woman." Certainly this gesture is by far the most violent shattering of gender coherence in Morris's repertory.

The last scene of *Dido* begins with Aeneas bringing the news of his impending departure. When he wavers and says he will stay in Carthage, Dido commands him to leave (No, faithless man, thy course pursue;/I'm now resolv'd as well as you). Their argument is translated into a dance in which her spiraling half-turns and sweeping upward arm movements of dismissal contrast with his spiking hops and rigid arms, one thrust out straight before him, the other bent sharply. At last he exits and Dido collapses in death, (Thy hand, Belinda: darkness shades me/On thy bosom let me rest/More I would, but death invades me/Death is now a welcome guest).

Although *Dido and Aeneas* focuses on Morris's body as a center of gender discontinuity and disruption, the dance also includes important, if less dazzling, destabilizing elements in the chorus. Consisting of ten male and female dancers, the chorus performs both traditionally male and female steps in various kinds of role reversals. For example, when Aeneas's crew is making ready to sail, all the chorus dancers play sailors and perform a rough-and-ready hornpipe, after which they throw their arms over each other's shoulders in comradely "male" fashion. All also do a small mincing step while holding the ends of their skirts in a traditionally "feminine" manner. Morris has used this kind of role reversal in many works, such as *Championship Wrestling after Roland Barthes* (1984) in which women punch-out opponents (both men and women), and *New Love Song Waltzes* (1982), where, among many examples, a man carries a woman tenderly onto the stage in his arms, and then a man carries another man in exactly the same fashion.

In all these multi-faceted ways then, Morris "troubles" gender in *Dido and Aeneas*, answering Butler's question, "Which possibilities of doing gender repeat and displace through hyperbole, dissonance, internal confusion, and proliferation the very constructs by which they are mobilized?" (1990: 31). Morris's answer is not simply through hyperbole and parody, but through fleshly style and through dance which so thoroughly focuses attention on the body as the primary site of gender. Most spectacularly in his taking on of two female roles, Morris breaks up the supposed coherence of gender, sexuality, and desire, demonstrating that "none of these dimensions of significant corporeality express or reflect one another" (ibid.: 136).

When *Dido and Aeneas* was premiered in Brussels it was met with consternation and loathing by the local press (Acocella 1993: 213–15). Much of the criticism had to do with gender issues – the fact that Morris shouted his homosexuality from the rooftops rather than being discreet about it, and how critics saw that homosexuality played out on stage. Several viewed the ballet as little more than a drag show with Morris as queen. Because Morris made a point of presenting gender issues through his own body both on and off stage, some viewers conflated Morris's public persona, which he had long controlled and theatricalized, with the double role he was playing in *Dido and Aeneas*.

If Morris offended some of the critics in Catholic Belgium, he received a far friendlier reception from the English and American press, who did not see his performance as a display of prurient behavior. However, this is not to say they accepted it without comment. Joan Acocella contends that Morris, in taking the part of a woman, depersonalizes Dido so that the audience sees her as a symbol of love rather than an individual (1993: 101). Although Morris does shift the focus away from Dido as a "woman" (that is as the particular), most of the press, both European and American, discussed the issue of gender in their reviews, raising the question of at least how direct their leap was to the symbolic. Many critics decided that Morris moved beyond gender in the work, but their reviews suggested a more ambivalent position in the ways in which they wrote about Morris's performance. For instance, Jann Parry of the *Observer* wrote, "The question of gender soon recedes in importance," but then goes on to say that, "Like Graham, his movements are spare and graphic; like Duncan, he has the courage to exploit his sincerity, at the same time knowing and naive" (1992). Alastair Macaulay of the *Financial Times* also compared Morris to Graham, saying, "Mark Morris . . . is the greatest modern-dance creator of dramatic female roles since Martha Graham" (1989). And Dale Harris of *The Wall Street Journal* reiterated the comparison to women dance pioneers: "Blending what looks like elements from Greek vase painting, photographs of Isadora Duncan, the early solos of Martha Graham and Nijinsky's *L'Après-midi d'un faune*, Mr. Morris has invented a style of movement that goes beyond the archaic to the primeval" (1989). However primeval Morris's *Dido and Aeneas* may be, however much it delves into the broad realms of good and evil, love and hatred, it is at its core about gender. Morris thrusts upon the audience an astonishing range of gender ambivalence within an intense atmosphere of desire. It is hardly surprising, then, that some critics condemned while others ignored or denied Morris's disquieting interpretation of the Virgil tragedy.

In *The Hard Nut* Morris examines gender in a different way than in *Dido and Aeneas*. Instead of centering the work on his own body (in *The Hard Nut*, he dances only two small roles), he uses his entire company to create a proliferation of gender identities. He also creates a more overtly parodic kind of theater, often through the use of drag. But although Morris uses drag, he makes it labor in conjunction with dance to question binary gender categories. He especially plays on ballet's highly developed vocabulary of male and female steps and conventions which stress heterosexual roles and male domination.

The Hard Nut, which premiered at the Théâtre Royal de la Monnaie, was Morris's last ballet in Belgium.[9] The work is based on the Pyotr Il'ych Tchaikovsky/Lev Ivanov ballet *Nutcracker* of 1892 and on the original story by E. T. A. Hoffmann. The traditional ballet is set in the nineteenth century and tells the story of a little girl who is given a nutcracker doll for Christmas. She dreams the doll comes to life as a handsome youth who takes her off to a land of sweets. Morris sets his version in the 1960s and not only deconstructs many of the solid bourgeois values of the original *Nutcracker*, but the rigid binary gender categories the ballet, as a product of dominant nineteenth-century society, promotes.[10] *The Hard Nut* opens with the Stahlbaum children, Louise, Marie and Fritz, gathered around the TV set in the den waiting for the Christmas party to begin. Louise, the eldest, is a sex-obsessed teenager. Marie is just on the verge of adolescence and Fritz, the youngest of the family, is a bratty boy of about twelve. The Housekeeper makes sure the children don't sneak into the living room until all is ready. Finally, the guests arrive and the party begins.

In the party scene, several of the major characters are in drag. Fritz, played by a woman, has a crew-cut and is dressed in shirt, vest, pants, and tennis shoes. The role of the female Housekeeper is performed by a man, as is the part of Mrs Stahlbaum. Travesty roles are a time-honored balletic device,[11] and one that is often used for the character of Mother Goose in the second act of traditional versions of *Nutcracker*. Yet although cross-dressing is important in this scene, Morris pushes movement beyond drag performance into a more virtuosic realm in order to call gender into question. In this sense he stresses Butler's concept of gender as an activity. Fritz is a good example. Once the party begins he assaults the room, using his body as a weapon. He hurtles himself to the floor like a break-dancer, rolling over on his back with an imaginary machine-gun to strafe the guests. He slides between people's legs as if they were goal posts, he cartwheels, somersaults, and generally creates havoc. His sneering face is much in evidence, especially when he's tormenting Marie. All of Fritz's gestures and movements have the abrupt aggressiveness and athleticism associated with boys. The way he is treated by others also is customarily reserved for boys. He is dragged from behind the sofa by one leg. He boxes with one of the guests, who cuffs him to the ground. Through both cross-dressing and movement Morris makes us question the performative aspects of gender. We see a "girl" who looks like a "boy" but still looks like a "girl," moving like a "boy," and we are struck by a series of jolts that constantly refocus our attention on the instability and performative aspect of gender. Fritz embodies Butler's contention that, " . . . identity is performatively constituted by the very 'expressions' that are said to be its results" (1990: 25). That is to say, the performativity of gender on the surface of the body causes identity rather than performativity being the result of a natural or interior core of gender identity.

The Housekeeper also deconstructs gender categories, but in a more overtly parodic way than Fritz does.[12] Esther Newton writes in *Mother Camp: Female Impersonators in America* that "Incongruity is the subject matter of camp, theatricality its style, and humor its strategy" (1979: 107). This is an apt description of the Housekeeper. The role was originated, and is still danced by Kraig Patterson, an African-American. His costume is a maid's uniform cut in back to a slim, elegant waist. The Housekeeper is a drag queen who has "become" a woman and savors every moment of it. She lovingly details and at the same time exaggerates all the aspects of performance that signify femininity, from raising an eyebrow to sniffing a perfume-infused magazine ad. Here is Butler's concept of gender as a set of repeated actions that come to signify "femininity." The Housekeeper dances on pointe, and pointe work is, of course, reserved for women in classical dance. One of the Housekeeper's defining movements is pas de bourrée, a series of tiny fluttering steps on pointe that emphasizes lightness and delicacy. Dance thus plays a critical part in the Housekeeper's confusion of gender, extending and enlarging the role of drag and at the same time playing on balletic conventions that reinforce compulsory heterosexuality. It is no accident that the family's Christmas gift to their maid is a new pair of pointe shoes.

Mrs Stahlbaum, a much more zaftig figure than the Housekeeper, wears a strawberry blonde wig with bangs, her hair tied back in a bun. Butler's "styles of the flesh" take on special resonance with this character. She, too, is camp, although as danced by Peter Wing Healey, she is less overtly exaggerated than the Housekeeper. Some of her humor derives from the incongruity of being extremely fluttery and dainty and at the same time extremely large – she towers over Mr Stahlbaum – but she elicits most of her laughs from poking fun at the stereotype of the neurotic suburban housewife. In this first scene, she performs mime almost exclusively, and it is a rich and suggestive mime, mocking fixed identity in a number of ways. For example, when Drosselmeyer, Marie's mysterious godfather, arrives at the party he attempts to deliver a lustful kiss to Mrs Stahlbaum's extravagant *décolletage*. Mr Stahlbaum dramatically intervenes, putting a stop to any further nonsense. Mrs Stahlbaum must content herself with a wistful kiss to Drosselmeyer's scarf as she takes it from him. The situation, then, is this: Mrs Stahlbaum, played by a "man," is attracted to Drosselmeyer, played by a "man." When Mr Stahlbaum, played by a "man," staunchly defends Mrs Stahlbaum's honor in the face of Drosselmeyer's lascivious kiss to her bosom, there is gender trouble aplenty.

Morris, who in this scene plays a drunken guest, offers an amusing send-up of heterosexual horniness, boozily chasing after any woman who comes his way. His costume includes the *de rigueur* bell-bottoms and boots of the 1960s, as well as an afro hair style and mustache. Considering Morris's well-known homosexuality (the nude *Village Voice* photo with an accompanying interview mentioning his sexual orientation was published at the time *The Hard Nut* was staged at the Brooklyn Academy in 1992), Morris's performance might be seen as a parodic act emphasizing the performative structure of heterosexual gender, especially the value male heterosexuality places on alcohol and woman-chasing as reinforcing cues. Morris, of course, accomplishes this gender parody without cross-dressing.

As the party progresses and the alcohol flows, inhibitions tumble. By the last dance, traditionally the "Grandfather Dance," here replaced by a driving version of the Bump, the guests are quite beside themselves. One young man yanks away the female partner of another man and substitutes himself, squatting ecstatically on the man's knee. Soon the men are embracing frantically as their female partners are forced to finish the dance together. The women are outraged, although eventually they are reunited with their men. In this sequence Morris demonstrates that there is little coherence between sex, gender, and desire, and he also shows these elements as shifting and unstable within a single individual. As Butler maintains, sex, gender, and desire exist in time, tenuously held together by a social regulation that, in this instance, becomes badly shredded.

The next scene takes place after the party. Earlier in the evening, Drosselmeyer gave Marie a nutcracker doll, which Fritz broke and Marie mended. Now she goes downstairs to make sure the doll is all right. In the darkness, she is attacked by rats. Suddenly, everything in the room grows to giant size and a battle ensues between the rats and a regiment of G.I. Joes headed by the Nutcracker. The Rat King is vanquished when Marie throws her slipper at him, but in the fight, she is knocked out. The Nutcracker is transformed into a handsome young man and Drosselmeyer appears. In most productions, once the Nutcracker has been transformed, he and Marie pass through the Land of Snow, where the Snow King and Queen dance for them. Morris uses Tchaikovsky's ecstatic music not for a heterosexual duet, but for a duet between Drosselmeyer and the young man, who is his nephew.

The dance starts with the two of them, separated by a scrim, executing identical steps. The scrim rises and they run in a half circle to meet. Drosselmeyer stands behind his nephew and in a gesture that will be repeated several times within the dance, places his arm around the young man's body, his hand over the youth's heart. In the language of balletic pantomime, placing one's hand over one's heart is a gesture of love for another person, and here, as Drosselmeyer places his hand over his nephew's heart, the gesture can be read as a sign of fidelity and love. Later in the dance, Drosselmeyer places his hand tenderly on the young man's cheek and the latter holds it there as they circle together. Throughout the dance, Drosselmeyer repeatedly lifts the youth and supports him for balances and promenades. In nineteenth-century ballet the pas de deux is a dance of love for a man and woman in which the man lifts and supports the woman. The dance is therefore a system signifying heterosexuality that was used to reinforce the codes and conventions of the dominant society. Here Morris challenges the relationship between gender, sexuality, and desire in a rather complex way. He attempts to show that a dance of love doesn't necessarily have to include desire and, even more poignantly, that interdictions against homosexuality are so oppressive that men are forbidden from acting out love for each other on the chance the performance of that love may lead to desire. Morris is attacking the fear of homosexuality that lies at the heart of heterosexual regulation, what Butler calls "the prohibitions that produce identity along the culturally intelligible grids of an idealized and compulsory heterosexuality" (1990: 135). It is part of the disciplinary production of gender that creates a false coherence along heterosexual lines and conceals any kind of gender discontinuities.

The Drosselmeyer pas de deux is followed by the Snowflake Waltz, originally and in most versions still an ensemble dance for a corps de ballet of women. Morris proliferates gender in this dance by including men along with women in the corps, and by dressing all the dancers alike in short tutus with bare midriff tank tops and ice-cream whirl caps that cover the hair. About half the dancers, both men and women, are on pointe; the others are barefoot. Tutus are only worn by women in classical ballet. However, identity confusion is created not only by male cross-dressing; it is created equally by the fact that men are performing a dance that in the classical ballet belongs to women. Having both men and women in the dance disrupts concepts of binary gender categories even more than an all-male corps de ballet would because it is more difficult to assign gender to the dancers. There are simply too many conflicting cues. In this dance, Morris proliferates gender to the point of erasing it altogether, since the spectator can no longer make gender attributions.

The second act of *The Hard Nut* combines elements of the E. T. A. Hoffmann story with the original ballet, incorporating the tale of Princess Pirlipat, which the Ivanov ballet eliminated. Here Drosselmeyer is sent in search of a nut, which when cracked will break the spell the Rat Queen has put on Princess Pirlipat. Drosselmeyer's travels about the world provide the opportunity to perform the national dances which in the 1892 version are done as entertainment for Marie and the Nutcracker Prince in the Land of Sweets. Morris confuses notions of identity in several of these dances. In the Chinese variation, for instance, he dresses a man and two women, all having the same small, slim body type, in similar costumes of tights and jackets, which might be worn by men or women. Morris puts them all on pointe, and gives them all the same petit allegro steps usually danced by women. For the French dance, two men, dressed as men in suits, and two women wearing dresses, are all put on pointe and given a dance in which bourrées (a woman's step) are heavily emphasized. In the Arabian dance, Morris assigns himself the role of the Odalisque, one of the most loaded icons of Orientalism and the single sexy number in traditional versions of *Nutcracker*. He surrounds himself with a quartet of men wearing voluminous robes and dark glasses. The dance is a hilarious parody of clichéd western ideas of the mysterious East, and of one of the classic objects of the male gaze, the seductive Oriental woman. "The Waltz of the Flowers," another women's ensemble number, is here performed by barefoot men and women dressed in knee-length strapless dresses. In all of these dances, Morris proliferates gender beyond the binary, and at the same time shows it to be, as Butler argues, a surface signification, a stylized representation rather than a core identity.

Drosselmeyer finally finds the magical nut back in the palace itself, Young Drosselmeyer cracks it and Princess Pirlipat becomes beautiful. However, Young Drosselmeyer accidentally kills the Rat Queen, at which point he becomes ugly. The now beautiful princess won't have anything to do with the now ugly nephew, but Marie steps forward and claims the young man, at which point he becomes handsome once more.

Together, they dance the Grand Pas de Deux, in classical ballet the romantic duet for the starring couple and the high point of the ballet. But Morris doesn't let them have the dance to themselves, he brings on the entire cast. This rejection of the heterosexual duet, one of the structural foundations of ballet, is a cornerstone of Morris's work (Acocella 1993: 102–6). Duets in his choreography tend to be fleeting and, as here, embedded within the group. Morris thus locates stability within the group rather than in the couple, locus of stability within the heterosexual matrix. On the matter of groups, Butler has little to say,[13] but certainly the dethroning of the couple is one of Morris's greatest challenges to heterosexual regulation.

Next, Young Drosselmeyer dances a solo, a classical ballet variation in which male heterosexuality is signified by large jumps and virtuosic turns. Marie then dances her variation, a classical ballet solo in which female heterosexuality is signified by petit allegro steps. Here Morris uses balletic conventions "straight," that is non-parodically, to define the couple's heterosexuality. As Marie's dance progresses, Young Drosselmeyer kisses her several times, a theme taken up again in the finale. In this last dance, the couple perform a series of steps and kisses and then Young Drosselmeyer lifts Marie just the way Drosselmeyer lifted him in the first act duet. He touches Marie's cheek as Drosselmeyer touched his. He places his hand on Marie's heart as Drosselmeyer did with him in the earlier dance. Marie repeats the gesture, and they each do it again. Here are the moves, the acts of love, Drosselmeyer instilled in his young pupil, transferred to another relationship and gender.

One might argue that after all, Morris has created a ballet that reinforces rather than subverts dichotomous gender roles. The central characters, Marie and Young Drosselmeyer, are clearly heterosexual. However, Morris is interested in disrupting assumptions about the duality of gender, not in destroying heterosexuality. *The Hard Nut* emphasizes that gender is an extremely varied activity that includes heterosexuality. Rather than being compulsory, heterosexuality in Morris's world is simply one more gender possibility. Neither is Butler trying to overthrow heterosexuality. She considers it impossible, in any event, because we exist within a heterosexual matrix where there is no beyond or before. We can't refuse the heterosexual power structure, we can only redeploy its power, which is what her goal is. She wishes to decenter heterosexual regulation, to make it obvious that heterosexuality is not natural but an idealized fiction, that there is no "real" gender but only imitations of imitations. She hopes to unmask compulsory heterosexuality, in part, through a proliferation of gender.[14] In *The Hard Nut* Morris creates a world in which individuals play the kind of dazzling array of gender roles Butler envisions. But Morris takes another step that Butler would probably have no interest in doing. He shows that all these varied individuals are capable of love, and all love counts equally. That is why the entire cast of characters dance in the Grand

Pas de Deux, even the villains. Here, gender finally yields to a human love in which all people can share.

This vision of a society that is open to myriad shapes of gender, where gender, which imposes categories of exclusivity, essentially melts away, is Morris's most utopian and for now his most profound statement on the subject.[15] Butler similarly feels that gender is illusory but she does not believe it will disappear. Her best hope is that the proliferation and denaturalization of gender will help shift power away from compulsory heterosexuality. However, subversive as these may be, Butler says proliferation and denaturalization are not enough to direct political struggle. At the end of *Bodies That Matter* we see her touching on a reformulation of kinship in ways that function supportively "as oppositional discourse" to compulsory heterosexuality (1993: 241). It may be that in the future Butler will develop this concept of family more fully, bringing her closer in practical terms to Morris's idealized vision of community.

NOTES

1 Although de Beauvoir separated a natural sex from a culturally constructed body, Butler contends that since de Beauvoir viewed the body as a "cultural situation" (a field of received and reinterpreted cultural possibilities), it might be possible, if one took her formulation to its "unstated consequences," to suggest that both sex and gender are cultural (Butler 1989: 128–34).
2 Neither can the writer avoid it. To try to speak about gender, as I do throughout this essay, without also speaking in terms of male/female, man/woman, masculine/feminine, is nearly impossible. However, when I do use these words, I hope the reader will understand that I am speaking in terms of performativity rather than a "true" or "real" gender. When I want particularly to stress the performative aspect of gender, I place quote marks around gender-specific words.
3 Butler does not define drag precisely, however, she uses the word primarily within the context of theatrical performance rather than to mean merely cross-dressing. She also makes the point that not all drag is subversive; rather it is a site of ambivalence, implicated in the regimes of power it contests (1993: 125). Drag also may be produced by heterosexual culture to bolster itself, as in films like *Tootsie* and *Victor, Victoria* (ibid.: 126).
4 A small but growing body of research is appearing on masculinity. See, for example, Rowena Chapman and Jonathan Rutherford (eds) *Male Order: Unwrapping Masculinity* (London: Lawrence & Wishart, 1988); Harry Brod (ed.) *The Making of Masculinities: The New Men's Studies* (New York: Routledge, 1992); Harry Brod and Michael Kaufman (eds) *Theorizing Masculinities* (Newbury Park, CA: Sage, 1994); Constance Penley and Sharon Willis (eds) *Male Trouble* (Minneapolis: University of Minnesota Press, 1993); and for masculinity viewed through performative theory, John Stoltenberg, *Refusing to Be a Man: Essays on Sex and Justice* (Portland, OR: Breitenbush Books, 1989).
5 *Dido and Aeneas*, a dance work in five scenes, was premiered March 11, 1989. Sets are by Robert Bordo, costumes by Christine Van Loon, and lighting by James F. Ingalls. Morris spent three stormy years in Brussels, often at loggerheads with the conservative Belgian press and public. When his contract came up for renewal in June 1991 he returned to New York with his company.

6 For the analyses of *Dido and Aeneas* and *The Hard Nut*, I depended on live performances, reviews, interviews, and video tapes. The video of *Dido and Aeneas* was a company tape made in Brussels in 1989 with the original cast. The video for *The Hard Nut* was created for *Dance in America*, PBS, in 1992 (distributed by Electra Nonesuch). This tape omits parts of the choreography, most notably Morris's Arabian solo in Act II.

7 Jameson calls postmodern pastiche a neutral practice, imitation "amputated of the satiric impulse" (1991: 17). However, Morris's Dido is too passionate, too heroic to be pastiche. It is anything but Jameson's "blank parody, a statue with blind eyeballs" (ibid.).

8 Acocella (1993) contends that the Sorceress is not a drag role for the same reasons Dido is not, that is because Morris does not attempt to hide his masculine gender cues.

9 *The Hard Nut* was premiered on January 12, 1991. The libretto is after E. T. A. Hoffmann's "Nutcracker and Mouse King" and Ivan Vsevolozhsky and Marius Petipa's scenario for the ballet *Nutcracker*. The production is based on the work of horror-comics illustrator Charles Burns. Costumes are by Adrianne Lobel, sets by Martin Pakledinaz, and lighting by James F. Ingalls.

10 However, Morris does retain an aspect of the original work commented upon many years ago by Edwin Denby. Denby pointed out that *Nutcracker* can be viewed as "a subconscious reverie beginning with a cruel sexual symbol, the nutcracker," (1986 [1944]: 273). This symbol of "savagely cruel impulses" is satisfactorily sublimated by the end of the ballet through a disciplining of the body represented by virtuosic dance (ibid.: 274). Certainly dance, in Morris's version, performs a similar task, spiraling, as the ballet progresses, into ever more complex and varied forms. At the same time, Morris dissolves the nutcracker's sexual cruelty, based in heterosexuality, through a proliferation of gender and his vision of community.

11 See Lynn Garafola, "The Travesty Dancer in Nineteenth-Century Ballet," *Dance Research Journal*, 17/2–18/1 (1985–86): 35–40.

12 In *Gender Blending: Confronting the Limits of Duality*, Holly Devor states that in a patriarchal society, women, who must be contained and controlled, are forced to distinguish themselves. When women don't clearly mark themselves, they can be taken for men (1989: 152). This may be why Fritz does not have to be greatly exaggerated to effectively parody gender stereotypes.

13 Butler begins to explore the realm of kinship and family in her analysis of the film *Paris is Burning*, where she sees the reconfiguration of kinship groups as a possible means of opposition to dominant power structures (1993: 240).

14 In "Variations on Sex and Gender: Beauvoir, Wittig and Foucault," Butler points out that Foucault "seems to suggest 'proliferation' and 'assimilation' as strategies to diffuse the age-old power game of oppressor and oppressed" (1989: 138). Butler also adopts proliferation as a strategy to explode binary assumptions.

15 Since choreographing *The Hard Nut* Morris has been less directly concerned with gender issues. Asked why this is, he said he has assimilated most of what he wants to say about gender into his work, and at least for now, he doesn't feel as pressed to make overt gender statements as he once did (personal interview January 18, 1994).

BIBLIOGRAPHY

Acocella, J. (1993) *Mark Morris*, New York: Farrar Straus Giroux.
Aloff, M. (1985) "Mark Morris Dance Group," *Dance Magazine* (December): 83.
Brod, H. (1995) "Masculinity as Masquerade" in Andrew Perchuk and Helaine

Posner (eds) *The Masculine Masquerade: Masculinity and Representation*, Cambridge, MA: MIT Press.

Butler, J. (1989) "Variations on Sex and Gender: Beauvoir, Wittig and Foucault," in Seyla Benhabib and Drucilla Cornell (eds) *Feminism as Critique*, Minneapolis: University of Minnesota Press.

—— (1990) *Gender Trouble: Feminism and the Subversion of Identity*, London and New York: Routledge.

—— (1993) *Bodies That Matter: On the Discursive Limits of "Sex,"* London and New York: Routledge.

de Beauvoir, S. (1973) *The Second Sex*, New York: Vintage.

Denby, E. (1986 [1944]) *Dance Writings*, Robert Cornfield and William Mackay (eds), New York: Alfred A. Knopf.

Devor, H. (1989) *Gender Blending: Confronting the Limits of Duality*, Bloomington: Indiana University Press.

Dunning, J. (1987) "Morris, in 'Mythologies,' Turns Words Into Dance," *New York Times* (May 5): C13.

Greskovic, R. (1992) "A Classic Nut Case: Mark Morris Tackles Tchaikovsky," *Village Voice* (December 15): 43–5.

Gruen, J. (1986) "Mark Morris: He's Here," *Dance Magazine*, (September): 46–50.

Harris, D. (1989) "Dance: Mark Morris's 'Dido and Aeneas,'" *The Wall Street Journal* (June 13): A18.

Hellman, E. (1987) "Mark Morris: The Rage of New York's Dance Scene Comes to Berkeley for Halloween," *San Francisco Sentinel* (October 23): 19.

Jameson, F. (1991) *Postmodernism or, The Cultural Logic of Late Capitalism*, Durham, NC: Duke University Press.

Kessler, S. and McKenna, W. (1978) *Gender: An Ethnomethodological Approach*, Chicago: University of Chicago Press.

Macaulay, A. (1989) "'Dido and Aeneas,'" *Financial Times* (March 30): 25.

Newton, E. (1979) *Mother Camp: Female Impersonators in America*, Chicago: University of Chicago Press.

Parry, J. (1992) "Charms of a Dido to Die for," *Observer* (August 23): 44.

Simpson, J. (1992) "Making the Right Moves," *Time* (April 13): 66–7.

Zeig, S. (1985) "The Actor As Activator: Deconstructing Gender Through Gesture," *Feminist Issues* 5, 1: 21–5.

10 Uncanny Women and Anxious Masters

Reading *Coppélia* Against Freud

Gwen Bergner and Nicole Plett

An old man in tattered, eighteenth-century dress shuffles across the stage toward the seated figure of a beautiful woman. A young man sits slumped at a table nearby. Four horns sound an anxious minor chord as the old man raises his arms in a commanding gesture over the motionless woman. This is the moment when the scheming Dr Coppélius believes he can bestow consciousness onto his pretty facsimile of a woman. The delicate creature shudders, rises, and – to the old man's incredulous joy – takes her first waltz steps. "I have made you and you are beautiful," the strange alchemist seems to exclaim – as he has exclaimed nightly, on stages across the world, for 125 years (Croce 1974: 77). Inseparable from the delight Coppélius takes in his creative powers is the anticipation that he will be master of his progeny. The inspirited woman, however, has plans of her own.

The nineteenth-century ballet *Coppélia* enacts a familiar male fantasy of perfectible woman that bears comparison to the way that this classical genre enjoins its female dancer to perform femininity. Yet just as Coppélius is undone by a willful Swanilda, ballet's control of the feminine is not absolute. *Coppélia*, then, may both amuse and alarm for the way that it consolidates, but also resists, the sex–gender system that produced it. Nestled within its comedic marriage plot lie a host of cultural anxieties – about the rise of science and industrialization, the survival of community structure, the deceptions made possible by woman's chimerical nature, and the threat posed by unregulated male desire.

The marriage of the betrothed lovers, Swanilda and Frantz, is nearly thwarted when Frantz becomes enamored of sinister Dr Coppélius's mechanical construction of woman, Coppélia. Coppélia comes from a long and worthy lineage of unsuitable, and often inhuman, brides in nineteenth-century romantic ballet such as *La Sylphide* (1832), *Giselle* (1841), *Ondine* (1843) and *La Péri* (1843), a line which continues in Russia with *Swan Lake* (1877). As the ballet opens, Frantz and Swanilda's union has already been sanctioned by the rituals of their community; their individual drama is staged within and around communal ceremonies of raising a new town bell and welcoming the local nobility to perform a group marriage. The threat to an orderly channeling of desire and fertility within marriage comes not from the witches of romantic ballets such as Madge of *La Sylphide* or Myrtha of *Giselle*, but rather from a rogue scientist and the vicissitudes of desire. Although the social order is reassuringly restored by curtain-fall, the narrative takes some unconventional turns before arriving at the wedding fête of Act III.[1]

Coppélia, or the Girl with Enamel Eyes (*Coppélia, ou La Fille aux yeux d'émail*), choreographed by Arthur Saint-Léon, with scenario by Charles Nuitter and Saint-Léon, and score by Léo Delibes, was commissioned by the Paris Opéra in 1867 and received its premiere there in 1870. Its success was "immediate and unequivocal" (Guest 1974: 244). By the turn of the century it had been introduced in St. Petersburg, New York, and London, while the original version remained in the Paris Opéra repertory for an unprecedented 711 performances over ninety years. Today it is found in ballet repertories throughout the world.[2] Our current interest comes not only from this historic record but also from pleasurable memories of *Coppélia*s past. This pleasure, we believe, is rooted in the artwork's complex and sometimes contradictory performance of gender and social structure. Our feminist project here is to amplify rather than repudiate a ballet that has endured in European-based cultures (perhaps most particularly in the lives of girls and women) for over a century.[3]

Swanilda, the ballet's uncharacteristically brave and brainy female principal, performs heroic deeds to recover her intended, thereby securing her marriage and, in a sense, a conventional feminine role.[4] She saves her fickle fiancé from the clutches of Dr Coppélius and the influence of his seductive automaton, Coppélia. Frantz has slighted Swanilda for the beautiful doll that Coppélius passes off as his daughter. Coppélius is at first outraged at Frantz's attentions to "his daughter;" he wishes to keep her to himself. He then attempts to capitalize on Frantz's obsession by stealing the young man's soul in order to animate the puppet. But Swanilda penetrates Coppélius's cloistered workshop to expose the automaton's inner works and rescue Frantz. She masquerades as the mechanical woman, violates Coppélius's book of secret knowledge, and awakens Frantz from his drugged sleep. Breaking with past balletic tradition as well as the convention of much folklore, *Coppélia* inverts conventional gender roles by making Frantz the sleeping beauty rescued by Swanilda's conquering love.[5]

But along with this innovative gender role reversal, *Coppélia* serves as a cautionary tale that aims to enforce the sex–gender system. Through the instrument of Swanilda, Coppélius is kept from artificially producing a perfect daughter whom he means to keep for himself and thereby reserve from the socially mandated economy of gender, marriage, and reproduction. And Frantz is spared the folly of his own misapprehensions, his blind desires. Supporting Swanilda and helping guard against the doctor's potentially incestuous relationship with this "daughter," is the village community which, in ensemble dances based on traditional folk dances such as the strident

Hungarian *czardas*, displays the cohesion and coercion necessary to rein in those who would circumvent the collective order.

Looking at the representations of the two "women," both objects of Frantz's desire, we can wonder how they occupy contrasting feminine roles as they compete for Frantz. Swanilda's technically dazzling and fluid movement compared to Coppélia's crudely articulated gestures, her rambunctious vivacity opposed to the doll's vacant elegance – what promises and threats does each kind of woman bring to Frantz and to the community? What questions about women's nature and male desire structure their juxtaposition? Frantz also finds a double in Coppélius; each performs identical gestures of obeisance before the form of the doll. What principles underlie their rivalry for possession of Coppélia? And if Swanilda's triumphant agency loosens the strictures of gender roles only to preserve conventions of marriage and class position, then what sort of intervention might the ballet make in cultural discourses of gender and performance?

To help answer these questions we would like to read *Coppélia* in light of its triangular relationship to two key texts. The first is the source of *Coppélia*'s scenario: E. T. A. Hoffmann's dark fantasy, "The Sandman," published in 1816.[6] The second is Sigmund Freud's essay, "The Uncanny" ("Das Unheimliche" 1919), which enshrines Hoffmann's tale as a quintessential literary work that elicits the sensation of uncanniness, a particular subset of the terrifying and strange. Specifically, Freud argues that "The Sandman" is uncanny because it arouses male castration fear. We begin our discussion of *Coppélia* by way of Freud's essay in order to show that the similarity between the horrific literary story and the comedic ballet resides in gender issues rather than atmosphere. We do not mean to argue that *Coppélia*, or even "The Sandman," is about castration in any literal sense. Rather, we consider Freud's discourse on castration a partial and metaphorical mapping of gender role dynamics which, along with feminist critiques of Freud's essay, provide a theoretical framework and conceptual vocabulary for analyzing the role of gender in *Coppélia*. We appropriate Freud's vocabulary as a means for articulating the cultural myths, archetypes, desires, norms, and dramatic effects of the ballet.

A long tradition of ballet commentary questions and even dismisses the ties between *Coppélia* and Hoffmann's "The Sandman." One critic suggests, for example, that Hoffmann's story merely provided the pretext for a decadent Opéra ballet that would include, as a novelty, the portrayal of a mechanical doll (Kirstein 1970: 170).[7] Furthermore, descriptions from such authoritative voices as Théophile Gautier, who reviewed the premiere and praised *Coppélia* as a "a charming ballet, lively, gay, witty . . . [a] graceful comedy" (Guest 1986: 336), and from Serge Diaghilev, who extolled it as "the most beautiful ballet in existence, a pearl which has no equal in ballet repertory" (Buckle 1979: 74), make it difficult to reconcile *Coppélia* with the macabre tenor of Hoffmann's tale. Yet despite the comic cast of its potentially frightening scenes and its happy ending of lovers reunited and wedding bells rung, the ballet's themes of weird science, deceptive automatons, and stolen souls suggest a deeper connection to Hoffmann's fantasy.

Both "The Sandman" and *Coppélia* offer willful male protagonists, Nathaniel and Frantz, respectively, who discard estimable fiancées in favor of mechanical dolls they believe epitomize sympathetic womanhood. Their misguided obsessions put the young men in the way of mortal danger. Frantz is threatened by the doll's "father"/creator, Coppélius, who would steal his soul to animate the doll; Nathaniel fears the doll's creator will steal his eyes. Although Hoffmann's heroine, Clara, is unable – despite repeated attempts – to save Nathaniel from the consequences of his fateful infatuation, *Coppélia*'s Swanilda rescues Frantz and marries him, breaking the mold of previous ballet heroines who tempt the hero to his death, or are themselves killed. The ballet and the story center, then, on paradigmatic gender issues marked by rivalries between sons and fathers, contested marriages, and questionable choices of feminine love objects. But more significantly, both narratives disrupt dominant norms of femininity that value passivity over agency by championing "real" women – flawed and assertive – over "perfect," impassive dolls. They also implicitly criticize the men who would look into women's eyes for a reflection of themselves rather than for the depths of a woman's own subjectivity.

Although Hoffmann's tale is framed by an unnamed narrator, first-person accounts from Nathaniel and his betrothed, Clara, both animate and complicate the narrative point of view. Nathaniel recounts the traumatic childhood event during which he secretly witnesses his father and Dr Coppélius, an evil and coercive associate, working on – presumably – alchemical researches. On discovering Nathaniel's hiding place, Coppélius threatens to pluck out Nathaniel's eyes. After his father has intervened and sent Nathaniel off to bed, an explosion kills the father while Coppélius escapes unharmed and disappears from the town. In young Nathaniel's mind, Coppélius's identity is alloyed with the fairytale character of the Sandman who plucks out the eyes of children who will not go to sleep. When, years later, as a university student, Nathaniel is approached by an oculist named Coppola, he is seized with the dreadful certainty that this man is really Coppélius and means him harm. Nathaniel's perceptive and level-headed fiancée, Clara, tries to disabuse Nathaniel of his consuming anxiety. Apologizing for her temerity as "only a simple girl," she offers rational explanations for his fantastical constructions and implores him to recognize that his fears originate in his own mind rather than in the world: "[T]hat uncanny power must surely go under in the struggle we must suppose takes place before it can achieve that form which is, as I have said, a mirror-image of ourself" (Hoffmann 1982: 96–7).

Annoyed by Clara's refusal to acknowledge that he faces real danger, Nathaniel replaces her in his affections with Olympia, the daughter of one of his university professors. Although Olympia says little, Nathaniel sees in the fixed stare of her eyes that his "whole being is reflected" (ibid.: 116). Unbeknownst to Nathaniel, Olympia is an automaton who lacks a mother, but has two "fathers": Professor Spalanzani who insinuates her into society, and the "repulsive" Coppélius, now passing as the oculist Coppola.[8] Eventually, Nathaniel discovers Spalanzani and Coppélius fighting over their creation. In his despair at losing the automaton, Spalanzani laments that his life's work is gone, including the eyes which he says, inexplicably, he had "purloined" from Nathaniel. This scene triggers Nathaniel's final breakdown. Although he returns to Clara, apparently recovered, he soon tries – unsuccessfully – to throw her from a tower, and succeeds in leaping to his own death.

If *Coppélia*'s relation to "The Sandman" is meaningful, then it proves illuminating to consider the ballet in light of Freud's essay, "The 'Uncanny,'" which takes Hoffmann's story as its specimen text. Freud's restless and ultimately unresolved investigation into the phenomenon of the uncanny amplifies Hoffmann's fiction by attempting to pinpoint the "common core . . . which allows us to distinguish as 'uncanny' certain things which lie within the field of what is frightening" (Freud 1961d: 219). As a provisional definition, Freud suggests that the uncanny is "that class of the frightening which leads back to what is known of old and long familiar," and promises to show "in what circumstances the familiar can become uncanny and frightening" (ibid.: 220). In the case of "The Sandman," Freud attributes the uncanny effect to its pull on "the anxiety belonging to the castration complex of childhood" (ibid.: 233). Freud interprets Nathaniel's fear of the Sandman/Coppélius and his recurring fantasy that his eyes will be stolen as a manifestation of the fear of castration at the hands of the father (ibid.: 230). However, in insisting that the story's impact lies in Nathaniel's fear of castration and of various father figures, Freud emphatically disavows the significance of the automaton, Olympia: "But I cannot think – and I hope most readers of the story will agree with me – that the theme of the doll Olympia, who is to all appearances a living being, is by any means the only, or indeed the most important, element that must be held responsible for the quite unparalleled atmosphere of uncanniness evoked by the story" (ibid.: 227). Freud clears Olympia from the scene even though a prior analysis of "The Sandman" by Ernst Jentsch (1906) – cited by Freud himself – locates the tale's uncanny effect precisely in the doll's ability to raise "'doubts whether an apparently animate being is really alive; or conversely, whether a lifeless object might not be in fact animate'" (Freud 1961d: 226). We would like to emphasize two aspects of Freud's interpretation: firstly, that class of the horrific which comprises the uncanny is, in fact, integrally linked to the formation of gender identity through its association with castration fear; and secondly, in linking the uncanny to, specifically, masculine gender identity, Freud excludes the figure of woman.[9]

But is the figure of the mechanical woman really dissociable from Nathaniel's fear of castration? In other writings, Freud claims that seeing the female form is instrumental in a boy's development of castration fear, an essential component of the Oedipal phase. Freud's theory explains the process through which children acquire gender identity and thus take up positions as subjects within the social order. The boy's initial attachment to his mother must be disrupted in order that he learn to direct his desire toward women outside the nuclear family. The father performs the function of disrupting the mother–son bond by threatening castration. Thus castration fear is a necessary and normal component of the child's Oedipal phase. But even though the father carries the threat of castration, Freud insists that the boy–child does not take the threat seriously until he is faced with the "reality" of girls' castration, that is, when he sees that girls lack a penis:

> For to begin with the boy does not believe in the threat [of castration] or obey it in the least. . . . The observation which finally breaks down his unbelief is the sight of the female genitals. . . . [N]ow his acceptance of the possibility of castration, his recognition that women are castrated, made an end of . . . the Oedipus complex.
>
> (Freud 1961a: 175, 176)

The "knowledge" that women are inferior stems from the ostensibly observable fact of their castration. The bias revealed by Freud's assertion that women are actually castrated does not preclude the possibility that boys are conditioned to interpret the sight of women's genitals in this way. In other words, the boy's coming to see women as castrated is more a matter of internalizing the symbolic significance of sexual difference than of recognizing biological reality.[10]

If the sight of woman suggests castration and, as Freud argues, there is a "substitutive relation between the eye and the male organ" (1961d: 231), then the theme of Olympia's lost eyes "acts as a representation of the male's infantile theory of sexuality: the female has no penis because she has been castrated by the father" (Todd 1986: 523–4). In other words, Olympia assumes the paradigmatic function of woman in signaling castration through the very condition of femininity. In her deft and brilliant recovery of the repressed figure of the feminine in Freud's essay, Jane Marie Todd connects the automaton Olympia to Freud's theme of castration:

> It is the loss of her eyes that makes of Olympia a creature less than human, and Freud had already set up the link between the eye and the penis. He was too quick to dismiss Jentsch's theory as inessential: Nathanael's castration complex reaches its crisis when he realizes that Olympia is inanimate, that is, when he sees that she has lost her eyes.
>
> (ibid.: 525)

Olympia's uncanny instrumentality in producing castration fear not only vindicates the rival theory Freud tried to debunk: that uncertainty about whether a figure is animate or inanimate produces an uncanny sensation, but also suggests that such uncertainty inheres, fundamentally, to the figure of woman. Since the male, who is not "castrated," is the standard for human, then all women – not only female automata – are excluded from that category. We can conflate the mechanical woman with femininity, in general, because Olympia is both automaton and quintessential woman. As Todd also points out, Olympia had made the rounds of respectable tea circles with "great success" (Hoffmann 1982: 121), her mute vacuity qualifying her as contemporary society's ideal of femininity.

The satiric tone Hoffmann takes to recount Olympia's social triumph in the tea circles ruptures the sinister atmosphere of his text and offers a critique of gender norms. High-society men, upon learning they have been duped by a doll, "demanded that their young ladies should sing and dance in a less than perfect manner" and "above all that they should not merely listen but sometimes speak too, and in such a way that what they said gave evidence of some real thinking and feeling behind it" (ibid.: 121–2). Imperfect graces and forceful personality are suddenly fashionable for women – although fashion is dictated by men's desire. Freud, however, discounts this section of the story, arguing that satire and the uncanny are inimical (1961d: 227). But the shift in tone from Nathaniel's lament to the narrator's mockery, suggests that what is uncanny for Nathaniel is laughable, in a sense, to an outside observer.

Furthermore, Hoffmann makes clear that Nathaniel's adoration of Olympia is fueled by his own narcissism. Nathaniel fantasizes that Olympia's lifeless eyes actually perceive him exclusively: "It was only for *me* that her look of love arose and flooded through mind and senses; only in Olympia's love do I find myself again" (1982: 117). The narrator's ironic distance and Nathaniel's glaringly solipsistic romanticism open up a space to critique Nathaniel's fear and society's consternation that the animate woman valued for her doll-like attributes should turn out to be, in fact, inanimate.

Freud, himself, names Nathaniel's "obsessive love for Olympia" narcissistic, but claims that it indicates a form of pathology wherein a "young man, fixated upon his father by his castration complex, becomes incapable of loving a woman" (1961d: 232 n.1). But, as Todd writes, this "veils everything that pertains to woman in Hoffmann's story and reduces 'The Sandman' to a father–son conflict" (1986: 523). Might Nathaniel's desire to make Olympia a mirror for his own image actually reflect normative masculinity? A long tradition of feminist theory argues, in fact, that masculine identity and patriarchal superiority depend on stripping women of subjectivity, on constructing woman as an Other that reflects man's image of himself.[11] Furthermore, the automaton's initially desirable, rather than frightening, aspect accords with Freud's claim that "the idea of a 'living doll' excites no fear at all" in a child and may indicate, instead, "an infantile wish" that a toy come alive (1961d: 233).[12] The masculine fantasy of creating the perfect, malleable woman is explored in a range of cultural productions which recall this "infantile wish." One of its early expressions is Ovid's Pygmalion, the king who breathes life into the ivory form of Galatea. "Not only has he created life, he has created female life as he would like it to be – pliable, responsive, purely physical" (Gubar 1985: 292).

There is, however, a double edge to an ideology that would interpret women's *difference* as *castration* in the process of shaping masculine gender identity. Although the notion of women's inherent "castration" contributes to male ascendancy, it also always portends male vulnerability. This vulnerability is not Freud's "castration fear" – the fear of being castrated "like women" – but rather the possibility that women are not, after all, castrated. If masculinity is propped against a false image of femininity without subjectivity, against what image will man then measure himself? That masculine identity rests on the denigration of femininity secures its very fragility. Nathaniel cannot tolerate Clara's insight and intelligence, her refusal to appear "castrated." He finds a reflection of his own being only in Olympia's vacant, yet more "feminine," eyes. Upon discovering that Olympia is not, after all, a real woman, Nathaniel's fantasy of woman as vessel for his own subjectivity is destroyed. He is driven to madness by the loss of this supporting feminine Other.

It appears that we have set up a contradiction: on the one hand, the female automaton conjures up Nathaniel's castration fear through the association of femininity with castration, and, on the other, the doll recalls an infantile desire for a non-threatening, feminine Other. Women's castration, it seems, is both a wish and a fear. This coincidence of apparent opposites is actually in keeping with Freud's assertion that the meaning of 'uncanny' "develops in the direction of ambivalence, until it finally coincides with its opposite" (1961d: 226). The German word *heimlich* (meaning cozy and domestic, the opposite of *unheimlich*, sinister and uncanny) "belongs to two sets of ideas, which, without being contradictory, are yet very different: on the one hand it means what is familiar and agreeable, and on the other, what is concealed and kept out of sight" (ibid.: 224–5). What begins by signaling the homey and familiar can also signal the secretive and withheld. Thus, "among its different shades of meaning the word '*heimlich*' exhibits one which is identical with its opposite, '*unheimlich*'" (ibid.: 224). Significantly, both connotations derive from the root of *heimlich* in the word for home, *heim*; the domestic realm provides comfort, but also conceals intimate matters from public view. Of course, women's equation with the domestic realm is equally ambivalent. The nineteenth century of Euro-America glorified women as the source of domestic comfort and intimacy, but restricted them to the home and barred them from the public sphere. If the uncanny is also, among its varied definitions, "everything . . . that ought to have remained secret and hidden but has come to light" (ibid.: 225), then the woman who ought to remain out of public view, but emerges from her domestic shroud, may elicit horror.

So far, we have posited Olympia as the link between femininity and the uncanny that is repressed in Freud's discussion of "The Sandman." But what of Hoffmann's other woman, Clara? Freud never mentions that Clara claims one of the tale's three narrative voices or that she plays the role of analyst to Nathaniel. Rather, Freud renders her passive: she is merely the "clever and sensible girl" forgotten by Nathaniel.[13] But if Olympia is the epitome of feminine passivity, Clara is, within the terms of the nineteenth century, a woman possessed of an independent mind. Clara sees through Nathaniel's fantastic fears, but Olympia does not see at all; in fact, Olympia exists to be seen by Nathaniel who first lays eyes upon her with the aid of a pocket-telescope. While Clara's eyes "penetrate our innermost heart" (Hoffmann 1982: 102), Olympia's are "completely lifeless" (ibid.: 116). Although Freud claims that Olympia acts as a double for Nathaniel so that the loss of her eyes signals the possibility of his own blinding/castration, Clara is threatening to Nathaniel precisely because she is not blinded/castrated; she does not yield to him the gaze. She elicits in Nathaniel the same fears Freud associates with castration; Nathaniel composes a poem in which Clara's eyes spring from her head like "blood-red sparks, singeing and burning" him (Hoffmann 1982: 105). So Clara, as well as Olympia, is connected to the themes of lost eyes and castration; she is "a female figure who embodies sexuality and castration and death," a figure Phillip McCaffrey calls the "Uncanny Woman" (1994: 96). Like the cultural logic that splits woman into the images of virgin and whore, Nathaniel's woman is split into the figures of passive Olympia and active Clara (the latter is even praised for her "wonderful Magdalen hair") – and both threaten the integrity of his identity (Hoffmann 1982: 102).

Although "The Sandman," like *Coppélia*, has male and female principals, commentators have ignored Clara's role. Yet Swanilda, Clara's counterpart in *Coppélia*, could never be overlooked because the ballet belongs to her in terms of both narrative and performance. We have discussed "The Sandman" and Freud's essay at length in order to draw out the importance of Swanilda's threat to male fantasies of femininity. Swanilda's refreshingly courageous character comes, in part, out of a French tradition traced to the late eighteenth century when French ballet scenarios increasingly employed "woman" as the symbol of motherhood and nature. Judith Chazin-Bennahum writes that during the revolutionary period, woman "also represented courage and defiance; she was often the heroine of the narrative, the valiant defender of men" (1988: 128). Even abstract national ideals were personified as heroic women in artworks such as Delacroix's "Liberty on the Barricades" (1830). During the romantic period, across the arts, this narrative pattern was largely subsumed by a new construction of masculine desire in which the woman became the inevitable victim of an art that demanded submission or death as the price of narrative closure.[14] *Coppélia*, the 1870 premiere of which marked the end of Second Empire ballet in France, shifts the representation of woman by providing for the heroine's survival and by replacing supernatural themes with scientific ones.

Of course the association of woman and nature does not begin with the nineteenth century, but, starting in the late seventeenth century, this hoary proposition found scientific validation in new taxonomies of plants and animals. With Linnaeus's coining of the term "mammal" in 1758, to demarcate a class of animals that includes humans, the lactating female breast became the "quintessential characteristic linking human-kind to animals" (Schiebinger 1993: 201). Thus began a shift in conceptions of sexuality and gender which culminated, at the time of the French Revolution, in a new gender hierarchy. "Eighteenth-century politics became body politics *par excellence,*" writes Londa Schiebinger, as scientists "took up the task of uncovering differences imagined as natural to bodies and hence foundational to societies based on natural law" (ibid.: 9). The grounding of sexual difference in the body played to the notion that nature – not men – prescribed the laws of society (ibid.: 38).

Coincident with the association of woman and nature arose the idea of the body as machine. "The then dominant metaphors for this body – clocks, watches, collections of springs – imagined a system that is set, wound up, whether by nature or God the watchmaker . . . [and] regulated by laws over which the human being has no control," writes Susan Bordo (1993: 265). The fantasy of the clockwork woman also encompasses the "vagina dentata" which, since the middle ages, had served as a literary and visual trope for the potentially murderous threat to men from women (Neumann 1994: 259). As a recurring construct of the patriarchal imagination, the female automaton literalizes this desire for – and fear of – an ideal and unchanging feminine Other.[15]

Within this context of difference, the ballerina body represented both an extreme construction of idealized femininity and a potential metaphor for mechanical perfection. As André Levinson wrote in 1925: "You may wonder whether I am suggesting that the dancer is a machine? But most certainly! – a machine for manufacturing beauty – if it is in any way possible to conceive a machine that in itself is a living, breathing thing, susceptible of the most exquisite emotions" (1992: 117). Reminiscent of Nathaniel's paradoxical desire for a living woman who acts like an *objet d'art,* Levinson's *danseuse* epitomizes woman as an organic construction that stages beautiful emotions, that manufactures and masquerades femininity. Even Swanilda's earthy role is performed by a ballerina required to embody a Coppélia-like ideal of femininity, suggesting the two apposed characters function as doubles.

Nineteenth-century anxiety regarding perceived threats to the dominant order from industrialization and colonial expansion resulted in a surfeit of fantasies involving gender, race, and class. "The images in culture began to shift, from the reveries of benevolent submission within a preordained hierarchy to nightmares involving powerfully constituted, monstrous Others threatening to overwhelm the weakened, victimized dominant order," writes Susan McClary in her discussion of the racialized Other in the opera *Carmen*, which received its premiere in Paris in 1875 (1992: 37). Perhaps the most influential of such monstrous Others that wreaked havoc on the social order is the man-made creature of Mary Shelley's *Frankenstein*; conceived in the laboratory of Dr Victor Frankenstein, the nearly human monster has come to bear his creator's – or father's – name. *Frankenstein*, which was published in 1817, a year after "The Sandman," resembles *Coppélia* in that it "intrud[es] secular science into a traditional Gothic framework that normally depends on supernatural machinery" (Levine 1987: 15). And, like *Coppélia*, *Frankenstein* worries the relation between developments in secular knowledge and the conventions of social life: "The apparent ideal in *Frankenstein* is the recognizable domesticity that Victor Frankenstein betrays," a betrayal that results in the murder of his bride on her wedding night (ibid.: 16). Presenting a nightmare of masculine reproduction, a human harnessing of powers heretofore reserved for nature or divinity (the full title of Shelley's work is *Frankenstein, or The Modern Prometheus*), "entails a transposition of the standard of moral judgment from the external world which ought to be reflecting a divine order, to the mind which is somehow forced to establish its own terms" (ibid.: 18). *Coppélia*, then, partakes of this representational trend marking a cultural moment when scientific practices begin to displace religious moral systems and to manipulate laws of nature, resulting in anxiety about the effect on social life at the level of the family.

From the opening scene, the drama of Coppélius and his enamel-eyed daughter is set against a backdrop of village ceremony and mating ritual. The location, Galicia, offers a nostalgic vision of rural community, long lost to the urban spectator of the 1870s; it also provides a rationale for the insertion of Central European folk dance. Several young men are decorating the village square for the upcoming *Fête de la cloche*, a festival which provides the ballet's overarching metaphor for social bonds expressed in folk dance and ritual celebration. Dr Coppélius, who dabbles in magic and alchemy, is a local object of suspicion. He lives with his sheltered daughter in a gloomy cottage on the village square, yet keeps himself apart from the web of social relations. His aloofness suggests that he is not bound by the same rules of exchange and rituals of courtesy as his neighbors. If men can reproduce outside the bounds of heterosexual alliances, then how will their desire and power be regulated? What will happen to the traditional kinship network that binds the community?

Coppélius's beautiful "daughter" Coppélia, positioned on her balcony overlooking the square, is approached first by Swanilda and then by Frantz. Swanilda opens with mimed gestures, inviting Coppélia to dance with her. This invitation is ignored and Swanilda dances alone – for a passive audience of one – her signature *valse lente*, a solo uncharacteristically accompanied by a big symphonic waltz. Swanilda both demands to be watched and invites participation with a recurrent beckoning arm gesture; when Coppélia fails to respond, Swanilda becomes angry and shakes her fists like a child. Her spectacular footwork and impetuous manner contrast with Coppélia's passivity. Frantz enters and sends his own affectionate gestures up toward Coppélia. He is undiscouraged by her aloofness which, it seems, only fans the flames of his ardor; he is content to look and demands no action from her.

The role of Swanilda is characterized, from the start, by rapid, technically difficult steps associated with the bravura Italian technique of the period. If Swanilda's mandate is to perform femininity, she does so by means of a dazzling, and painstaking, ballet technique. Her small, rapid pas de bourrées piqués, articulated pointework, and multiple entrechats – precise and detailed like the "feminine" art of needlepoint – culminate, in Act III, with her famous (and famously punishing) hops en pointe along a diagonal path traversing the entire stage.[16] Although small and precise, her steps require strength and speed, paradoxically enacting an aestheticized femininity through demanding physicality. Swanilda's rival Coppélia is, by contrast, not much of a dancing role: in Act I the doll sits and reads; in Act II she sits and reads; and in Act III she is ruined, reduced to nothing more than a stuffed muslin form. Coppélia's role is further impoverished by the fact that her pseudo-mechanical dance of Act II, to the delicious dotted notes of Delibes's *Valse de la poupée*, is performed – unbeknownst to the viewing audience – by Swanilda masquerading in Coppélia's party dress.

A short mimed sequence in Act I serves as an allegory for the ballet's object lesson. Swanilda admires and catches a butterfly which she shows to Frantz, who takes the delicate creature from her and pins it to his shirt. Whereas Swanilda is thrilled by the butterfly's beauty and movement, Frantz wants to entrap and immobilize it, using it, ultimately, for his own adornment.

Following the quiet butterfly interlude, the young people arrive at the square. Their joyful mazurka, performed in couples, establishes the rhythm of social interaction. Color and activity fill the stage as the dancers move in long, grounded strides, sweep their arms and feet outward, and click their heels together sharply – all contributing to a lively picture of community cohesion. The only shadow comes from Frantz's attraction to Coppélia – that cipher of femininity – which has disrupted the lovers' betrothal. This note of discord occasions the solemn *pas de la paille* or Ear of Wheat Dance, in which Swanilda questions Frantz's love and fitness for marriage. Together with their friends, the couple shakes a ripe ear of wheat three times and listens for the rattle that would affirm Frantz's loyalty. But it is silent. This is Swanilda and Frantz's first duet, and he supports her in slow promenades en attitude and her signature arabesque penchée, movements characteristic of the simpler, more subdued vocabulary of the French school.

Figure 10.1 Coppélia: Giuseppina Bozzacchi in Act I, Scene 2, 1870. (Photo courtesy of the Dance Collection, New York Public Library for the Performing Arts, Astor, Lenox and Tilden Foundations)

This vocabulary is further constrained by the fact that Frantz, originally danced in travesty, would not have lifted his partner. As Lynn Garafola observes, "there is a lexical and stylistic dichotomy between Swanilda's dancing as a woman alone and her dancing as part of a couple."[17]

After Swanilda and Frantz's duet, the dark mood lifts and the gathering is crowned by the dancing of the *czardas*, a powerful line dance grounded by long, low steps, that starts out with stately dignity and builds its kinesthetic pull through a progressively increasing tempo to end on a giddy, joyful note. The play that occasions the young people's dances reflects traditional mating rituals, and the collective aspects of boy culture and girl culture are emphasized throughout. As night falls, the young men act together to harass old Dr Coppélius. And when Swanilda sneaks into his house she takes all her girlfriends with her; they hold hands and make a great chain that links them physically in their common adventure.

In opposition to the young people's rehearsals of the rites of heterosexuality, Coppélius occupies himself with his "daughter," keeping himself apart, and keeping her at home. He withholds his "daughter" from the marriage market that is institutionalized by the nobility's offer of a dowry to girls who marry at the fête. The village society is structured by the practice of exchanging women among groups of men according to historically and culturally specific rules. The form of such "traffic in women" in nineteenth-century European culture is, in the most general terms, the exchange of daughters between men of different nuclear families, but within the same class stratum. Women are exchanged among men in order to consolidate bonds between and among groups of men; families are allied through inter-marriage. This practice of circulating or trafficking in women, suggested by classic texts in anthropology (on kinship patterns), psychoanalysis (on the Oedipus complex), and Marxism (on women's role in the reproduction of the labor force), has been analyzed by feminists as a primary means by which women's lack of agency is codified and institutionalized.[18] Luce Irigaray, working from Freud and Lévi-Strauss among others, writes, "The passage into the social order, into the symbolic order, into order as such, is assured by the fact that men, or groups of men, circulate women among themselves, according to a rule known as the incest taboo" (1985: 170).[19] The traffic in women not only describes the system of heterosexuality, but also marks a conjunction of the sexual economy with the material economy, the correspondence between women and wealth, gender and goods (ibid.: 172).

Act II takes place in Coppélius's workshop, a secretive space where the rules and safety of society are suspended.[20] Here Coppélius attempts to animate the doll with a soul stolen from the drugged Frantz. But the man of science is duped by a canny Swanilda. In this dramatic climax, Swanilda, by impersonating Coppélia, exploits Coppélius's illusions of omnipotence and his proprietary stance toward his fabricated daughter. Under the alchemist's influence, she pretends to come to life in a series of little gestures

– arm movements, shoulder shrugs, and raised legs, culminating in the tell-tale blinking of the eyes – all performed to the same staccato melody. Coppélius partners her in a series of fledgling, floppy movements that, in their very excess and lack of control, parody the classical pas de deux. As soon as the doll "comes alive," Coppélius hands her a mirror. But she, not content to sit pretty and admire her looks, discards the mirror and begins to traipse through the workshop, touching the maestro's inventions. "In desperation, he pushes her back on to her pedestal, and wheels her into the alcove," writes Ivor Guest (1974: 240).

But Swanilda refuses to be enshrined, and escapes once more. Coppélius tries to occupy her first with a Spanish mantilla and then with a Scottish tartan, which prompt her to dance sparkling variations on these two national dances. This ploy, however, provides only temporary respite, for when the automaton is inspired with a soul, she exhibits an active and outwardly directed desire. Freeing herself of his trifling costumes, impertinent Swanilda/Coppélia mocks, breaks, and ruins things. She desecrates the doctor's book of secret spells – that potent source of patriarchal power – by trampling on it. And she liberates Frantz. If Coppélia as automaton is a perfect invention of woman, then the "flaw" in her animate counterpart, Swanilda, dictates precisely her ability to resist patriarchal authority. As Swanilda rebels against Coppélius's paternal authority, she destroys his fantasy of a sentient yet submissive daughter. Like Dr Frankenstein, Coppélius does not anticipate his creature's individual will which propels it out of his control in search of a mate.

As Swanilda and Frantz flee, hand-in-hand, from the workshop, Coppélius cradles the shell of his doll-daughter now stripped of her feminine trappings. Swanilda, in wreaking vengeance on the inanimate doll, has "kill[ed] the aesthetic ideal through which [women] themselves have been 'killed' into art" (Gilbert and Gubar 1979: 17). Coppélius, a still form at the center of the stage, is derided by the manic activity of his surviving puppets. Punished for his inappropriate object of desire, he becomes, by the ballet's end, a figure of pathos.[21]

Once Swanilda has defeated Coppélius, the ballet's action is restored to the public space. The wedding fête and village festival of Act III mark the restoration of women to circulation within established patterns of village life. The celebratory pageant comprises seven small allegorical plays in the form of *divertissements*: Waltz of the Hours, Dawn, Prayer, Work, Hymen, Discord and War, and Peace. These morality plays, performed by the villagers, blend a didactic agenda with the cathartic possibilities of the carnivalesque. The festivities are interrupted by Coppélius, who arrives protesting his victimization; whereupon Swanilda offers to pay for the broken doll with her dowry. But the nobleman stops her and hands Coppélius a purse, as if to compensate him in cash for the loss of his "daughter." The story's resolution is sealed by the pageant's eighth *divertissement*, originally choreographed as a solo for Swanilda, that now provides the opportunity for a conventional grand pas de deux for the wiser, wedded lovers, Swanilda and Frantz.

We would like to close with a meditation on the enigma of Swanilda as a classical role that both resists and reinscribes conventional femininity. Since Romanticism, ballet has been construed as an inherently feminine art form – from the prohibition of the male dancer in the 1830s to Balanchine's oft-quoted dictum: "ballet is woman." Moreover, "in ballet, the female form has long been inscribed as a representation of difference: as a spectacle, she is the bearer and object of male desire" (Daly 1987–8: 57). To what extent, then, can Swanilda's role as active heroine be separated from the fact that the ballerina who dances the role occupies a position of essentialized femininity? How can Swanilda be distinguished from Coppélia if she, too, is required to display in movement the conventionally feminine characteristics of "softness, fragility, speed and multiplicity" (Kirstein, quoted in Daly 1987–8: 60)?

At the climactic moment when the necromancer sets Swanilda, as the newly animated Coppélia, on her feet, the distinction between the autonomous woman and the mechanical doll blurs. In an endless series of inversions between the substance and surface of femininity, an obedient dancer portrays the autonomous Swanilda impersonating an automaton becoming a woman invested with free will. A quotation from Arlene Croce's review of Balanchine's 1974 production reveals how this scene also collapses the distinction between the story of *Coppélia* and its own means of production:

> [Coppélius is] the strangest of all alchemists, seeking to transform his beloved twice over: doll into woman, woman into ballerina. Swanilda must become as totally manipulatable, totally perfectible, as a Balanchine ballerina. She must be a work of art, and then burst out of her mold.
>
> (1974: 77)

Coppélius, as would-be creator of a feminine paragon, strives for the same end as Balanchine, the quintessential *maître de ballet*. Each desires to make a female form that exceeds woman in its distillation of pure femininity. Swanilda/Coppélia, in order to appear a "real" woman, must achieve the supreme artifice of the *première danseuse*. She must enliven her role with a unique virtuosity, the source of which, paradoxically, is always attributed to the master.

The infinite regression toward an illusion of feminine essence enacted by Swanilda's masquerade as Coppélia exposes both the doll and other constructions of woman as simulacra, that is, as copies for which there is no original. But the question remains: can the dancer as representation of woman ever "burst out of her mold"? Can she seize the role from the master who imagined it? Swanilda's capacity to change places with the idealized, objectified Coppélia, and to fool both the doctor and Frantz, locates the possibility of feminine masquerade in male desire. What else but such desire can support Gautier's baffling assertion, in reference to Frantz's mistaking a doll for a real woman, that "it is possible sometimes to be so deceived" (Guest 1986: 335)? The play of desire, then, provides leeway for women's agency. It suggests, as well, that those who require women to act in a prescribed fashion can expect to be deceived.

NOTES

Acknowledgments: The authors wish to thank Lynn Garafola and Ellen W. Goellner for their generous support of this work.
1 *Coppélia*'s narrative intrigue, comic situation, triumphant heroine, and common setting suggest ties to the early and enduring *ballet comique*, *La Fille mal gardée* (1789), which was revived at the Opéra with a new score in 1828, and also link it to a line of romantic "village" ballets, replete with happy endings, such as *Nathalie, ou la laitière suisse* (1821). Both these roles were counted among the Romantic ballerina Fanny Elssler's most successful. We thank Lynn Garafola for this information.
2 Note on major productions: *Coppélia* was performed eighteen times before the Opéra was forced to close in August 1870, one month after the outbreak of the Franco-Prussian war. The Opéra re-opened during the summer of 1871, and the ballet was revived on October 16, remaining in the repertory until 1961 (Guest 1970: 32). After 1872, Acts I and II only were performed in Paris (Guest 1974: 242). A measure of the ballet's initial, and continued, success has been attributed to Delibes's score (Guest 1986: 334). In 1884, Petipa re-choreographed *Coppélia* in St. Petersburg where it was presented at the Bolshoi Theater. In 1894, this production was revised by Enrico Cecchetti and Lev Ivanov at the Maryinsky Theater. In 1933, Ninette de Valois invited Nicholas Sergeyev, the former regisseur of the Maryinsky Ballet (1904–17) who had fled Russia after the revolution, to stage *Coppélia* for London's Vic-Wells (later Royal) Ballet. It is this latter production – Sergeyev's *Coppélia* based on the Petipa-Cecchetti-Ivanov production and as performed by the Royal Ballet – that is most widely known. In 1974, George Balanchine choreographed a new *Coppélia* for New York City Ballet. Working closely with the Maryinsky-trained Alexandra Danilova, Balanchine made a three-act work to Delibes's entire score, noting that "the first dance drama of really uniform excellence deserves no less!" (Balanchine and Mason 1977: 138).
3 For an intriguing discussion of special ties between ballet and girls, see Novack (1993: 34–48).
4 Laurence Senelick observes that "performance ... has traditionally been a medium of reconcilement and mediation rather than one of rejection and alienation. ... Oppositions and differences, which in everyday life might arouse anxiety, tension, or hostility, are given a hearing that often resolves the conflict or at least provides a fresh alternative" (1992: xiii).
5 Further complicating *Coppélia*'s representation of gender and power is the fact that the role of Frantz was created for Opéra star Eugénie Fiocre performing *en travesti*. By the 1860s, principal male roles were commonly danced *en travesti* in Paris and London, a shift occasioned by the privatization of ballet and resulting pressure to appease popular appetites for feminine spectacle. At the Opéra, Frantz's role was danced by a woman well into the twentieth century. In her groundbreaking article, "The Travesty Dancer in Nineteenth-Century Ballet," Lynn Garafola argues that, "in appropriating the male role, the travesty dancer stripped that role of power" (1985–6: 38). She further

suggests that the *danseuse en travesti* "invokes both the high poetic and the bordello underside of romantic and post-romantic ballet" (ibid.: 35). Unfortunately, a full discussion of the implications of Frantz *en travesti* is beyond the scope of this paper.

6 "Der Sandmann" was published in the collection of tales, *Nachtstücke* (Hoffmann 1982: 13). "Der Sandmann" also comprises the first act of Offenbach's opera, *Les Contes d'Hoffmann* (1881). The opera, in turn, is the source for Michael Powell and Emeric Pressburger's film, *The Tales of Hoffmann* (1951), choreographed by Frederick Ashton, which moves Olympia's (Moira Shearer) graphic dismemberment to center stage.

7 Gautier observed in 1871 that Nuitter had departed from his ostensible source, "But no matter! . . . Hoffmann is not a sacred text" (Guest 1986: 335). This line of thought has been validated and perpetuated by ballet historian Ivor Guest: "Nuitter had been inspired by one of Hoffmann's tales, *Der Sandmann*, but the resemblance between this and the scenario of *Coppélia* went no further than the name and vocation of Coppélius" (1974: 238).

8 The manner of reproduction is certainly at issue here: Hoffmann borrows Spalanzani's name from an eighteenth-century doctor who pioneered artificial insemination in animals (McGlathery 1985: 229).

9 Jane Marie Todd's "The Veiled Woman in Freud's 'Das Unheimliche'" cogently argues that "[t]wo motifs, in particular, are regularly pushed aside by Freud: the central figure of woman . . . and the related theme of seeing and being seen" (1986: 521).

10 Freud's account of how gender identity develops can seem fantastical since women are not actually castrated and boys are not actually threatened with castration. Lacan's reading of Freud's Oedipal scenario as, in effect, an allegory for the structures of desire and authority within a given social order may be helpful. Lacan argues that Freud's concept of castration functions as a metaphor for how the child internalizes the regulatory mechanisms of culture. The child takes up either a masculine or feminine position in relation to the metaphor of castration. This assumption of gender occurs through the Oedipal crisis when the father enforces the incest prohibition by interrupting the narcissistic mother–child dyad. We would argue that although the "lack" produced by this disruption constitutes both masculinity and femininity, the social order accords men greater authority. Thus the metaphor of girl's castration signals women's lack of power and authority within the social structure, while the metaphor of boy's castration fear signals that men are accorded greater cultural authority as long as they adhere to prescribed norms of masculinity. See also "Some Psychical Consequences of the Anatomical Distinction Between the Sexes" (Freud 1961b: 248–58).

11 Exemplary of this tradition of feminist theory is Simone de Beauvoir's *The Second Sex* (published originally in France in 1949):

> [M]an represents both the positive and the neutral, as is indicated by the common use of *man* to designate human beings in general; whereas woman represents only the negative, defined by limiting criteria, without reciprocity. . . . Thus humanity is male and man defines woman not in herself but as relative to him; she is not regarded as an autonomous being. . . . She is defined and differentiated with reference to man and not he with reference to her; she is the incidental, the inessential as opposed to the essential. He is the Subject, he is the Absolute – she is the Other.
>
> (1980: xxi–xxii)

De Beauvoir notes that the tendency to divide the world into a Self–Other duality is universal to human thought, although not always or only attached to gender.

12 The resurgence of Nathaniel's infantile wishes and fears about women, occasioned by Olympia, accords with Freud's statement that an "uncanny experience occurs . . . when infantile complexes which have been repressed are once more revived by some impression" (1961d: 249).

13 Todd discusses Olympia as the "veiled woman" of Freud's essay (1986); McCaffrey argues that Olympia is the "Uncanny Woman" (1994). Both note that Freud pushes aside the figure of woman in his elaboration of a theory of the uncanny, but neither extends that claim to Freud's treatment of Clara and neither includes Clara in her/his discussion of what makes the figure of woman uncanny.

14 For more on the subject of the death of the female protagonist and narrative form see Gilbert and Gubar (1979: 3–44), de Lauretis (1984: 103–57), Clément (1988).

15 This compressed chronology of the history of thought on sexuality and the body is based on Walkowitz (1980), Jordanova (1989), Outram (1989), Laqueur (1990), and Schiebinger (1993).

16 In her 1870 début as Swanilda, the 16-year-old Giuseppina Bozzacchi was applauded by critics for the ladylike moderation of her movement. Albert de Lasalle was relieved to see that she "does not leap about and do all those dangerous *cabrioles* which have become fashionable in these past few years" (Guest 1974: 245). Paraphrasing Lasalle, Guest writes that Bozzacchi's "pointe work was rapid, precise, firm, yet delicate" (ibid.). However, this kind of post-romantic pointework required great strength and the additional support provided by the boxed shoe which came into use in the 1860s.

17 Lynn Garafola, personal correspondence, March 30, 1995.

18 For the foundational text on this subject see Rubin (1975).

19 Freud discusses the institution of the incest taboo as the key to modern social structure in "Totem and Taboo" (1961c). He posits that early in the history of civilization, a taboo against sexual relations between mother and son was instituted so that sons would not be tempted to engage in parricide. This institution of the incest taboo is repeated on the individual level in the life of every male as he passes through the Oedipus complex. Significantly, the form of incest Freud presumes a danger is that between mother and son. By this time, Freud had long renounced the seduction theory and never again seriously addressed the problem of father–daughter incest.

20 In the first production, the other mechanical figures of the workshop included: "an old white-bearded Persian . . . a menacing negro, a cymbalist sitting on a cushion . . . and a large Chinaman with a dulcimer" (Guest 1974: 240). Such types hark back to the exoticism that was as important to romantic ballet as the supernatural.

21 In this century, Coppélius has been frequently portrayed as a comedic figure. Writing in London in the 1940s Cyril Beaumont entreated Sadler's Wells (later The Royal) Ballet, to cease this new interpretive practice, to "please, spare us the comic" (1946: 33). Balanchine, in his 1974 production of the ballet, is credited with investing Coppélius's character with more pathos than was then customary. See Croce (1974: 75–7); Reynolds (1977: 318).

BIBLIOGRAPHY

Balanchine, G. and Mason, F. (1977) *Balanchine's Complete Stories of the Great Ballets*, Garden City, NY: Doubleday.

Beaumont, C. W. (1946) *The Sadler's Wells Ballet*, London: C. W. Beaumont.

Bordo, S. (1993) "'Material Girl': The Effacements of Postmodern Culture," in C. Schwichtenberg (ed.) *Madonna Connection*, Boulder, CO: Westview Press.

Buckle, R. (1979) *Diaghilev*, London: Weidenfeld & Nicolson.

Chazin-Bennahum, J. (1988) *Dance in the Shadow of the Guillotine*, Carbondale: Southern Illinois University Press.

Clément, C. (1988) *Opera, or The Undoing of Women*, trans. Betsy Wing, Minneapolis: University of Minnesota Press.

Croce, A. (1974) "I Have Made You and You Are Beautiful," *The New Yorker* (August 5): 75–8.

Daly, A. (1987–8) "Classical Ballet: A Discourse of Difference," *Women and Performance* 3: 57–66.

de Beauvoir, S. (1980) *The Second Sex*, New York: Vintage Books.

de Lauretis, T. (1984) *Alice Doesn't*, Bloomington: Indiana University Press.

Freud, S. (1961a) "The Dissolution of the Oedipus Complex," in *The Standard Edition of the Complete Psychological Works*, J. Strachey (ed.), London: Hogarth Press, 19: 173–9.

—— (1961b) "Some Psychical Consequences of the Anatomical Distinction Between the Sexes," in *The Standard Edition of the Complete Psychological Works*, J. Strachey (ed.), London: Hogarth Press, 19: 248–58.

—— (1961c) "Totem and Taboo," in *The Standard Edition of the Complete Psychological Works*, J. Strachey (ed.), London: Hogarth Press, 13: ix–162.

—— (1961d) "The 'Uncanny,'" in *The Standard Edition of the Complete Psychological Works*, J. Strachey (ed.), London: Hogarth Press, 17: 217–52.

Garafola, L. (1985–6) "The Travesty Dancer in Nineteenth-Century Ballet," *Dance Research Journal* 17/2–18/1: 35–40.

Gilbert, S. M. and Gubar, S. (1979) *The Madwoman in the Attic*, New Haven, CT: Yale University Press.

Gubar, S. (1985) "'The Blank Page' and the Issues of Female Creativity," in E. Showalter (ed.) *The New Feminist Criticism*, New York: Pantheon.

Guest, I. F. (1970) *Two Coppélias*, London: Friends of Covent Garden.

—— (1974) *The Ballet of the Second Empire*, Middletown, CT: Wesleyan University Press.

—— (1980) *The Romantic Ballet in Paris*, London: Dance Books.

—— (ed.) (1981) *Letters from a Ballet-Master: The Correspondence of Arthur Saint-Léon*, London: Dance Books.

—— (ed.) (1986) *Gautier on Dance*, London: Dance Books.

Hoffmann, E. T. A. (1982 [1816]) "The Sandman" in *Tales of Hoffmann*, trans. R. J. Hollingdale, Harmondsworth: Penguin.

Irigaray, L. (1985) *This Sex Which Is Not One*, trans. C. Porter, Ithaca, NY: Cornell University Press.

Jordanova, L. (1989) *Sexual Visions*, Madison: University of Wisconsin Press.

Kirstein, L. (1970) *Movement and Metaphor*, New York: Praeger.

Laqueur, T. (1990) *Making Sex*, Cambridge, MA: Harvard University Press.

Levine, G. (1987) "The Pattern: *Frankenstein* and Austen to Conrad," in H. Bloom (ed.) *Mary Shelley's* Frankenstein, New York: Chelsea House.

Levinson, A. (1992) "The Spirit of Classic Dance," in S. J. Cohen (ed.) *Dance as a Theater Art*, Princeton, NJ: Princeton Book Company.

McCaffrey, P. (1994) "Freud's Uncanny Woman," in S. Gilman (ed.) *Reading Freud's Reading*, New York: New York University Press.

McClary, S. (1992) *Georges Bizet: Carmen*, Cambridge: Cambridge University Press.

McGlathery, J. (1985) *Mysticism and Sexuality in E. T. A. Hoffmann*, Berne: Peter Lang.

Neumann, E. (1994) *The Fear of the Feminine and Other Essays on Feminine Psychology*, trans. B. Matthews, Princeton, NJ: Princeton University Press.

Novack, C. J. (1993) "Ballet, Gender and Cultural Power," in H. Thomas (ed.) *Dance, Gender and Culture*, London: Macmillan.

Outram, D. (1989) *The Body and the French Revolution*, New Haven, CT: Yale University Press.

Reynolds, N. (1977) *Repertory in Review: 40 Years of the New York City Ballet*, New York: Dial Press.

Rubin, G. (1975) "The Traffic in Women: Notes on the 'Political Economy' of Sex," in R. Reiter (ed.) *Towards an Anthropology of Women*, New York: Monthly Review Press.

Schiebinger, L. (1993) *Nature's Body*, Boston: Beacon Press.

Senelick, L. (ed.) (1992) *Gender in Performance*, Hanover, NH: University Press of New England.

Todd, J. M. (1986) "The Veiled Woman in Freud's 'Das Unheimliche,'" *Signs* 11, 3: 519–28.

Walkowitz, J. (1980) *Prostitution and Victorian Society*, Cambridge: Cambridge University Press.

Part III
Histories Reconsidered

11   *American Document* and American Minstrelsy

Susan Manning

When Martha Graham premiered *American Document* at the Bennington Festival in 1938, none of the critics who reviewed the work considered her choice of a minstrel show frame odd. Original, yes, but not odd. Typical was the comment by Owen Burke in *New Masses*, who characterized the dance as "an episodic theater piece built rather loosely along the lines of a minstrel show" – and here Burke quotes Alain Locke's *The Negro and His Music* – "the minstrel show from which 'much that is typically American in mood and sentiment was precipitated'" (Burke 1938: 29). Burke's citation to Locke is the closest one comes in 1938 to a black voice commenting on *American Document*, a black voice ventriloquized by a white writer, appropriately enough for a work framed as a minstrel show, complete with Walk Arounds, End Figures, a Cross-Fire, and an Interlocutor.

Of course, from the perspective of the present, the minstrel show frame for Graham's *American Document* seems very odd indeed and demands investigation. In particular, I want to focus on the implications of white and mostly female dancers physicalizing the historical experience not only of African-Americans but also of Native Americans within the performance. To pursue this inquiry I first will reconstruct the work and then will place the work in relation to the practice of blackface minstrelsy, a practice that originated in the 1830s and that survived as a form of professional entertainment into the early years of the twentieth century. Since the staging of *American Document* deliberately rejected the performative convention of blackface, the work cannot be construed as a continuation of minstrelsy in any literal sense. Nonetheless, the question remains of how Graham's work, created just a decade or two after minstrelsy had disappeared from the professional stage, related to its precedent and referent.

Did *American Document* simply reiterate the racist assumptions of the earlier genre, appropriating black culture for use on the white stage? So implied Halifu Osumare, a contemporary black choreographer and critic, at a recent forum (Osumare and Lewis-Ferguson 1991: 67). Or did Graham's work intentionally reverse the racist implications of blackface minstrelsy, as a white dance historian recently has argued (Costonis 1991)? I would like to suggest that neither position adequately describes the complicated politics of *American Document*. Nor do such either–or formulations adequately describe the tradition of blackface minstrelsy, if one agrees with Eric Lott's brilliant study *Love & Theft: Blackface Minstrelsy and the American Working Class* (1993). Although Lott focuses on the origins of blackface minstrelsy in the antebellum period and I am focusing on a single work that composes part of the afterlife of minstrelsy, his insistence that scholars find ways to move beyond the binaries that have characterized the critical history of minstrelsy resonates with my own interpretive approach to *American Document*.

To reconstruct Graham's work from the fragmentary evidence that survives – a libretto published in *Theatre Arts Monthly* in 1942, silent film footage of a few sections, photographs (most especially those included in Barbara Morgan's 1941 portfolio), programs and reviews of the premiere and subsequent performances, oral history with participants and spectators – is to confront the instability and evanescence of dance texts. Although the surviving evidence makes clear that *American Document* underwent changes from its first performance at the 1938 Bennington Festival to its New York premiere later that same year to the version presented on tour in 1939–40, it is not possible to track the changes precisely. Nor is it possible to determine the exact relation between the libretto published in 1942 and the earlier versions of the work in performance. Nonetheless, enough evidence survives to document the work's larger choreographic structure. Read in tandem, the libretto and the other evidentiary sources reveal the performative strategies that underlay the work in its changing realizations from 1938 to 1942. In all its incarnations *American Document* deployed the minstrel-show frame and an all-white and mostly female cast, and it is these elements that ground my interpretation of the work's figuration of race and gender.

Strikingly, the inscription of race and gender evident in the performances from 1938 to 1940 and in the 1942 libretto broke down in subsequent versions of the work – its revival in 1944 and a free adaptation staged in 1989. Toward the conclusion of this essay, I will comment on the significance of the stage history of *American Document*. But first I will reconstruct the work in its earlier incarnations and analyze its performative strategies in relation to the practice of blackface minstrelsy.[1]

The dance begins with a Walk Around, Graham's adaptation of a minstrel show procession. Once all the dancers – Graham, her male partner Erick Hawkins, and twenty-odd other female dancers – have circled the stage and bowed to the audience, the Interlocutor – a male actor – introduces the action:[2]

Ladies and Gentlemen, good evening.
This is a theatre.

The place is here in the United States of America.
The time is now – tonight.
The characters are:
  The dance group, led by Sophie,
  You, the audience,
  The Interlocutor – I am the Interlocutor,
  And Erick and Martha.
(Graham 1942: 566)

The dance group exits, leaving Hawkins and Graham to perform a "Duet of Greeting," a brief excerpt of which survives on film. Performing in unison, the two walk side by side, angling their arms across their chests as if stiffly waving and bending forward in an arabesque with hands and feet flexed. As captured on film, this passage seems to stylize the bow executed earlier by the entire company.

The group then returns for a "Cross-Fire," transforming the verbal badinage of blackface minstrelsy into what the libretto describes as a series of "strong, assertive" leaps across stage (Graham 1942: 566). The Interlocutor concludes the opening:

These are Americans.
Yesterday – and for days before yesterday –
One was Spanish,
One was Russian,
One was German,
One was English.
Today these are Americans.
(ibid.: 566–7)

Note that the European lineages given were accurate reflections of the ethnic composition of the dance group.

The Interlocutor continues, introducing the first episode titled "Declaration."

An American –
What is an American?
1776 –
Five men wrote a document.
Its name rings like a bell.
Here it comes:
Declaration!
(ibid.: 567)

Two End Figures punctuate the Interlocutor's words and build suspense for the recitation to come by running "swiftly" across the stage, their diagonal runs accompanied by a "snare-drum roll" (ibid.: 367). Then, as the Interlocutor proclaims passages from the Declaration of Independence, the other dancers enter singly and walk across the stage, occasionally stopping as if to listen more intently to the words. Sophie Maslow and Hawkins are the last to enter, and after the Interlocutor has finished his recitation, the two lead the other performers in a "Dance of Declaration." A photograph by Barbara Morgan shows the lead dancers with their right hands raised overhead, as if taking an oath, with groups of female dancers flanking them on both sides. As captured by the camera, the women appear to transform the central couple's gesture into motion, jumping in arabesque with their right arms angled strongly across their chests and bending backward with right arms curved over arching torsos.

Rephrasing the question that opened the first episode, the Interlocutor introduces the second episode, titled "Indian Episode" in performance, retitled "Occupation" in the printed libretto:

> America – what is America?
> It is a great continent, a new world.
> I do not remember,
> You do not remember . . .
> We do not remember the Indian prairie
> Before these states were.
> But my blood remembers,
> My heart remembers.
>
> (ibid.: 567–8)

Graham then performs a solo dance titled "Native Figure." A photograph by Barbara Morgan shows her standing with her right arm raised overhead, her left arm stiffly cradling her left knee to her chest. The gesture of her raised arm varies the meaning of the oath-taking gesture performed by Maslow and Hawkins. In contrast to the thrusting quality of the straight elbows and palm-front hand positions adopted by Maslow and Hawkins, Graham's elbow is slightly bent and her hand is softly cupped. Together with her downcast eyes and inward focus, Graham's gesture suggests a meditative quality that corresponds with the text's emphasis on the action and emotion of remembering.

The group then performs "Lament to the Land," dancing in counterpoint with the Interlocutor's recitation from Red Jacket of the Senecas:

> Listen to what we say.
> There was a time when our fathers owned this great island. . . .
> But an evil day came upon us. Your forefathers crossed the Great
>   Waters, and landed on this island. . . .
> They wanted more land . . .
> They wanted our country.
> Listen to what we say.
> You have got our country.
>
> (ibid.: 568)

Photographs by Barbara Morgan show the female dancers in varied positions, sitting and striking the floor with cupped hands, kneeling and bending toward the floor with curved arms outstretched, standing and gazing upward with one arm floating overhead and the other arm reaching to the side. All of the dancers' actions seem defined by their relationship to the floor, a metaphor for the land to which the title refers and to which the text makes frequent reference.

A Walk Around marks a break before the next episode, "The Puritan." The Interlocutor repeats the opening question, "An American – /What is an American?" (ibid.: 569). This time he answers juxtaposing lines from Jonathan Edwards's sermons with verses from the Song of Songs. Set as accompaniment to a duet by Graham and Hawkins, the juxtaposed lines suggest, according to the stage directions printed in the libretto, "the conflict that took place in Puritan hearts when faced with the choice of a simple life or an angry life of denial" (ibid.: 570). The Interlocutor speaks in alternating tones:

> We may read in men's foreheads as soon as e'er they are born the
>   sentence of Death. And we may see by men's lives what hellish
>   hearts they have.
> I am my beloved's
> And his desire is toward me. . . .
> God shall set himself like a consuming, infinite fire against thee,
>   and tread thee under his feet, who has by sin trod Him and His
>   glory under foot for all thy life.
> How beautiful are thy feet in sandals,
> O Prince's daughter.
>
> (ibid.)

Silent film footage shows excerpts from Graham and Hawkins's duet. In contrast to the unison dancing of their earlier "Duet of Greeting," the two partner one another, creating shapes with two bodies that could not be made by one body alone. As captured by the camera, the two stand facing one another and circle their arms overhead, his coming behind hers and catching her in a back sway. The sway turns into a release, and she spins around him, ending in a fall to his feet. Then she sits upright and raises her arms overhead, as if celebrating his power to make her swoon. He responds with a spread-eagle jump and pulls her to standing. In this passage the explicit eroticism of Graham and Hawkins's dancing echoes the sensuality of the spoken lines from the Song of Songs and counters the sexual repression of the spoken lines from Jonathan Edwards's sermons.[3]

Once again a Walk Around marks a break before the next episode, titled "Emancipation." This time the Interlocutor changes the wording of his opening query:

> The United States of America – what is it?
> It is a nation of states. . . .

One state has corn,
One state has gold,
One state has cotton.
Once, more than one state had slaves.
Now, no state has slaves.
Now every state has one deep word. . . .
Emancipation!

(ibid.: 571–3)

Then the group dances, pausing midway through to listen as the Interlocutor recites the words of Abraham Lincoln: "That government of the people, by the people, and for the people shall not perish from the earth" (ibid.: 573). The group dance ends, according to the stage directions, with the performers "in a semicircle, looking up in an ecstatic gesture, both arms spread to the side" (ibid.). In this position – the semicircle recalling the spatial arrangement of the traditional minstrel show – the dancers listen once again to the Interlocutor reciting the words of Abraham Lincoln: "That all persons held as slaves shall be then, thenceforward and forever free" (ibid.). The group exits, and Graham and Hawkins conclude the section with an "Ecstatic Duet."

Photographs by Barbara Morgan of the "Emancipation Episode" show an off-centered quality that sharply contrasts the compositional symmetry of her images of "Declaration," "Indian Episode," and, to a lesser extent, "Puritan Episode."[4] In a photograph of the group (Figure 11.1) some of the women fling themselves in the air, their bodies nearly parallel to the floor, while other women hold their bodies close to the floor, as if struggling to free themselves from their weighted position. In between these two extremes are other women, some jauntily tilting their torsos to one side, one woman kneeling and looking upward, with her hands interlaced over her eyes. As captured by the camera, the kneeling woman could be praying or covering her eyes, as if not wanting to see. This interpretive ambiguity marks the photograph as a whole: in enacting the historical experience of African Americans, are the women celebrating their freedom – in physical terms, the transcendence of the weightedness of the body and, in narrative terms, the release from slavery – or struggling to attain their freedom?

Yet another Walk Around marks a break between sections and introduces the final episode, titled "After Piece" in production, retitled "Hold Your Hold" in the libretto. The episode begins with three women dancing as the Interlocutor recites:

We are three women.
We are three million women.
We are the mothers of the hungry dead.
We are the mothers of the hungry living.
We are the mothers of those to be born.

(ibid.: 573)

Figure 11.1 American Document: the Martha Graham Dance Company in the "Emancipation Episode." (Photo: © Barbara Morgan, courtesy of the Willard and Barbara Morgan Archives)

A photograph by Barbara Morgan evokes the textual linkage of three women with three million women by superimposing two images. Both images show the three dancers isolated from one another, each inhabiting her own space and contracting her body in an attitude of despair. The women's poses project an uncontrolled quality that surpasses even the off-centeredness of the photographic imagery of "Emancipation Episode."

Once the trio of women exits, Hawkins enters and, for the first time in the work, performs a solo. A photograph by Barbara Morgan shows him in full stride, body upright, arms and legs straight and extended. This photographic image suggests that Hawkins's solo restabilizes the work after the disruption of the women's trio. As Hawkins dances, the Interlocutor recites:

> This is one man.
> This is one million men.
> This man has a faith.
> It is you. . . .
> This man has a fear.
> It is you. . . .
> This man has a need.
> It is himself,
> And you.
>   (ibid.: 574)

Graham returns and performs a solo, and then the group re-enters. The Interlocutor offers one last answer to his question, "What is America?," with a ringing declaration, "Democracy!" (ibid.). The group performs a final dance reminiscent of their dance in the first episode, and the circular structure of the work reaches closure with a Walk Around and the Interlocutor's parting words, "Ladies and gentlemen, may we wish you goodnight" (ibid.).

As my reconstruction makes clear, *American Document* made reference to the format of blackface minstrelsy through the processional entry of the Walk Around, the semicircular spatial arrangement of the dancers, the Interlocutor's direct address to the audience, the designation of End Figures, and the segmentation of the work into distinct episodes, including a Cross-Fire and an After Piece.[5] Yet despite these clear references to the format of the minstrel show, Graham eschewed the defining convention of minstrelsy, namely, blackface impersonation. Unlike blackface minstrels, Graham's all-white cast did not caricature the speech and movement patterns of persons of color. Rather, *American Document* relied on the choreographic strategy of textual illustration, substituting metaphorical gesture for the mask of blackface.

Graham's metaphorical gesture figured race in different terms than did the mask of minstrelsy. In minstrelsy, the white performer put on the mask of blackness. As Eric Lott has noted, this strategy of impersonation allowed for an ambivalent identification between the (white, male) performer and the (black, male) subject as well as for the white performer's degrading parody of the African-American. In Lott's argument, this ambivalent identification occasioned the "simultaneous drawing up and crossing of racial boundaries" (Lott 1993: 6), at least in antebellum minstrelsy.[6] In other words, the act of masking doubles the identity of performer and subject and, in the case of minstrelsy, unsettled the binary of black and white that has defined race in American culture. But at the same time the theatrical device of masking ensures that the identity of the performer remains separate from the identity of the mask. Thus, spectators of minstrelsy could remain certain that the performer's mask of blackness did not alter his essential whiteness. Indeed, as Lott argues, the performers' adoption of blackface helped create a common identity of whiteness among minstrelsy's working-class audiences. In so doing, blackface minstrelsy reasserted the binary of racial difference.

In *American Document* Graham's dancers did not put on the mask of blackness. Rather they put metaphorical gestures into motion, enacting a series of identities that defined race and ethnicity as non-verbal languages that could be transmitted from one body to another. Or, differently stated, Graham's work defined race and ethnicity as a series of identities that could be transmitted through a single dancing body. Recall the gesture of the upraised right arm. In "Declaration" it symbolized the promises made by the signers of the Declaration of Independence. In "Native Figure" the gesture became part of a bodily metaphor for the spiritual bond between the Native American and the land. As captured by Barbara Morgan's camera in an image not previously described, the upraised arm went off-center in Graham and Hawkins's "Ecstatic Duet," visualizing the emotion and action of jubilation. In this way, variations on a single gesture took on a myriad of meanings in relation to the spoken text.[7]

Graham's performative strategies of textual illustration and metaphorical gesture staged race in contradictory ways. From one perspective, racial and ethnic identity became fluid, as each dancer moved through a multiplicity of roles, her gestures alternately symbolizing the historical experience of the Founding Fathers, of Native Americans and African-Americans, and the contemporary experience of men and women in the depression era. Spectators could read – and based on the evidence of reviews, did read – the varied episodes on many levels and in relation to one another. Thus, the geographic dispossession experienced by the Native American resonated with the social dislocation experienced by many Americans during the 1930s. And the celebratory tone of the "Emancipation Episode" reflected as much on the historical experience of African-Americans freed from slavery as on the experience of Anglo-Americans freed from the sexual mores of Puritanism.

Yet the fluidity of each dancer's identity did not mean that conventional stereotypes of race and ethnicity disappeared. On the contrary, the dancers deployed images of the Native American and the African-American long familiar in white American culture, such as the Native American's spiritual bond with the land and the African-American's association with bodily (and sexual) freedom. Moreover, the fluidity of racial and ethnic identity moved in only one direction, for it was the white body that enacted the experiences of persons of color, and not vice versa. In *American Document* only the white body possessed the privilege of becoming the universally American body. Thus, however much Graham's performative strategy of textual illustration through metaphorical gesture departed from the mask of blackface, her work reiterated minstrelsy's paradoxical staging of race. Like minstrelsy, *American Document* unsettled the binary of racial difference through the white dancers' multiple roles and fluid identities. Yet like minstrelsy as well, *American Document* reasserted the binary of racial difference through its one-way representation: only the white body could take on alternate racial and ethnic identities.

This one-way representation of racial identity was characteristic of American modern dance in the 1930s. *American Document* was not the only work to cast white dancers as metaphorical Native Americans and African-Americans. Indeed, there seemed an entire genre of dances at the time that did so, including Helen Tamiris's solo cycle *Negro Spirituals* (1929) and her 1937 group dance *How Long Brethren?*, the most successful production staged by the Federal Dance Project; Ted Shawn's *John Brown Sees the Glory* (1933) and Charles Weidman's *Lynchtown* (1936); and Graham's own 1931 masterpiece *Primitive Mysteries*, a work based on religious practices she had observed among Native Americans and Hispanics settled in New Mexico. That the racial politics of these works occasioned so little comment at the time evidences the white spectatorship that had been a given in modern dance since the time of Isadora Duncan. As Francis Fergusson, Graham's literary collaborator on *American Document*, baldly stated when asked about race relations at Bennington in an oral history interview, "We had no Negro problem. . . . There were no Negroes around" (Fergusson 1979: 54).

Contrary to Fergusson's view, there were "Negroes around" in the formation of American modern dance. During the 1930s African-American choreographers were beginning to establish an independent genre that later became known as black concert dance.[8] In 1937, the year before the premiere of *American Document*, a group of African-American choreographers – Alison Burroughs, Asadata Dafora, Katherine Dunham, and Edna Guy – presented a concert in New York titled "Negro Dance Evening" that anticipated the development of black concert dance over the next three decades (Perpener 1992: 114–16). Performing theatricalized versions of African and Caribbean dances and dances of social protest, the African-American choreographers introduced the possibility of black spectatorship into a genre that had presumed white spectatorship.

Yet the introduction of black spectatorship did not reverse the one-way representation of racial identity that marked the work of white choreographers during the 1930s, for the African-American choreographers were not interested in the potential of the black body to represent whiteness. On the contrary, African-American choreographers were intent on choreographing visions of blackness. And so the underlying representational trope remained: whereas the white body could represent a universal body, the black body could represent only a black body.

Just as an analysis of the figuration of race in *American Document* leads to a discussion of the larger racial politics of American modern dance, so too does an analysis of the figuration of gender in Graham's work lead to a consideration of the larger gender politics of American modern dance. Indeed, *American Document* represented an important moment of change in the gender politics of Graham's work and, by extension, in the practice of American modern dance.

Before *American Document* Graham choreographed for an all-female group. The works she created for her company – from *Heretic* (1929) to *Primitive Mysteries* (1931) to *Chronicle* (1936) – presented women as representatives of humanity. Her female dancers did not dance Woman but Humankind. *American Document* continued this representational strategy in "Declaration," "Indian Episode," and "Emancipation Episode." In these sections Graham made the female dancer the subject and agent of American history. Judging from the reminiscences of Sophie Maslow, the dancers found this an empowering experience. As Maslow recalls the experience of performing the work:

> [*American Document* was] a dancer's dream because you really ran the gamut. . . . When the Declaration of Independence was spoken and you came walking out, you felt heroic and you felt that the Founding Fathers were in you; and then when the dance of the Indians started, it had a feeling of being related to the earth, that [the earth] was your home, the home you had lost. Then there was a dance called Emancipation Proclamation that was about the blacks [gaining] their freedom, and that had a most joyous quality; then there was a dance based on what President Roosevelt said at the time about one third of the nation being ill-housed, ill-clothed and ill-fed, and then you were tragic. So what more could you want in one dance? It was terrific. Everything was there, all the different facets you would want in a single program.
>
> (Maslow *et al.* 1981)

In Maslow's memory there seemed nothing incongruous about a group of women alternately illustrating the words of the Founding Fathers, Red Jacket of the Senecas, Abraham Lincoln, and Franklin Delano Roosevelt. (Whether or not Roosevelt was exactly quoted or not will be discussed later.) Maslow's experience performing in Graham's group dances since 1931 had accustomed her to thinking of women as capable of representing the diversity of human experience.

In *American Document* a male dancer entered Graham's company for the first time, and Hawkins's presence altered her staging of gender. Almost always when Hawkins appeared onstage, the female dancers represented not humanity in general, but women in particular. The one exception to this came in the opening episode, "Declaration," where Hawkins shared the leadership of the group with Maslow without casting the women in gender-specific roles. But as the work progressed, the women with whom he shared the stage became limited to gender-specific roles, as did Graham in the erotic "Puritan Duet" and the celebratory "Ecstatic Duet" and as did the trio of women in the "After Piece" who came to represent "three million women . . . mothers of the hungry dead."

In works choreographed after *American Document*, gender-specific identities for male and female dancers became the rule in Graham's choreography. In fact, her choreography came to assign certain movements to men – large, thrusting, open, phallic movements – and other movements to women – small, closed, circling-back-on-themselves movements. Or, more accurately, her narrative dances from the 1940s and 1950s derived their drama from the exchange of "masculine" and "feminine" movement qualities between male and female dancers. For example, in *Errand Into the Maze* (1947) the female protagonist vanquishes her male antagonist once she integrates the boldness of his movement quality into her own originally more circumscribed movement.

Viewed in retrospect, *American Document* juxtaposed Graham's earlier representational trope of Woman as Humankind with her later representational trope of Woman as the (Jungian) Feminine. This juxtaposition inflected the paradoxical staging of race in *American Document*. For the collective of white female dancers moved more easily from one racial and ethnic identity to another than did Hawkins, the sole male dancer. Although Hawkins performed with Graham in the "Ecstatic Duet" following the all-female group dance in "Emancipation," he otherwise left the enactment of alternate racial identities to Graham and the all-female ensemble. His roles followed a more narrow continuum than did the women's, for his appearances were clustered within the Anglo-inflected episodes of "Declaration," "Puritan Episode," and "After Piece." In other words, the male dancer held onto the identity of whiteness, while the female dancers were allowed to cross racial boundaries. In this way the division between the male soloist and the female collective underlay the work's paradoxical staging of race.

The surviving evidence suggests that this interplay of race and gender marked both the performances of the work from 1938 to 1940 and the libretto published in 1942. Yet, despite the common figuration of race and gender, the production and the libretto reveal differing political agendas. Toured across the country in the last years of the New Deal, *American Document* carried a reformist message. Published during the dark years of World War II, the libretto for Graham's work bespoke a fervent patriotism.

The changing Zeitgeist had much to do with the shift, yet so too did the revisions Graham made to distance the printed libretto from its earlier realization in performance.[9]

The surviving evidence suggests that the major textual changes between the production and the libretto came in the "Emancipation Episode." Reviews of the 1938 version mention topical references that were cut from the printed libretto.[10] According to George Beiswanger's account of the Bennington premiere in *Theater Arts*, "Emancipation Episode" opened with the Interlocutor "[calling] to mind 'things we are ashamed of . . . Sacco-Vanzetti, share-croppers, the Scottsboro boys . . . ' to the eloquent accompaniment of the group dance" (1939: 54).[11] These references gave a timeliness to the work that underscored its relevance to contemporary crises and that led reviewers to interpret the work as reformist in intent. (The topical references – and the dramaturgy of textual collage – also recalled the most notable reformist genre of the period, namely, the Federal Theater Project's Living Newspaper.) Writing in *The Nation* Lincoln Kirstein describes the ending as "a finale of contemporary self-accusation, a praise of our rights, and a challenge to our own powers to persist as democracy" (1938: 230). In *Dance Observer* Henry Gilfond describes the ending as "a militant testimonial to our love and loyalty to democracy in these trying and threatening days of 1938" (1938: 101).

The reviews by Beiswanger, Kirstein, and Gilfond view the work's conception of democracy in dynamic terms. The reviews imply that although democracy was not always realized in the past, it remains a vital principle in the present. Yet for the potential of democracy to be realized, the spectator must take action. Owen Burke's account of the New York premiere in *New Masses* most clearly evokes this vision of the work, and so it is worth quoting at length. Commenting on the changes between the Bennington premiere and the first production in New York, Burke notes the heightened political impact of the work:

> A surer knowledge of purpose has come to the composition, both in text and performance. Loose ends have been drawn in, the work is tighter, more firmly integrated. The opening Declaration (of Independence) remains unaltered but the "Indian Episode" with its poignant "Lament for the Land" takes on current significance, brings to mind migratory workers, the increasing ranks of the jobless – land becomes a symbol of security and the composition connects with the streams of refugees leaving their fascist-invaded lands and homes. The "Indian Episode" loses its nostalgia.
>
> The "Puritan Episode" comes into its own. Originally a love duet and interlude, it becomes an integral section of the composition, gains depth and meaning as a manifestation of the rebellion of reason against the tyranny of the church of Cotton Mather.
>
> "Emancipation Episode," built on Negro themes (musically and choreographically both), adds to it Lincoln's "government of the people,

by the people, for the people, shall not perish from the earth." To jubilee it brings the knowledge that the struggle for Negro liberation was (as is today the struggle for Negro rights) part and parcel of the constantly urgent struggle for democracy.

The climactic Declaration (of faith in the American people), originally a solo, now draws the whole cast into what amounts to a mass chant and call. Picking up from "After Piece 1938" with its jobless, its lack of security, its growing class-consciousness, and its will to democracy, the choreography takes on tone, climbs in its militant Declaration to a magnificent climax – compelling, demanding that the American people remember its tradition, collect its strength, remember that their country was conceived and molded in the struggle for democracy, that it carry forward.

(1938: 29)

The topical references in the production of *American Document* perhaps explain an odd incongruity between the archival documentation of the work and its oral history. In the passage quoted earlier, Sophie Maslow describes the "After Piece" as "a dance based on what President Roosevelt said at the time about one third of the nation being ill-housed, ill-clothed and ill-fed" (Maslow *et al.* 1981). Yet the printed libretto does not include Roosevelt's well-known phrase, nor do reviews mention its inclusion. And not only did Sophie Maslow relate the closing section of the dance to Roosevelt's Inaugural, so too did Pearl Lang in an independent interview. Lang also remembered Roosevelt's phrase in relation to the trio of women in the final section, who "came right out of the Depression and the New Deal" (Lang *et al.* 1988). Although it is possible that the production did quote Roosevelt, this seems unlikely, for all the programs from 1938 to 1940 contain a note on textual sources that does not list Roosevelt. What seems more likely is that the dancers were recalling Graham's allusion to Roosevelt in the lines she herself wrote, "We are three women./We are three million women."

In contrast to the reformism of the production stands the patriotism of the libretto published in 1942. Whereas the reviews of the production conceptualize democracy as a dynamic principle, the libretto presents democracy in more static terms. In the libretto democracy becomes the origins and the endpoint of American history, a principle perhaps violated in the past but one fully realized in the present of war-time America. Yet even the violations of the democratic ideal become transmuted in the libretto, transmuted into nostalgia for the noble Indian and into celebration of the Emancipation Proclamation. In the climactic passage of the closing section, retitled "Hold Your Hold!," the libretto breaks into a chant:

America! Name me the word that is courage.
America! Name me the word that is justice.
America! Name me the word that is power.

America! Name me the word that is freedom.
America! Name me the word that is faith.
Here is that word –
Democracy!

(Graham 1942: 574)

This passage may well have been spoken in the earlier production as well. But in the context of the printed libretto, the passage does not ask the spectator to take action in order to realize democracy but rather to assent to its ritual celebration. That the outbreak of war had much to do with this shift is suggested by the unsigned prologue to the printed libretto. The prologue recounted Graham's inspiration for the work:

She had been listening to the vicious and terrifying words sent over the air from the Axis countries. It occurred to her that our own country – our democracy – has words, too, with power to hearten men and move them to action. The words she remembered are in this libretto.

(ibid.: 565)

Given the cuts evident in the libretto, the "words [Graham] remembered" no longer included "things we are ashamed of . . . Sacco-Vanzetti, share-croppers, the Scottsboro boys" (Beiswanger 1939: 54).

Yet however much the political import of the published libretto departed from the political effect of the production, both relied on a common figuration of race and gender. What is striking is how the same tropes of race and gender supported such differing interpretations of the work's national politics. Underlying both production and libretto was the performative convention that only the white body could represent the universally American body, a convention that marked American modern dance in the 1930s. In *American Document* this convention crossed a moment of transition in the staging of gender in Graham's choreography, a moment when the female dancer gave up her performative claim to represent humanity and took up the performative task of representing Woman in relation to Man.

As a coda to my discussion, I would like to reconstruct two subsequent versions of the work, first, its revival in 1944 and, second, Graham's free adaptation done in 1989. Both versions broke down the figuration of race and gender evident in the original production and libretto, but in strikingly different ways. Whereas the 1944 revival introduced token integration into the casting, the 1989 adaptation reversed the earlier versions' focus on the female subject.

In 1944 Graham revived *American Document* as part of a two-week retrospective season in New York. Given this context, reviewers focused on how Graham's subsequent works had surpassed *American Document*, a critical judgment that has survived in the Graham literature until the present. Performed only twice, the revival cast fourteen women in addition to Graham and Hawkins and featured Merce Cunningham as the Interlocutor. The surviving evidence is equivocal about whether the revival more closely resembled the patriotic design of the printed libretto or the reformist impulse of the earlier production. On the one hand, reviewers interpreted the work as a straightforward statement of patriotism, thus suggesting an affinity with the printed libretto. Interestingly enough, the review that makes this clearest takes a critical attitude toward the changed tone of the work. In the *New York Herald Tribune* Edwin Denby wrote:

> Originally [*American Document*] seemed at least to conceal some sting of protest and to present our history as much for its disgraces as for its strength. At present it seems intended merely as smug glorification. It is monotonous as dancing and in sentiment varies from hollow solemnity to mawkish sentimentalism. The opening of Miss Graham's Indian solo and one sentence quoted from Jonathan Edwards are the only thirty seconds of interest; the rest seems as insincere as those patriotic full-page advertisements in color in the slick-paper magazines.
>
> (1986: 230)

Denby's interpretation of the "smug" patriotism of the work stands in sharp contrast to Owen Burke's interpretation of the militant reformism of the 1938 New York production.

Yet on the other hand, the program for the 1944 revival reveals a distinct departure in casting that takes the reformist impulse of the earlier staging in a new direction. No longer is the ensemble limited to Americans of European ancestry, for Yuriko, a Japanese-American, appears in the dance group. Yuriko had arrived at the Graham School the year before, just after her release from an internment camp in California. *American Document* marked her debut with Graham's professional company, inaugurating an association that has lasted until the present day (Horosko 1991: 109). At a time when the United States government considered Japanese-Americans as enemy aliens, Graham included an Asian-American in a dance ensemble that represented the American body politic. Yet no reviewer at the time commented on the change.

Yuriko's presence in *American Document* raises questions applicable to Graham's repertory until the present day, for the revival introduced the token integration that has characterized the Graham Company until the present, not only of Asian-Americans since 1944 but also of African-Americans since 1952, the date when Mary Hinkson and Matt Turney joined the company. Does the token integration of the company break down the racial trope established in the 1930s and present bodies of distinct ethnicities yet a common humanity? Or does the token integration in an odd way extend the racial trope of the 1930s, framing the Asian-American and African-American bodies within the company as "separate yet equal" or as symbolically "white"?

By 1989, the year that Graham staged a free adaptation of *American*

Document, the token integration of her company had been an established convention for decades. Thus it is not surprising that the adaptation cut the work's minstrel-show frame, for it no longer made sense to present the white body as the universally American body. As the program noted, "The *American Document* of 1989 is neither a revision nor a revival of the 1938 ballet. Rather, Martha Graham has taken as her departure some of the original text and movement and created an entirely new work set to a contemporary score by John Corigliano." The "original text," derived from the printed libretto, included passages from The Declaration of Independence, Red Jacket of the Senecas, Jonathan Edwards, Song of Songs, and Abraham Lincoln. To these passages, the 1989 production added quotations from Joseph Campbell, Martin Luther King Jr., and John F. Kennedy.

Strikingly, the 1989 adaptation reversed the figuration of gender in the original production. Mikhail Baryshnikov was the featured performer, while a young actress took the role of the Narrator, as Graham now termed the Interlocutor. The chorus included equal numbers of men and women, in keeping with Graham's choreographic practice since the 1960s. The reviews are unclear about the structure of the work, although they do note that three soloists – Joyce Herring, Maxine Sherman, and Peter London – framed Baryshnikov's appearances "as a sort of Everyman who weaves in and out of the action" (Gale 1989: 7). Indeed, most reviews were devoted to recapitulating the structure of the original production, because as Tobi Tobias stated in *New York Magazine*, "[Graham's reworking] . . . is so disconnected and conceptually inchoate, it can be understood only in the light of its original" (1989: 156).[12]

"In the light of its original," however, the 1989 adaptation is notable for the way its focus on a male protagonist radically altered the gender politics of Graham's earlier works, not only the works from the 1930s that presented women as representatives of humanity but also the works from the 1940s and 1950s that defined Woman in relation to Man. The 1938 *American Document* stood at a point of transition between these two representational tropes for gender. The 1989 *American Document* reversed both tropes, presenting the male dancer as the central consciousness and as the subject and agent of American history. It is hard to know what to make of this swerve in Graham's late choreography. Yet the turn does illuminate the figuration of gender in her earlier works, just as a consideration of the original *American Document* illuminates the racial politics of American modern dance at mid-century.

NOTES

1 The following reconstruction relies mostly on the printed libretto and on the visual evidence of photographs and silent film clips, sources that enable an analysis of the performative conventions employed by *American Document* in the period from 1938 to 1942. Although reviewers' descriptions also have

informed my visualization of the work, I reserve specific reviewers' comments for my subsequent discussion of the stage history of the dance. Graham compiled the libretto in collaboration with Francis Fergusson, then head of the drama department at Bennington and later a professor of dramatic literature at Princeton and Rutgers. Graham herself wrote much of the bridging material between sections, and Fergusson contributed passages from his own writings as well as working with Graham on the textual collage. The typography of minstrel terms in my reconstruction follows the usage recorded in the libretto and in programs for the work.

My reconstruction does not address the relation between the dance and the music, first, because the original score composed by Ray Green is not published or available in manuscript, and, second, because the silent film footage obviously offers no sense of the relation between music and movement. However, reviews of *American Document* and published interviews with Green offer some details, such as that the music was scored for piano and snare drum, that it was based on American and African folk songs, and that it made reference to the drum rolls and fanfares of a minstrel show. See Beiswanger (1938), Diamond (1940), Kriegsman (1981), and Costonis (1991). Nor does my reconstruction describe the costumes, designed by Edythe Gilfond, and sets, designed by Arch Lauterer. Photographs in Barbara Morgan's 1941 portfolio show the costume silhouettes, and Costonis's 1991 article in *American Music* provides additional details on the costuming and the architectural set. However important these production elements, they were not constitutive of the performative strategies emphasized in my reconstruction, except in the negative sense of not involving blackface. For the sake of clarity and brevity, my reconstruction thus omits design details.

2 The Bennington premiere cast twenty-one women in addition to Graham and Hawkins, the New York City performance twenty-two women in addition to Graham and Hawkins. The touring version involved a female ensemble of ten to twelve dancers. Houseley Stevens Jr. took the role of the Interlocutor in performances from 1938 to 1940. (Program files, Martha Graham Company, Dance Collection at the New York Public Library for the Performing Arts).

3 This passage is included on the PBS documentary titled "Martha Graham: A Dancer Revealed." The silent film footage at the Dance Collection includes, in addition to the excerpts from the two duets described here, passages of group dancing. However, which group sections were filmed cannot be ascertained with certainty, beyond the prancing walk identified in still photographs as a Walk Around.

4 It is important to note that Morgan's photographs constitute an interpretation of the dance. After viewing a work repeatedly in rehearsal and performance, she would choose moments to light and photograph in her studio. Thus, my reading of Morgan's photographs is an interpretation of an interpretation. Yet her visual interpretations often seemed to capture the underlying choreographic principles of Graham's dances. In terms of *American Document*, Morgan's photographs provide more insight into Graham's choreographic strategies than do the silent film clips. For an account of Morgan's working method, see Maslow and Morgan 1983.

5 In the late nineteenth and early twentieth centuries a conventional minstrel show began with a Walk Around, as performers two by two strutted around the stage and ended posed in a half-circle facing the audience. The Interlocutor then greeted the audience and proceeded to engage the two "end men," typically called Tambo and Bones, in a comic repartee called the Cross-Fire. After this opening came an olio, a section of vaudeville-type acts and then a final After Piece, a dramatic skit often farcical in tone. For further discussion of the form of the minstrel show, see Costonis (1991) and Lott (1993).

6 Lott's limitation of his study to the antebellum period is crucial to his argument, for he does not have to follow the complexities that ensued after the Civil War, when female performers and African-American performers took up the practice of minstrelsy.

7 The variations on the gesture of the upraised right arm also can be seen as alternatives to the Hitler salute. In 1936 Graham had refused an invitation to perform at the Berlin Olympic Games because many members of her company were Jewish. Given this context, she may well have deliberately reworked the movement motif of the Hitler salute when choreographing *American Document*. For this insight, I am indebted to Danielle Robinson.

8 Although individual Native Americans have entered the field of modern dance, there has never been a collective movement among Native American choreographers comparable to that among African-American choreographers of modern dance.

9 For a different analysis of the admixture of reformism and patriotism in the work, see Graff (1994).

10 In addition to the topical references, the libretto cut poems of Walt Whitman that were included in the stage version performed from 1938 to 1940. However, it is unclear which poems were included in "Emancipation Episode" or how they inflected the reviewers' interpretation of the politics of the work.

11 In *American Dancer* Albertina Vitak and in *Dance Observer* Henry Gilfond also mentioned the references to Sacco and Vanzetti and the Scottsboro boys, though, interestingly enough, not the reference to share-croppers.

12 Tobias's assessment was echoed by other reviewers, who wondered aloud whether the production was staged simply as a vehicle for Baryshnikov and as a draw for the benefit audience at the opening night of Graham's 1989 New York season. The reviewers could make little sense of what Clive Barnes termed "the jingoistic maelstrom of parades and events" (1990: 26) beyond its pastiche of the earlier version and other works from the Graham repertory. As Joan Acocella wrote, "Almost every theme, step, feeling, or technical device that was ever important in Graham's sixty-year oeuvre is reiterated – with no logic, no development. The piece is a list" (1989: 71).

BIBLIOGRAPHY

Acocella, J. (1989) "The Empress' Old Clothes," *7 Days* (October 18): 71.

Barnes, C. (1990) "Martha at 95," *Dance & Dancers* 478: 26–9.

Beiswanger, G. (1938) "Music at the Bennington Festival," *Dance Observer* 5, 7: 102–4.

—— (1939) "The New Theatre Dance," *Theatre Arts Monthly* 23: 41–54.

Burke, O. (1938) "An American Document," *New Masses* (October 18): 29.

Costonis, M. (1991) "Martha Graham's *American Document*: A Minstrel Show in Modern Dance Dress," *American Music* 9, 3: 297–310.

Denby, E. (1986) *Dance Writings*, New York: Alfred A. Knopf.

Diamond, D. (1940) "With the Dancers," *Modern Music* 17, 2: 116–20.

Fergusson, F. (1979) "Bennington Oral History Project," transcript of unpublished interview, New York: Columbia University Oral History Office.

Film Archive, Martha Graham Dance Company, Dance Collection at the New York Public Library for the Performing Arts.

Gale, J. (1989) "An 'American Document,'" *The Independent Press* (October 11): 7.

Gilfond, H. (1938) "Bennington Festival," *Dance Observer* 5, 7: 100–2.

Graff, E. (1994) "Dancing Red: Art and Politics," *Studies in Dance History* 5, 1: 1–13.

Graham, M. (1942) "Dance Libretto: *American Document*," *Theatre Arts Monthly* 26: 565–74.

Horosko, M. (1991) *Martha Graham: The Evolution of Her Dance Theory and Training 1926–1991*, Pennington, NJ: a cappella books.

Kirstein, L. (1938) "Martha Graham at Bennington," *The Nation* (September 3): 230–1.

Kriegsman, S. (1981) *Modern Dance in America: The Bennington Years*, Boston: G.K. Hall.

Lang, P. *et al.* (1988) "The Creative Process: Graham, Humphrey, and Limon," video recording of television show titled *Eye on Dance* aired on WTTW on May 19, 1988, Dance Collection at the New York Public Library for the Performing Arts.

Lott, E. (1993) *Love & Theft: Blackface Minstrelsy and the American Working Class*, New York: Oxford University Press.

Maslow, S. and Morgan, B. (1983) "Sophie Maslow/Barbara Morgan: Dialogue with Photographs," *Massachusetts Review* 24, 1: 65–80.

Maslow, S. *et al.* (1981) "The Early Years: Martha Graham and Modernism," video recording of conference held at State University of New York at Purchase, Dance Collection at the New York Public Library for the Performing Arts.

Morgan, B. (1941) *Martha Graham: Sixteen Dances in Photographs*, New York: Duell, Sloan & Pearce.

Osumare, H. and Lewis-Ferguson, J. (1991) *Black Choreographers Moving: A National Dialogue*, Berkeley: Expansion Arts Services.

Perpener, J. (1992) "The Seminal Years of Black Concert Dance," unpublished Ph.D. dissertation, New York University.

Program files, Martha Graham Dance Company, Dance Collection at the New York Public Library for the Performing Arts.

Tobias, T. (1989) "Flags Flying," *New York Magazine* (October 23): 156–7.

Vitak, A. (1938) "Dance Events Reviewed," *American Dancer* (October): 13, 39.

12 The Culture of Nobility/The Nobility of Self-Cultivation

Judy Burns

By Delsarte Culture, that aids in establishing
outer harmony and inner poise, we may
at last approach our marble ideals in expression.

Emily M. Bishop (1892: 34)

THE CULTURE OF NOBILITY

On November 25, 1892 Genevieve Stebbins gave a Delsarte matinee to benefit the National Christian League for the Promotion of Social Purity. Performing pantomimes and recitations on Greek and Oriental themes, as well as her signature statue poses in which she melted from one famous classical image to another (*New York Times* 1892: 9), she manifested what Ruth St. Denis later remembered as the serenity and coordination of an angel or goddess (St. Denis 1960). Stebbins's blend of spirituality, classical culture, artistic aspiration, and consummately controlled, graceful movement would surely have seemed to be the epitome of nobility, the very model of deportment, for the ladies and gentlemen who comprised the membership of the National Christian League. Dedicated to improving the moral tenor of life, the members of that socially concerned organization helped women find economic alternatives to prostitution, encouraged paternal responsibility, pressed for legislation that would make adultery a crime, and sponsored edifying entertainments at which young men and women could socialize (National Christian League 1892–3: 9, 12, 13–14, 17).

Stebbins was one of the most prominent practitioners and teachers of Delsartism in America, but during the 1880s and especially the 1890s, there were many others, both professional and amateur. Indeed, Delsarte in its many manifestations was, for a time, a craze among middle- and upper-class Americans, especially women. As a system of expression, its rules were grafted onto popular theatrical and educational forms, including tableaux vivants, pantomimes, recitations, physical education exercises, and temperance military drills. The results were performed in countless lecture halls, church basements, and school auditoriums. Delsarte expressive exercises for the body were also taught separately as refined, spiritualized physical culture to thousands of American women.

Most contemporary research focusing on the "pure" movement principles behind Delsarte's philosophy, as expounded by such major American Delsartians as Stebbins, has considered how American Delsarte influenced the development of modern dance (Ruyter 1979; Shelton 1981; Jowitt 1988). As a consequence, modern scholars have by definition paid little attention to American (re)construction or transformation of these laws. Furthermore, while some scholars have acknowledged that modern dance, with its high art aspirations, sprang from a mongrel mixture of what would conventionally be considered high and low culture (e.g. Kendall 1979), most recent studies have tended to shun the many self-proclaimed Delsartians whose teachings were less profoundly "artistic," more pragmatic, more eclectic, more fragmentary, or frankly commercial. Neither have they paid serious attention to numerous well-documented Delsarte performances, except those that clearly anticipate modern dance in its most serious aspect, or to Delsarte physical culture apart from its significance to early art dance.

All these neglected examples of Delsarte performance have most often been viewed as trivializations of American Delsarte's high artistic aims, and relegated to the status of crackpot oddities or arcane jokes. To be sure, they were frequently seen the same way in their own time (Baker 1889; Wilbor 1891: 250). Yet the many and varied manifestations of Delsarte in America – the ways in which it was used and abused, recycled and reconstructed – are valuable evidence of the complex cultural values of the time, especially in regard to class and gender. In the many manifestations, "authentic" and "inauthentic," of American Delsarte, practitioners enacted a variety of conflicting, and conflicted, aspirations for social- and self-improvement.

Delsartism itself entered the United States swathed in idealism. The actor and director, Steele MacKaye, had studied with the French teacher and aesthetician, François Delsarte, in Paris between 1869 and 1870 (MacKaye 1927: 135), absorbing the master's Christian-based philosophy of expression in which the triune nature of humanity demonstrated the divine source of art and expression. MacKaye learned about the interdependence of mind, body, and spirit (or the mental, vital, and moral), and about how three different sections of the body signify these three aspects of human nature. He absorbed the meanings of various placements of the body – or parts of the body – in space, all codified in groups, or multiples, of three. He even developed his own set of physical exercises to facilitate the expression of Delsarte's concepts.

When Steele MacKaye introduced Delsarte's aesthetic theories to the United States in 1870, many educators and religious and civic leaders invited MacKaye to lecture and demonstrate Delsartian principles to their constituents. Edgar S. Werner, editor of an important journal for orators and teachers of expression, lauded Delsarte's "science of expressive man," and added,

It lifts the actor out of the experimental rut of mere chance on to the plane of fruitful method, furnishing him with the formulae that . . . enable him to progress alon[g] an ascending scale of excellence, as he becomes more and more thorough in the practice of his art as scientifically governed.

(*The Voice* 1884: 67)

Beyond raising the status of theater in the United States, Delsarte's system did not rely solely on intuition or genius: its principles could be taught to anyone. One can see the practical Yankee minds ticking away as some Delsartians lauded the system's efficiency: "An actor surrenders ten years of life to the acquisition of that which, systematically taught, could be better gained in a year or six months' time" (ibid.).

During the 1870s Delsarte found its American application as a system of training for actors and orators, but its full potential was not felt to be realized. Perhaps still moved by Durivage's claims, Werner and others were interested in how Delsartism could benefit society as a whole. In raising such an issue, Werner reflected the practical scientific bias of his time. But also, as Stebbins was to note later ([1895]1902: 339–40), there was ample precedent for studying the social benefits of art in John Ruskin's writings, for Ruskin struck a chord with Delsartism in his assertion that the pursuit of art enriched and ennobled individuals, and raised them beyond the limits of social rank.

William Alger, one of American Delsarte's first and most idealistic proponents, was also one of the first to propose it as a system of physical culture for the general public, and he believed that the benefits would be unlimited. Delsarte, he claimed, would become "the basis of a new religion, destined to perfect the children of men, abolish deformity, sickness, and crime, and redeem the earth" (1885: 56). Alger's extremely optimistic claims grew out of a belief that Delsarte would address long-standing American anxieties centering around the survival of traditional American values and ways of living. Since the 1820s American leaders had been preoccupied with what they perceived as a decline in the strength and forcefulness of the Anglo-American stock. The second generation of post-Revolutionaries were anxious about their ability to carry out the promise of the nation for which their illustrious forefathers had fought (Green 1983: 7; 1986: 10–16). Urbanization was breaking up the old extended families. Industrialization meant that men no longer worked in the home and that women increasingly did not contribute materially to the family economy but cultivated leisure instead (Green 1983: 6–7). The first wave of immigration introduced different cultural practices, and Anglo-American religious values were not nearly as rigorous as those of the Calvinists a century earlier. The increase in sedentary "brain work" jobs in offices, and the growth of prosperity and educational opportunities meant that Americans were also not living as physically challenging a life as the Puritans had. Neurasthenia became the disease of the American middle class (Green 1986: 103–4, 138–40).

Educated Americans were mindful of the republican view of history, according to which the course of civilizations was a series of rises and declines. They remembered Rome's fall, which they associated with unthinking luxury, and when they thought about the astonishing economic growth of the period they lived in, combined with its physical and spiritual laxness, they worried. For if industrialization seemed to point to America's future greatness, it also held the seeds of her decline (Lears 1981: 4; Green 1983: 114–15; 1986: 15–16). The financial panics of the pre-Civil War period seemed to give some credence to this view and so millenarian religious activity flourished by leaps and bounds (Green 1983: 8; 1986: 29).

Physical culture also flourished. As a number of writers have noted, nineteenth-century Americans considered the individual body to be a sign of broader social values, especially the health of the political and social state (Gallagher and Laqueur 1981: vii; Green 1986: ix). And so Americans set out, literally and aggressively, to bolster social values by making and remaking individual bodies. Health cures, like religious retreats, became the rage, and calisthenics were taught in the schools, as well as practiced at home. The beginnings of women's higher education raised fears that women's delicate constitutions would be damaged by too much "brain work," and so women's physical culture also received particular attention at this time (Solomon 1985: 56–7; Green 1986: 185).

It is important to note that the republican interpretation of history corresponds nicely with pre-Revolutionary, "traditional" Calvinist religious beliefs. According to the Puritan conception of grace, individual men could do almost anything to lose grace, but nothing in particular to win it. In a harsh world, grace came in God's time and of God's accord. People looked continually for signs of God's favor and found it manifested in the physical conditions of an individual or a body politic. Whatever improved the outward state was interpreted as manifesting God's favor.

By the early nineteenth century Protestant dogma changed somewhat. Pre-ordination and infant damnation were set aside (Green 1983: 35; 1986: 10). Dogma admitted the possibility that an individual's good works could actively win grace; a belief in man's essential perfectability began to prevail. In this context, individual responsibility for obtaining grace was magnified (Lears 1981: 17–18; Green 1986: 28) but material conditions still remained the measure. Americans, in other words, still looked for signs; and weakened bodies, neurasthenic constitutions, and financial reverses were not perceived as signs of grace for middle-class urban, industrial America. On the other hand, all the health cures and religious conversions did not seem to solve the problem either.

Beginning in the 1850s several new currents of ideas began offering hope. Liberal economists popularized Adam Smith's economic theories, asserting that the pursuit of industrial capitalism promoted the good of the whole society (Lears 1981: 18–19). Material progress was, by definition, accompanied by and equivalent to moral progress. This view obtained further support from positivism, the belief that the universe was governed by deterministic scientific laws that could be revealed through human inquiry (ibid.: 20), thus leading to ever greater rationality. Herbert Spencer's evolutionary theory of history, that "cultures evolved from homogeneous warlike clans to heterogeneous peaceful commercial civilizations" (ibid.: 21) completed the reassuring portrait of urban capitalist centers evolving towards ever greater harmony and perfection.

Together these theories provided a practical, secular substitute for Calvinist theology, a mechanical, closed system that, once started, promised to perform like a self-winding clock. Middle-class Americans, it would seem, could rest assured that their country was moving inexorably toward its destiny of greatness and grace. But by the 1870s the closed system was showing some cracks as unprecedented waves of immigration challenged cultural and economic patterns, and strikes and labor unrest broke out.

In proposing Delsarte as a system of physical culture for both men and women, the Rev. William Alger specifically located the need for Delsarte gymnastics within the context of the old republican anxieties:

> How greatly it is needed one fact shows, namely, the steady process which has long been going on of lessening beauty and increasing ugliness in the higher classes of society, lessening roundness and increasing angularity of facial contour. The proof of this historic encroachment of anxious, nervous wear and tear displacing the full grace of curved lines with the sinister sharpness of straight lines, is given in most collections of family portraits, and may be strikingly seen by glancing from the rosy and generous faces of Fox and Burke, or of Washington and Hamilton, to the pinched and wrinkled visages of Gladstone and Disraeli, or of Lincoln and Seward.
>
> (Alger 1885: 56)

Old-fashioned gymnastics, by which Alger presumably meant German gymnastics or military drill, would not repair the "historic encroachment of anxious, nervous wear and tear" because they only utilized straight-line movement. Alger based his argument on the Delsartian doctrine that man has three natures – vital, mental and moral – and that these are represented in different movements within space: vital movements are excentric; mental, accentric; and moral, concentric. The straight line movements of conventional gymnastics overdeveloped the excentric and accentric natures, or the vital and the mental. These were precisely the two aspects of the "higher classes" which were already overworked by modern urban culture, which Alger considered "perverted and sick" (ibid.). On the other hand, Delsarte gymnastics, with their curving and spiral lines, cultivated the spiritual nature and healed the deficiencies of modern life by promoting a harmonious balance between the three aspects.

The body values Alger advocated echoed the holistic physical culturists of his time, who warned that overall flexibility was more healthy than the selective cultivation of brute strength in a few body parts. But Delsarte was even superior to those "unmeaning" systems of calisthenics in that it was expressive.

> This style of gymnastic alone recognizes the infinitely solemn and beautiful truth that every attitude, every motion, tends to *produce* the quality of which it is the legitimate expression.
>
> (ibid.)

Drawing upon the embryonic psychology of the day, Delsartians asserted that not only did movement express inner states, it also caused them:

> ... motion causes emotion. Stand in a stooped attitude, with sunken chest and hanging head, hold the position for a few moments; how mean you feel! Now stand with upright body, raised chest and head and see if you do not feel like another person.
>
> (Morley 1887: 7)

Along with that recognition went an awareness that other people read an individual's character through nonverbal cues as surely as they interpreted an actor's performance by means of his attitudes and gestures. If, as Delsartians believed, the practice of Delsarte gymnastics could change one's character, then there was a clear mandate to consciously choose and shape one's physical habits. The need was particularly acute for children, who were still only partially ravaged by civilized values and were closer to the natural state. Margaret Morley, who taught in Chicago, asked:

> Is it not our duty to practice those motions whose expression is noble, is elevating? Is it not our duty to see that the physical training of our children shall tend to make them express good and beautiful things?
>
> (1887: 7)

And the students of Mary V. Lee, who supervised the physical culture classes at the Oswego (New York) Normal and Training School learned "to give expression to the higher nature":

> By having every movement taught in harmony with law; by having graceful, rhythmic movements repeated before the pupils till they see the grace; by having these imitated till they feel the grace; by arousing noble feeling and then giving its natural gesture expression; by arousing noble feeling and calling for its expression. ..
>
> (Arnold 1887: 175)

THE CULTIVATION OF CULTURE

But, as far as Alger's evangelistic claims went, all the wishing, and the striking of attitudes, did not undo the real psychological, physical and social problems of late-nineteenth-century, middle-class, urban-industrial Americans. The unfortunate fact was that the movement values Delsarte promoted – grace, poise, flexibility, relaxation and organic succession – belonged to an earlier, gentler era. If physical culturists of the Civil War era had promoted the all-around man, moderate overall development of the entire body, spiral as well as straight line movements and flexibility rather than brute strength (Green 1986: 193), by the 1880s men were joining the National Guard to protect the (middle-class) law and order. Weight-lifting, selective development of body parts and a general "he-man" look were becoming fashionable. Men like Sandow and Bernarr Macfadden were only interested in posing as Greek statues to show off their bulging muscles. And although Herbert Spencer soothingly counseled the adoption of relaxation ("We have had something too much of the gospel of work. It is time to preach the gospel of relaxation" (Spencer 1882: 359; Bishop 1892: 56)), for the average businessman this translated to an occasional vacation.

These physical characteristics, in turn, represented changes in lifestyle for men. Alger's and MacKaye's cultivated habits, their dedication to art, their widespread learning and their flowery, sentimental styles of writing and speaking were less and less typical of men in general. Sandow and Macfadden, the latter a heroic version of the ninety-pound weakling who became a he-man, symbolized the successful self-made businessman who was becoming a male ideal. By the turn of the century, America would be on the verge of an unprecedented expansionist phase, proving its "manifest destiny," and Teddy Roosevelt, outdoor man and big game hunter, would embody a central male ideal (Green 1986: 208, 235–7, 242–5).

Increasingly, Delsarte movement values, and Delsartian values in general, fell within the domain that had been coded as "female" by nineteenth-century middle-class Americans. Specifically within the context of urban business culture, women were seen as the counterbalance to:

> the heartless world of capitalist competition. . . . According to conventional wisdom, the male world of work was tough and demanding; the female world of home was comfortable, reassuring, and adorned by "the finer things of life." In the transition to an urban market economy, women . . . became the guardians of culture and morality. Remaining aloof from the emerging market society, Victorian housewives were encouraged to shelter their children from the corruptions of the marketplace and comfort their exhausted husbands.
>
> (Lears 1981: 15)

As "guardians of culture and morality," women were associated with "culture" in three senses.[1] First, woman was culture in the horticultural sense of "cultivation." Women were associated with benign "natural" imagery, as opposed to the "tooth and claw" imagery of the business world. The foremost duty of a new wife, says an 1899 manual, was to provide for her husband "the single spot of rest which a man has upon the earth for the cultivation of his noble sensibilities" (Green 1983: 27–8). The Victorian home, women's domain, was likened to a garden, often filled with plants (ibid.: 37). A pregnant woman was also told to think of herself as a garden, providing the good soil in which her baby could grow (ibid.: 33); and a child who was given "brain-work" too early was referred to as "forced," like a bulb (ibid.: 27–8).

Second, women were the keepers of culture in that they were expected to be accomplished in the arts, crafts, and music. The display of their accomplishments proclaimed their leisure for these pursuits, and therefore their husbands' financial success (ibid.: 93). Their refinement also affirmed the allegedly moral underbelly of capitalism by suggesting that the pursuit of wealth led to the accumulation and display of beauty, the practice of a "superior" lifestyle.

Finally, as cultivators of "man's noblest sensibilities" and tenders of future generations, women also became guardians of the very culture that urban capitalism was destroying. In particular, women were the repositories of an earlier generation's moral values, including its religious piety, its sense of right behavior, and its ideals for humanity. Mothers were charged with the task of instilling these values in their sons and daughters, not through any direct means but by acting as silent, shining examples. Women, as men's "better selves," were thus positioned as a potential counter-culture, but with little power.

The literature of the period is filled with sentimental tributes to this type of femininity and feminine influence (Douglas [1977] 1988: 3–13); Delsarte performance, in turn, drew strongly on the sentimental literary tradition. Participating in the nineteenth-century American anxiety for locating themselves within valued historical traditions – but in the context of separate spheres – women began looking for role models, and certain aspects of Greek tragedy and myth were an important source. Probably the all-time favorite classical image of woman for Delsartians was Niobe, the mother who refused to worship the gods because she claimed that her children were as perfect as the deities. To teach her a lesson, the gods killed her children and turned her to stone. Other typical subjects were "The Sacrifice of the Minotaur," "The Sacrifice of Iphigenia," "The Sacrifice of Irene," and "The Fate of Virginia," the Roman maiden who was murdered by Appius Claudius, and commemorated in a poem by Thomas Macaulay.

As should be evident from the list above, Delsartians chose primarily those characters who fit the genteel upper-middle-class morality, favoring saintly – or at least devoted – mothers, dutiful daughters, and blameless virgins wronged by evil men, the very figures and values the National Christian League for the Promotion of Social Purity sought to protect. With their bodies, Delsarte performers enacted the various types of culture/cultivation that were considered women's sphere. Evoking their horticultural role, their bodies resembled vines, spiraling, twining, flowing

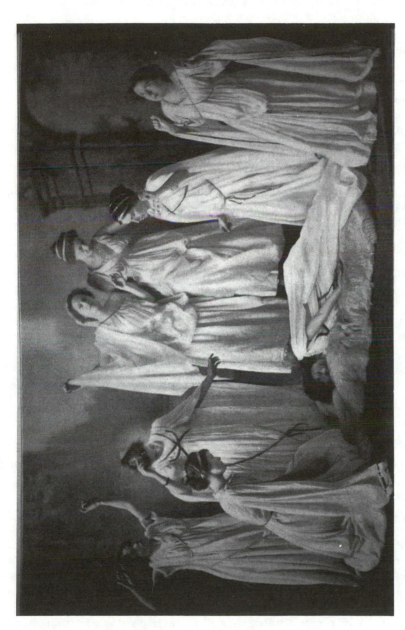

Figure 12.1 "The Fate of Virginia." *Werner's Voice Magazine* (May 1899) XXIII, 3: 198. (Photo courtesy of the Billy Rose Theater Collection, New York Public Library for the Performing Arts, Astor, Lenox and Tilden Foundations)

organically. At the same time, they did not just cultivate the arts or nurture cultural traditions: through performance, they literally *became* the arts. Instead of just playing roles, in a reversal of Pygmalion, they reverted to marble sculpture.

They became silent, shining examples par excellence. This is especially apparent in the way many Delsarte tableaux were laid out spatially. Usually a half circle of women surrounds a central figure who has either collapsed in someone's arms or lies decoratively sprawled on the ground. The surrounding women show their responses to the situation; they gasp, they mourn, they plead with some unseen deity, or commend the unfortunate's soul to a better place. Their sole dramatic function, in fact, seems to be to react and, in so doing, to cue the viewer's response to the appropriate moral. At the same time, they are so decoratively arranged, they make a picture of such varied poses and interesting lines and balances of masses, that the viewer's eyes linger over them. Seldom do we see women in actual conflict with the fates or persons who oppress them, only at the moment of their noble death or defeat. Their role, then, is not to redress wrongs, not to truly challenge the system, but rather to offer passive reproach. The movement values that were widely understood to be appropriate for Delsarte performance only heightened this sense of acquiescence: relaxation that often was indistinguishable from limpness, and a statuesque stillness that was supposed to contain the germ of movement just arrested, but more often was only frozen, static. Like the sentimental women's literature of the period, much Delsarte performance served nostalgically to evoke the "better selves" that urban industrial society was fast leaving behind (Douglas [1977] 1988: 12). It is in this context that we can understand the penchant of sentimental literature and performance for casting women in sacrificial roles.[2]

THE CULTURE OF SELF-CULTIVATION

Ann Douglas has written of "the drive of nineteenth century American women to gain power through the exploration of their feminine identity as their society defined it" ([1977] 1988: 8). This was a double-edged proposition. As we have seen, Delsarte performance largely constrained women within roles that played out genteel – and somewhat dated – middle-class ideas about women's sphere. On the other hand, Delsarte did give women a forum for performing outside the home, and such performance was not restricted to genteel theatrical realms. By the time Delsarte was taken up by large numbers of women, women were beginning to insist on extending the exercise of their "legitimate" sphere into many parts of the larger world, for its own moral good, as well as their own greater fulfillment. Women were becoming teachers in significant numbers, claiming the job as their natural, motherly right. Women were also attempting to influence public policy on moral issues, to enforce moral standards and to redress social injustice. For example, the Women's Christian Temperance Union, whose program included prohibition and women's suffrage, was founded in 1874, and the National Christian League in 1886.

One might say that women were looking for cracks through which they could wedge their influence into the outer world without making too much of a fuss; Delsarte provided a perfect opportunity. It spoke to their leisure and their cultivation of the arts. It reflected their approved role as cultivators of future generations, and many women, including women whose families had lost their male breadwinner to the financial reverses of the period, were able to support themselves as Delsarte teachers. Women, as the primary consumers of health and rest cures over the course of the century, also saw health as their legitimate sphere. "Women are the natural disciples of this 'Gospel of Health,'" asserted Julia and Annie Thomas. "It is preeminently their sphere, first as mothers or nurses, then as teachers . . . " (Thomas and Thomas 1892: 5).

Emily Bishop, Assistant Director of Physical Culture at Chautauqua and one of the most prominent teachers of Delsarte physical culture, was to practical Delsartism what Stebbins was to artistic Delsartians. Bishop appreciated the beauty of the expressive system she taught, but her concerns were considerably more down-to-earth than Stebbins's:

> Unusual circumstances led to the conversion of the Delsarte expression exercises into health agencies; experience had proven that along this line it is possible to give "the greatest good to the greatest number." Where one person is interested in "art for art's sake," one hundred are interested in "health for health's sake."
>
> (Bishop 1892)

Bishop was interested in making women healthier and she expressed this in purely economic terms: "we should treat our strength as we do our income, getting the most and best for the amount expended" (ibid.: 254). Delsarte was the best way to accomplish health, Bishop felt, not just because it was beautiful, but because "grace is economy of force; awkwardness is physical extravagance" (ibid.: 28).

Just as Genevieve Stebbins gave her expression students images to help them feel the movements they were required to perform, Bishop gave students images to guide the exercises that would remake their bodies. In her bestselling *Americanized Delsarte Culture* Bishop counseled her readers, "Keep the thoughts concentrated as much as possible on some result to be obtained by the practice" (ibid.: 43). Bishop called her system psycho-physical culture, a reminder that Delsarte gymnastics were not just mechanical exercises:

> The gymnastics of exercise have relation to physical growth; the gymnastics of expression have relation to the growth of the mental and emotive natures, as well as to the growth of the physical. Whereas the

one uses motion exclusively, the other uses motion as related to emotion or to a mental state.

(ibid.: 20)

Thus, the images she suggested were not directly pragmatic, but rather idealized mental and emotional states. To counteract the tension of urban, industrial life, for example, Bishop recommended a simple exercise in which the arms were raised over the head, accompanied by the words "relaxation, repose, rest" repeated several times (ibid.: 62). To cure insomnia she urged her readers to lie completely still and repeat, like a Christian mantra, the phrase, "God is love" (ibid.: 143).

Her teaching method in some ways resembled late-twentieth-century sensory awareness training, encouraging students to enter imaginatively into the joints and muscles of their bodies. But in spite of this forward-looking aspect of her work, Bishop reflected and slightly distorted a good deal of the liberal positivist dogma. Her economic justification of the pursuit of grace, for example, provided another version of the credo that moral and material good coincided; at the same time, her reasoning made the pursuit of physical culture an economic duty.

Echoing the era's unbounded faith in the power of science to bring about unending improvement she optimistically asked:

Is it too much to ask of science that she shall interpret the gestures, attitudes, bearings, tones and inflections of man and disclose the laws by which these expressions, the faculties, nay, more: how the thoughts, passions and emotions can be influenced?

(ibid.: 192)

She showed a thoroughgoing admiration for Herbert Spencer's sweeping optimism, and imitated his thought by constructing her own evolutionary scheme in which the present age would surpass any before it in its balanced attention to all aspects of man. With a remarkably selective grasp of history, she characterized the Greeks as body worshippers, the people of the "Dark Ages" as religious ascetics who abused body and intellect, and the Reformation as a period in which the intellect predominated. As to the late nineteenth century, she advised, "It is believed that we are now on the threshold of the age of symmetrical culture; a culture that seeks the harmonious use, expression and growth of all the powers" (ibid.: 18). In fact, Bishop rang a rather subtle change on Alger's idealism about the ability of Delsarte to remake humankind in a nobler form. For Bishop, and virtually all of the other teachers of Delsarte physical culture, the emphasis shifted from utopian social aspiration to an individualized sort of "be-all-that-you-can-be" self-cultivation.

Self-improvement, whether in the form of rest-cures, physical culture, or home-study courses, had a long tradition among middle-class Americans. That desire was also deeply rooted in traditional religious conceptions of how grace was obtained, and it was firmly tangled up with business culture as well. Thus, Emily Bishop could quote Herbert Spencer in one of her chapter headings: "All breaches of the laws of health are physical sins . . . " (ibid.: 32). One can see how her readers might find, in this uncompromising statement, a mandate for bodily vigilance, perpetual dissatisfaction, and an endless questing for improvement almost Calvinist in quality.

This type of language and sentiment was also commonly associated with women's reform projects like the Women's Christian Temperance Union that used the passive influence of piety to encourage changes in individual behavior and public policy. While it is not known whether Bishop was a member, it appears that other Delsarte-associated teachers, like Julia and Annie Thomas, were. Just as Delsartians believed that the body expressed God's being through the soul, so the W.C.T.U. viewed the body as the temple of the spirit, requiring the most reverent of attentions. The Thomases' idiosyncratic 1892 *Psycho-Physical Culture* was dedicated:

> To parents, especially to mothers, to whom is intrusted [sic] the laying of the foundation of these wonderful temples;
> To teachers, on whom such great responsibility rests for assistance and direction in the continuation of the building of the temple;
> To the members of the W.C.T.U., who are bravely working for the abolishment of the great evil which more than anything else defiles, defaces and deforms the temple . . .
>
> (Thomas and Thomas 1892)

So if, as current scholars point out, religious or patriotic concepts such as duty were being used by the neophyte advertising industry to encourage women to buy the latest dress or book or brand of baking soda, and by philosophers and statesmen to prop up the social order, it is also important to note that women were employing the same ideas and language to try to promote what they saw as productive social reform.

But perhaps most important, the concept of realizing one's potential that the Delsarte physical culture manuals promoted had specific meanings in the context of middle-class women's (as opposed to men's) lives. By the mid-1880s, women were the primary students and practitioners of Delsarte physical culture and performance forms (Bishop 1892). While middle-class women were certainly privileged in comparison to the working-class women of the cities, they nevertheless were sufficiently hampered by social and cultural constraints that they had a long way to go to realize their full potential. Bishop, for example, describes the value Delsarte's expressive exercises could have for the many women who were stepping outside the sphere of the home:

> Many persons in everyday affairs of life, in society, in business, appear stupid who are only timid; they have not possession of their nerve-and-muscle machines.

Why do women feel trepidation when they are to read a paper at a literary society, or to give a five minutes talk at the "Club"? Because they are conscious of their instruments of expression – conscious of hands, attitudes, voice, even dress. Fear is born of this self-consciousness, they dare not do what they are capable of doing. When by self-knowledge and self-discipline, women shall gain habitual, easy control of their bodies, they will have achieved an important emancipation.

(ibid.: 29–30)

This need for "control of their bodies" was very real. Although many women of the younger generation were engaging in other forms of physical culture or had taken up tennis or bicycling, for many, many women American Delsarte was an important introduction to their physical capacities.

Bishop took civilized culture to task for its generally repressive effect on natural self-expression:

Conventionality has much to answer for, not the least part of which is the enslavement of women to its false standards of culture. Society has said, and some fashionable "Finishing (?) Schools for Young Ladies" still say, that culture consists in repression, not expression . . .

(ibid.: 185)

In that very binary – "expression"/"repression" – lurks one of the social paradoxes of Delsartism in America. Delsarte's ideas were seen as a way of restoring "natural" deportment – in movement, speech, manner – to classes of people who, either because of extensive training in artificial social behavior or because of the pace of modern life had lost their connection with the spontaneous inner self. Yet Delsarte itself was a method of actor training as potentially elaborate as any society etiquette. It could easily be argued that if Bishop and other Delsartians were freeing women's bodies from "repressive" social mores, they were doing so by substituting another equally rigid system of discipline that was also heavily interlarded with all sorts of civilized culture (as opposed to "natural" self-expression). As we have seen, in her own writing, Bishop associated the concepts "self-discipline," "control," and "emancipation," and preached a nearly Calvinistic attention to the body.

Such an attitude is evident, as well, in the self-conscious self-surveillance some Delsartians, and others, advocated in dress reform and the pursuit of the "natural" female body. Just as Greek statues were models of nobility for Alger and of artistic expression for Stebbins, so classical marbles provided an image of the unfettered female body to Delsartian physical culturists. The Thomases even stated this assumption with republican overtones:

Competent judges of all civilized and cultured nations have for a long period agreed to regard the Apollo Belvedere and the Venus de Milo as standards of beauty for the entire human race. Although at the present time no one can be found whose physical conformation is not marked by one or more defects, yet there must have been a period in man's history when physical perfection characterized the human family. This, however, was subsequently more or less marred by over-indulgence of the passions and appetites, and the diseases and infirmities consequent thereon, which nature at every new birth endeavors to correct.

(1892: 229)

As a solution, they recommended, "The study of physical perfection – embracing proportion, symmetry, simplicity, variety, grace, and strength, and its development – should be made a part of the curriculum of every school" (ibid.: 228).

Werner's Magazine published many articles on dress reform during the late 1880s and 1890s, including some quite graphic illustrations. Reflecting the trend in physical education of the time towards the measurement of bodies and establishment of ideal norms, *Werner's* even reprinted an article from a popular journal that compared the measurements of the average American woman with those purported to belong to the Venus de Milo (1892: 24). And the Thomases advocated:

> that the board of education be instructed to purchase some statuary representing the female form in perfection, so that the girls might know what a perfectly developed woman is, and to place one in every schoolroom; then we would have mirrors all around that they might see their own forms reflected, and make comparisons.
>
> (Thomas and Thomas 1892: 14)

This image of self-surveillance, of young women constantly measuring themselves against their marble models, is both inspiring in its idealism and chilling in its own repressiveness and impossibility. Cultural critics have noted that the encouragement of dissatisfaction with the present state, and quest for unattainable goals was manipulated in the nineteenth century into the beginnings of consumerism; Ann Douglas's *The Feminization of American Culture* and T. J. Jackson Lears's *No Place of Grace* have presented sentimentalism and anti-modernism as insincere and ineffective responses that, rather than challenging industrial capitalism, served to prop it up. These charges could certainly be leveled at Bishop. She railed against the stresses of urban industrialism, including "the pace that kills" (1892: 57), but offered solutions that were little more than bandaids of the imagination, what we today would call stress- and image-management. And she participated in a system in which women could never be satisfied with their present state, but were always goaded to greater perfection.

But others pushed Delsartism much further in the direction of escapism and consumerism. The most important example is undoubtedly the particular brand of Delsarte-influenced aestheticism that Henrietta and Edmund Russell promoted. However much orthodox Delsartians looked askance at the Russells (*Werner's Voice Magazine* 1890: 5), there is no doubt that the couple found a ready audience in leisured women conditioned to believe that the cultivation of the arts was their natural sphere. Influenced by the English arts and crafts movement, itself a nostalgic reaction against the impersonal, unspiritual ugliness of urban industrial England, Edmund Russell preached the gospel of beauty and the individual cultivation of self-as-art-object through dress, personal ornament, household decoration, Eastern philosophy, good literature. Yet this gospel was frequently trivialized and commercialized: for example, the Delsartian balance of the three aspects of man was translated into knowing which clothing colors went with brown or blonde hair, which dress cuts "harmonized" with a stout or slim figure. The desire to develop a noble character was transformed into a rather privileged, hothouse type of beauty cultivation. If Delsartian performance transformed women's bodies into Greek statues, Russell remade women, their possessions, and surroundings into elaborate theatrical settings that made the everyday world of industrial cities seem far away. He broke down, and at the same time, absolutely literalized, the fine line that had both separated, and cross-fertilized life and art in other American Delsartians' work.

During the 1890s *Werner*'s ran a number of Russell-inspired articles with titles like "Expression in Jewelry," "Expression Through Bronze," and "Expression in Wall Decoration." In 1891 and 1892 *Werner*'s ran its own Russell-influenced beauty column, "Beauty and Artistic Dress" by Helen Potter. Potter's column was divided into three sections. In the first, "The Lecture Room," she gave inspirational talks on subjects such as dress reform or the need for the national interest in physical culture to be tempered by moral development. "The Studio," the second section, contained exercises that were little more than pretty, precious poses accompanied by the thinking of "good and elevated thoughts" (Potter 1892: 65) and the wafting of arms in an unconscious parody of the Delsarte "feather" movement, an unfortunate inheritance from Henrietta Crane Russell, Edmund's wife (*Werner's Voice Magazine* 1890: 5).

The third section of Potter's column, "The Toilet" offered hints on beauty culture, such as patterns for "artistic hygienic" dress, clothing that tried to satisfy the requirements both of dress reform and fashion. There seemed to be a dress for every conceivable occasion, complexion, and build in Potter's pages and, reflecting Edmund Russell's travels, they also appropriated the styles of numerous ethnicities. Many of the designs frankly looked like theatrical costumes; some appear to have been the leisure clothes of famous performers like Sarah Bernhardt and Marie Bonfanti. In one instance, the same dress was even presented, little altered, in two different columns. In one it was called "Stage Dress, Special Design for a Stout Lady," and in another, "Evening Dress for a Stout Lady." The theatrical effect was further enhanced here and there by a list of make-up necessary for amateurs.

In this version of Delsarte-inspired aestheticism, all the world is a stage, in its narrowest sense. The interpenetration of the realms of art and life does not lead to ennoblement or spiritual refinement, or even to practical improvement, as it did in the case of the physical culturists, but rather to an obsessive degree of self-cultivation, that was a constant testimony to one's currency, in several senses of that word. First, one demonstrated that one was *au courant*, and as a corollary, one embodied an entire economy in which one demonstrated not just familiarity with all the "best" people and cultural icons, but also the ability to imitate or become them. And as a not-insignificant aside, one demonstrated that one had the means to do so. The emphasis is frankly acquisitive: the artistic life, in this context, is cultivated, but it is also purchased and collected. While Stebbins and others saw the Greek marbles as symbols of the potential for human nobility in its most profound sense, and the Thomases used Greek statues as models of proper feminine proportions to correct the possible influence of fashionable bad habits, for Potter the Greek statues simply offered the lure of a desirable image, much as women might, and did, model themselves after a famous actress. And the exercises in which Potter's readers imitated gods and goddesses were described in the language of modern beauty magazines: "of practical personal import to develop your powers" (Potter 1891: 270).

In fact, the artistic perfection that Potter urged her readers to cultivate masked a disturbing escapism and an utter lack of contact with the real problems of the urban industrial world. Although Potter cited the many contemporary instances of corruption in high office as a sign that moral education was needed to counterbalance physical and intellectual development, her "moral education" is little more than narcissistic self-cultivation and capitalistic acquisitiveness in disguise. This quest for the perfection of art in life perhaps reflects one logical conclusion of Spencer's evolutionary ideas, but it is Calvinism – and Delsarte – gone badly awry.

THE CONSTRUCTION OF CLASS

The Delsartian injunction to remake the body along noble lines addressed a variety of class anxieties that seem to have preoccupied the middle and upper classes in the latter part of the nineteenth century. These anxieties had their roots both in the economic instability of the period and in the floods of immigration. Americans with longstanding lineage in the nation worried about which cultural groups would dominate the future of the United States, and manifested their concern by performing popular- and home-theatrical versions of the dialects and customs of non-WASP groups. They were also fascinated with the allegedly healthy posture, natural grace and boundless energy of the immigrants, as opposed to the tired neurasthenia of the white collar "brain workers" (Green 1986: 138–9).

Anxiety about the future of American culture also showed itself in an obsession with the allegedly flourishing birth rates of the immigrants, and with the declining birth rates for urban and suburban WASPs (Green 1983: 8; 1986: 224). Physical culture for women was one of the solutions proposed to make middle-class super-mothers, and the Thomases presented this solution draped in heroic Roman splendor:

> At the time the Romans were giving so much attention to physical development in order that they might have magnificent warriors; every attention was given to the training of young men, but still they did not meet that perfect ability desired. This caused them to infer that the imperfectly developed physique of the mothers must be the barrier to the desired end, and so a course of athletic training was established for women and girls, and no nation has produced such perfectly and symmetrically formed men and women as was the result of this training. The Roman matron and Roman warrior are synonymous terms.
>
> (1892: 5–6)

When we consider that this statement was made at a time when middle-class men were training in order to put down strikes by workers who were mainly immigrants, the Thomases' construction of American women as Roman matrons is not perhaps as benign as it might seem.

Delsartians seem to have shared the period's fascination with the Americanization of immigrant groups, which they sometimes discussed in terms that suggest Lamarckian inheritance. Helen Potter demonstrated this in one of her columns:

> How do we know [a person's ethnic background]? Because they show it. Their thoughts, lives, and habits running for a long period in one channel have made of them distinct peoples. They look the distinct nationality in face, form, dress and manner. But if they live here under new conditions of thought and government, they change. Their children and grand-children become Americanized, until, after a few generations, the old manner of looks are altogether lost, and they become Americans, and speak of their ancestors as we do of our English forefathers, and with the same feeling.
>
> (1891: 270)

Some social reform segments of the middle class were not content just to cultivate themselves. Unwilling to wait for time to take its course, they took an aggressive stand on the assimilation of immigrant groups to middle-class mores. The National Christian League for the Promotion of Social Purity, for example, the organization for which Genevieve Stebbins gave a benefit, was in 1892 already talking about kindergartens to keep the poorest children "out of the paths of temptation," classes in which young women could be taught to earn their living by means other than prostitution, and the encouragement of early marriage in the working classes as a way of decreasing "vice" (National Christian League 1892–3: 12, 16). After the turn of the century, they were firmly committed to eugenics, which they referred to as "spiritual and scientific mating" (National Christian League 1904: 18).

Delsartians generally did not go as far as the social reformers. However, that they did consider Delsarte as a tool for assimilation was evident in the somewhat confused belief that if children were trained in Delsarte, "there would be no bias of birth or custom to overcome in later years" (Morgan 1889: 9). At one and the same time, these remarks illustrate a cherished American faith in the democratic experiment, together with an endorsement of what amounts to cultural retraining of body, mind, and spirit in an upper-class, Northern-European-biased communication system.

However, most Delsarte practitioners were not immigrants, but upper- and middle-class people with roots in the United States: society ladies interested in "defining and confirming the authority of high society" (Banta 1987: 652), provincial middle-class women cultivating refinement, or the newly rich trying to "display the outward behavior that suggested the qualities of the lady and the gentleman" (ibid.: 635). As such, Delsarte was a marker of the extreme social mobility of the time, both its hopefulness for those "on the rise," and its anxiety for the currently privileged. A number of Delsarte manuals seem to have had a subtext of using the very codification of Delsarte to distinguish, even exaggerate, the markings of class, and to characterize and extirpate lower-class behavior in favor of deportment that evoked either the Greek past or the English aristocracy. This was, after all, a period of obsession with lineage (Green 1986: 223), and specifically with what was perceived as the "correct" lineage for America and Americans. Elite Americans busily tried to (re)construct the nation's history and its holidays, such as Thanksgiving, to reflect an impeccable genealogy that extended from the Greeks and Romans, to England and thence to the United States. Individuals eager to demonstrate their place in this lineage founded the Daughters of the American Revolution in 1890. Even *Werner's Magazine* stressed the honorable heritages of the Delsartian performers Kate Weaver and Leotta.

Delsarte offered not just a chance, but a mandate, to remake bodies of "the best type"[3] that resonated with the anthropometric and physiognomic studies of the time. And some Delsartians, like their social science counter-parts, strayed into ethnic and racial stereotyping. Anna Morgan, for example, interpreted dilated nostrils as "anger" within the context of her own culture, but also asserted that a nose "cast in an heroic or graceful mould [a classical Greek or Roman model?] is rarely found dissociated with some other admirable qualities of heart or mind" (1889: 47). On the other hand, a receding brow and projecting cheekbones signified "mental density," and "[h]eavy, sensuous lips, square, massive jaws, and a thick neck leave room for conjecture as to the prevailing traits of the person possessing them" (ibid.: 47–8). This particular reading of character from appearance had its seeds in François Delsarte's own words, when he advised the Philotechnic Society that there is a difference between "the swift and flexible movements of an elegant organism and those evolutions clumsily executed by the torpid limbs hardened by constant labor" (Stebbins [1895] 1902: 124).

In cultivating the ideal body, the movement values Delsarte training fostered – grace, flexibility, poise, economy of gesture – were associated with nobility in the sense of the Northern European aristocrat. For a student of acting who might portray a peasant type, such observations could be useful; but in the American Delsarte manuals they took on different overtones. When Stebbins asked her readers in *Society Gymnastics* to cultivate "the poise of Greeks" and to behave "like gods and heroes, superbly calm in their inner nature, whatever might be the outer tempest" (1888: 11–12), one feels that she was not just offering images of supreme repose, but potential models of aristocratic aloofness and superiority. And when she cast the elevating benefits of Delsarte in explicit class terms, an unmistakable sense of smugness crept in: "If mere physical work were all that is necessary, our mechanics would be models of bearing, and washerwomen would have the presence of duchesses" (ibid.: 7).

Perhaps part of the confusion existed because Delsarte's ideas on the relative expressiveness of different classes appear to have overlapped with Herbert Spencer's ideas about the evolution of societies from simple to complex. When Stebbins, quoting Delsarte, but echoing Spencer, counseled: "[T]he higher classes have a gamut of expression subtler than those of the lower" ([1895] 1902: 124), her readers might think, with some satisfaction, about their own bearing in comparison to the less cultured attitudes and mannerisms of the many working-class immigrants.

In Anna Morgan's *An Hour with Delsarte* (1889) these ideas about shaping the body were given an ever-so-slightly cruder and more explicit twist. Drawing on phrenological and physiological research, Morgan built an image of the ideal human being, discarding at every turn images that she associated with the lower, generally non-WASP classes:

> Undue prominence of the abdomen [in Delsartian terms a sign of overabundant sensuality] need not be confined to the lower classes . . . one would have no difficulty in finding it in the upper grades of society, where it is unpardonable.
>
> (1889: 13)

Like her contemporaries in many fields, Morgan constructed a rough evolutionary model, in her case, one for looking at movement values along gross cultural and ethnic lines. Standard Delsartian analysis would say that movement in a straight line – the movement of much manual labor – was considered lower down the evolutionary scale than movement in the curved or spiral line that American Delsarte valued. So Eleanor Georgen demonstrated the difference between a lady's curtsey and a maid's: the lady's curtsey makes full use of at least two dimensions in space, while the maid's is a simple, one-dimensional up-and-down bob (Georgen 1893:

81–2). Morgan asserted that the limbs, the primary vital or sensuous zone of the body, reached their greatest physical power in the "inferior races" (1889: 45–6). She seemed to suggest that the forte of the "inferior races" was mere brute strength. On the other hand, the "advanced races," whom Morgan specifically labeled "intellectuals," or "highly sensitive organisms" were characterized by their flexibility (ibid.: 46, 47). It is hard not to see in this phrase a reference to the middle-class urban industrial "brain workers," with their neurasthenia, the very group that had been perceived as progressively weakening over the course of the century. But in Morgan's version, Delsarte does not just democratically ennoble, or physically condition and improve. Rather, it affirms the a priori superiority of the "brain workers." It is as though she were saying, "We know they're the 'best type.' We just have to get them to behave that way."

> Art is the tendency of the fallen soul
> toward its primitive purity or its final splendor.
>
> François Delsarte (1902: 65)

T. J. Jackson Lears has written of the anti-modernist impulses that arose in the late 1800s as reactions against the social and scientific optimism and the economic rationalism of the nineteenth century. As we have seen, many of the ways Delsarte was used by Americans speak to what Lears calls a "crisis of cultural authority" (1981: 5) in the United States, or a series of crises that revolved around the effects of immigration, business culture, economic mobility and instability, the changing roles of women, and the diminishment of religious faith. Certainly, much of the rhetoric surrounding Delsartism in America sounds anti-modernist: the evocation of a more-perfect past, a turning to aestheticism, critiques of overcivilization and urban industrialism, the privileging of "feminine" realms of experience, and the quest for what Lears calls "authentic experience" (ibid.) in the form of dramatic endeavors, and more natural and spontaneous expression. Then too, the cultivation of spiral movement and organicity, the focus on breath and voice, the insistence on spirituality all point to the Orientalism that pervaded some anti-modernism.

Yet if Delsarte harked back to an historical ideal, it was the Greece of Apollo, not Dionysus. For all its yearnings to promote change, Delsartism ultimately had more in common with the very systems it sought to combat, above all because it was a rational system. Not only did some of its practitioners loosely use the language of economic rationalism. Delsarte, which its practitioners often proudly called a "science," itself attempted to rationalize some of the least-understood elements in American society, notably the infant social sciences, especially psychology and sociology. While Delsarte manuals often contained some critique of what Lears calls "the internalized morality of self control," and called for relaxation, nevertheless, they substituted a system of self-discipline and self-conscious-ness that was at least as elaborate as its Calvinist and Victorian predecessors, and that mandated the harmony of mind and emotions. Although Delsarte claimed to be a means of restoring "natural" self-expression, it had far more in common with what Lears called "the drive for efficient control of nature under the banner of improving human welfare" (ibid.: 57). Furthermore, the very idea of self-improvement that found such varied manifestations in American Delsarte, presupposes an optimistic rationalism. Delsarte, with its actor's compendium of significant gestures, postures, and roles, provided a technology by which the elite could maintain their hegemony and, at the same time, people of different genders, classes, and cultures could potentially be assimilated into a harmonious social fabric. In this regard, American Delsarte's emphasis on precise recipes for balance, integration, organicity, both in posture and in color, resonates, both magically and ironically, with the social dislocations of the period.

The fact that American Delsarte is pervaded by rationalist elements does not make it any the less anti-modern. Lears observes that much anti-modernism was "a muddle" (ibid.: 57), and American Delsarte was no exception. That muddle was evidence of the ambivalence of the ruling bourgeoisie to the real social and cultural changes that would have to be enacted to seriously address anti-modernism. And perhaps more importantly, it was testimony to the complexity and persistence of the problems facing American culture then and now.

NOTES

1 The following observations owe an obvious debt to the discussion of culture in Raymond Williams's *Keywords: A Vocabulary of Culture and Society* (1983: 87–93). For an example of some of these usages in contemporary literature see Alice Ives *et al.*, *Our Society: A Complete Treatise on the Usages that Govern the Most Refined Homes and Social Circles*, Detroit, MI: Darling Bros & Co., 1891, especially 368–401.

2 In making this point, I do not wish to imply that Delsarte was never used to portray "strong women's" roles. For a more detailed analysis of the varieties of Delsarte performance, see my master's thesis, "Niobe and the Amazons," New York University, 1989. I am also aware that this discussion avoids the entire issue of melodrama which is quite important in understanding women's performance of Delsarte.

3 This phrase is a deliberate echo of Martha Banta's chapter, "Looking for the 'Best' Type," in *Imaging American Women: Idea and Ideals in Cultural History*. While Banta's focus is the search for types of the American Girl, it contains a useful consideration of the period's classification and differential valuation of ethnic and racial types, particularly the elevation of the "Anglo-Saxon" type and the denigration of Southern Europeans, Blacks, and Native Americans as inferior (1987: 111–21). Another important backdrop for any study of classical influences on Euro-centric constructions of American lineage is Martin Bernal's *Black Athena: The Afro-Asiatic Roots of Classical Civilization*, New Brunswick, NJ: Rutgers University Press, 1987, especially chapters VI and VII.

BIBLIOGRAPHY

Alger, Rev. W. B. (1885) "A True System of Gymnastics," *The Voice* (April): 55–6.

Arnold, S. L. (1887) "The Delsarte Gymnastics in the Public Schools," *The Voice* (November): 175.

Baker, G. M. (1889) *Forty Minutes with a Crank; or, The Seldarte Craze*, Boston: Walter H. Baker & Co.

Banta, M. (1987) *Imaging American Women: Idea and Ideals in Cultural History*, New York: Columbia University Press.

Bishop, E. M. (1892) *Americanized Delsarte Culture*, Meadville, PA: Hood & Vincent.

Delsarte, François (1902) "Delsarte's Address Before the Philotechnic Society of Paris," in G. Stebbins, *Delsarte System of Expression*, New York: E. S. Werner.

Douglas, A. ([1977] 1988) *The Feminization of American Culture*, New York: Anchor Press.

Gallagher, C. and Laqueur, T. (eds) (1981) *The Making of the Modern Body*, Berkeley: University of California Press.

Georgen, E. (1893) *The Delsarte System of Physical Culture*, New York: Butterick Publishing Co.

Green, H. (1983) *The Light of the Home*, New York: Pantheon.

—— (1986) *Fit for America*, New York: Pantheon.

Jowitt, D. (1988) "The Search for Motion," in *Time and the Dancing Image*, New York: William Morrow & Company, Inc., 69–102.

Kendall, E. (1979) *Where She Danced*, New York: Alfred A. Knopf.

Lears, T. J. J. (1981) *No Place of Grace: Antimodernism and the Transformation of American Culture 1880–1920*, New York: Pantheon Books.

MacKaye, P. (1927) *Epoch: The Life of Steele MacKaye*, New York: Boni & Liverwright.

Morgan, A. (1889) *An Hour with Delsarte*, Boston: Lee & Shepard.

Morley, M. W. (1887) "Gymnastics for Children," *The Voice* (January): 7–8.

National Christian League for the Promotion of Purity (1904) Constitution and By-Laws with Reports of the Fourteenth Annual Meeting, March 26, 1904, New York: David Brown.

—— (1913) Constitution and By-Laws with Reports of the Twenty-Third Annual Meeting, March 27, 1913, New York.

National Christian League for the Promotion of Social Purity (1893), Constitution and By-Laws, with President's Address and Secretary's and Treasurer's Annual Reports for 1892–3, New York.

New York Times (1892) "Entertained by Miss Stebbins" (November 26): 9.

Potter, H. (1891) "Beauty and Artistic Dress," *Werner's Voice Magazine* (November): 269–71.

—— (1892) "Beauty and Artistic Dress," *Werner's Voice Magazine* (March): 64–6.

Ruyter, N. L. C. (1979) *Reformers and Visionaries*, Brooklyn, NY: Dance Horizons.

St. Denis, R. (1960) Interview with Walter Terry, Phonotape No. *MGZT 7-57, New York Public Library Dance Collection.

Shelton, S. (1981) *Divine Dancer: Biography of Ruth St. Denis*, Garden City, NY: Doubleday.

Solomon, B. M. (1985) *In the Company of Educated Women*, New Haven, CT: Yale University Press.

Spencer, M. (1882) "The Gospel of Relaxation," *Popular Science Monthly* (January): 354–9.

Stebbins, G. (1888) *Society Gymnastics and Voice Culture*, New York: E. S. Werner.

—— ([1895] 1902) *Delsarte System of Expression*, sixth edition, New York: E. S. Werner. New York: Dance Horizons.

The Voice (1883) "Which Is the Better?" (November): 168.

—— (1884) "The Delsarte System: Furnishing a True Science of Acting and Oratory," [E. S. Werner], *The Voice* (May): 66–7.

Thomas, J. and Thomas, A. (1892) *Psycho-Physical Culture*, New York: Edgar S. Werner.

Werner's Voice Magazine (1890) "False Delsartism," (January): 5.

—— (1892) "Women's Waists," (January): 24.

Wilbor, Elsie S. (1891) "Delsarte Echoes from Chautauqua. 'Americanizing' Delsarte," *Werner's Voice Magazine* (October): 250–2.

Williams, R. (1983) *Keywords: A Vocabulary of Culture and Society*, New York: Oxford University Press.

13 Jazz Modernism

Constance Valis Hill

Jazz is the product of a restless age: an age in which the fever of war is only now beginning to abate its fury; when men and women, after their efforts in the great struggle, are still too much disturbed to be content with a tranquil existence; when freaks and stunts and sensation are the order – or disorder – of the day; when painters delight in portraying that which is not, and sculptors in twisting the human limbs into strange, fantastic shapes; when America is turning out her merchandise at an unprecedented speed and motor cars are racing along the roads . . . and the whole world is rushing helter skelter in unknown directions.

R. W. S. Mendl (1927)

During the 1920s, jazz swept Paris like a whirlwind, its speed and syncopated rhythm echoing the mood of a society turned upside down by global war and massive technological change. Jazz affected not only social life in the post-war era, but art, music, literature, and, not the least, dance. This essay will look at the ways in which ballet choreographers working in Paris responded to the urgent rhythms of the Jazz Age.

By 1920, Europe had already experienced the cakewalk and was weathering a ragtime craze in which syncopated rhythms cut traditional time "in tatters." But the arrival of jazz, with its intricate propulsive rhythms, polyphonic ensemble playing, improvisatory solos, and melodic freedom was an altogether more profound upheaval.

After sampling such revues as *Laissez-les tomber!* (Let Them Drop!) of 1917, Parisians may not have fully understood the new American form, or even how to spell it,[1] but they knew it meant energetic dancing, full body movement, and personal expression. Like ragtime, Parisian jazz music was rarely improvised, but its fiercely insistent beat, built-in syncopation, and deliberately pitched notes made a dramatic contrast to the painstaking formalities of European dance music. It was the dancing, then, and not strictly jazz music that became the reigning obsession of the Parisian Jazz Age.

In 1918 Comte Etienne de Beaumont, that inveterate host of extravagant soirées, staged a "Great Negro Fête," the first private party in Paris to feature American jazz supplied by American soldiers on leave from the front. Parisian socialites weren't the only ones snapping their fingers and trotting to jazz. The general public turned out nightly by the thousands to dance the one-step and foxtrot. The streets and alleys of Montmartre became the center of Parisian jazz, turning the area into a trans-Atlantic reflection of Harlem. But everywhere in Paris, there was a band playing a rough version of swinging jazz rhythms that made people want to move.

Artists, too, were stricken with jazz fever. Piet Mondrian, whose friends dubbed him "The Dancing Madonna," painted stylized steps by day and danced to the current rhythms of jazz by night. Blaise Cendrars used African motifs and jazzlike compositional patterns in his writings; Erik Satie transposed ragtime clichés into his score for the ballet *Parade*; Igor Stravinsky, inspired, he wrote, "by the passion I felt for jazz which burst into my life suddenly after the war ended," (1936b: 78) composed *Ragtime*.

The twenties saw a profusion of ballets inspired by jazz and American themes, including Jean Cocteau's *Le Boeuf sur le toit*, set in an American bar during Prohibition; Jean Wiener's *Arc en ciel*, accompanied by the croons and shouts of a black banjo player; Jean Börlin's *Within the Quota*, to music by Cole Porter; Bronislava Nijinska's *Impressions de Music Hall* with ballet dancers doing the charleston on pointe; and Leonide Massine's *Crescendo*, which boasted a chorus of tap dancers "jigging to the tune of cocktails and jazz" (Massine 1968: 165).

Despite the infatuation with *rhythm américain*, the French often misunderstood and misused jazz. "So," according to pianist Jean Wiener, "you got jazz bands whose only purpose was to make as much noise as possible – bells, klaxons, drums, revolvers. The music was absolutely foreign to the French at that time" (Goddard 1979: 16). Because the French were not always clear on the new American form, some historians maintain that ballet choreographers used jazz simply for modish decoration. Lynn Garafola writes in her history of the Ballets Russes, "Jazz served as background; like a Chanel swimsuit, it gave the action of the ballet an aura of chic modernity" (1989: 112).

However, twenties choreographers were not only attracted to trend-setting dances, like the charleston, that could be tossed into an otherwise traditional ballet. Although some dance makers clearly relished this easy kind of appropriation (and their handiwork was much in evidence), serious choreographers responded to more fundamental jazz elements. They explored the structural and dynamic aspects of jazz music such as speed, dissonance, polytonality and polyrhythms that accented, pulsed and even suspended time. They assimilated the parts of jazz dances that isolated body parts, squared the port de bras, and created new body dynamics. By the end of the decade, these choreographers' experiments had infiltrated the dance vocabulary as well as dancers' bodies. Leonide Massine spoke for many choreographers when he said in a 1925 interview with *The Dancing Times*,

(Jazz) is an art form which represents the speed of modern life. . . . It has as much melody as the valse and the quadrille and it has rhythm, the essential part of it . . . we cannot resist or get away from jazz, because we cannot avoid our own life. . . . Modern choreography finds its highest expression in jazz.

(1925b: 1139)

JAZZ WITH A FRENCH ACCENT

Jean Cocteau wrote in 1919:

I listen to a jazz band at the Casino de Paris. . . . The Negroes . . . lash about, waddle . . . to blows of the trumpet and rattle. A dance tune – broken, sparring, in counterpoint – rises from time to time to the surface. The hot hall, full of painted girls and American soldiers, is a saloon in movies of the Far West.

(1919: 4)

This show for American soldiers was inspiration for Cocteau's *Le Boeuf sur le toit*, first performed at the Comédie des Champs-Elysées on February 21, 1920. Subtitled "The Nothing-Doing Bar" and set in an American bar during Prohibition, the ballet–farce was inhabited by a Negro Boxer, Black Dwarf, Lady of Fashion, Redheaded Woman, Bookmaker, Barman and Policeman who, like "divers at the bottom of the sea," moved in deliberate slow-motion against rapid-paced, syncopated rhythms. The dancers, wearing oversized masks and wielding blown-up props, were acrobats, clowns and dwarfs from the Cirque Medrano who improvised dances within the framework of the musical score by Darius Milhaud. Georges Auric's foxtrot, "Adieu New York," performed by the tap dance team Footit and Jackley, opened the program; and "American Cocktails," not drinks but a jazz band specializing in popular American tunes, played in the foyer during intermission.

Experiments with jazz had already been made by Erik Satie, in "Ragtime du Paquebot" from *Parade* (a ragtime dance syncopated with the sounds of a typewriter, roulette wheel and revolver shots) and by Stravinsky in *Ragtime*. But it was Milhaud who would use jazz more extensively in orchestrations for the ballet. First exposed to popular Brazilian music and carnival melodies in Rio de Janeiro in 1917,[2] he returned to Paris after the war's end, tantalized by the rhythms of tangos, maxixes, sambas and Portuguese fados. The score for *Boeuf* was a fantasia of these rhythms, played in rapid sequence with a recurring rondo-like theme between each of the airs. In Brazil, Milhaud became fascinated with dancers who amused themselves by improvising words to a tune repeated over and over again, and "the monotony of their never-ending chorus, with its insistent rhythm" was hypnotic (Milhaud 1953: 74); this he effected in his score for *Boeuf*, in which syncopated rhythms of the maxixe and tango were run "from one hand to the other" (ibid.: 74) in an endless propulsion of rhythm.

By moving dancers and props in a sustained slow-motion, against the irregular beats and the rapid pace of the music, Cocteau created a poly-rhythmic scenography. It was a visual counterpart to the "dance tune – broken, sparring, in counterpoint," he heard at the Casino de Paris. In slow-motion, to the tempo of a slow blues, the Bookmaker does a triumphant little dance to a samba, the women dance a tango, the Gentleman and Bookmaker play a game of dice to a samba, the Policeman turns with the grace of a ballerina to the lively syncopations of a maxixe; and when by mistake the Policeman is decapitated, the Redheaded Woman in a Salomé-like dance shakes his head to the rhythm of maracas as though it were a cocktail.[3] "I wanted *Boeuf* to be the opposite of everything the Ballets Russes represented," Cocteau declared. In his "spirit of contradiction, which is the form of the spirit of creation" (Ries 1986: 60) he discovered rhythm, which became the basis for his experiments with movement and physical forms of expression.

Cocteau and his circle of modernist composers, known as Les Six,[4] were searching for a leaner and more economical musical style that permitted angular and dissonant harmonies and greater rhythmic freedom. They frequented the Bar Gaya where Jean Wiener played syncopated music with sensitivity and an especially light rhythm. With partner Vance Lowry, an African American saxophonist and banjo player, Wiener would segue from fashionable foxtrots to Bach, and then invite the group to *venez jas ce soir* ("come 'jazz' tonight"). "We arrived early and stayed late," recalls Milhaud, "There was always one part of the evening when we were all alone and free to make music to our hearts' content" (1953: 120). Their improvisations bore theatrical fruit at the Théâtre Michel in 1921: *Caramel mou*, subtitled "Shimmy for Jazz-band," was performed by the black dancer Johnny Gratton to words by Cocteau and music by Milhaud. As Gratton improvised, his feet shuffling close to the ground "avec une réligieuse gravité," Milhaud played piano and Cocteau intoned over the music: "J'ai connu un jeune homme malheureux en amour, qui jouait les Nocturnes de Chopin sur le tambour" (Auric 1979: 177). The juxtaposition of dancer, piano, and poet, with its random cross-rhythm of taps, keyboard and vocal˙explosives, duplicated the improvisational framework of jazz musicians.

It was the freedom of the jazz solo, and its flagrant self-expressiveness, that attracted these modernists. At the Casino de Paris, Cocteau heard "a cataclysm in sound . . . strange squawks from the saxophone, grotesque little cries from a muted cornet and violent perversions of time on the pianoforte" (1926: 14). Listening to the "new music" in London, Darius Milhaud marveled at how "the saxophone breaking in, squeezing out the juice of dreams, or the trumpet, dramatic or languorous by turns [and] the lyrical use of the trombone, glancing with its slide over quarter-tones in crescendos of volume and pitch" (1953: 119) intensified feeling. The new orchestral timbre enforced rhythmical irregularity, allowing musicians the freedom to duplicate animal sounds, such as horses whinnying and tigers growling. The expressive possibilities of each instrument within the ensemble, along with the constant use of syncopation in the melody and its contrapuntal freedom, led Milhaud to consider the idea of adapting jazz timbres and rhythms into a chamber work.

In 1922, after a trip to New York where he spent countless evenings in Harlem clubs absorbing jazz, Milhaud wrote:

> Against the beat of the drums, the melodic lines crisscrossed in a breathless pattern of broken and twisted rhythms. . . . This authentic music had its roots in the darkest corners of the Negro soul, the vestigial traces of Africa. Its effect on me was so overwhelming, I could not tear myself away.
>
> (ibid.: 127)

A year later he was invited by Swedish producer Rolf de Maré to create a new ballet, in collaboration with scene designer Fernand Léger, choreographer Jean Börlin and writer Blaise Cendrars, whose subject was the creation of the world as represented in African folklore. At once, Milhaud recognized the opportunity to arrange his orchestra like those he had heard in Harlem. Utilizing seventeen solo instruments including jazz saxophone, his score for *La Création du monde*, performed by Ballets Suédois at the Théâtre des Champs-Elysées in 1923, had shocking polytonal harmonies, dissonant "wrong-notes" and a cacophony of rhythmical effects described as "going back to tom-toms, xylophones, bellowing brass and noise" (Häger 1990: 190).

When the curtain rose on near blackness to reveal an inchoate mass of dancers, the giant figures of Mzame, Mebere and Nkwa, African gods of creation, gradually materialized and chanted magical incantations. Out of the central mass of entwined bodies, and to the accompanying squawk and thunder of brass and percussion,[5] life commenced to erupt: trees shot up, leaves fell from their branches and, touching the earth, metamorphosed into huge insects; birds (transported by ballerinas en pointe) flew, and crane-like creatures (ballet dancers on stilts) stalked the earth. Against the abrupt shift of melodic and percussive themes, each creature evolved individually until, at last, human appendages began to appear – a leg, a torso, and finally a complete man and woman. Léger's designs for the gods, birds, and creatures were conceived on the basis of geometric motifs and primary colors. Their abstract forms were shifted and juxtaposed by masked dancers in a mechanical choreography that gave the stage a physical dynamism. The multiple backdrops of clouds and mountains revealed a "syncopated" sense of rhythm, through the drastic alternation of color, the transition from negative to positive space in depicting contiguous parts of a scene, the spacing between objects of altering height and the many adjacent right angles (Brender 1986: 130). The orchestra further enhanced the syncopation by playing independently of the dancers' steps, which in turn were deliberately out of time with the music and independent of the rhythm of Léger's mobile forms. In this kaleidoscope of shifting shapes and color constellations, a totally abstract choreography was created involving pure forms of movement freed from the limitation of the human body.

La Création du monde opened possibilities for music and movement, rhythm and form, to unfold side by side as equal and autonomous entities. Confessing to "exploiting the jazz style unreservedly, blending it with a classical feel" (Häger 1990: 191), Milhaud smeared his melody with a crude and sliding counterpoint. His counter-rhythms worked so strangely against each other they suggested the polyrhythms of African music.

Africa was present, too, in Börlin's choreography which was inspired by Sub-Saharan sculpture, as evidenced by an earlier Ballets Suédois solo, *Sculpture nègre* (1920), in which he emulated the forms and mass of African sculpture in a series of cubist plastiques. Although Börlin was a Fokine-trained dancer,[6] critics commented that he resisted the classical style of the *danseur noble*, used his head, arms and legs in slightly angular positions and was weighted in his movement (Paillot 1924: n.p.). Little is written about Börlin's choreography for *Création*, or the "Adam and Eve pas de deux" he danced with Ebon Strand at the climax of the ballet. But Cendrars, in eulogizing Börlin, compared his dancing to that of "a mulatto, Negro" and praised his rhythmic invention, which was surely the ballet's most salient feature:

> With your Swedish peasant feet, you are the exact opposite of the Ballets Russes. You've thrown a monkey wrench into the French balletic tradition as it has come down to us from the *ancien régime* and Italianism via St. Petersburg. . . . You've discovered rhythm, the beautiful rhythm of today.
>
> (Brender 1986: 134)

The evidence is circumstantial, but taken altogether – Börlin's being compared to an African American dancer, Milhaud's jazz-orchestrated score, Cendrars' Africanist sources, Léger's "syncopated" designs – the artistic collaborators of *La Création du monde* succeeded in creating their vision of a jazz ballet.

JAZZ AS L'ESPRIT NOUVEAU

One of the many speculations about the origin of the name "jazz" was that it was a slang term for speed.[7] "The whole idea of speed was in the air," Marcel Duchamp observed (Kern 1983: 124).[8] "Life is more fragmented and faster-moving than in previous periods and artists are seeking a dynamic art to depict it," Léger wrote (ibid.: 118). Jazz expressed the swift and breathless excitement generated by the rushes of the moving picture, the dynamism of airplanes and fast cars, the synaptic dash-and-dot phrasing of the telegraph. Its sudden shifts in tempo and new percussive textures gave an overall impression of the excitement and unpredictability of contemporary life. "All modern dances look dull next to this powerful, sustained concentration of speed" exclaimed Mondrian (Troy 1984: 640), who painted "Foxtrot A&B" and "Broadway Boogie Woogie." These artists were responding to the pulse of a changing world, as were the artistic collaborators of *Le Train bleu*, presented by Diaghilev's Ballets Russes at the Théâtre des Champs-Elysées in June 1924. Sleek in line, swift in motion, and "full of references to the crazes of the 1920s, from sunbathing and snapshots to movies and maillots" (Morris 1990: 10), the ballet was the embodiment of the Jazz Age. Cocteau's scenario of the young and fashionable frolicking on the Côte d'Azur blended the insouciance of the Parisian élite with the athletic prowess of Jazz-Age youth. Milhaud's score for *Le Train bleu* accelerated the tempos of popular music-hall songs and ballroom dance rhythms. Pablo Picasso's enlarged gouache for the front curtain captured the freedom of women running hand-in-hand along a sandy beach. And Henri Lauren's cabana beach set, "Coco" Chanel's twenties sportswear, and Nijinska's choreography, which mined the expressive possibilities of athletics and ballroom dance, all combined, observed Frederick Ashton, to bring "the modern world onto the stage" (Vaughan 1977: 8). "The first point about *Le Train bleu*," Diaghilev wrote, "is that there is no blue train in it. This being the age of speed it has already reached its destination and disembarked its passengers."[9] Neither a train nor plane, which passes over the beach, are physically present in the ballet. But these symbols, as well as the speed, gaiety and freedom so often associated with the Jazz Age, are personified. In the opening rush of activity, couples dance the tango, beach boys flex their muscles and swagger like strongmen, and bathing beauties dive into the arms of their partners, their legs fluttering like fish out of water.[10] The chorus of Gigolos jog and somersault while the Poules, in the spirit of the newly-liberated woman, kick legs like flappers doing the charleston and flirt with whomever they please.

But it is ballet that is truly liberated in *Le Train bleu*. Nijinska uses steps (double tours, entrechats and indeed the whole academic vocabulary) with astonishing freedom. The pas de bourrée, which once represented a girl's joyous scamper, is now used as an instrument of flirtation and gains a new seductive expression. Virtuosic steps, once belonging to the solo *danseur*, are now delivered by all the men in the corps with a sporty bravado. Variations in Beau Gosse and Perlouse's pas de deux become displays of one-upsmanship in which each tries to outdo the other. Nijinska has turned ballet into a sport, and in doing so finds a new choreographic voice. In the Tennis Champion's solo, ballet's attitude is translated into a preparation for swinging the tennis racket; penché arabesque is the illusion for stroking the ball; and jetés are darts across the court. In the finale, there is a duel between the (Golfer's) club and (Tennis Champion's) racket and the crowd watches, alternately moving in slow and fast motion. Stopping from time to time to pose before flashing cameras, the dancers reinforce the idea that *Le Train bleu* is a snapshot of the 1920s: it presents a world filled with speedsters and sportsters in tune with the quickstep of modern life.

This melding of speed, athleticism, and modernity with classical dance was only the beginning of Nijinska's absorption of jazz themes. When Stravinsky conducted his *Ragtime* (1917) for eleven solo instruments at the Paris Opéra in May 1925, it is possible that Nijinska, who was living in Paris, heard it for the first time. Shortly after, she created *Jazz* to Stravinsky's score, presenting it in August 1925, for the premiere of her new chamber company, Théâtre Choréographique Nijinska. *Jazz*, or *The Savage Jazz* as it was initially titled, saw the choreographer and her partner in blackface (their faces and bodies covered with dark liquid makeup), dancing to ragtime syncopations. While the character dance was "inspired by the twenties craze for black American art and culture" (Baer 1986: 52), there are earlier sources. Nijinska remembers seeing a performance of a "brown ballet," *L'Africaine*, in a summer resort theater near St. Petersburg in 1897, in which all the dancers "wore brown, heavy, wool-knitted tops and tights, big brass earrings and enormous black woolen wigs, their lips outlined broadly in red paint and their eyes in white and black" (Nijinska 1981: 25).

Alexandra Exter's designs for *Jazz* are remarkably similar to Nijinska's description of the "brown ballet." While the suggestion of blackface in the costume sketch (Baer 1986: 54) recalls the nineteenth-century minstrel performer, the costumes were very much of the twenties: a drop-waist, large red and white polka dot dress for Nijinska, and a rectangular tunic in broad red and white stripes for Eugene Lapitsky. Exter's manipulation of color reflected a fascination with "color interrelationship, co-intensity, rhythmization and the transition to color construction based on the laws of color."[11] The interplay of the diagonals and dots in the costumes with the syncopated rhythms of Stravinsky's score was surely intentional, and indicative of Exter's desire to thrust herself into modern life.[12] There is no record of Nijinska's choreography to know if the steps and movement patterns for *Jazz* were executed with a distinctly angular line. But given the peculiar use of instrumentation and syncopated rhythms that Stravinsky used with the utmost freedom and fantasy in his score,[13] how could Nijinska not have responded to those offbeat accents, irregular beats, and dotted quavers that produced the overall quality of swing? We know, at the very least, that Nijinska was exploring angularity and rhythm in other works of the period. *Les Noces* (1923), for instance, with its flexed and parallel feet, straight-legged jumps, speed and driving swing of the legs, invites comparison to jazz dance. Although its human assemblages, constructed pyramids and movement in simple, geometric planes are clearly influenced by Russian constructivism, they do share a similarity in form with the black Broadway chorus lines of *Shuffle Along* (1921).

Figure 13.1 Jazz: Alexandra Exter's costume design for Eugene Lapitzky and
Bronislava Nijinska, 1925. (Photo courtesy of the Fine Arts Museums of San
Francisco and the Nijinska Archives)

Nijinska was obviously familiar with some ragtime jazz dances – Cocteau had taken her to music halls in preparation for *Le Train bleu*, and Nijinska's *Impressions de Music-Hall*, a one-act ballet performed at the Paris Opéra in 1927, featured the reigning *étoile* Carlotta Zambelli backed by a line of chorus girls, on pointe, dancing a ragtime cakewalk. Nijinska herself confesses in her *Early Memoirs* that her first dance lessons came from Jackson and Johnson, a pair of African-American tap dancers who toured through Europe as music-hall artists:

> My first dancing lessons were from the two American tap dancers. They brought a small plank to our home one day, spread sand on it and taught me how to dance on the plank. . . . When Vaslav saw how quickly I picked up the routine and its rhythms he joined the lessons. He was surprised to find it was not as easy as it looked.
>
> (1981: 25)

"What interested Stravinsky and the others was above all the syncopated rhythms," says Jean Wiener (Goddard 1979: 277). From jazz, Stravinsky borrowed rhythmic principles which he broke down, tore apart, and fused again, making them independent nuclei for his musical discourse. Similarly, syncopated tap rhythms left an indelible impression on Nijinska, her response to jazz leading to the development of the rhythmic element in her choreography. The speed, offbeat accents, downward drive of weight and syncopated pas in her enchaînements were distillations of a classical technique that had absorbed black jazz dance and rhythm.

JAZZ EMBODIED

In 1925, Josephine Baker made her European debut and a new wave of jazz mania swept over Paris. Straight from New York, *La Revue nègre* opened at the Théâtre des Champs-Elysées with a virtually unknown cast. But in its fusion of African-American jazz and African art that was embodied by its star, Baker, the all-black musical revue symbolized a new cubist sensibility that savored angles and fragments, juxtaposition and frenetic energy. Straight out of the tap chorus lines of *Shuffle Along* and *Chocolate Dandies*, Baker played her body the way a jazz musician plays an instrument, as a series of fast and frenetic changes in tempo and dynamics. She waddled onto the stage, flat-footed and with her knees bent like an isosceles triangle, contorting her body and splaying her arms and legs as if they were dislocated. The rhythms of the music seemed to come from somewhere inside her. "It was she who led the spellbound drummer and the fascinated saxophonist in the harsh rhythm of the blues," André Levinson wrote, "It was as though the jazz, catching on the wing the vibrations of the body, was interpreting word by word its fantastic monologue. The music is born from the dance, and what a dance!" (Rose 1989: 31)

Sliding down her partner's back in "Danse Sauvage," Baker did a "stomach dance," an improvised combination of the shimmy, shake and mess-around, all popular black New York dances. The way she flung her arms and legs in the charleston signified liberty, freedom and the throwing off of old restraints. If, before 1914, French ideas about blacks were shaped by images of Africa as the "dark continent" peopled by dangerous and immoral savages; Paris after the war (due to African participation in the war effort and contact with American soldiers) viewed blacks as "noble savages" blessed with unfettered primitive spontaneity. The "discovery" of Baker, like the discovery of all things "nègre" by the European avant-garde, reflected modernism's affinity for the primitive. "The abstract, almost esoteric art of blacks is one of the most satisfying expressions of the contemporary spirit of anxiety," Paul Guillaume proclaimed after seeing Baker (Stich 1990: 209). Baker's figure, for the architect Le Corbusier, was matched only by the monumental, almost Egyptian, concrete grain elevators rising from the American plains. Singing "Baby" in a "stupid variety show," there was such an intense and dramatic sensibility in Baker's performance that Le Corbusier was moved to tears: "There is in this American Negro music a lyrical contemporary mass so invincible that I could see the foundation of a new sentiment of music capable of being the expression of the new epoch" (ibid.: 185).

BLURRED BOUNDARIES

The idea, first proposed by the futurists, that high art was corrupt and that cinema, circus, music-hall, and jazz held the keys to a new theatrical poetic, had materialized by the mid-twenties. Jean Wiener's ballet, *Arc en ciel*, which "styled movement to jazz rhythms," placed the black banjoist Vance Lowry onstage, strumming "first softly, then stridently, in the manner of a black coon shouter" (Malkiel 1925: 3). Jean Börlin, in *Within the Quota* for Ballets Suédois, "sacrificed ballet steps to the foxtrot, shimmy and those body-jerking dances performed in soft shoe" (Hagar 1990: 212). Cole Porter's musical score for *Quota* alternated the blues with the throbbing rhythms of ragtime, creating what was considered a new style of movement – "American rhythms worked into ballet form" (Orledge 1975: 25).

Dancers routinely shuffled back and forth between the concert and variety stage; the line demarcating the two blurred. The Théâtre des Champs-Elysées, "home of the grand ballet," became a stylish music hall and began catering to popular taste, under the management of Rolf de Maré (who produced *La Revue nègre*). While in London, West End music-halls and producers of variety shows, like Sir Oswald Stoll, had no compunction about combining ballet dances with animal and acrobatic acts on one program. Leonide Massine, settling in London after the financial disaster of the Ballets Russes' *The Sleeping Princess*,[14] worked as a freelance choreographer for West End musicals. Massine's "Togo: or, the Noble Savage," for the musical revue *You'd Be Surprised* which was subtitled "A Jazzaganza in two acts and fifteen surprises," was accompanied by the Savoy Havana Band playing a "saturnalia of syncopation." *Crescendo*, which Massine choreographed for C. B. Cochran's *On With the Dance*, had a score by Noël Coward that was a composite of jazz melodies. "The so-called classical mode is out of touch with modern life," Massine told *The Dancing Times* in 1925 about this new jazz ballet. "To make dancing vital, we must learn all we can from the Italo-French school of 300 years ago and transpose it into . . . modern jazz. We have to alter the direction of the ancient school and, by adapting its form and its steps, create a new spirit representative of the spirit of the age" (1925b: 1139).

George Balanchine also worked the music halls in the 1920s, and his early choreographies for Ballets Russes used contemporary ideas borrowed from popular culture. *Barabau* (1925) was a broad and earthy knockabout farce inspired by popular songs; *La Pastorale* (1926) told the tale of a Telegraph Boy who falls asleep beside his bicycle and wakes to find a film company at work on location; and in *Jack in the Box* (1926), ballerina Alexandra Danilova was cast as "The Black Dancer" in an acrobatic adagio. Balanchine himself donned blackface to dance the role of "Snowball" in *The Triumph of Neptune*. His choreography was described by Cyril Beaumont as "full of subtly contrasted rhythms, strutting walks, mincing steps and surging backward bendings of the body, borrowed from the cake-walk" (1951: 269). Jazz and musical theater were not new to Balanchine. One of his earliest choreographies was a ballet to Stravinsky's *Ragtime* for a school concert in 1920. In 1921, he created *Foxtrots* for his company, Young Ballet, as part of a demonstration concert in Petrograd, and in 1923, he devised movements to poems set to music for cabaret entertainments. The next year, when the Young Ballet went on a tour to Germany and decided not to return to the Soviet Union, the company went to London to perform in popular music halls. For the Opéra de Monte-Carlo in 1925, Balanchine choreographed *L'Enfant et les sortilèges*, with a score by Ravel that is usually cited as the composer's first use of ragtime jazz. Like Stravinsky, Balanchine was especially adept at assimilating jazz themes into his evolving choreographic style. It was a style which Levinson described in 1926 as a "wild exaggeration and mockery of the Classical School in which harmony, balance and grace of line were intentionally excluded and choreographic beauty disregarded" (Acocella and Garafola 1991: 67). In a review of *Pastorale* he charged that "the very articulation of the musical rhythm, in which double measures dominate" denied the slow development of the adagio and great arc of leaps through the air (ibid.).

Between 1929 and his arrival in the United States in 1933, Balanchine had several opportunities to take his jazz inspiration in new directions. "What Is This Thing Called Love" for C. B. Cochran's *Wake Up and Dream* (1929) was choreographed to music by Cole Porter and a short jazz number for Stoll's Variety Shows (1931) had the recorded music of Jack Hilton and His Dance Orchestra. In *Cochran's 1931 Revue*, Balanchine worked with the

Broadway choreographer and African American jazz tap dancer Clarence "Buddy" Bradley, who had devised dance routines for such stars as Gilda Gray, Ruby Keeler, and Eleanor Powell. From Bradley, Balanchine observed how simplified rhythms in the feet and black vernacular dance steps could reshape the body and add new dynamics to musical theater dance.[15] Even before his association with Bradley, Balanchine was influenced by jazz in such works as *Le Bal* (1929), in which he created angular poses with bent elbows and knees, turned-in positions of the legs, and syncopated steps. But more than an isolated ballet step turned jazzy, it was the synthesis of Jazz Age cultural influences that by the twenties' end pushed Balanchine to the threshold of a fully neo-classic style.

JAZZ MODERNISM

There is no one "ism," be it cubism, futurism, constructivism or expressionism, that single-handedly "modernized" ballet, giving it angularity and a downward drive of weight and speed while fracturing the timing of the phrase and turning in the feet. But we must not ignore the phenomenon that had ballerinas, en pointe, performing black American social dances on the concert stage – the shimmy, that torso-shaking dance done to blues music that isolated body parts; the leggy charleston, which tilted the torso to the horizontal to splay the arms and legs; and the snake-hips, which dropped the center of weight into the pelvis. These dances profoundly altered the line and form of the ballet dancer, as Jean Wiener observed, "Que la mode du jazz change les danses, qu'elle modifié la silhouette des danseuses, rien de plus naturel" (1984: 40).

White audiences discovered black social dances in New York with *Shuffle Along*, and in Paris with *Revue nègre*. As Nijinska did in *Le Train bleu*, whites emulated these dances; they removed the sexy hip and pelvic thrusts, making them, instead, more athletic. And as the dances moved from the dance-hall to the concert stage, they began to show more leg, utilizing more of the torso, legs, and hips in an opened-out display of the body. The turnout and high extension of the ballet dancer enhanced the line and dimension of these social dances as they were translated through the classical technique and adapted to the concert stage.

"Jazz is rhythm and meaning," Henri Matisse wrote in the introduction to his collection of "syncopated compositions" entitled *Jazz*. In the rhythmic procession of black-on-white images through the book, punctuated at precise moments with exciting clashes of color, Matisse created what he felt was the visual counterpoint of jazz music. The Paris choreographers of the twenties were inspired in the same way Matisse was. They responded to the dark rhythms, rolling counterpoints, happy staccatos, and jolting dissonances of jazz, as the cubists and primitivists[16] had responded to African and Oceanic artifacts a decade or two earlier. Although these choreographers were inspired by jazz, they didn't invent an entirely new movement idiom. Rather, they translated jazz through their first language, classical ballet, and in the process of that translation ballet was transformed. But not because ballet dancers did the charleston. The transformations in ballet that jazz instigated were more fundamental than that, though not immediately visible in the Parisian twenties.

Ultimately, it is the American ballet dancer, "who tends more toward rhythmic abandon, with movement that is sharper, more objective and less reliant on emotionalism and the grand manner" (Krokover 1956: 9) on whom jazz has had its most visible effect. Only in American ballet, which has "more to do with sport and jazz than czars and ballerinas," Lincoln Kirstein writes, is there "elegance in the ordinary" (Van Vechten 1974: xvii). In America, starting in the thirties with Balanchine, who altered ballet's line, attack, speed, weight, and phrasing, jazz in its transatlantic round-trip came home to roost.

NOTES

1 Some claim that jazz was "discovered" in New York circa 1917, with the first recording of the all-white Dixieland Jazz Band, though there was a richer and more developed form of jazz being played by black musicians in New Orleans ten years earlier and various tributaries of jazz that can be traced back to the Civil War. Marshall Stearns says that "jas," "jass" and later "jazz" first turned up in Chicago, in the middle teens, with other words descriptive of musical styles with origins in Negro slang (boogie, swing, rock), and that jazz had an unprintable meaning related to sex or fornicating (Stearns, 1968: 22).

2 In 1917, at the age of 25, Milhaud was awarded a scholarship to study music in South America. His experiences in Rio inspired *Saudades de Brazil* (1921), influenced by popular South American rhythms rather than folk music, and the score for *L'Homme et son désir*, performed in Paris by Ballets Suédois on June 6, 1921.

3 It is possible to follow the general action of the ballet by matching the sequence of the scenario in "Le Boeuf sur le toit," *Drama Review*, Michael Kirby (ed.) (September, 1972), 27–45, with Milhaud's score for *Le Boeuf sur le toit*, EMI, Orchestre National de France, CDC-7 47845 2, 1978.

4 Les Six consisted of composers Arthur Honegger, Louis Durey, Germaine Tailleferre, Darius Milhaud, Georges Auric, and Francis Poulenc.

5 Although the choreography is not extant, it is possible to visualize how the action of the ballet interplayed with the music by following the scenario as described in Häger (1990: 190) and listening to Milhaud's score for *La Création du monde* conducted by Leonard Bernstein, EMI CDC-7478452.

6 Börlin studied at the Royal Theater in Stockholm and entered its corps in 1905. Studying under Fokine, he was appointed soloist there in 1913. He left the company in 1918 to continue study with Fokine in Copenhagen and in 1919, he studied at the Dalcroze Institute in Geneva.

7 (Kern 1983: 124); "Some say jazz is a slang term for noise, while others say it means speed or haste. . . . 'Jazzbo' is the name given in the United States to the final scene of a vaudeville entertainment." (Mendl 1927: 46).

8 Duchamp's "Nude Descending a Staircase" was inspired by E. J. Marey's chronographs (studies of birds in flight) and E. Muybridge's serial photographs (studies of bodies in motion).

9 Serge Diaghilev quoted (translation by Frank W. D. Ries) in program to Oakland Ballet's "Best of the Ballets Russes" presented on February 15, 1992 in Landis Auditorium of Riverside Community College, Riverside, California.

10 This analysis of the ballet was made from studying a videotape of the Oakland Ballet's *Le Train bleu*, reconstructed, staged, and directed by Irina Nijinska and Frank W. D. Ries after choreography by Nijinska. I also attended a performance of the ballet when it was performed on February 15, 1992 in Landis Auditorium of Riverside Community College in Riverside, California.

11 Exter quoted in *The Avant-Garde in Russia 1910–1930: New Perspectives*, Exhibition Catalogue, Los Angeles: Los Angeles County Museum of Art, 1980: 151.

12 Exter's composition emphasized diagonality, "a quality described as a symbol of the Russian avant-garde's desire to thrust themselves into modern life" (Ronny H. Cohen, "Russian Avant-Garde Drawing," quoted in Baer 1986: 52).

13 In *Ragtime*, Stravinsky concentrates on the peculiar jazz use of the flute, clarinet, horn, cornet, trombone, violin, viola, double bass, and percussion, adding to them the cymbalon, ordinarily used by gypsy orchestra. Igor Stravinsky, *Stravinsky: Ragtime*, conducted by Neeme Jarvi for the Royal Scottish National Orchestra and Orchestre de la Suisse Romande, Essex, England: Chandos CHAN 9291, 1994. Enchanted by its popular appeal and its fresh novel rhythms "which so distinctly recalled its Negro origins," Stravinsky requested a pile of popular ragtime jazz music be sent to him from America. His impressions of this music led to the creation of *Ragtime* (Stravinsky 1936a: 130–1).

14 London impresario C. B. Cochran produced *The Sleeping Princess*, which opened at the Alahambra on November 2, 1921 and closed, due to financial failure, on February 4, 1922. Diaghilev retreated back across the Channel, leaving behind unemployed dancers from his company to find work in the commercial theater.

15 Clarence "Buddy" Bradley went to London in 1930 to choreograph the Rogers and Hart musical *Evergreen* and ended up staying for thirty-eight years. Through him, American vernacular dance was literally transplanted onto the English musical stage. Bradley choreographed twenty-nine musical numbers for *Cochran's 1931 Revue* and Balanchine, two (Hill 1992: 77–84).

16 William Rubin defines primitivism as "the interest of modern artists in tribal art and culture as revealed through their thought and work" (1984: 1).

BIBLIOGRAPHY

Acocella, J. and Garafola, L. (eds) (1991) *André Levinson on Dance: Writings from Paris in the Twenties*, Middletown, CT: Wesleyan University Press.

Auric, G. (1979) *Quand j'étais là*, Paris: B. Grasset.

Baer, N. (1986) *Bronislava Nijinska: A Dancer's Legacy*, San Francisco: Museum of Fine Arts.

Beaumont, C. (1951) *The Diaghilev Ballet in London*, London: Adam and Charles Black.

Brender, R. (1986) "Reinventing Africa in Their Own Image: The Ballets Suédois," *Dance Chronicle* 9, 1: 119–47.

Cocteau, J. (1926) *Call to Order*, trans. Rollo H. Myers, London: Faber & Gwyer.

—— (1972) "Le Boeuf sur le toit," *The Drama Review* 16, 3: 27–45.

Garafola, L. (1989) *Diaghilev's Ballets Russes*, New York: Oxford University Press.

Goddard, C. (1979) *Jazz Away From Home*, London: Paddington Press.

Häger, B. (1990) *The Swedish Ballet*, New York: Harry N. Abrams.

Hill, C. V. (1992) "Buddy Bradley: The 'Invisible' Man of Broadway Brings Jazz

Tap to London," Proceedings of the Society of Dance History Scholars, Fifteenth Annual Conference, University of California at Riverside, February 14–15.

Kern, S. (1983) *The Culture of Time and Space 1880–1918*, Cambridge, MA: Harvard University Press.

Krokover, R. (1956) *The New Borzoi Book of Ballets*, New York: Alfred A. Knopf.

Law, A. (1980) "The Revolution in Russian Theater," in *The Avant-Garde in Russia*, Los Angeles: Los Angeles County Museum of Art.

Malkiel, H. (1925) "Paris Modernists Rebel Against Outmoded Ballets," *Musical America* 25: 3, 17.

Massine, L. (1925a) "Crescendo," *The Dancing Times*: 953–6.

—— (1925b) "Sitter Out," *The Dancing Times*: 1139.

—— (1968) *My Life in Ballet*, London: Macmillan & Company.

Matisse, H. (1973) *Jazz*, New York: George Braziller.

Mendl, R. W. S. (1927) *The Appeal of Jazz*, London: Philip Alland & Company.

Milhaud, D. (1953) *Notes Without Music*, New York: Alfred A. Knopf.

—— (1973) *Ma Vie Heureuse*, Paris: Editions Belford.

Morris, G. (1990) "*Le Train bleu* Makes a Brief Stopover," *New York Times* (March 4): 10, 29.

Nijinska, B. (1981) *Early Memoirs*, New York: Holt, Rinehart & Winston.

Orledge, R. (1975) "Cole Porter's Ballet *Within the Quota*," *Yale University Library Gazette* 50, 1: 19–29.

Paillot, F. (1924) "Jean Börlin à l'exercise," *La Danse*: n.p.

Ries, F. (1986) *The Dance Theater of Jean Cocteau*, Ann Arbor: University of Michigan Press.

Rose, P. (1989) *Jazz Cleopatra: Josephine Baker in Her Time*, New York: Doubleday.

Rubin, W. (1984) *Primitivism in Twentieth Century Art*, New York: Museum of Modern Art.

Stearns, M. and Stearns, D. (1968) *Jazz Dance*, New York: Macmillan.

Stich, S. (1990) *Anxious Visions: Surrealist Art*, Berkeley, CA: University Art Museum.

Stravinsky, I. (1936a) *Chronicle of My Life*, London: Victor Gollancz, Ltd.

—— (1936b) *Igor Stravinsky, An Autobiography*, London: Calder & Bojari.

Troy, N. J. (1984) "Figures of the Dance in De Stijl," *The Art Bulletin* LXVI, 4: 639–56.

Vaughan, D. (1977) *Frederick Ashton and His Ballets*, New York: Alfred A. Knopf.

Van Vechten, C. (1974) *The Dance Writings of Carl Van Vechten*, Paul Padgette (ed.), New York: Dance Horizons.

Wiener, J. (1984) "Le Mouvement même de la vie," *Jazz Magazine* (January) 325: 40–1, 82–3.

Part IV
Cultural Crossings

14 Observing the Evidence Fail

Difference Arising from Objectification in Cross-Cultural Studies of Dance

Sally Ann Ness

Dance, as an object of cross-cultural study, has produced a dazzling array of methodological activity. "How might one best approach the task of understanding a dance (or "Dance" or "The Dance" in general, for that matter) that does not originate from or exist within one's own culture?" In the century or so that cross-cultural researchers and students of dance have been struggling with this question, no clear paradigm-setting answer has emerged. With respect to the question of how best to deal with the observable aspects of dance, for example – a key methodological question in this field of study – answers have ranged from a "no attention necessary" stance (the "and then they danced" ethnographic approach that has been so thoroughly critiqued in contemporary culturally focused dance research),[1] to the employment of elaborate perception-enhancing instruments, both conceptual and technological, intended to ensure a rigorous "objectivity" with respect to the culturally different dancing in question (an interest now also subject to critique from postcolonial, poststructural, and critical cultural studies sectors). The methodological range in the specific area of cross-cultural dance observation has been so great that a common ground for discussion and debate has been difficult to achieve.

Variations notwithstanding, however, the task of learning, across cultural divides, what it means and what it is to dance has always entailed some method of identifying, conceptualizing, or constructing a recognizable and documentable "thing" or referent called "(the) dance."[2] This conceptual "dance–object," generally speaking, has become knowable to the researcher during the research process via a variety of attributes, some of them perceptual, some symbolic, some historical, some otherwise defined. Ultimately, the dance–object becomes evidence, in some or all of these respects, for or against various theories – of dance more and less general, or of dance as a part of culture, of history, of human communication, of cultural symbolism, or of dance in relation to some other interest generated by the researcher's particular cross-cultural learning agenda. The activity of objectifying (i.e., creating a conceptual object out of) dance cross-culturally has had and continues to have practical, ethical, and theoretical consequences for the field of study, and, in this regard alone, its methodological variations (and the research agendas driving them) have merited careful attention and scrutiny.[3]

It is the variable history of this activity of objectifying dance in a cross-cultural research context, and then, of making certain kinds of evidence or knowledge out of "its" study, that I wish to reflect on in this essay. It is now such a rich and complex history that I cannot even begin to make a sketch of it in its totality, but can only examine closely a few (to me) extraordinary moments. I do so, not to find order in the chaos, or to recommend one objectification over the others. Instead, I raise these cases in point, out of the past and of the present, to reflect upon their differing capacities for representing moments of cultural difference in acts of dance.

What I am calling "cultural difference" occurs at that moment when a conceptual object – in this case the dance–object – however preconceived, *fails* to represent the researcher's understanding of the very practices they seek to identify by it and to study. These moments of failure register nothing other than the brute fact of difference, differences in world view, differences in what Bourdieu has called *habitus*[4] or what Wittgenstein might have called logic – differences in the conceptual results of the under-standings gained from participating in given sociocultural environments. When such failures are themselves defined and included in a researcher's record as a significant finding, they document the limits of cross-cultural comprehension and/or cultural translation.

Such recordings of cultural difference are of profound importance to cross-cultural study. They make visible, however imperfectly, the unstable, confused, and dynamic territory of cross-cultural working experience, the process of the *crossing* of cultural divides. The "territory" of the cultural divide, that which lies in between the researcher's own cultural productions and those of the dance they seek better to comprehend, which they understand as different from their own, becomes apparent in these representational failures.

These fields of cultural difference, not easily illuminated, are, perhaps, the only ground from which to appreciate the actual extent and significance of the transcultural movements researchers achieve and perform in their dance studies. In comparing these moments of cultural difference, pro-duced in various ways by different kinds of dance–objects and the cross-cultural evidence they generate, the radical potential of dance as a producer of the grounds for cross-cultural transgression begins to come into view. While these are grounds where some might fear to tread, given their colonizing legacy and potential, they are also the grounds that can enable new forms of tolerance, understanding, and cross-cultural respect at profoundly personal levels of awareness.

DIFFERENCES VIA ANTI-SUBJECTIVITY:
E. E. EVANS-PRITCHARD'S STUDY OF AZANDE DANCE

A landmark moment in cross-cultural dance history occurred in 1928 with the publication of E. E. Evans-Pritchard's short article, "The Dance." Published in Volume One of the international journal *Africa*, by one of British social anthropology's most highly respected leading figures, this article set forth the radical proclamation that dance had been given a marginal place in ethnological inquiry which was "unworthy of its social importance" (1928: 446). By its own exemplary though self-consciously abridged analysis of the *gbere buda* "beer dance" of the Azande people of Sudan[5] the article provided a substantial justification for the general pursuit of cross-cultural dance research as a viable inroad for cultural study.

Evans-Pritchard's study proposed an anti-subjective strategy of dance–object making, "anti-subjective" with respect to the *researcher's* subjective participation in the learning process. The forms of cultural difference produced by this strategy in Evans-Pritchard's work were both embodied and symbolic. They precluded any potential for the researcher, implicitly defined as bodily unqualified, ever to experience the dance as an authentic culture bearer might. Evans-Pritchard's anti-subjective approach to cross-cultural study also, paradoxically, constructed a dancing body of the culturally different dancer that was unproblematically observable, and in its observable characteristics, assumed to be universal as an essentially anatomical object. While the dancing experience he studied was cross-culturally un-assumable, and evidence of its distinctive effects could only be gathered by discussion with participants and attendance at dance occasions, the dancing body was transculturally, transparently, and immediately available for cross-cultural analysis.

In the opening lines of this article, Evans-Pritchard characterizes "the dance" as a distinctive object ("the" marking the dance–object so conceived as a general pan-cultural phenomenon). Noting that dance typically is conceived of as happening *during* or *in* other "things" such as "occasions" or "events," Evans-Pritchard challenges this view of dance as applicable to the cultural practices he seeks to understand. He argues that if such an idea of dance is predominant in the mind of the observer, the account of such practices as he himself is encountering in Africa would lack apparent details that are of most value to what he terms the "theoretical worker" of cross-cultural study. "The dance" in Evans-Pritchard's view is to be observed and studied primarily as being "an occasion." Understanding the bodily act of dancing as an institutionalized occasion enables the theoretical worker to better estimate its actual meaning and nature across cultural divides.

Such a conceptualization might be expected to lead the observer away from the real "it" of dance as typically conceptualized – the corporeal and choreographic component – and toward the details of "its" contextual setting. The dance is understood as something *with* a context or occasion, of which it can be studied independently. However, Evans-Pritchard's analysis of the *gbere buda* highlights and foregrounds the observation of its choreographic and corporeal detail. Photographs of the dance are included in the study that illustrate various aspects of choreographic structure. Included, too, are diagrams of the group formations employed in the dance that depict the exact placement of individual bodies on the dancing ground. The text's narrative also includes observations of typical individual actions performed during the dance, noting the active body parts engaged and their positions if gestural positions are held, the directions in which they tend to move, the "stereotyped steps" regularly performed and even the relative involvement of one skeleto-muscular group – the abdominal muscles. Moreover, Evans-Pritchard calls attention to the inadequacy of even this level of observation for pursuing the questions of social organization and cultural values that are the focus of his inquiry, and calls for subsequent study that might report on the choreographic structures of the dance in even more detail so as to adequately address these and "other interesting problems" (1928: 458) for the study of Azande culture.

This descriptive detail of "the dance" is presented as evidence supporting Evans-Pritchard's main arguments about the distinctive cultural structures

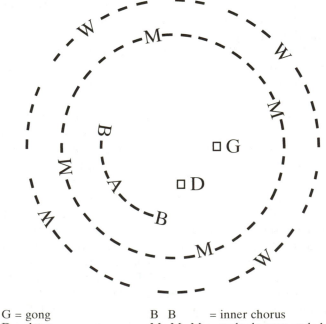

G = gong	B B = inner chorus
D = drum	M M M = male dancers and chorus
A = soloist	W W W = women dancers

Figure 14.1 E. E. Evans-Pritchard's diagram for the Zande beer dance. (Source: Evans-Pritchard 1928: 452)

and values of the Azande nation. Evans-Pritchard argues that within the embodied structures of the *gbere buda* dance, at both individual and collective levels, there is evidence of mechanisms by which a culturally distinctive style of Azande leadership both originates and functions. The dance, Evans-Pritchard explains, occasions displays of virtuosity – in gong playing, in vocal and verbal play, and in its additional muscular movements. Such displays tend to become competitive and disruptive, particularly between individuals engaged in courting behaviors who are participating in the dancing. These displays are tempered in the dance via the use of segregated group formations and the clear choice of soloists who lead the dance, gong playing, and singing rhythms and patterns. The leadership of soloists in the dance functions to maintain a degree of discipline and formal collective cohesiveness in moments when competing individual motivations are likely to produce conflicts, disruptions and, if unchecked, social and cultural chaos. In this respect, Evans-Pritchard argues, the dance embodies leadership and formal discipline. It is not symbolic of some abstract leadership principle that it "represents." It literally creates and personifies leadership in action. Likewise, the circular choreographic forms, the rhythmic structures of singing and dancing, and the sequential movements of the bodies participating are all evidence of the way in which the Azande style of governance is originated and employed in actual practice.

The use of such choreographic observations illuminates Evans-Pritchard's conceptualization of "the dance–object," not as something that might be abstracted from something different called "an occasion" or "an event" or "a context," but rather an understanding of the dancing itself as a site of cultural occasion-making. The occasion is produced in the choreography. Cultural difference is illuminated in this article via this definition of the dance–object and, to a limited extent, via the bodies it entails.

Evans-Pritchard defines the *gbere buda* dancing specifically as being something more than essentially muscular movement. He describes "the dance" as a concerted synthesis of gong playing action, singing, and additional non-instrumental "muscular movement," a definition that reads awkwardly throughout the article and appears not to make sense in its confounding of the standard European categories of music, song, and dance. The manner in which these three "elements" are integrated into a dancing activity, Evans-Pritchard reports, is "difficult to understand" (1928: 447), but he maintains that the *dance* of the *gbere buda* would be inconceivable without all elements simultaneously evident, and without the collective positioning of these activities in the forms of concentric, gender-coded circles that are carefully documented in his diagrams. Cultural difference becomes apparent in the discussion as the standard categories are shown inadequate but nonetheless indispensable in rendering a cross-cultural account of *gbere buda*.

The dancing body as well as the dance becomes a limited source of difference. Evans-Pritchard notes that any *gbere buda* dance involves certain distinctive kinds of Azande bodies, bodies marked by their placement in the dancing as male and female, as existing at a range of different age sets, and as belonging to a single residential community. The bodies involved in the dance are not simply anatomical organisms, but are themselves socially constructed, possessing characteristics of age, sex, and residential locality. Part of "the occasion" of the dance is dancing with and experiencing such a socially defined body. In this respect Evans-Pritchard tacitly acknowledges the cultural difference between the dancing bodies and his own, and the ways in which his own participation in and subjective understanding of "the dance" is limited. His body can never know the dancing as that of a lifetime resident might.

There are clear limits to Evans-Pritchard's own abilities to observe, describe, and define the *gbere buda* and its dancing bodies, and account for the cultural difference entailed in such an undertaking. His method of observing the dance element of "muscular movements," for example (ibid.: 451), consists of noting body parts that are active and various directions they appear to take in a three-dimensional spatial realm ("moves hands and arms up and down, shakes his head backwards and forwards, leans from side to side, lifts and lowers his shoulders . . . "). The bodies are observed mechanistically, in eurocentric spatial and anatomical terms. Even after remarking upon how distinctively the social body of the dancer is constructed, as noted above, the individual dancing bodies Evans-Pritchard observes appear to bear no trace of those differences. Moreover, there is no indication given in the discussion that there might be some alternative means of characterizing the movement processes in ways that might more closely approximate the culture bearer's lived experience of them.

This strategy might not bear comment, given the pioneering nature of the study, were it not for the fact that one of Evans-Pritchard's main arguments about the social function of the dance focuses on an aspect of it that he is apparently incapable of documenting due to the observational orientation he assumes toward Azande dancing bodies. One main social function of the *gbere buda*, Evans-Pritchard claims, is to embody the emotional antithesis of mourning and thus serve as a balance to the mourning process. However, despite the claim that the dance is centrally concerned with the experience of these positive emotions, Evans-Pritchard makes no record of observing any evidence of such emotions in the "dance elements." Furthermore, no accounts of any emotional experiences of the dance that might have been elicited from discussion with its performers are provided in the narrative. The only observations reporting anything that might be even vaguely linked to this emotional aspect is one remark noting that the dance involves "exercising" muscles, the abdominal muscles in particular (ibid.: 451). Any indications of emotional dynamics evident in the "muscular movements" are condensed into the single notion of "exercising."

This gap in the observational record limits Evans-Pritchard's argument concerning the emotional social function of the dance, even while the argument itself assumes that some apparent emotional element must be evident in its performance. The gap, moreover, goes unproblematized. The emotional dimension of the dance is characterized by default as not available for observation, in contrast to the spatial and anatomical aspects of the choreography. Emotional experience is apparently hidden from the observer's objective gaze, located, perhaps, somewhere "inside" the dancing body. In this respect, the dance is accounted for as a phenomenon that involves emotion without manifesting it in any observable way, an objectification of the dance that works against Evans-Pritchard's own theoretical projects.

It seems important to note that despite Evans-Pritchard's primary interest in observing for the graphic details of the dance–object, certain assumptions about the body of a dancing culture-bearer and about how it might be comprehended by a culturally unfamiliar but "scientific" observer intervene and curtail the observational process and any self-conscious methodological critique thereof. That Evans-Pritchards doesn't note his own observational limitations, even when they occur to the detriment of his expressed research agenda, is puzzling, given that he is quick to note similar limitations in analogous processes of observing and describing musical elements of the dance, in particular the singing performance process and its elemental structures.[6] It is in this respect, I would submit, that a disciplinary concern in maintaining a certain kind of researcher anti-subjectivity underlies and governs Evans-Pritchard's methodological awareness, compelling an observational focus on features of the dance that are apparently emotion-free, and which can be identified and recorded without emotional experience being referenced or engaged. Evans-Pritchard's specific observational interests release him from attending to indicators of emotional processes that might possibly bring into play his own subjective (and assumed to be inherently distorting) cultural biases. His method allows him to stay invested instead in the relatively neutral activity of following traceforms through abstract space and identifying moving body parts. Paradoxically, however, this very method reduces Evans-Pritchard's ability to understand the dance–object he so observes or even to mark his own limitations for so doing. In the attempt to limit a subjective/biased distortion by keeping his own culturally unqualified body from participating in the research process, the object-oriented goals of the research are also constrained. Ultimately, while Evans-Pritchard's study of a dance–object makes apparent some forms of embodied cultural difference, the anti-subjective observational strategy applied to the study of individual dancing bodies assumes a universal object that precludes the recognition or encountering of such difference.

Evans-Pritchard's study of the *gbere buda* fundamentally changed the way in which dance as an object of cross-cultural study could be conceptualized, investigated, and understood. As a consequence of this recharacterization, "dance" had the potential to become something more than an essentially physiological and psychological phenomenon. "Dance" became recognizable as a source of evidence for originating as well as for supporting theories of social structure and social organization, an important source of insight into such central cultural phenomena as the principles of leadership and discipline, and of the emotional and spiritual relationship between life and death. In his profound rethinking of what kind of a "thing" dance was, Evans-Pritchard also began to call into question some European assumptions about the nature and meaning of dance – an achievement made possible by his close observation of the site-specific details of "the dance" among the Azande people. His work in this respect anticipated a question subsequent dance researchers have asked about the reality of such a thing as "dance" actually existing pan-culturally, given how fundamentally eurocentric the concept is in origin.

ANTI-ETHNOCENTRIC FORMS OF OBJECTIVITY: DIFFERENCES PRODUCED VIA PAN-CULTURAL DANCE–OBJECTS

The late 1960s and 1970s produced two extraordinary dance scholars, Judith Lynne Hanna and Adrienne Kaeppler, whose work, in very different ways, enlarged and diversified the means by which dance as an object of cross-cultural study might be conceptualized. While the two dance scholars share little in terms of the theories of dance they originated, both were trained in cultural anthropology during a period of its history when researcher objectivity – a neutral perspective opposed to the subjective and chauvinistic position of "ethnocentrism" – was considered a unifying value throughout the discipline. Debates of this time raged between "ideationalists" and "behavioralists" over whether or not "Culture" could best be studied objectively via the direct observation of human action or via the elicitation of rules and codes of human thought. Prevailing cultural anthropological studies modeled themselves after the experimental designs of cognitive science, communication theory, and linguistics, exploring the diversity of conceptual frameworks across cultures via the use of linguistic componential analysis and other forms of cognitive mapping, seeking to discover universal human laws of communication and intelligence as well as to comprehend the vast diversity of human logic systems. In this intellectual climate, both Kaeppler and Hanna forged innovative cross-cultural theories of dance, each highly objective in the anti-ethnocentric sense, designed specifically to avoid imposing western viewpoints on the practices and traditions of non-western cultures. Comparing their approaches reveals that, while cultural difference is registered and illuminated differently in each case, the anti-ethnocentric orientation produces a general effect of its own as well, with respect to the paradoxes of cultural "translation" it seeks to transcend.

**Semiotic Objectivity: Judith Lynne Hanna's Model of
Dance Communication**

Judith Lynne Hanna's models of dance and dance communication, published most prominently in the 1979 book, *To Dance is Human: A Theory of Nonverbal Communication*, emerge from an attempt to develop an overarching analytical understanding of dance of pan-cultural magnitude and scope. The dance–object Hanna conceptualizes endeavors to integrate the widest possible range of theoretical perspectives on "dance" into a single, all-encompassing model of dance and its meaning-making movements. Although Hanna acknowledges that she, herself, is "a Westerner" and "obviously influenced by [her] culture"(1979b: 18), the undertaking of such a pan-cultural construction is a task that idealizes objectivity in the anti-ethnocentric sense.

To summarize, Hanna defines dance as "human behavior composed, from the dancer's perspective, of: 1) purposeful, 2) intentionally rhythmical, and 3) culturally patterned sequences of 4a) nonverbal body movements, 4b) other than ordinary motor activities, 4c) the motion having inherent and aesthetic value" (ibid.: 19). "Dance" in this definition is essentially a matter of bodily action, first and foremost a physical experience for "the" dancer. Hanna also argues that dance in all cultures is *communicative* behavior, comparable to a nonverbal "text" or "coding device" which can be modeled in relationship to its cultural "context." This dance–object is integrated into what Hanna defines as a cross-culturally viable semiotic model of human communication.

The model of dance communication is conceived as a flow chart systematizing linkages and various feedback and feedforward loops between all elements of the communicative network that involve the dance–object. The main nodes within this network consist of: 1) catalysts – individual, social, historical, phylogenetic, or physical – which determine the occasions of dance and its varying elemental components ("who dances, why, where, and how," ibid.: 78); 2) audiences, and 3) dancers/choreographers, who are identified as "encoding–decoding" nodes with respect to the dance performance; and, 4) the dance–object – identified as a "medium–channel" – along with "adjunct channels" of music, song, and costume (ibid.: 79).

The relationship between the dance–object and the audience and dancer/choreographer nodes are cast in a wide variety of linguistic, psychological, and communication theory terms. Syntactic, semantic, and pragmatic levels of "encoding/decoding," for example, are recognized and incorporated into the model. The "syntactic" level incorporates many of the processual movement concepts of Labananalysis in order to represent body movement structures as they might be sequenced and combined into the equivalents of dance "grammars."

The extraction of information from the dance–object is conceived as potentially involving any one or several of the entire array of human

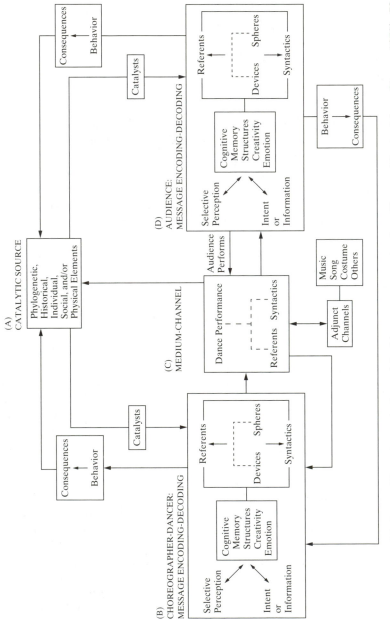

Figure 14.2 Judith Lynne Hanna's semiotic model of human communication. (Source: Figure 4 from Hanna 1979b: 79; by permission of University of Chicago Press)

intelligence-producing faculties: memory, cognition, emotion, learned and inherited communication capabilities, creativity, and social experience. The encoding/decoding process is also elaborated in terms of an array of six "devices," either conventional or autographic in reference, that are evident in the dance–object and which convey different forms of meaning within a variety of seven potential "spheres" of reception or interpretation, ranging from the specific movement, to the pattern of the whole performance, to the socio-cultural event involving the performance (1979b: 41–7). The model attempts to take into account every possible communicative and interpretive process known to the various fields of communication studies from virtually every discipline and to diagram with maximum flexibility the possible movements of information throughout the network(s) involving the dance–object, its catalysts, dancers and choreographers, and audiences.

Hanna reviewed the most substantive debates of the time regarding the nature and significance of dance, and incorporated both sides of each question as possibilities in her overarching scheme. Dance was not necessarily cognitive or affective, but could be either or both. Dance was not necessarily creative or traditional, conservative or innovative, reflective or influential, representational or presentational, mental or physical, but could be either or both, to different nodes on the information network or to all at once, or to some or all in some kind of sequence. From its generative processes, through its occasions of performance, and on to its reception and the consequences following from them, the rules, devices, operations, and transformations of dance were conceptualized as variable and, thus, their understanding required site-specific study. Virtually no prior assumptions about the network of cultural understanding in which the dance–object was involved could rest unchecked. The model thus marked virtually all aspects of dance's meaning-making capacities and processes as open to investigation.

While the model's voracious eclecticism may have seemed maddeningly contradictory to theorists specializing in any one of the many fields Hanna drew from, its very open-endedness was one of its greatest inherent assets as a methodological tool for anti-ethnocentric objective cross-cultural study. In the abstract, the model provides an infinite number of possibilities for representing cultural diversity with respect to the origins and inspirations of dance, and its understanding and interpretation by all who might participate in whatever active or passive way in its practice. The array of questions a cross-cultural researcher is compelled to ask, in seeking to identify and define for a specific situation the actual equivalents of the dance–object, its catalysts, its agents of performance and its audiences, and their dynamic interrelationships with respect to various spheres of meaning, guarantees that a wide variety of perspectives and viewpoints are taken into account in the course of cross-cultural study. The array of possibilities for "encoding" devices elaborated in the model also insures that researchers do not impose preconceived interpretative scenarios onto the dance practices studied, but rather observe for and discover objectively the processes by which culturally different dance meanings are conveyed. As dance anthropologist Jill Sweet remarked in a response to Hanna's theoretical work, Hanna's model takes researchers "beyond static and functional studies which invariably [conclude] that a particular dance contributes to the social solidarity of the group, reflects the social order, or portrays a particular mythic or legendary story" (Sweet 1979: 329). Instead, researchers are intended to follow the trail of communicative signs throughout a cultural network wherever they might lead, having no particular biases or expectations about the specifics of the route taken toward constructing meaning. Virtually any realm of human life or socio-cultural action is potentially involved in the network in a wide variety of ways.

The dance–object itself is also observed by Hanna as providing various kinds of evidence of a cultural network. As with the model of communicative processes, Hanna's model of body movement processes (which constitute the dance–object) attempts to incorporate a comprehensive array of concepts derived from those formulated in various fields of body movement studies.[7] The general areas of "space," "rhythm," "dynamics," and "use of the body" are each defined in terms of eclectic and expandable sets of movement variables, any one or combination of which might serve as a "device" or encoding element of some kind in its own communicative network (1979b: 245–6). In the area of space alone, for example, the model recognizes such diverse movement variables as the direction(s) of focus of the performer's eyes and body, the direction(s) of body movements (in a three-dimensional spatial environment), the forms and amplitudes of group shapes, and the levels used in body movement (high, middle, and low). Any one of these variables or several together might combine to serve as a metaphor, a metonym, an icon, or one of the other "devices" conveying meaning within one of the dance network's nodes or spheres. Hanna observed, for example, that the circular group forms employed in some dances of the Ubakala people of Nigeria were a metaphoric device representing the concepts of safety, solidarity, and stability (ibid.: 94). Likewise individual dancers' leaping steps, which displayed a marked upward and downward spatial form, were observed as metaphoric devices representing masculine gender roles (ibid.: 94–6).

Along these specific communicative lines the dance–object is understood in Hanna's theory as having an infinite potential for making meaning. Cross-cultural study necessarily involves the formulation of graphically detailed move-by-move reconstructions of the dance–object. Different movement variables serve as different devices for different nodes within different spheres of the network. The researcher must abandon ethnocentric preconceptions about what kind of device or what sphere of reception might involve the dance–object or any of its movement components, and, instead, observe the dance–object and its components for evidence of its potentially numerous relationships with virtually any realm of life. The opportunities for inquiry with regard to different movements, their individual features, their communicative references, and their encoding and decoding processes are almost too numerous to imagine.

As critiques coming from within cultural anthropology of such totalizing semiotic models have noted, the adherence to one level of anti-ethnocentric objectivity paradoxically ensures the failure of objectivity at more foundational levels of understanding. Researchers are prone to become lost inside their own vast typologies, falsely assuming that whatever information may become apparent to them via their employment of universally applicable concepts might also constitute a "translation" of interpretive or explanatory understanding. Hanna's model of dance communication is, of course, not immune to such a critique. It assists the researcher in modeling cultural diversity and crossing cultural boundaries with respect to what kinds of devices, what particular dance–object features and structures, and what individual communicative networks might become apparent to the observer at specific cultural sites. However, it also forestalls the exploration of cultural diversity with respect to the vast array of constituent concepts on which it is itself dependent for organizing its observations. It does not, for example, call into ethnocentric question the array of semantic devices or spheres of meaning, or general categories of dance features, or, perhaps most critical, the key concepts of "audience," "choreographer," "catalyst," and "dance performance." Paradoxically, the near-perfect flexibility and eclecticism of the model makes its capacity for defining such inherent conceptual ethnocentrism all the more difficult to address and examine. By appending more and more concepts originating from within the model's own cultural discourses, the structure of the model itself is less and less likely to be understood as vulnerable to being ruptured by the cultural difference actually encountered at any specific instance of application. The researcher is more and more likely to become sealed inside the model's overarching paradigms, continually finding solutions to problems posed by individually observed dance–objects and their apparent communicative networks through recourse to the vast array of featured alternatives already formulated and awaiting application.

Hanna's own application of the model to her research on the dance of the Ubakala culture of Nigeria (which remains its only in-depth application) as published in her 1979 text exemplifies this predicament. The creative process of crossing back and forth between cultural realities that was required in order to apply the model to the specific study is not foregrounded in the account. No excerpts of the cross-cultural discourses that led to the general observations framed by the model are recounted verbatim or in graphic detail. Instead, the process of constructing a model-reinforcing object, a culturally translated experience, is the central project of the writing. The study culturally "double-crosses" Ubakala dance in this respect. It represents Ubakala dance via a western conceptual scheme that characterizes apparent non-western patterns of meaning-making.

While Hanna's model is fashioned so as to suppress evidence of cultural difference in favor of producing a discourse of cultural translation, ultimately, I would argue, the semiotic network of the dance–object is very effectively designed to produce evidence of cultural difference as well. Hanna's study itself, as predominantly "translated" as it is, foregrounds some organizing moments of cultural difference. The very notion of "dance" that Hanna defines, for example, fails to represent adequately the specific practices of the Ubakala. Hanna is brought by her own translating efforts to a recognition that what the Ubakala do merits the label "dance-play" instead of simply "dance." The hyphenated concept, its hyphen foregrounding its own conceptual imperfection, achieves something of what Evans-Pritchard's occasion/dance writing does, confounding commonsense definitions of both concepts and joining them in a manner that illuminates an absence of reason, reason not available without crossing into a different cultural reality.

As vast as the model's potential for "translation" is, so too is its potential for indicating, tracking, and producing experiences of cultural difference, if each of its concepts were to be employed with the awareness that it was not a problem solving, but a problem generating device, not a permanent fixture in the researcher's stockpile of analytical instruments, but an array of temporary signposts, not an end, but a beginning to cross-cultural discourse that might be initiated by its own (mis)application. Such a failure-driven use of the model would also allow it to remain more fundamentally true to the anti-ethnocentric projects it was intended to pursue.

Structuralist Objectivity: The Ethnoscientific Model of Adrienne Kaeppler

There is, perhaps, no scholar in the field of cross-cultural dance study whose work has been more effective in illuminating the richness of cultural difference made visible via the representational failures of a dance–object than Adrienne Kaeppler. Kaeppler, working also from a perspective of rigorous anti-ethnocentric objectivism, probed the limits of that orientation by challenging the general capacity of the concept "dance" to serve as a vehicle of cross-cultural representation and understanding. "Dance," Kaeppler has argued – most forcefully in her 1985 article, "Structured Movement Systems in Tonga" – is an inherently ethnocentric concept. To attempt to involve it in the study of practices of cultures in which it does not originate is to risk a distorted view of those practices. However, Kaeppler's studies of the (non)dance practices of Tonga have demonstrated lucidly that the failure of the "dance" concept can be extremely productive. Its (mis)application can open up a cross-cultural research process to a consideration of alternative conceptualizations of the practices that a dance-oriented culture bearer might potentially construe as "dance." The limitations of the dance–object in Kaeppler's Tongan studies enables the introduction of a wide array of Tongan concepts into her analytical discussion. These repeatedly jar and torque the anti-ethnocentric cultural frame of reference and create a profoundly cross-cultural textual domain. The approach also allows Kaeppler to attempt, at least in theory, to give Tongan cultural discourse the last conceptual word.

Kaeppler's ethnoscientific method of analyzing Tongan dance cross-culturally borrows heavily from structural analysis used in linguistics (1967: vi; 1972: 174–6). As with such structural linguistic approaches, a series of levels of observation of the dance–object are identified and differentiated. These are defined as 1) the kinetic level of observable body movement, initially identified and notated by the researcher via "culture-free" observational typologies (Kaeppler identifies Labanotation in particular in this regard), 2) the "kineme" or smallest unit of movement recognized as meaningful by performers, 3) the "morphokineme" which consists of combinations of kinemes that exhibit a cohesiveness or integrity and are recognized as "dance movements" – in Kaeppler's terms "the smallest unit that has meaning in the structure of the movement system" (1972: 185), 4) the "motif" level, which consists of a combination of morphokinemes and forms a short entity in itself (ibid.: 202), and, finally, 5) the "dance genre" level, or totality of the movement practice observed, considered as a sequential ordering of all structural elements involved (1967: vi; 1972: 214).[8]

Relying on the "etic/emic" distinction which posits that a cross-cultural researcher's ethnographic "etic" perspective differs significantly from a participant "emic" interpretive perspective, Kaeppler's kinemic method first attempts to identify and describe minimal units of action evident in culture-free and cross-culturally observable processes of body movement. Subsequently, through discussion with practitioners, such etic observations are used to elicit emic representations of practitioners' experiences at the kinemic, morphokinemic, motif, and dance genre levels of description and analysis. What Tongan dancers recognize as significant in their "dance" becomes knowable through this dialogue regarding the etic objectifications and their emic constructions and interpretations.

With respect to Tongan cultural practices in particular, Kaeppler finds, for example, that Tongan conceptualizations and objectifications of what might be construed as "dance" – particularly as defined in relation to other "non-dance" practices – differ markedly from those produced by non-Tongan observational frameworks. In order to define the cultural difference indicated by this conceptual mismatch, Kaeppler (1985) employs the concept of the "structured movement system," considered a more abstract and less ethnocentric notion than "dance," and describes such systems and their cultural significance. Using this strategy, Kaeppler demonstrates how such apparently "non-dance" Tongan activities as formal speech-making (involving gesturing), *kava*[9] mixing, and the actions involved in making a public ceremonial presentation of pigs and foodstuffs

to ranking authority figures, all involve formalized body movements
imparting information about social relationships that exhibit underlying
conceptual linkages, in relation to which the cultural significance of Tongan
"dance" activities is generally understood by Tongan culture bearers. In
contrast to a dance-centered view of Tongan cultural life, Kaeppler
observes that such Tongan concepts as *"faiva"* (roughly translated, "skill-
requiring activity") and *"katoanga"* ("festival" or "celebration") are more
central to organizing and understanding the full array of practices and
traditions that a dance-oriented cross-cultural researcher might want to
investigate. Kaeppler's cross-cultural study of Tongan *faiva* shows that all
that a dance-oriented researcher might want to understand across cultural
divides is not accessible through a narrow investigation of the closest
Tongan equivalents of the concept of "dance," which Kaeppler glosses as
"tao'olunga" or *"faiva* that emphasises [sic] the performer rather than the
poetry" (1985: 117) of a formal, choreographed *hiva Kakala* or "sweet
song" speech-making event.

By studying, not what is "dance" in Tongan culture, but, rather, what is
the *cultural equivalent* of the western dance–object in Tongan cultural
practice, Kaeppler's cross-cultural studies have exposed an immense
ground of cultural difference. A non-Tongan reader sorting through
Kaeppler's findings is bombarded at every turn with original Tongan
concepts – concepts of activities, events, movements, movement elements,
and social actions – which serve as reminders of the limits of the English-
speaking culture bearer to comprehend or fully translate Tongan lifeways.
The terms, when read so as to form a concrete vocabulary for defining a
world of social action, create a web of interrelated events and processes
radically different in design and composition from the web of social action
a dance observer might weave in order to investigate "its" cultural significance. The "dance–object" in this respect becomes evidence of cultural
difference by virtually every aspect of its social character.

While the social actions performed by Kaeppler's dance–object
illuminate cultural difference, the dance–object also consists of a bodily
aspect as well. The body of the dance–object in Kaeppler's method tends
to serve as evidence, not of cultural difference, but of common human
identity. The body of the dance–object becomes apparent mainly in the etic
phases of research, those involving a detailed accounting of observable
movement patterns. Culture-free body parts are defined in terms of the
human skeleton. Head, torso, arms, lower arms, hands, legs, hips, thighs,
knees, and feet of Tongan dancing bodies all are observed as having
movement patterns whose spatial traceforms, sequencing, and combination
can be identified and recorded (1972: 177–85). In this regard, the body
of the dance–object is construed as basically similar to that objectified in
Evans-Pritchard's and in Hanna's studies. Kaeppler's approach assumes
an ahistorical and universal human body existing in abstract geometrical
three-dimensional space, that can perform movement structures, functions,

roles, and other such elements. This etic observable body does not undergo cross-cultural reconceptualization as do its movement patterns at subsequent levels of "emic" analysis in Kaeppler's method. The etic body remains an underlying conceptual given on which cross-cultural study develops. In this respect, Kaeppler's strategy does not escape the ethnocentric problem it identifies with respect to the "dance" concept. It shifts the paradoxes of conceptual ethnocentrism onto the concept of the "body" as well as onto the concepts of "movement," and "structured system."

Limitations of the universal dancing body aside, however, Kaeppler's strategy accomplishes much of critical value with respect to the dance–object it ultimately abandons. While the concepts of "body," "movement," and "structure" lead to anti-ethnocentric cultural "translations,"[10] the notion of the inherently Western dance–object foregrounds and keeps apparent a cultural divide. The failing dance–object and its persistent presence in Kaeppler's analysis consistently mark and establish her cultural crossing, maintaining a vital oppositional relationship with respect to the practices observed in Tonga, whose very vulnerability to misrepresentation as "dance" identifies them as cross-culturally research-worthy. While the observable bodies of Tongan dance and their capacity for producing "structured movement" are not called into cultural question – are left as evidence of universal human similarity or common ground – virtually every other element that might conceivably be construed as "dance"-related becomes potential evidence of cultural difference. In this regard, Kaeppler's anti-ethnocentrist orientation produces the opportunity to strategically employ an avowedly ethnocentric conceptual object oppositionally, so as to identify evidence by contrast of a dissimilar cultural system, indicating the traces of a more profoundly cross-cultural equivalent.

SUBJECTIVE MEANS TO DIFFERENCE: THE REFLEXIVE DANCE–OBJECT OF AVANTHI MEDURI

I look now at a dance–object constructed in the service of a very different sort of culture-crossing endeavor. Despite their differences, Evans-Pritchard, Hanna, and Kaeppler all share in their writing a similar cultural predicament. All are self-defined as culturally different from the dance they study. All seek to gain understanding via the observation of dancing bodies also defined as culturally different from their own. All value forms of non-subjectively defined observation as methods ensuring the least distorted understandings possible in their cross-cultural endeavors. All encounter cultural difference via the failures of such an anti-subjective/objective pursuit. In the reflexive subjective work of dance theorist Avanthi Meduri, however, a radically different cross-cultural project ensues. Meduri's strategy, which I will discuss as it is represented in her article, "Bharatha Natyam – What are You?," identifies the dance–object and the body it involves as culturally her own. In this crossing, the researcher who crosses is herself a dancing subject. Dance is not the object of a foreigner's gaze alone. The dance–object is characterized as existing in foreign cultures, both in contemporary India and in non-Indian European and American contexts, but it is also situated within a familiar body, a cultural "self." The dance–object is the potential, though failing, bridge of a cultural crossing that moves in the reverse direction from those discussed previously. Even more important, Meduri identifies the differing cultural contexts between which cultural difference becomes apparent as also respectively her own. Her study thus includes no object or territory marked as culturally mysterious or unfamiliar.

Despite the lack of exotic territory, however, questions regarding the nature of the dance–object and the cultural difference its study produces do not disappear. Cultural difference is encountered and illuminated subjectively, and the dance–object becomes an object of an even more problematic and ambiguous sort as it becomes evidence of this cultural difference. In Meduri's essay dance is evidence of cultural difference via its practice, as opposed to its direct and formal observation.

Meduri begins the article with an account of the manner in which she, as a young student of the Bharata Natyam tradition, received knowledge of its history from her dance teachers. She learned stories of the dance's past, literally sitting at their feet. Her understanding of the dance as a cultural insider is established initially via this near-classic narrative of cultural transmission: she, a young "native" learns from her elders an established, unambiguous culturally marked dance tradition. Meduri articulates questions with respect to this received wisdom, questions remembered in part from her own adolescence, about the validity and meaning of the dance history transmitted and its ambiguous relevance for contemporary performance contexts. These questions stimulate a more lengthy account of Bharata Natyam's dance literature, beginning with a summary of its originating text, the *Natya Shastra*. Meduri's historical account emphasizes the close relationship evident between Indian classical dance and Indian philosophy (aesthetics, ethics, and ideology) in pre-contemporary times (1988: 4). This discussion shows how the traditional Indian temple and its cultural life were critically important to the existence of dance itself in the time of the *devadasi* temple dancers, who are described as having reached the height of their glory in the ninth through twelfth centuries AD. The history of the dance begins to grow problematic with the decline of the temple culture and the corresponding "corruption" of the *devadasi*. It becomes increasingly so with the reinventions of the tradition staged by "respectable" women of the early twentieth century, whose efforts to recuperate the now stigmatized tradition in part contributed to its destruction as a distinctive spiritual experience.

The article shifts to an analysis of the paradoxes generated by contemporary performance contexts, whose secular environments fail to support the philosophical vision and ancient aesthetic still inherent in the dance form. For the Bharata Natyam dancer today, Meduri argues, the task of embodying both the traditional Indian figure in performance along with the contemporary professional dancer off stage creates a tension and a split identity that is painful to endure. The dancer's body in this way is characterized as a body that contains not only observable moving parts, but a personality as well, a body that makes theory, has pain, and questions with feeling its cultural predicament. The article ends with a call for a post-colonial aesthetic, one that "can describe and evaluate the secular reality of dance in all its marvelous multiplicity" (ibid.: 20).

The dance–object conceptualized in Meduri's work is ambiguous, continually changing in character. When discussing Bharata Natyam historically, Meduri initially defines it as a shared embodiment of verbal texts and concepts. Bharata Natyam (ibid.: 3) is conceptualized as the performance by one dancing body of *nrtta* (non-narrative sculpturesque poses and movements) that produces *rasa* (aesthetic delight) in spectator bodies. This is not a causal, linear production with *nrtta*/dancing body at one temporal end (beginning) of the performance process and *rasa*/watching bodies at another. The dance–object is defined as something meant to be co-created and which is existent only when co-experienced. Fusions of the kinesthetic and the visual, as well as the ideological and the physical are its essential substance. "It" cannot be watched dispassionately, nor can the viewing body and its emotional presence fail to change the dancing body's performance. Thus conceived, the dance–object appears fundamentally different from those available to study via anti-ethnocentric objectivism. It is performed so as to be observed, but observed so as to be felt.

As Meduri's dance history proceeds to the early twentieth century, the dance–object changes character somewhat. Initially it is represented as a living organism of sorts, a kind of cultural outgrowth. Meduri asks early on in the discussion, "would the dance survive on this [secular] platform, cut off from the ritual roots of the temple?" (ibid.: 7). Like a plant with stem and roots, the dance–object is initially defined as vitally dependent on a specialized cultural environment, as well as on multiple bodies.

When Meduri recounts the competing reinventions of the tradition that occurred in the early twentieth century, she articulates a somewhat different conceptualization of dance. In this section, she discusses multiple dance–objects, conceived variously by those whose stake in the revitalization of the "corrupt" dance tradition were far from identical. Here, the dance–objects reported appear as formulas, the products of mental definitions that are projected onto obedient bodies. She describes the educated Brahmin agents in this conflict, for example, as "bringing their own philosophical and ideological biases to bear on bharatha natyam . . . radically altering an ancient art form of the temple" (ibid.: 11).

The dance–object of Meduri, the dancer herself, is a more volatile construction than any yet mentioned, whose problematic conceptualization constitutes the main effort of the article, as its title suggests. Meduri includes a poem at one point that asks the dance–object to define itself, questioning whether it might best be conceived as a vision, or as a memory, or as a "dance at the heart that does not move" (ibid.: 9). Ultimately, with the array of historical, contemporary, and subjective manifestations taken into account, Meduri's personal dance–object appears in the text as something like a living membrane. It exists as a formal entity, but it exists so as to be formally altered by the living, thinking flesh that constitutes it and/or the environments affecting and supporting it. It can absorb new materials/bodies or release them and reshape itself to adapt to changing circumstances. It is evidence of flux, of changing bodies, changing circumstances, changing environments, but also, and essentially, evidence of a qualified formal continuity. Its formal operations remain basically unaltered even while its constituent material and performance environment continually changes. Indeed, Meduri's account includes relatively little discussion of the observable forms of Bharata Natyam choreographies. Given her interests, they aren't relevant. The historical and contemporary record are not marked in terms of such observable changes, but rather by the manner in which the changing performance environment affects the lived experience of the dance.

Meduri's self-conscious and subjective perspective might seem to preclude any encounter with cultural difference. If such difference, as I have defined it, can only be perceived via realizing the failure of a conceptual strategy, how can one fail to conceive of one's *self* and one's own experience? However, the reflexive perspective actually works in Meduri's article to foreground cultural difference. The problems of translation with respect to Bharata Natyam's understanding in the contemporary world are all the more sharply defined by Meduri's own familiarity with them and her personal experience of them. "Indian dance today," she writes, "functions ... in the gap between philosophic vision and everyday reality" (ibid.: 4). The "gap" Meduri identifies is a territory of cultural difference.

More than one such cultural gap opens up in the article. There is the divide between Meduri and her dance's past history, a cultural divide between the present and the past in India itself. There is a cultural divide as well between Meduri and her dance ancestors, both the *devadasi* temple dancers, and the dance heroines who revitalized the art form in the early twentieth century. The lineage of dancers is itself twisted and torqued by the changing historical circumstances of performance. Yet another divide opens between Meduri and her contemporary audiences. She describes herself as a dancer "always reaching out," reaching "out to her audience, sometimes across the vast geographical distance between the East and West" (ibid.: 15). Finally, there is the divide between Meduri the traditional dancer on stage, dancing the stories of the gods, and Meduri the modern woman inhabiting intelligently and ambitiously the contemporary secular cultures of India and the United States. Meduri places herself and her reader on the dancing side of this gulf, watching the divide open between her learned practice and the "contemporary world" she otherwise inhabits. The subjective perspective does not produce a self-obsessed reverie, but rather a heightened awareness of cultural divides, divides no less real for having no unknown mysteries represented on either side, divides all the more evident as a felt experience for having been located within an "individual's" cross-cultural life history.

Meduri the dancer, as well as Meduri the contemporary, secular, cross-cultural observer of the dance, fails to develop an articulation across cultural divides in this writing. However, the failure does not result from some absence of understanding, but rather out of the awareness that the divide itself is a consequence of the convergence of fundamentally different cultural systems. From this perspective, the cultural difference ultimately appears, not as a void waiting to be bridged, a conceptual ocean between cultural continents that the culturally unfamiliar researcher is seeking eventually to cross or translate, but rather as a gap enlarged by the very act of attempted contact, a cultural trench deepened by the collision of dissimilar landscapes. The problems Meduri articulates with respect to the cross-cultural translation of the dance–object into the contemporary environment are not solvable problems. They result, not from the application of a flawed but potentially modifiable conceptual framework, but from the meeting of cultural frameworks that are themselves conceptually incompatible. Meduri's work begins to resemble Kaeppler's in this regard but powerfully indicates as well how actively the body participates in this failure of translation.

Meduri's study necessitates a new perspective on the cultural difference it illuminates. The cultural difference encountered is understood as an objective reality, not the result of a subjective or conceptual mistake. Cultural difference becomes apparent in the study as a circumstance that must be tolerated, as opposed to being overcome, an outcome to be studied in and of itself, as opposed to being treated as the consequence of a temporary misunderstanding. Cultural difference is not the consequence of a researcher's failure to be objective in this sort of cross-cultural study. It is a condition generated by circumstances beyond the dancer/researcher's control, but one which is also contingent upon her activities and bodily participation.

CONCLUSION

I wonder, as I review these cross-cultural dance writings, at my own experience of partnering them as a reader. There are moments in which I come away feeling as though I have been a partner in what I myself understand as a dance, a dance across cultural divides with the objects of study they conceptualize. I am shaken as I read by the moments of difference they produce, moments when I am otherwise dancing right along. I feel the movements of failure, as I seek to cross into territories that are not my own. I would estimate that my body responds more animatedly to the failures than to the lucid observations of dancing presented in fully translated form. This close and moving understanding of difference is gained via the authors' appreciation of and careful attention to body movements, embodied knowledge, and/or lived experience.

The divergent strategies reviewed above reveal the vital fact that "dance" typically has been made into a conceptual object as it has been thought onto bodies, living human subjects. Differences in approach notwithstanding, the cultural difference made visible (or invisible) via such dance writing is cast in terms of the human being itself. The field of study in general produces awareness of cultural difference at very personal, one might even say intimate, levels.

In Meduri's essay, cultural difference, as well as dance, becomes a personally felt experience. Difference becomes a pain in the heart; it produces headaches and disturbs peace of mind. In Kaeppler's kinemic approach, difference is located in the study of personal, culturally conscious action, in the webs of understanding that interrelate activities involving the culturally structured participation of arms, legs, torsos, feet, and hands. It is difference acted out in the gestures and postures of Tongan-speaking and Tongan-moving human bodies. In Evans-Pritchard's writing, difference is expressed in part as a personal conceptual experience, as Evans-Pritchard struggles in vain within his own thought process to come to terms with the dance–object through standard English concepts. Evans-Pritchard also locates cultural difference in the dancing individuals he, ultimately, can only study as an observer and can never himself personally know or subjectively become. The dancing person Evans-Pritchard conceptualizes is one in which the experiences of being a self residing permanently in a specific cultural community motivate and define the occasion happening in the dancing. Finally, in Hanna's semiotic model, difference is potentially located in any of the vehicles or channels of signification that entail the dance–object and its dancing bodies. This entailment is not conceived as a superficial association or involvement of the dancing participants, but rather one achieved via communicative linkages that engage the most fundamental aspects of the dance movement patterning and its bodily agents of production – the "grammar" or "syntax" of choreography constituted by foot steps, head turns, hand shakes, and other such corporeal maneuvers.

Cross-cultural dance research presents great potential for the study of cultural difference. It illuminates the diversity of cultural experience in profoundly personal terms. It reveals, in the most concrete discourse conceivable, the talk of physical experience – body talk – the impossibilities of merging culturally defined systems of understanding human thought and action. It foregrounds the manner in which bodily participation in given forms of symbolic action produce forms of wisdom, necessarily distinctive, necessarily culturally specific in their interpretation, forms of human under-standing without corresponding representation across cultural divides. In so doing, cross-cultural dance research raises the possibility that the most basic forms of human wisdom can only be deeply (and perhaps never fully) understood "cross-culturally" when the limits of their translation are defined through interactive failures. Moreover, the active grounds of cross-cultural translation and the origination of such understandings must be studied for their own sake, in their own terms, that is to say, choreographically.

NOTES

1 See for example the critical discussions of Royce (1977: 38), Novack (1990: 7), Cowan (1990: 5), Kaeppler (1978), and Ness (1992: 239).
2 I include the parenthetical "the" in this statement in order to recognize and incorporate in this discussion the theoretical work of those researchers, notably Paul Spencer (1985: 2), who have used the definite article to specify a notion of dance in which dance is understood as being essentially an institutionalized product of socio-cultural processes, and to distinguish this sort of conceptual-ization of dance from one that is primarily concerned with individual dancers and their dancing experiences. The distinction between "dance" and "the dance" has been an important one in the history of cross-cultural dance theory.
3 For discussions of methodological issues arising in cross-cultural dance research, see Kurath (1960), Royce (1977, especially pages 38–63), Hanna (1979a), Spencer (1985: 1–46), and Ness (1992: 236–40).
4 *Habitus* is defined by Bourdieu as the systems of shared dispositions that tend to reproduce, through creative yet regular applications of their generative principles of practice, the objective structures constitutive of a particular type of socio-cultural environment. A given *habitus* is not a mechanistic recipe for executing the rules of social structure, but rather an intelligent adaptive system of responses and understandings generated from the embodied inculcation of the material conditions of social existence that human beings are inevitably subjected to by virtue of their having been born into specific socio-cultural environments. See Bourdieu (1977: 72–95).
5 The Azande cultural communities Evans-Pritchard studied during his field work were located in what was at that time the "Anglo-Egyptian Sudan." The area today is located in southwestern Sudan, bordering on the Central African Republic and on Zaire.
6 In his discussion of the musical element of Azande dance, Evans-Pritchard notes that he has "very little knowledge of music." In a footnote he reports that, when he tried to get two Azande musicians to set down a notation of songs by Azande singers, "the attempt was a failure" and the use of a phonograph would be essential for any future recording effort (1928: 448 n.1). His own powers of observation and description are characterized as consciously dependent on the Azande practitioners' expertise. Without their descriptive notations, his study is paralyzed. Evans-Pritchard also notes later in this discussion that, with respect to European missionaries' attempts to translate African song lyrics into European hymn tunes, African singing proved generally untranslatable into European modes of song description and composition. Likewise, he notes that European hymn lyrics are impossible to translate into an African language and singing mode, given that the muscular movements African singing necessarily

entails cannot be incorporated into hymn singing (ibid.: 449 n.1). Evans-Pritchard is able to comprehend limits and even to define some objectively generated forms of cultural difference with respect to translating incompatible "song–objects" across African–European cultural divides. With respect to any analogous translation of "body–objects" across such divides, however, his awareness of such problems of translation ceases.

7   Hanna (1979a: 323) emphasized as well that the model stood ready for adjustment and expansion as evidence of new forms of body movement and new features of movement were conceptualized and made available.

8   Kaeppler stresses that only the kinemic and morphokinemic levels are likely to have pan-cultural significance. Higher levels are more variable (1972: 176). For my purposes, this observation is not particularly salient, given that the methodological issues I seek to address occur at the transition between the kinetic and kinemic levels of analysis. Interestingly, Kaeppler's model tends to characterize the kinetic observation process as something other than a level of analysis, starting level "one" with "kinemic" characterizations (ibid.). This strategy effaces the most critical and problematic level transition of the etic/emic ethnoscientific approach.

9   In Kaeppler's words (1985: 116) "*kava*" is defined as "infusion of the root of the pepper plant, *Piper methysticum.*"

10   Interestingly, Kaeppler records these translated observations with indexical labels instead of proper or general names. These abbreviated labels serve effectively to mark the "translated-ness" of their referents and to differentiate the observations from more natural (ethnocentric) "dance talk." The forty-six kinemes Kaeppler documents, for example, are classified with such labels as "L1" (forward step), "W2" (flexion of the wrist), and "A17" (hand on head). The employment of these abbreviated labels in Kaeppler's analyses, which interrupt the flow of her discussion, neither preserving the Tongan emic discourse, nor replacing Tongan concepts with fully fledged English concepts, achieve, and define, implicitly a territory of difference in her work. The primitive indices indirectly indicate the limits of the cross-cultural discourse Kaeppler is attempting to carry on.

BIBLIOGRAPHY

Bourdieu, P. (1977) *Outline of a Theory of Practice*, Cambridge: Cambridge University Press.

Cowan, J. K. (1990) *Dance and the Body Politic in Northern Greece*, Princeton, NJ: Princeton University Press.

Evans-Pritchard, E. A. (1928) "The Dance," *Africa* 1: 446–64.

Hanna, J. L. (1979a) "Movements Toward Understanding Humans Through the Anthropological Study of Dance," *Current Anthropology* 20, 2: 313–39.

—— (1979b) *To Dance is Human: A Theory of Nonverbal Communication*, Austin: University of Texas Press.

Kaeppler, A. L. (1967) "The Structure of Tongan Dance." unpublished Ph.D. dissertation, University of Hawaii.

—— (1972) "Method and Theory in Analyzing Dance Structure with an Analysis of Tongan Dance," *Ethnomusicology* 16(2): 173–217.

—— (1978) "Dance in Anthropological Perspective," *Annual Review of Anthropology* 7: 31–49.

—— (1985) "Structured Movement Systems in Tonga" in P. Spencer (ed.) *Society and the Dance: The Social Anthropology of Process and Performance*, Cambridge: Cambridge University Press.

Kurath, G. P. (1960) "Panorama of Dance Ethnology," *Current Anthropology* 1: 233–54.

Meduri, A. (1988) "Bharatha Natyam – What Are You?" *Asian Theatre Journal* 5, 1: 1–22.

Ness, S. A. (1992) *Body, Movement, and Culture: Kinesthetic and Visual Symbolism in a Philippine Community*, Philadelphia: University of Pennsylvania Press.

Novack, C. J. (1990) *Sharing the Dance: Contact Improvisation and American Culture*, Madison: University of Wisconsin Press.

Royce, A. P. (1977) *The Anthropology of Dance*, Bloomington: Indiana University Press.

Spencer, P. (1985) "Introduction," in P. Spencer (ed.) *Society and the Dance: The Social Anthropology of Process and Performance*, Cambridge: Cambridge University Press.

Sweet, J. D. (1979) Remarks made in "Comments" section of "Movements Toward Understanding Humans Through the Anthropological Study of Dance," *Current Anthropology* 20, 2: 329.

15 Cross-Cultural Differences in the Interpretation of Merce Cunningham's Choreography

Miwa Nagura

In the 1970s, Miyabi Ichikawa, one of Japan's foremost dance critics, wrote extensively about the work of American choreographers. His criticism, translated for the first time here, provides an opportunity to see the West viewed from the perspective of the East. It also makes possible an examination of some of the difficulties of writing across cultural boundaries. That these boundaries exist, despite increased intercultural understanding, is beyond doubt. Dance clearly manifests different styles, techniques, and meanings in different cultures, and these differences act as a veil through which a critic sees. In this essay, I will look at cross-cultural differences in American and Japanese dance criticism by closely examining Ichikawa's texts on Cunningham from the 1970s and comparing his analysis with that of various Americans.

Ichikawa (b. 1937) is an internationally known dance critic, recognized especially for his writing on butoh. He lived in New York from April 1966 to September 1968 and also in 1974 for a short period. His goal in these travels was to become better acquainted with the American performing arts, in particular modern and postmodern dance. His visits came at a time when the Japanese were intensely curious about American culture. It is important to remember that a close relationship between the U.S. and Japan was established only after World War II. In addition to Japan's geographical remoteness, her isolationist policy during the Edo era (1601–1867) and her imperialist period from the beginning of the twentieth century through World War II kept American influences at bay. It was not until the signing of the Treaty of Peace for Japan with the United States and other nations in 1951 that cultural exchanges between the two countries became common.[1]

As for American modern dance, it developed and flourished from the 1920s through the 1940s, years in which Japan had scant contact with U.S. culture. By the time the Japanese encountered modern dance in the 1960s, it was a mature form with many diverse styles. Japanese critics felt they had much catching up to do in order to understand current dance trends.

Ichikawa returned to Japan just as opportunities were increasing for American dance companies to appear in his country. He wrote extensively on American dance and was soon acknowledged as a leading authority on the subject. The Merce Cunningham Dance Company's second Japanese tour in 1976 (the first was in 1964), coincided with Ichikawa's most active period of writing.

CHANCE, INDETERMINACY, AND IMPROVISATION

Among Ichikawa's Japanese publications are *Koui-to-Nikutai* (Action and Bodies) (1972), *American-dance Now: Modern Dance and Post-modern Dance* (1975), and *Buyo-no-Cosmology* (The cosmology of dance). *Koui-to-Nikutai*, a collection of essays written for Japanese magazines from 1969 to 1972, includes three essays on American contemporary dancers – Yvonne Rainer, Anna Halprin, Alwin Nikolais – and one on the development of modern dance. *American-dance Now* was the first book in Japan completely devoted to modern and postmodern choreographers: Martha Graham, Nikolais, Cunningham, Alvin Ailey, Halprin, Rainer, Trisha Brown, and Meredith Monk. The book, whose publication coincided with the Grand Union's first performances in Japan at the end of 1975, went far in helping the Japanese understand current American trends. *Buyo-no-Cosmology* is another collection of Ichikawa's essays for Japanese magazines, spanning the years 1973 to 1980. The book includes one article on Cunningham's aesthetics, written in 1976 right after his company appeared in Japan.

The chapter on Cunningham in *American-dance Now,* is titled "Dance of *Guzen-sei* (chance) and *Sokkyo-sei* (improvisation)"; it outlines Cunningham's signature choreographic methods. *Guzen-sei* means occurring unexpectedly or being accidental, as does chance in one of its English meanings. *Sokkyo* means improvising on the spot. It originally referred to poets who improvised verses in traditional Japanese verbal performances. The improvisational dance of postmodern choreographers was also coined *Sokkyo*. Ichikawa's title is misleading because *guzen-sei* may not clearly convey the characteristics of chance as Cunningham used it; and of course, Cunningham rarely used *sokkyo*, that is, improvisation, in his dances. An examination of how Cunningham's methods of dance-making have been translated into Japanese points out a difficulty in conceptualizing his choreographic methods within the Japanese language.

Cunningham, influenced by composer John Cage, his long-term collaborator, has favored chance methods as a way of opening up movement possibilities beyond those he might customarily invent. When he uses chance methods, he prepares elaborate charts for such elements as body parts, directions, the duration of movements, and the order of choreographed sequences. Then he composes a dance by selecting elements from the charts through arbitrary means. These include coin-tossing, dice-throwing, or hexagrams from the *I Ching* (Chinese book of changes).[2] Cunningham finds chance methods valuable because, as he explains:

When I choreograph a piece by tossing pennies – by chance, that is – I am finding my resources in that play, which is not the product of *my* will, but which is an energy and a law which I too obey. . . . The feeling I have when I compose in this way is that I am in touch with natural resources far greater than my own personal inventiveness could ever be, much more universally human than the particular habits of my own practice, and organically rising out of common pools of motor impulses.

(1978: 311)

Chance choreography is often considered to be fortuitous because of its random selection process. Once the movements are selected, however, the choreography is rehearsed accordingly, becomes permanent, and can be repeated like conventional choreography. Cunningham's use of chance methods is, therefore, only methodological. He uses chance as a tool to choreograph movements he would not otherwise have thought of.

Along with chance, Cunningham experimented with the idea of indeterminacy in a few of his dances in the late 1950s and early 1960s. For him, indeterminacy gave his dancers "a certain freedom, not about the movements themselves but about tempo, direction, and whether to do certain movements or not" (Cunningham and Lesschaeve 1985: 150). In a dance in which indeterminacy was an element, Cunningham set the framework of choreography but would let spontaneous possibilities shape the dance at the moment of performance on stage. Indeterminacy is characterized as "open form" (Klosty 1975: 13; Brown 1968: 22) since the choreography is not entirely set, or "live chance" (Johnston 1971: 157) because chance elements are left for the dancers to select while on stage.

In the chapter, "Dance of Chance and Improvisation," Ichikawa introduces Cunningham's chance methods: "Cunningham has broadened the realm of movement by applying the methods of *guzen-sei*, by which he determines choreography by tossing a coin" (1975: 50, trans.).[3] Ichikawa, however, often uses another term, *fukakutei-sei*, to describe chance methods, although this literally means "indeterminacy" (*fu* connotes negation, *kakutei* means an act of determining, and *sei* is a suffix pertaining to a characteristic):

Cunningham has had an impact on the world of modern dance in several respects. He applied *fukakutei-sei* to his creative process. This method seems to have been influenced by John Cage. Cunningham wrote out various elements, tempi, directions of movement, kind of movement (running, jumping, pirouette, solo or unison, etc.) on a chart and determined a combination by tossing a coin. He also numbered parts of the body and made movements in a similar way. This way of dance-making produced an unexpected sequence and sometimes resulted in a very dramatic dance.

(ibid.)

Ichikawa's description corresponds to Cunningham's chance methods, but Ichikawa considers them indeterminate. For Cunningham, indeterminacy is, of course, another choreographic method and differs from chance.

Following the above quotation, Ichikawa explains how chance is applied:

> Our imagination is limited by our intelligence or social environment. There is almost no way to avoid such limitations. In the case of dance, certain ways of combining steps and movements, or structuring a dance piece are taken for granted. Cunningham overcame the limitation in imagination by applying *guzen-sei* and succeeded in achieving a superior imaginative space. The dances made by *guzen-sei*, such as *Untitled Solo* and *Fragments*, were choreographed in the 1950s. He then came to choreograph strictly in the 1960s.
>
> (ibid.)

In this passage Ichikawa is right when he says that Cunningham aims at finding unexpected movement through chance methods, but the distinction he makes between *guzen-sei* and strict choreography is not accurate. His understanding of Cunningham's choreographic strategies can be summarized this way: dances choreographed by chance methods are not strictly set, therefore, their structure is indeterminate (*fukakutei*) and they bring unexpected sequences (*guzen*) into a performance. His use of *guzen-sei* is problematic; if *guzen-sei* represents chance, it has to be used as a concept which is different from *fukakutei-sei* or indeterminacy. The distinction between *guzen-sei* and *fukakutei-sei* is crucial because Cunningham unequivocally distinguishes between the two. The confusion of chance and indeterminacy comes from a connotation of *guzen-sei* in the Japanese language; that is, *guzen* implies indeterminacy.

Having noted that Cunningham's dances are indeterminate, Ichikawa introduces improvisation as "another method of his choreography in addition to *guzen-sei*." He takes *Field Dances* as an example, although Cunningham, himself, does not consider the work to be improvisatory, but rather indeterminate:

> Cunningham expanded the possibility of improvisation as much as he could. He showed somewhat simple movements and let dancers go on or off stage at will. *Field Dances* in 1963 is an example. This is another way of unleashing the imagination from conventional forms.
>
> (ibid.)

What Ichikawa calls improvisation is actually indeterminacy in Cunningham's sense because movement sections are prepared prior to a performance, among which the dancers spontaneously choose. This is different from improvisation, which occurs spontaneously during a performance without preparation beforehand.

Ichikawa also uses *Story* to exemplify Cunningham's combined uses of chance and improvisation although it is, in fact, an indeterminate dance:

Improvisation and *guzen-sei* were sometimes used at the same time. In *Story* (1963), Cunningham transformed the stage into a dressing room. Each dancer insisted on his or her own individuality without any central focus of attention on stage. The accumulation of each dancer's movement formed the dance piece as a whole. But this work fell into a kind of anarchic state. It was said that the dance was abandoned because dancers on stage collided with one another. *Guzen-sei* was then given up because Cunningham realized that the method was not effective unless dancers with rich improvisational ability and imagination were able to dance in a suitable environment.

(ibid.)

Being unable to grasp Cunningham's dance-making philosophy, Ichikawa thinks that Cunningham gave up chance and improvisation because they did not effectively support his fundamental choreographic tenets, while in fact, Cunningham continues to use chance methods in his dances.

I think that Cunningham's concept of improvisation, *guzen-sei*, simultaneity, and everyday movement came from his long-term friendship with John Cage. However, Cunningham is not as radical a philosopher as Cage; he is merely a Dionysian dancer who has no other desire than making his dances out of his passion for movement and having his dancers dance his works. . . . Contrary to Cage, Cunningham accepts these concepts only as methodology. Now in the 1970s, Cunningham is trying to discard them. Perhaps, he has decided that they are not effective in his dance-making.

(ibid.: 51, trans.)

Ichikawa interprets correctly that Cunningham's interest in chance is only methodological. However, his analysis of Cunningham as Dionysian is not appropriate, since Cunningham is, if anything, Apollonian in the extent to which he controls his work. Spontaneity is kept to a minimum, and even giving the dancers some limited choice in what movement they would execute on stage, was soon abandoned. As Roger Copeland points out:

Cunningham's use of chance is diametrically opposed to the sort of improvisation which lies at the heart of abstract expressionism. Cunningham is not attempting to break through the resistances of the intellect so as to unleash "natural" impulses buried within him. Quite the contrary: he utilizes utterly impersonal mechanisms (coins, dice, the I Ching, etc.) so as to avoid what might otherwise "come naturally." This is why so many dancers complain that Cunningham's choreography is often excruciatingly difficult – if not impossible – to perform: it doesn't *come naturally* to the human body.

(1983: 317)

Ichikawa's confusion about chance, indeterminacy, and improvisation may have been due, in part, to the scant information available to him in the 1970s on Cunningham's dance principles. Even when he was dealing with Cunningham's own words, the information could have caused him to make a skewed interpretation. This is clearly seen in Ichikawa's essay on Cunningham's book, *Changes* (1968) in the Japanese magazine, *Geijutsu-Techo*, in 1970. *Changes* is not really a suitable introduction to Cunningham's aesthetics; for the book – an assemblage of charts Cunningham used for chance operations, concert programs, short essays, notes for particular dances, and photographs without page numbers or a logical order to follow – does not contain any explanation of Cunningham's chance methods or of his philosophy. Due to a lack of explanation, Ichikawa regarded the charts in the book as Cunningham's dance notation:

> Cunningham disagrees with dance notation such as Labanotation. Dance notation is all about a description of steps. Using this type of notation means accepting formalist aesthetics, which puts absolute importance on strict choreography. Cunningham does not use such a notation of steps. He only determines a space or a consistent situation. ... His notation ... is definitely different from traditional notation because it is a description of a whole theatrical space rather than steps.
>
> (1970: 160–5, trans.)

Ichikawa believes that the charts portray situations in which dancers improvise, but not steps or precise choreography. This interpretation leads him to relate the charts to improvisation:

> In Cunningham's company, most parts of the dance are left up to the dancers' spontaneous movement rather than to a strict choreography. It would be explained by Cage's words: "Although a situation is determined, its contents are given shape by indeterminate improvisation."
>
> (ibid.: 160, trans.)

Ichikawa thinks the charts are similar to the scores for the indeterminate music of Cunningham's collaborators – namely, Cage, David Tudor, and Toshi Ichiyanagi – which are concerned with "the production of sound and are different from traditional musical scores" (ibid.). Ichikawa's comment on the musical scores is accurate, but his correlation of the scores with Cunningham's charts is misguided.

In addition, Ichikawa also finds similarities between Cunningham's charts and Lawrence Halprin's movement notation (ibid.: 165). Halprin, a California landscape architect and husband of Anna Halprin, created his own method of movement notation called "Motation" out of his interest in the relationship between space and movement.[4] Motation aims at bringing a graphic system to a kinetic environment for landscape planning or a performance.

The system is a tool both for recording existing events or to create new conditions. It is a scoring system for motion through space, just as musical notation is a scoring system for sound. Its uses are the same. As a musical score can describe a piece of music that then can either be heard in the mind's ear or actually played, so Motation can describe motion through spaces that can either be seen through the mind's eye or moved through in actuality.

(Halprin 1965: 130)

Motation indeed shares some similarities with chance methods, in that it can be used as a tool for creating choreography. Having noticed the similarity between the two, it is understandable that Ichikawa might consider Cunningham's charts as notation describing a particular space or situation in which movement takes place. In addition, certain postmodern dance choreographers in the 1960s, such as Steve Paxton and Carolyn Brown, experimented with scores to teach movement to their dancers. Ichikawa, having known that Paxton and Brown studied with Cunningham, finds their scores similar to Cunningham's charts. Ichikawa's correlation of Cunningham's chance methods with various postmodern dance activities misleads the reader as to the true nature of Cunningham's methods.[5] Certainly, Cunningham's innovative approach to choreography offered many possibilities to postmodern dancers. Ichikawa, while living in New York from 1966 to 1968, encountered some of the new dance that was influenced by Cunningham and in the 1970s wrote many articles in Japan about postmodern dance in the United States. It seems, however, that his relatively short stay only led to partial understanding.

A lack of reliable secondary information was another problem Ichikawa faced in interpreting Cunningham's choreography. Calvin Tomkins's *The Bride and the Bachelors*, published in the United States in 1968 and consisting of articles he wrote as art critic for *The New Yorker*, was one of the few references Ichikawa could turn to when writing his book, *American-dance Now*. *The Bride and the Bachelors*, which includes a chapter on Cunningham, was published in a Japanese translation in 1972. Ichikawa's explanations in his "Dance of Chance and Improvisation" are often similar to Tomkins's. For example, Ichikawa describes the processes of chance choreography very much as Tomkins does (Tomkins 1968: 260). Ichikawa may well have had to depend on Tomkins's book as a valuable secondary source. Tomkins methodologically distinguishes chance from indeterminacy, and indeterminacy from improvisation, and he writes that works like *Field Dances* and *Story* have strict limits in their degree of indeterminacy (ibid.: 275–6). Nevertheless, his depiction of indeterminacy, in which he mentions the dancers' spontaneous choice of movements during a particular performance, might have seemed to Ichikawa to be based on improvisation.

Because he had not seen many Cunningham dances nor been exposed to

Figure 15.1 *Event #9:* Merce Cunningham and Dance Company, 1968. (Photo: James Klosty)

the opinions of numerous critics, it was extremely difficult for Ichikawa to fully understand the key concepts of chance and indeterminacy and express them in Japanese. Such complex ideas do not contextually translate into Japanese. As Talal Asad argues, there are limitations to reproducing the structure of an alien discourse within a translator's own language (1986: 141–64).[6] There is no equivalent word in the Japanese indigenous vocabulary for Cunningham's chance, and because Ichikawa did not fully understand Cunningham's use of the word, he could not explain it. By using *guzen-sei*, a literal translation of chance, he inadvertently distorted Cunningham's meaning.

EXPRESSIVITY

Ichikawa's essay, "The Aesthetics of Non-Expressivity" in his book, *Buyo-no-Cosmology*, written after Cunningham's company performed *Event #163* in a Kyoto gymnasium in 1976, exemplifies another pitfall in cross-cultural dance analysis: the different aesthetic bases from which critics write. In this essay, Ichikawa characterizes Cunningham's dances as non-expressive in contrast to Martha Graham's highly expressive choreography.

> Cunningham was once one of the principal dancers of the Martha Graham Dance Company. Graham is known for her creation of a dance style which expresses various emotions. Cunningham, however, came to disagree with such an expressive dance. In search of independence of physical movement, he went to the School of American Ballet to study under George Balanchine. Balanchine was called a "neo-classic" choreographer and favored abstract ballet. There, Cunningham learned Balanchine's aesthetics, which prioritized lines and forms as the absolute principles of dance. At present, Cunningham's creativity seems to come from a non-expressive aesthetics of line and form.[7]
>
> (1983: 118–19, trans.)

Ichikawa also mentions similarities between Cunningham and Balanchine in his earlier publication, *American-dance Now* by quoting Cunningham:

> Cunningham commented on his departure from Graham: "I don't work through images or ideas. I work through the body. I don't even want to think that dancers' movement means something. That is the reason why I thought I could not dance with Graham. That is, she always taught me to think that a particular movement means something specific. I thought such a notion was nonsense."[8] There is no doubt that this comment denied introspectiveness and affirms the aesthetics of abstract ballet.
>
> (1975: 50, trans.)

Although Cunningham rejects Graham's notion that movement has specific meaning, "non-expressivity" does not represent his style; for he believes that movement itself is expressive. Rather than denying expressivity,

Cunningham introduced a new concept of expressivity to American dance:

> I don't think that what I do is non-expressive, it's just that I don't try to inflict it on anybody, so each person may think in whatever way his feelings and experience take him. I always feel that movement itself is expressive, regardless of intentions of expressivity, beyond intention.
>
> (Cunningham and Lesschaeve 1985: 106)

Ichikawa positions Cunningham at the polar opposite of Graham. This interpretation excludes the possibility of another kind of expressivity; it can only lead to an absence of expressivity:

> Cunningham, deprived of emotions, destroyed plots and talked about his distrust of total art. Through destructive processes, he returned to the physical body and movement, and buried himself in abstract ballet. ... The body and movement stood alone [without emotions or plots] like a building which miraculously remained unburnt in a city which had been reduced to ashes.
>
> (1972: 201–2, trans.)

Cunningham's Events, in which segments from several repertory pieces are assembled to construct a single ninety-minute dance, persuaded Ichikawa that Cunningham's work was non-expressive. This occurred despite the fact that Cunningham himself created his Events out of the belief that movement is expressive in itself and doesn't need to be supported by the production elements that originally surrounded it, such as music, decor, titles, and costumes.

In his essay, Ichikawa points out his reasons for asserting that Cunningham's Events lack expressivity:

> What Cunningham wants to present [in an Event] is the non-expressivity of dance movement. Strictly speaking, in spite of the fact that any movement can be expressive, his movement does not reflect any particular thing or theme. There is no emotional expression, such as agony, joy, or absoluteness, nor a narrative which derives from a Greek tragedy, for example.
>
> (1983: 118, trans.)

Ichikawa also comments that "Cunningham focused on non-expressive dance in response to the current trend in postmodern dance, and dance which opposes the extremely expressive dance seen in Graham's choreography" (1976: 74, trans.). He interprets Cunningham's movement as intentionally abstract:

> Cunningham would say, "The audience can interpret the dance in whatever ways they want to because we do not impose a certain image upon the audience; in other words, an interpretation of our dance is totally open to the audience." His belief that movement ... should not

be determined by anything else seems to have led him to make such abstract movement.

(1983: 118, trans.)

This approach to Cunningham dances may be convincing to Ichikawa because he believes Cunningham's choreography is akin to Balanchine's abstract ballets. This belief is not limited to Ichikawa, since Cunningham has been nicknamed "the barefoot Balanchine" in Japan. Yet, Balanchine's abstract ballets are not analogous to Cunningham's dances for many reasons, none more obvious than that for Balanchine dance is inspired by music, whereas for Cunningham, dance and music are different entities which happen to take place at the same time. It's not clear why Ichikawa attempts to position Cunningham linearly between the extremes of Graham's and Balanchine's styles, but it may be because Graham and Balanchine were leading American dance figures and better known in Japan in the 1970s than Cunningham. Such a comparison, however, misrepresents the new dimension of expressivity Cunningham advocated.

In general, Ichikawa considers "expressivity" "a style of modern dance"(1983: 98, trans.). In the chapter about the history of American modern dance in *Buyo-no-Cosmology* (ibid.: 95–105) he discusses a number of distinguished choreographers ranging from Isadora Duncan to various postmodernists. A major key in his analysis is the way choreographers express their inner emotions or "introspection" through the body. Choreographers whose dances lack introspection (who are not concerned with expressing emotions or specific meaning) he calls "abstract." To Ichikawa, Graham's choreography is based on introspection while Cunningham's originates from a kind of anti-introspection which produces abstraction. Ichikawa considers dance movement a symbolic intermediary through which communication takes place between choreographers/ dancers and audience. "Even though modern dance simply insists on its introspectiveness," Ichikawa writes, "if the body does not express the introspection and is not communicative, it [the choreography] is considered to lack expressivity" (ibid.: 100, trans.). That is, he does not consider Cunningham's dances to be communicative. In his view, movement has to symbolize a specific feeling or narrative.

On the contrary, Cunningham's dances do communicate in a way Ichikawa has not acknowledged. For example, Susan Foster, in her study of modes of communication in dance, states that Cunningham's dances communicate in a reflective mode: as movements reflect themselves, they "inevitably reflect the viewers in the process of searching for and producing meaning for the dances" (1986: 76). Marcia Siegel, although she disagrees with Foster's categorization, believes that dance, including Cunningham's, communicates, even though theory cannot easily explain how this is done (1988: 24).

Ichikawa has a strong interest in the symbolic system of dance. In his essay "Dance as Symbol" (1983: 217–25), he refers to German philosophers such as Ernst Cassirer, Gerhard Zacharias, Carl Jung, Ernst Groce, and Max Dessoir, as well as Russian dance critic, Akim Volynski.[9] Ichikawa was especially influenced by Volynski and Zacharias's concept of "the body as a microcosm" in their analyses of symbolic movement in ballet. With this notion, Ichikawa argues that dancers are "prototypes who symbolize the dynamic, spatial, and time harmony of the universe" (ibid.: 218, trans.).

Susanne Langer's philosophy also undoubtedly influenced Ichikawa in his application of a symbolic system to American modern dance. Langer defines "expression" as "the function of symbols" (1953: 26) and "art" as "the creation of forms symbolic of human feeling" (ibid.: 40). As a protégée of Cassirer, Langer's theory must have appeared convincing to Ichikawa. Three of her books – *Philosophy in a New Key* (1942), *Feeling and Form* (1953), and *Problems of Art* (1957) – became available in Japanese translations in 1960, 1970–1 (in three volumes), and 1967 respectively. Some of Langer's concepts can be applied to Cunningham. For example, she categorizes symbols as discursive and non-discursive (1953: 29). Visual forms are non-discursive symbols, which "do not present their constituents successively, but simultaneously, so the relations determining a visual structure are grasped in one act of vision" (1942: 93). By applying this idea, Ichikawa analyzes Cunningham's choreography as follows:

> Cunningham thinks it is wrong to attribute movement to a particular narrative meaning because any movement constantly connotes meaning. His belief coincides with Susanne Langer's semantic analysis [of dance]. . . . In her book, *Feeling and Form*, she points out two kinds of form: literal and intuitive. Dance, together with music, is an intuitive form and an untranslatable, non-discursive symbol. Cunningham's theory of dance, in the same way, seems to emphasize the non-discursive nature of movement and seeks an independent meaning of dance by means of executing movement.
>
> (1983: 100, trans.)

Ichikawa's assumption that expressivity is connected to emotion is also close to Langer, who contends that "all dance motion is gesture, or an element in the exhibition of gesture" and is "always motivated by the semblance of an expressive movement" (Langer 1953, 174). Ichikawa presumes that gestures are the essential components of dance, through which emotions are conceptualized and expressed:

> Both languages and gestures are symbols and different from signs because signs are intrinsic responses to feelings. Symbols acquire meaning through the process of conceptualizing feelings. . . . The content of a dance is not determined by what the movements indicate. Dance obtains its content when the things to be expressed are conceptualized into gestures.
>
> (1983: 218, trans.)

This opinion is in line with Ichikawa's other belief that movement symbolizes a certain thing. He can relate the expressivity of dance to emotions because he thinks that dancers conceptualize feelings through gesture. It should be noted that in Japanese traditional dance and Kabuki, movement is made up of a combination of gestures, which are particular codes of emotional or indicative expressions.

Ichikawa's notions of expressivity share many similarities with the ideas of John Martin and Louis Horst, whose theory and criticism helped define American modern dance during the 1930s and 1940s. Martin was dance critic for the *New York Times* from 1927 to 1962, seminal years in the history of American modern dance. His book, *The Modern Dance*, published in 1933, was one of the first to attempt to define American modern dance as a form. Horst was musical director of Graham's company, a composer, and editor of *Dance Observer*. He influenced a number of dancers, choreographers, and actors through his dance composition classes, conducted from 1928 to 1964, and through his theory of composition, based on thematic coherence and variation.

For Martin, movement is "the link between the dancer's intention and your [the audience's] perception of it" (1933: 12) and "a medium for the transference of an aesthetic and emotional concept from the consciousness of one individual to another" (ibid.: 13). "Metakinesis," which he considered one of the unique aspects of modern dance, is the association between the physical and the psychical. As in German expressionist dance, where the dancer's feelings are made visible through movement, Martin contends that movement is "the result of some personal, mental, psychological characteristics" (ibid.: 16). He believes modern dance should pursue movement forms that express an inner compulsion (ibid.: 6). Similarly, Horst, who studied in Germany, favored expressing emotions through movement, especially inner emotions and the workings of the subconscious (Horst and Russell 1961: 90–5). In modern dance, he believed that emotions must be "transposed into a form, a significance, which will deliver back to an audience the motivating idea" (ibid.: 142).

The theoretical concepts supported by Langer, Martin, and Horst form the basic tenets of expressivity in American modern dance, tenets which Cunningham challenged.

> Dance is not emoting, passion for her, anger against him. I think dance is more primal than that. In its essence, in the nakedness of its energy it is a source from which passion or anger may issue in a particular form, the source of energy out of which may be channeled the energy that goes into the various emotional behaviors.
>
> (Cunningham 1978: 311)

NEW DIRECTIONS IN AMERICAN CRITICISM

With Cunningham's revolution and the experiments of postmodern choreographers in the 1960s, American critics began to expand the meaning of "expressivity" (Carroll 1981). Jill Johnston, dance critic for the *Village Voice* in the 1960s, was particularly influential on later dance criticism. She refers to Cunningham's expressivity in movement as a "shift of focus – from representation to the concentration on materials" (Johnston 1992: 34). With this approach, emotion in Cunningham's dances is "created by motion rather than the reverse," and therefore, "each movement means only itself and it moves you by its pure existence, by being so much itself" (ibid.: 35). The following excerpt from Deborah Jowitt's review of a Cunningham Event in 1978 clearly shows a perspective that is markedly different from Ichikawa's: "Events provide an opportunity for Merce to acknowledge ... that movement can function differently in different contexts, just as gestures in life acquire different meaning from the circumstances in which they occur" (Jowitt 1985, 30).

During the 1960s, art in the United States changed because of political, sociological, and cultural shifts within the society. Now the world's richest nation, the U.S. enjoyed new-found confidence. Americans were willing to take risks and open the doors to new ideas. Developments such as the civil rights and free speech movements called the establishment into question, producing an atmosphere of openness and experimentation that had not existed before. At the same time, events such as the Cuban Missile Crisis added to the general anxiety about the future that was an underlying theme throughout the Cold War. Due to these conflicting elements, artists in the sixties came to make works that addressed multiple realities from multiple viewpoints. American interest in Asian philosophies, already established by the beat generation in the 1950s, found many more advocates in the next decade. John Cage incorporated precepts of Zen Buddhism into his work and created a new style of music. For example, he advocated the idea that "expressing nothing is expressing something." This concept could help explain the shift in American modern dance from representing something absolute, such as a story, an emotion, or a theme, to allowing movement to have multiple meanings.

Sally Banes notes that dance not only reflects society, but also produces it (1994: 43–4). Cunningham's dances not only addressed the evolution of American culture and society, but also encouraged American dance critics to seek alternative interpretations. Consequently, dance criticism in the United States in the late 1960s discarded traditional theoretical modes in order to deal with new styles of contemporary dance. How American critics responded to Cunningham's dances over the years demonstrates changes taking place in dance criticism itself.

American dance critics in the 1950s and the early 1960s, such as Martin and Horst, disapproved of and ignored Cunningham's works. His name did not even appear in Horst and Russell's *Modern Dance Form in Relation to the Other Arts* (1961). Critical response to Cunningham remained unfavorable until Johnston approached his work from a different standpoint.[10] However, Johnston was not alone in creating a new kind of criticism. Susan Sontag, an extremely influential voice for change, emphasized form in art rather than content (1966: 102–4). She proposed that the function of criticism should be "to show *how it is what it is, even that it is what it is*, rather than to show *what it means*" (ibid.: 104). Her critical perspective corresponded well with Cunningham's aesthetics.

Dance styles and dance criticism, then, have evolved reciprocally in the United States. In Japan, on the other hand, political, sociological, and cultural shifts – from the feudal era to the pre-war imperial era, then to post-war democracy – produced a very different way of looking at dance. During the decades of modernization and westernization from the end of the nineteenth century through World War II, Japan had close contact with Germany while American influences were kept at bay.[11] A number of Japanese students went to Germany at this time to study, particularly literature and medical science, in order to narrow the intellectual and technological gap with the West. Ougai Mori (1862–1922), a Japanese novelist, studied in Germany and later established the expressionist school of literature in Japan. He was acclaimed for his highly romantic novels, some based on his experiences in Germany, others dealing with events in Japanese history. It was, then, through expressionism that Japanese writers conveyed the subject matter of the modern age. Similarly, dance styles in Japan were westernized while traditional dance was denounced as trivial and far-fetched. "In Japan," Ichikawa writes, "it was mandatory that everyone abandon nonsensical dances as seen in Kabuki, and to make dances which had rational plots based on modern consciousness" (1991: 125, trans.).

German *Ausdruckstanz* of the 1920s and 1930s had a significant influence on the creation of what was later called "modern dance" in Japan. Before World War II, new dance styles in Japan were called "*Neue Tanz*" or "new dance," after the German. The term, "modern dance" came from the United States after World War II and was used for German-influenced dance as well as American modern dance. Ichikawa points out the influence of German modern dance on Japanese choreographers, such as Kouya Eguchi, who studied in Germany from 1931 to 1933 and taught butoh dancer, Kazuo Ohno. *Ausdruckstanz*, especially the dance of Mary Wigman which Eguchi often discussed with Ohno and Tatsumi Hijikata, was a significant influence on the rise of butoh in the 1960s (Ichikawa 1989: 14–19). Since Japanese dance was inspired by German modern dance, a critical approach in Japan was formed within the framework of German expressionist dance and criticism.

Japan's close relationship with the United States was established only after 1951 after the signing of the peace treaty. Just as in the pre-war period, when Germany had influenced Japanese artistic and intellectual life, American culture now came to the fore. However, despite the change of critical approaches in the United States in the late 1960s, the new criticism was not easily accessible to the Japanese because of geographical distance and differences in language. When dance aesthetics in the United States developed beyond the theories of Martin, Horst, and Langer, the Japanese remained essentially unaware of the new directions being taken. During the 1960s, when Americans were inspired by Asian philosophies and arrived at new stylistic junctures in dance, the Japanese ironically were trying to catch up with American culture and consequently praised the "Americanness" of the dances they saw. Following this trend, Ichikawa attempted to understand Cunningham's dances within the theoretical framework of traditional American modern dance and expressionistic German modern dance even though they were, in fact, irrelevant to a clear analysis of Cunningham's work. Poignantly, this resulted in creating a great gulf between him and American dance critics of the day.[12]

Through this examination of Ichikawa's criticism, I have attempted to show some of the reasons dance may be interpreted differently in different cultures. Clearly, reliable secondary sources and a relevant theoretical basis are particularly crucial for an effective contextualization of foreign dance forms. But a host of other elements also contribute to the critic's ability to understand the arts of another culture, and these elements can be far beyond an individual's control. Despite valiant efforts to understand dance of another culture, we must accept the fact that critical viewpoints will always be bound by the writer's own cultural context.

NOTES

1 Prior to the treaty, American culture was brought into Japan during the United States' occupation (1945–51). After 1951, along with the economic recovery from the devastation of World War II, Japanese interest in American culture grew rapidly.

2 *Sixteen Dances for Soloist and the Company of Three* (1951) was Cunningham's first application of chance methods in determining the order of choreographed sequences. *Suite by Chance* (1953) was the first dance in which movement itself was constructed by chance methods from a large series of charts.

3 Quotations from Ichikawa's Japanese publications are my translation and designated as "trans." throughout the essay.

4 Motation consists of a horizontal track which maps the path of travel within an environment, a vertical track which charts what performers will see as they move, and two columns for distance and speed.

5 Ichikawa also uses the term *guzen-sei* to characterize the work of the Living Theater, a New York-based experimental theater group in the 1960s. He says the group performed *guzen-sei* theater in which improvisation is an essential element (1972: 200, trans.). Such a use of the term blurs the meaning of chance methods specific to Cunningham's application.

6 Asad argues the issue of cultural translation in terms of westerners' ethnocentric interpretations of Third World cultures. However, I believe his approach

also can be applied to cross-cultural interpretations working in the opposite direction.

7 Although rarely encouraging her company members to study ballet, Martha Graham suggested to Cunningham that he take classes at the School of American Ballet and introduced him to Lincoln Kirstein, director of the school. Cunningham attended Balanchine's classes, but studied primarily with others such as Anatole Obukhov and Pierre Vladimirov (personal communication, David Vaughan, June 1995).

8 This quotation probably comes from Tomkins's *The Bride and the Bachelors* (1968: 246). Indeed, Tomkins also links Cunningham with Balanchine: "Cunningham's work had less in common with the modern dance choreography of Graham and Jose Limon than it had with the dazzling neoclassicism of George Balanchine" (ibid.: 263).

9 Some of these writers' books are available in Japanese. For example, The Japanese translation of Zacharias's *Ballet – Gestalt und Wessen* was published in 1965 while no English translation is available. Volynski's *Buch der Jubel* was originally published in Russian. Part of the book was translated into German and appeared in the German magazine, *Der Tanz*, in the series from June 1931 to March 1936. It was also included in Zacharias's *Ballet – Gestalt und Wessen*. The book was then published in Japanese (publishing date unknown) whereas only an excerpt appeared in English in *Dance Scope* in 1971 (Spring: 16–35), and a section, "The Vertical: the Fundamental Principle of Classical Dance," in Copeland and Cohen (eds) *What Is Dance?* in 1983 (255–7). Ichikawa has said that *Buch der Jubel* is necessary reading for Japanese dance critics. He also said that *Ballet – Gestalt und Wessen* influenced him greatly, particularly elements having to do with Jung's psychoanalysis and archetypes (personal communication). Such Jungian elements are often referred to in Graham's dances.

10 Johnston's contribution to a new direction in dance criticism, which can embrace Cunningham's aesthetics, is well described in Banes's *Writing Dancing in the Age of Postmodernism* (1994: 3–9).

11 For example, Japan's first constitution, the Meiji Constitution, was adapted in 1889 from the German constitution. Hermann Roessler, a German adviser to the Japanese Foreign Office, helped implement it. Hirobumi Ito (1841–1909), Japan's first prime minister, attended a course of lectures by the German authoritarian fanatic, von Gneist, during his visit to Germany and listened to Lorenz von Stein in Vienna. Japan's close relationship with Germany continued until the end of World War II.

12 Another factor that might have contributed to differences between Japanese and American criticism in the 1960s and 1970s is that German books were translated into Japanese that were not translated into English and consequently had no influence in the United States while having an impact in Japan.

BIBLIOGRAPHY

Asad, T. (1986) "The Concept of Cultural Translation in British Social Anthropology," in J. Clifford (ed.) *Writing Culture: The Poetics and Politics of Ethnography*, Berkeley: University of California Press.

Banes, S. (1994) *Writing Dancing in the Age of Postmodernism*, Hanover, NH: University Press of New England.

Brown, C. (1968) "On Chance," *Ballet Review* 2, 2: 7–25.

Carroll, N. (1981) "Post-modern Dance and Expression," in G. Francher and G. Myers (eds) *Philosophical Essays on Dance*, Brooklyn, NY: Dance Horizons.

Copeland, R. (1983) "Merce Cunningham and the Politics of Perception," in R. Copeland and M. Cohen (eds) *What Is Dance?: Readings in Theory and Criticism*, Oxford: Oxford University Press.

Cunningham, M. (1951) "The Function of a Technique for Dance," in W. Sorell (ed.) *Dance Has Many Faces*, New York: The World Publishing Company.

—— (1968) *Changes: Notes on Choreography*, New York: Something Else Press.

—— (1978) "The Impermanent Art," in R. Kostelanetz (ed.) *Esthetics Contemporary*, Buffalo, NY: Prometheus Books.

Cunningham, M. and Lesschaeve, J. (1985) *The Dancer and the Dance*, New York: Marion Boyars Publishers.

Foster, S. L. (1986) *Reading Dancing: Bodies and Subjects in Contemporary American Dance*, Berkeley: University of California Press.

Halprin, L. (1965) "Motation," *Progressive Architecture* (July): 126–33.

Horst, L. and Russell, C. (1961) *Modern Dance Forms in Relation to the Other Modern Arts*, Princeton, NJ: A Dance Horizon Book.

Ichikawa, M. (1970) "Cunningham's *Changes: Notes on Choreography*," *Geijutsu-Techo*, (March): 158–65.

—— (1972) *Koui-to-Nikutai*, Tokyo: Tabata Shoten.

—— (1975) *American-dance Now: Modern Dance and Post-modern Dance*, Tokyo: Parco Shuppan-Kyoku.

—— (1976) "Merce Cunningham Dance Company," in *The Art of Music*, Tokyo: Ongaku-no-Tomo.

—— (1983) *Buyo-no-Cosmology*, Tokyo: Keisou Shobou.

—— (1989) "Butoh: The Denial of the Body," *Ballett International* 12, 9: 14–19.

—— (1991) "Modern Dance," in *Dance Handbook*, Tokyo: Shinshokan.

Johnston, J. (1971) *Marmalade Me*, New York: E. P. Dutton & Co.

—— (1992) "Two Reviews by Jill Johnston," in R. Kostelanetz (ed.) *Merce Cunningham*, Chicago: A Cappella Books.

Jowitt, D. (1985) *The Dance in Mind*, Boston: David R. Godine, Publisher.

Klosty, J. (ed.) (1975) *Merce Cunningham*, New York: Saturday Review Press.

Langer, S. (1942) *Philosophy in a New Key*, Cambridge, MA: Harvard University Press.

—— (1953) *Feeling and Form*, New York: Scribner.

—— (1957) *Problems of Art*, New York: Scribner.

Martin, J. (1933) *The Modern Dance*, New York: A. S. Barnes.

Siegel, M. (1988) "The Truth About Apples and Oranges," *The Drama Review* 32, 4: 24–31.

Sontag, S. (1966) *Against Interpretation, and Other Essays*, New York: Farrar, Straus & Giroux.

Tomkins, C. (1968) *The Bride and the Bachelors: Five Masters of the Avant Garde*, New York: Penguin Books.

16 Dance Discourses
Rethinking the History of the "Oriental Dance"

Joan L. Erdman

"Oriental dance" was an occidental invention. Not created to steal initiative from the Orient, "oriental dance" was initially a term used by Europeans and Americans to describe innovative and balletic dances which were eastern in theme, content, mood, costume, musical accompaniment, inspiration, or intent. By the 1920s, oriental dance conjured up expectations of exotic movements, glittering costumes, flowing lines, sublime dedication, and minor mode or strangely tuned music. Certain features were perceived as essential: fluid boneless arm and shoulder motion, rhapsodic spirituality, costumes composed of swirling gossamer drapery and opaque veils, elaborate and wondrously vibrant jewelry, and hand movements intended to signal more than graceful positioning. Dancing feet were often bare, women's midriffs were usually uncovered, and men danced bare chested in draped or bloused pantaloons.

Once oriental dance became a genre, created by western devotees with eastern ideas and values and extended by dancers from places that seemed to Europeans oriental, the style influenced dancers who arrived in Europe *from* the Orient,[1] and also dancers *in* the Orient.[2] In the early twentieth century when Diaghilev brought his Ballets Russes to Parisian audiences, oriental arts were already admired and sought by connoisseurs. Then and later, artifacts of Art Nouveau and Art Deco were heavily influenced by oriental design, particularly by japonaiserie. Japanese prints were in the collections of Degas, Monet, and Whistler. Earlier, Romantic artists like Ingres and Delacroix had sought sources for their fantasies in North Africa and the Near East, while writer Pierre Loti aroused Parisians' literary interests with his novels of women secluded in harems. Oriental arts were composed of strange and exotic figures,[3] redolent of veiled and mysterious women, surprising the eye with vibrant color and elaborate design, with an aesthetic valuing the harmony of movement and stillness. Interest extended from and to scholarship, with departments of oriental languages established at universities on the continent and in Great Britain. Even before Diaghilev, Frank Kermode notes, "The circus, the vaudeville, the *bal*, were serious pleasures; the primitive, the ugly, the exotic were in demand."[4] In America, as in France, international exhibitions and world fairs brought exotic dancers, curious music, novel artifacts, and strange scents from the East. Thus the opportunity to promote programs of oriental dance at the beginning of this century occurred in an atmosphere of curiosity and yearning for exotic entertainment, where dancers represented living embodiments of the unfamiliar.

Salomé (and her veils) had became a touchstone for the exotic feminine in Paris, in operas and ballets, in plays and paintings – particularly those of Gustave Moreau, and in the works of Aubrey Beardsley. When, in 1893, Loie Fuller succeeded in attracting a devoted and aristocratic audience for dances rippling with flowing veils and shaded with colored lights, using a "Hindu skirt" sent to her by young officers in India,[5] a connection between gauzy drapery and the mysterious East had already been established. Maude Allen debuted in Vienna in 1903 with her "Vision of Salomé," which was no doubt seen in Paris soon after. The 1909 season of Diaghilev's Russian dancers, with their elaborate costumes, exquisite sets, and extraordinary themes, brought to ballet what had already been viewed on the stages of music halls and in the Folies Bergère: the exotic Orient.[6] Only four years earlier, in March 1905, Mata Hari, known socially in Paris as Lady MacLeod, had been presented in the round upstairs library of the Musée Guimet as a temptress of Lord Shiva, with the deity represented by a half life-size carving from the museum's collection.[7]

Historical continuities can be traced from the Ballets Russes to classical Indian dance through Pavlova and the collaborator she selected for her "Dances Orientales" – Bengali art student Uday Shankar, through the Théâtre des Champs-Elysées built for the Ballets Russes and used for Uday Shankar's first company performance in Paris, through the sets and costumes of Nicholas Roerich to Shankar's father, Shyam Shankar Chaudhuri, who was his friend, and through the visit of Pavlova to India and Rukmini Devi's founding of Kalakshetra in Madras. These relationships place India's 1930s renaissance in dance within the compass of oriental dance and its history.

What constituted the "East", or the "Orient," in a particular country was dependent on national perspectives and linguistic discourse, as well as colonial extensions. In France, the Orient encompassed North Africa, Arabia, Turkey, Russia, China, India, Java, Japan, and all adjacent Asian lands. For the English the East extended from the Arabian peninsula to the Pacific Ocean, but rarely included North Africa west of Egypt. In Holland both Indians and Indonesians were considered *Indian*, leading to conflation of their dance arts as Hindu, and disregard for distinctions between Buddhist, Hindu, and Muslim cultures. But in all parts of Europe, and in all European languages, the genre oriental dance was intended to encompass as yet unknown dances of India.

In India, however, oriental dance meant dance from Europe. Dances with oriental themes were initially performed in India by Europeans or Europe-based Indian dancers, including the Denishawn Company on their

1926–7 tour, and a few years later by Uday Shankar, returning to India after ten years in Europe. These oriental dances were never mistaken by Indians for their own dance forms; rather they were appreciated attempts by artistes to stage dance with Indian themes and costumes.[8] Until Indians rediscovered their own dance arts in the 1930s, foreigners in India were only shown entertainments at Maharajahs' and Nawabs' *mardana* evenings, accounts of which depict audiences composed of mostly bored and ethnocentric East India Company officials and haughty invitees who found the events tedious. The discovery (by persons other than the native performers and their traditional patrons) of indigenous Indian dance genres awaited the arrival of European *dancers* in the early twentieth century, although dialogues between eastern and western arts and aesthetics had begun many centuries before.[9]

This paper explores the impact of western ideas of oriental dance on the history of Indian dance, and suggests that contemporary Indian dancers have only recently and consciously begun to disavow the complex values of western orientalism, and their impact on dance in India.

For dance, the history of orientalism differs from what is described by Edward Said in *Orientalism*, where the arguments are derived from and focus on politics, archaeology, literature, and visual arts. While it is true that twentieth-century Indian dance is a historical consequence of the idea of oriental dance, which did in fact originate in Europe, the dialogue between oriental dance (European) and classical dance (Indian) was a complex interchange of expectations and discovery. *Actual* Indian dance influenced programs of western artists only after their interest in the feminine divine principle and in the play of the gods provoked Ruth St. Denis and prima ballerina Anna Pavlova to seek authentic Indian dance and dancers in India in the 1920s. Mata Hari, St. Denis, Loie Fuller, and Pavlova had adapted eastern themes recreated from contacts and researches into Indian arts. None except Mata Hari claimed to be presenting "Indian dance," and despite the fact that this Dutchwoman's dance was based on her experiences in Java, not India, no one in Europe knew the difference.

Claims of "authenticity" – audiences were expected to believe that if the dancer was oriental the dance must be authentic – were fashioned with little if any knowledge of India's *devadasi* or *tawa'if* traditions. For the few dancers who traveled to India and sought indigenous dance forms, the showy (and tawdry) street dances of the Kathaks (filmed by Ted Shawn), the sitting dances of the *thumri* artists, the rarely approachable tribal and village festival dances, the inaccessible temple dancers designated as prostitutes, and an absence of opera and staged dance performances left foreign visitors with only fragmentary information.

But it was mainly the interest of westerners in indigenous Indian dance which encouraged India's westernized elites to search for their own traditions and reconstruct them for staged public performances.[10] That is, staged performances of oriental dance in India preceded Indian efforts to discover their own regional dance traditions and bring them to the public.

Of course, many princely courts, outside the view of Indians living in British-ruled presidencies, continued to maintain dancers who performed within their state households and temples, but in many cases the interest of these royals in classical music and dance had been subordinated to new technologies and sports by the beginning of the twentieth century.[11]

FROM ORIENTAL DANCE TO INDIAN DANCE

Despite its status as a genre, "oriental dance" was characterized by ambiguous boundaries, an inconsistent record, and an anecdotal discourse. In order to write its history, one must search in dance writings and beyond into literary passages, biographical accounts, political tracts, art and performance histories, as well as reports by participants and observers. No longer can one read such texts naively, as if they were *true*. Rather one must consider them as viewpoints particular to their times and places, as are ours. This is not to deny universals in dance, but to acknowledge contextual and temporal biases.

In such a project, an anthropological perspective suggests that understanding the past is parallel to understanding "the other": anthropology moves across space, and history through time. Transnationalism has made such "otherness" reflexively complex; what is "the other" when one belongs to more than one place? Thus there is an enormous corpus of relevant and factual writings from inventors and perusers of the oriental dance traditions to review and consider, as well as data from concomitant sources including photographs, paintings, costume designs, recordings and musical scores, and concert programs.

Since there are contemporary concerns, especially among those scholars who begin with texts rather than performances, about the likelihood that "factual data" exist, let me be clear from the outset what constitutes the data in my inquiries. Since 1977, when my research on dancer and choreographer Uday Shankar began, I have studied materials in library holdings, special and private collections, archives, memorabilia, and all other documentation relevant to the writing of a history of Shankar and his role in the dance. In addition, I have interviewed family members, performing artists, connoisseurs, devotees, and others who knew or saw or were affected by Shankar and his art.

Factual data may or may not be *true* in the sense that it represents a singular correct interpretation of what happened. But it is crucial to any history, and without it such statements as "Uday Shankar attended the Royal College of the Arts in London from 1920 to 1923" should be suspect, although the fact that someone thought it to be true is another kind of "factual datum." So also are opinions, explanations, and other representations data; any writer must sort out the relevant and significant from the marginal and suspect. The issue is by what criteria one does so, and whether the author reveals these criteria to readers.

My position is that arts flourish when their histories are known; artists need to be able to quote and cite their antecedents, to partake of or modify or rebel against known traditions, to innovate consciously in a genre or create a new tradition *knowing* their works are a departure. Poets read poetry, painters visit art museums, dancers can now watch films and videos. An awareness of what is important to watch, to consider, to understand, stems from familiarity with the history of one's art.

Unfortunately, India's dance in the twentieth century is without a critical history;[12] fortunately, Indian classical dance has been sustained and promoted in this century by denying that it is oriental dance (in the European sense), and by efforts to recreate and embody its actual and indigenous ancient heritage, which can also be seen as retronymic histories.[13] In fact, Indian dance has flourished in twentieth-century India, and has been subject to historical reinterpretation since at least the early 1930s.

TOWARDS A NEW HISTORY OF INDIAN DANCE

Writings about Indian dance in the modern era, by those familiar with its forms and genres, can be traced to Ragini Devi's 1928 *Nritanjali, An Introduction to Hindu Dancing* and Projesh Banerji's 1942 *Dance of India*, which included a brief foreword by Uday Shankar.[14] These publications mark the beginning of an era of English language description of India's dance styles by dance experts, and follow earlier comments on dance and dancers by travelers and officials dating from the seventeenth century. The rediscovery of Sanskrit and regional language texts (shastras) on Indian dance occurred mainly after Indian independence (1947). Dance descriptions, relating dance to temple sculptures and literary citations,[15] and differentiating among the styles designated as "classical dance" continue to be published.[16] All these works accept the renaissance or revival of Indian dance as commencing in the twentieth century when classical dance forms were "discovered" by nationalists seeking India's indigenous roots. The authors thus continue a theme originating in the latter half of the nineteenth century before India's independence movement.

Most writers on Indian dance[17] offer descriptive accounts of the genres of dance resulting from the rediscovery and exploration of regional dance. In each genre there was an effort to develop repertoire, costuming, and makeup, the goal being to stage dance programs for the public which would be proper for the middle classes and for Brahmins to attend. Regional dance arts were appropriated from their hereditary traditions (*parampara*) by these nationalistic and higher castes, who accepted a western interpretation of temple dancers as prostitutes, and strategized to save the dance while replacing traditional dancers with proper young women.

Only now, nearly fifty years after Indian independence, is a critical approach emerging. In her recent dissertation on "Temple 'Prostitution' and Community Reform: An examination of the ethnographic, historical and textual context of the devadasi of Tamil Nadu, South India", Amrit Srinivasan broaches political contexts for the revival of Tamilnadu's dance tradition, known as *sadir nautch*. This dance was transmuted, Srinivasan argues, into Bharata Natyam in the 1930s, amidst nationalist, reformist, Theosophical, revivalist, and purist goals, and issues which were missionary-driven and concerned with temple administration. Her analysis acknowledges the secularization of temple dance in the early twentieth century, and begins to address the history of the dance in India. Avanthi Meduri's paper, "Bharatha Natyam – What Are You?" and her forthcoming dissertation should take us further along this historical and analytic pathway.

Based on research in Europe (1986 and 1990), India (1980, 1983–4 and 1987), and research and interviews in the United States (1980–92), my current work focuses on the years between the World Wars as critical in the recognition of the category known as "oriental dance," but also problematic in its tracing its creation and the intentions of its use. In order to explore the relationship between oriental dance and classical Indian dance, we can trace the chronological development from dances thematically "Indian" or "Hindu" (Mata Hari, Ruth St. Denis, Pavlova) to dances argued to be "authentically Indian" (Nyota Inyoka, Uday Shankar,[18] Menaka, Ram Gopal) to dances based on ancient texts (*Natya Shastra*) and sculptures, now accepted as "classical Indian dance." By acknowledging a relationship between the idea of oriental dance and the politics of colonial and post-colonial culture, Indian dance history can recognize contemporary choices as contextual and outcomes as created. The alternative, to limit historical accounts to the bounds of antiquity and authenticity as determined by the past and its rediscovery, seems untenable in contemporary India.[19]

A critical history of Indian dance in the twentieth century must acknowledge European orientalism, exotic influences on modern dancers, especially Ruth St. Denis,[20] which in turn influenced Indian dancers, as well as the post-World War II positioning of dance by independent India as a representative of ancient heritage and high cultural rank in the world of new nations. By choosing, before and especially after independence, to mine the past for the dance of the present, Indian dancers, teachers, and scholars invented a new dance tradition based on claimed antiquity, asserted authenticity, well-intentioned chauvinism, and middle-class purity. Through these values, classical dance training and performance (up to the point of marriage) was established as a suitable domain for proper Indian women, and western approbation was secured for this extension of oriental dance as a process of indigenous rediscovery.

Within the twentieth century the category called oriental dance has dissolved into the particular dances from India, Japan, China, Korea, Bali, Thailand, and other nations of South Asia and the Far East. No longer can one speak of "oriental dance" except as a catch-all, a stereotypical classification, or a historical recreation for a program. The Indian part of oriental dance has replaced thematically based choreographies depicting Indian *nautch* and representations of the exotic and erotic divine with tradition-based solo classical performances which find their legitimacy in the ancient *Natya Sastra*. Scholarship on Indian dance has moved from textual explorations and descriptive accounts of dance genres to sharp and sometimes bitter indigenous Indian critiques charging sexism and mis-representation in the recreation of India's classical dance traditions. Recent writings on the politics of dance, especially those by Avanthi Meduri, Sadanand Menon, Rustom Bharucha, and Amrit Srinivasan, suggest that scholars are in the process of constructing a new Indian dance history for the twenty-first century.

This new discourse is not the first reinterpretive effort, nor can we assume it to be the last. In fact, critiques of westerners' ideas of oriental dances in India came quickly on the heels of their invention, from three major sources: 1) indigenous dancers, 2) visitors to Asian cultures,[21] and 3) sophisticated and upwardly mobile Brahmin middle classes[22] in India who discovered Indian gurus as authentic experts in their arts. On the one hand, Uday Shankar, Menaka, and Ram Gopal, by extending the search for genuine dance traditions begun by Pavlova and Denishawn dancers in India, were all artists claiming greater authenticity than the original "oriental dancers" who were Europeans. Each of these Indian dancers learned, to a greater or lesser degree, classical forms from Indian masters, and produced programs which mediated between what westerners had come to expect as oriental dance and the ways in which it was presented in indigenous Indian contexts.[23] On the other hand, the discovery of India's dance gurus, in villages of Tamilnadu and Kerala, in princely courts and temples, and in distressed and sometimes less than proper circumstances, by an increasingly conscious and patriotic urban middle class, led to a renaissance in India of the dance and its dissemination to newly Sanskritized[24] urban families and students.

Invented around the turn of the century, by the 1930s the idea of oriental dance had become a segue to ancient treasures of the East, which were rediscovered, and in India reinvented to be taught to high-class young girls for their debuts into society. Unlike oriental dance in Europe, which was an exotic performance genre witnessed by *avant garde* and *outré* Europeans, on a proscenium stage or in a variety revue, the rediscovered Indian classical dance was an essentially non-professional movement, leading to an embodiment of India's cultural heritage in young, upwardly mobile, and high-class women during a period of intense nationalism. Indians, in India, astutely named their forms to reflect regional traditions and new ideas: Bharata Natyam (literally "Indian dance-art"), Kathakali (story-telling art), Kathak (story-dance), Manipuri (after its region of origin), and then Odissi, Kuchipudi, Chhau, Mohini Attam, etc. The dance discourse in India was particular, discriminating, autochthonous, and the provenance of each form local, or locally based with national and classical aspirations.

SHANKAR AND THE DANCE RENAISSANCE

To Indians at home oriental dance was an art admired by naive westerners and westernized natives, in performances promoted by western dance connoisseurs, something *from Europe*, not from India. In India by 1934 Uday Shankar and his Company of Hindu Dancers and Musicians were perceived as presenting oriental dance from Europe, not quite Indian, and certainly not authentic. Before forming his first company, Shankar had choreographed dances for himself and European partners in London and in Paris, and presented them in England, Germany, Italy, Holland, and France. After ten years in the west, Shankar visited India in 1930, accompanying his Swiss patron the sculptor Alice Boner.

After touring around India, he was received in Calcutta with some curiosity and considerable reservation. What was this young Bengali Brahmin trying to do by dancing on stage in a style praised in Europe as authentically Indian? Was this *Indian* dance? If so, what kind? It was definitely not the modern Manipuri of Rabindranath Tagore's theatrical performances, which some Bengalis knew. But when they saw Shankar dance, they liked it, and the initially skeptical Indian musicians invited to perform with him agreed to provide accompaniment in Calcutta and on Shankar's European tour.[25] Somewhat unorthodox themselves, having been trained by Ustad Allauddin Khan of Maihar to perform as an orchestra, these musicians suited Shankar's needs exactly. But after a triumphant Shankar company tour in India in 1932, his next visit to India was greeted with dissatisfaction and disillusionment by newly minted Indian connoisseurs. These viewers had now found what they regarded as truly authentic Indian dance, taught by *guru*s and *natuvanar*s and *ustad*s. In South India connoisseurs had renamed the traditional temple dance Bharata Natyam, with enthusiasm for its status as the true classical Indian dance. In the modern era the explosive florescence of Indian classical dance that took place in the 1930s created an entire new infrastructure for dance. Dance schools and *gurukula*s were started, conferences and performances were arranged. Teachers, musicians, students, *devadasi*s, and *tawa'if*s came forward or were rediscovered. Competitions, *arangetram*s, reviews, photographs, and films were produced and accepted by a growing public audience. Emphasis was placed on decorum and propriety of character. Wealth was diverted to support dance and dancers, and organizations to classify and sponsor dance learning and performance were founded by industrialists, scholars, and religious societies. Their excitement about the antiquity of indigenous arts was reinforced by the value of these arts in affirming both India's claim to be an ancient civilization and Indians' nationalist aspirations.

Eventually, after Indian Independence in 1947, when India's cultural policy was being developed to provide government patronage for the arts in this new nation, nationalists offered support to two genres: 1) the revived and recreated "classical dances" based on regional styles; and 2) the collection of folk dance forms from countless regional and local cultures of the new nation.[26] What became known as "Shankarstyle", promulgated through the Uday Shankar India Culture Centre at Almora in the years 1939 to 1942, and continued by innovators such as Narendra Sharma and his Bhoomika Dance Company, Sachin Shankar and his Bombay-based Ballet Unit, Sri Ranga Ballet group under Shanti Bardhan, the short-lived Zoresh Dance Institute run by Zohra and Kameshwar Segal in Lahore, and later the schools of Amala and Uday Shankar in Calcutta, was subordinated to the documentation of how India's ancient heritage qualified its artists to be embodiments of *shastra* and *sanskriti* – a classical civilization. Popular political celebrations paraded folk artists brought to the new capital at New Delhi from all parts of India (often in recreated choreographies and modified costumes unrecognizable to their local audiences). Aspiring dancers of proper social status and training were showcased for dignitaries at diplomatic soirées and for tourists in huge hotels, as well as pictured on colorful promotional calendars. The new democratic republic attracted dancers and dance institutions to its capital at New Delhi, close to the sources of government patronage and the commodification associated with tourism.

TOWARDS NEW CRITIQUES

Having been discovered by non-traditional dance students, and having trained daughters of wealthy families, the generations of traditional teachers, mostly male *natuvanar*s and *ustad*s and *guru*s began to send their male offspring to other professions. Only a few new major male teachers emerged,[27] but the female pupils of the first generation trained by male experts grew into young women. Many married and gave up dance altogether, while others turned to teaching as a way of continuing their dedication to dance while caring for a husband and children. Coming on stage as a married woman was looked upon with considerable distaste by most husbands and extended families, although presenting an annual program with one's students became an acceptable performance arrangement.

Scholarship was another path for a young woman interested in continuing her dance, and in some cases the findings of a thesis or dissertation were incorporated into performances with astonishing results.[28] Women dedicated to dance as a career found it difficult to combine their art with marriage and child-bearing, physically and emotionally, as well as socially, though some did succeed. Dance expertise accompanied Indian diaspora to England, France, Canada, the United States, South Africa, and other countries, with students trained in India opening schools as married women abroad. And scholarship led dancers into new theoretical and political realms, in and out of India, especially after the impact of Edward Said's *Orientalism*, the trendy popularity of French critical historians and literary critics, and feminist theories.

Yet only in the 1980s did the recreation of classical dance begin to be questioned from within. What entered the discourse were voices of dancers, trained to accept the myth of their art's antiquity, its ritual *arange-tram*s and costumes and programs, who were also educated in institutions which promoted critical thinking and historical research. No doubt they were also galvanized by an emerging feminism in India, and by various efforts to bring together Indian and foreign dancers in dialogues and exchanges. Gradually these artists recognized that their dances, and others which had qualified for "classical" status, were *contemporary* interpretations and interpolations based on restricted repertoires and knowledge of temple *devadasi*s, extensions of the expertise of *gotipua*s and *natuvanar*s, and that of court dancers and musicians.[29] Such a critique was not seen as diminishing the achievement of these teachers and their disciples; rather it fostered a sense of having been betrayed. Their belief that the dance they were taught was *the* ancient dance turned out to be not quite accurate. Like arts in all traditions, the vitality of the dance was dependent upon continuous reinterpretation and reembodiment by contemporary artists.

The questions which arose in the 1980s were not unrelated to Said's consideration of *orientalism* as a complex invention of the West, nor were they immune to feminist critiques of implications of the myth of ancient heritage, to subaltern analyses of India's denied and unheard voices, or to post-colonialist reassessment of power relationships and their discourses. In India, the interrogation of received lore coincided with an attempt to create dialogues among dancers of different genres, in India and world-wide. At a 1984 international dance conference in Bombay, sponsored by a private indigenous institution (National Centre for the Performing Arts) and a forward-looking dance connoisseur at Max Mueller Bhavan, non-Indian dancers were brought together with innovative Indian group choreographers and classically trained solo dancers. Madras-based choreographer Chandralekha, in an astounding modern presentation based on indigenous forms including Bharata Natyam and yoga, challenged those whose conservatism denied status to original choreography in India. A few other experiments were deemed less successful. More recently, conferences in Delhi, programs in Madras, and gatherings in Toronto (1993) and elsewhere, have shown that a new energy for inventive choreography, Indian *and* modern,[30] is evident in works of Chandralekha, Shobana Jeyasingh (London), Mallika Sarabhai, Daksha Sheth, Uttara Asha Coorlawala, Astad Deboo, Anita Ratnam, Roger Sinha, Janaki Patrik (New York), to mention only a few in a burgeoning diversity of choreographic fascinations.

If there were any doubt that "antiquity as legitimacy" is being challenged by "the future as potential" in Indian dance, one has only to remember that dance is integral to its times and is conceived in the context of its times. No communicative art can be made or performed in a vacuum; nor is dance anywhere merely an art for art's sake, though some modern dance teachers train their students as if this could be the case. Walter Sorell's *Dance in Its Time* argued for a history of western dance which placed events, ideas, and issues in temporal and spatial contexts. Indian dancers await a critical history which takes up contemporaneous discourses along with dance performances and lives of dancers and choreographers (and perhaps critics).

Such a history has provocative questions to raise. Is the new Indian choreography a "new orientalism" – in the sense that it combines western sensibilities, technological sophistication, and international audience appeal with indigenous Indian themes and/or movement?[31] How do contemporary choreographies differ from the passé Shankarstyle? Or are they related to it? Contemporary exponents of Shankarstyle have either revived his dances (Amala Shankar, Mamata Shankar) or moved into new choreography based on Shankar's movements and ideas (Tanushree and Ananda Shankar, Sachin Shankar, Narendra and Bharat Sharma). But the works of Chandralekha (who appeared with her company at Jacob's Pillow and St. Mark's Church for Dance Theater Workshop in summer 1994), Uttara Asha Coorlawala, Daksha Sheth, Astad Deboo, Roger Sinha, Ann-Marie Gaston, Mallika Sarabhai, and Janaki Patrik are based on combinations of learned techniques including western modern and ballet, Indian dance genres, and other movement forms such as yoga and martial arts.

Or is Indian modern dance a reassertion of indigenous ingenuity – in the sense that there is no reason why India's dancers should look only to the past for inspiration? Why not look ahead? For some viewers, daring to look forward and outside indigenous traditions leads to dance which is condemned as derivative – a critique sometimes applied to India's contemporary painting by those who regard Rajput miniatures as India's highest achievement, and betray an ethnocentric resentment for an eastern *modern* art. For others, using Indian themes, movement, timings, and choreography to create an art dance, with appropriate art music, and a visual and kinetic language as Indian as are the classical forms, is a beckoning invitation.

DECONSTRUCTION AND RECONSTRUCTION

A significant challenge for dance historians is the effort to remove unacknowledged blinders. No longer can any historian of Indian dance simply record what is danced or seen, as if it is only (or purely) a recreation of ancient heritage. No more can the works of an Indian dancer be considered without inquiring what kinds of technical training, whether modern or indigenous, classical or western, has contributed to the dancer's choreography and repertoire. No history of Indian dance can avoid confrontation with the actual events which resulted in the modern myth of ancient heritage, and the chronological complexities which led to its popular acceptance.

One major question is whether such contemporary histories will seek to destroy the myth, and thus disparage the great renaissance in Indian dance which has been the result of its propagation. Or will they instead seek to understand the values and by-ways which have led to voiced contemporary critiques, and the paths that are being opened for dancers today?

What goals can we champion for dance history in the coming decades? My suggestion is exemplified by this discussion of the history of the oriental dance, based on observations and study of the role of Indian dancer/choreographer Uday Shankar in the evolution of this genre. As Edward Said has eloquently established, the idea of the "Orient" is an outsider's viewpoint. In South Asia it is paralleled by an outsider's view of persons from the subcontinent as "Indians", even though *among themselves*, they identify as Gujaratis, Bengalis, Tamils, Maharastrians, Oriyas, Malayalees, Hindus, Muslims, Parsis, Brahmins, Rajputs, Sikhs, or even Ambedkar-converted Buddhists, etc. An undifferentiated view of "the Orient" may be a convenience, a naiveté, a consciousness, blissfully unaware of diverse realities. The representation is not unlike that of "Third World" in the minds of Americans, who take their "First World" status so for granted that they never need articulate it. Just as "the West" and westernization have come to be coterminous with modernity and modernization, thereby extending ethnocentric imperialism and disregard for the particularities of indigenous mixtures, so also the delightful complexity of India's dance scene can be misconceived by arguably innocent western viewpoints. We need to stop and ask how dancers and dances from India's peoples articulate their identities. Must they continue to use western discourse, such as extensions of the idea of an *oriental dance* to describe their art? How can we create dialogues which present and preserve the ever-increasing intricacy of cross-cultural dialogues?

My current work on Uday Shankar, begun in the late 1970s when re-discovery of India's early twentieth century dance history was in its infancy, has led me to recognize that development of a history of Indian dance in this century is essential for those who would move forward. Replacement of the myth of antiquity with histories of modernity is a formidable task, requiring not only new research in arenas not always seen as relevant (e.g., opera archives in Europe, court and temple records in India, newspapers and journals, key connoisseurs and patrons, etc.), but also new thinking about what was seen as appropriate in the context of its times. We need to remember that such new thinking, if propelled *only* by current theoretical trends, may be as mythical as the subject matter it considers. Recognition of past events as connected to other occurrences in *their own* times is essen-tial, as in the connection, for instance, between nationalist enthusiasm and the naming of Bharata Natyam – literally, Indian dance. Or the connection between Uday Shankar's *Labor and Machinery* and films of Charlie Chaplin such as *Modern Times* with their comedic critique of industrialization. Or between the orientalist projection of a "spiritual East" and the acceptance of dance as religious art. Looking back (for anthropologists and historians) and looking ahead (for dancers and choreographers) are intimately related projects, which will put the *oriental dance* in its place and times, and give contemporary dance from India its own space to amaze and entice new audiences and critics.

The twenty-first century history of "oriental dance" can no longer be defined by a mainly western perspective, but is shaping up as a lively transnational discourse. For Indian dance a critical history must not only recognize occidental invention of oriental dance but also incorporate an analytically conscious account of the Indian rediscovery of ancient dance forms. Pivotal to this emerging history is the period in the 1920s and 1930s when internationalism propelled the popularity of the *oriental dance* back to India and engendered the invention of a modern tradition in Indian dance.

NOTES

1 See my description of the influence of oriental dance on Uday Shankar in "Performance As Translation: Uday Shankar in the West."
2 See, for example, the oriental dance of Ram Gopal, in the film *Lord Shiva Danced* (1948, sponsored by Burmah Shell).
3 See, for instance, Partha Mitter's description of European reactions to the arts of India in his *Much Maligned Monsters*.
4 Kermode, "Poet and Dancer Before Diaghilev" in Roger Copeland and Marshall Cohen (eds) *What is Dance? Readings in Theory and Criticism*, Oxford: Oxford University Press, 1983: 150.
5 This event and its antecedents are described by Loie Fuller in her book, *Fifteen Years of a Dancer's Life*.
6 In her account of the Ballets Russes in *Diaghilev's Ballets Russes*, Lynn Garafola points out that most of the Ballets Russes programming before World War I was "orientalist extravaganzas." "The French wanted exoticism, and Diaghilev, with an eye to the box office, obliged. Each year thereafter exotic ballets – either Eastern or Russian in theme – filled one or, more often, two new repertory slots . . . " (1989: 43).
7 An account of this performance is given in Russell Warren Howe's *Mata Hari. The True Story* (1986: 40–2).
8 Shankar's dance was initially appreciated as a native effort, but in a few years his oriental dance was replaced by genres indigenous to Indian communities that budding Indian critics and politically motivated nationalists deemed to be more authentically and classically Indian.
9 In his study of European responses to depictions of multi-armed deities and erotic temple sculpture, Partha Mitter indicates that Marco Polo's return to Europe from travels in the East initiated an era of descriptive accounts. Dancers on the Coromandel coast of India were discussed, for instance, as "nuns", and pictured in a later fourteenth-century manuscript as "*Danse des servantes ou esclaves des dieux*" (Mitter, 1978: 3–4).

10 The two exceptions to the rediscovery of indigenous dance by westerners are Rabindranath Tagore's attempts to bring Manipuri dance into Calcutta dramas and musicales, and the interest of a few ethnographers in tribal dances as part of their studies of "primitives."

11 See, for example, my description of the last decades of the *Gunijankhana* in the princely state of Jaipur (Rajasthan) in *Patrons and Performers in Rajasthan: The Subtle Tradition.*

12 Rina Singha and Reginald Massey's 1967 *Indian Dances: Their History and Growth* offers brief histories of Dasi Attam (Bharata Natyam), Kathakali, Kathak in a volume that also describes Manipuri, Odissi and other styles of Indian dance. However, they employ a traditional bardic strategy of encapsulating and mythologizing earlier periods into condensed episodes, providing research-based and/or anecdotal histories only for the contemporary era.

13 I have adapted the term "retronymic history" from the idea of a *retronym*, a word created to specify an earlier item after the invention of a later one, e.g., an apartment house, to distinguish it from a house. "Retronymic histories" parallel the anthropological concept of "secondary rationalizations." That is, such histories are created to respond to questions asked after the fact. Statements are retronymic or secondary rationalizations when they attempt to explain something more fully that was intelligible at the time of its inception, but has become unclear due to later values or inventions. In these days of deconstruction and ideology-based scholarship, "retronymic history" is an analytic necessity.

14 Ananda K. Coomaraswamy's earlier *The Dance of Siva: Fourteen Indian Essays* (London [1924] 1985) was actually a set of art history papers, with the title essay describing the role of Siva as manifestor of primal rhythmic energy, as Nataraja, Lord of the Dance, not a description of dance as practiced in India at the time.

15 Kapila Vatsyayan's path-breaking *Classical Indian Dance in Literature and the Arts* argues for the integration of Indian aesthetic theory, classical Indian literature and dance, and classical sculpture, in a single cultural whole. Her analysis and insights have evoked scholarly studies of Indian dance which attempt to go beyond description, and her study provoked Indian dance scholars to research ancient and classical forms and bring them into their dances. Anne-Marie Gaston's *Siva in Dance, Myth and Iconography*, and Frederique Marglin's *Wives of the God-King. The Rituals of the Devadasis of Puri* are excellent examples of this genre, as is Saskia Kersenboom-Story's *Nityasumangali. Devadasi Tradition in South India.*

16 See, for example, Leela Samson's *Rhythm in Joy. Classical Indian Dance Traditions* with magnificent photographs by Avinash Pasricha, and *Dances of the Golden Hall* photographed by Sunil Janah and written by Ashoke Chatterjee. MARG has also produced a series of books on particular styles of classical Indian dance, as well as a volume on *The Performing Arts*, guest edited by Dr Narayana Menon (Bombay: MARG, 1982), which includes articles on dance styles as well as theater, folk traditions, and tribal dances. In 1957 *MARG* published one of the earliest collections of articles on *Kathakali* (XI, 1), under the general editorship of critic and novelist Mulk Raj Anand.

17 See, for instance, Kay Ambrose (1950), Enakshi Bhavnani (1965), Rina Singha and Reginald Massey (1967), Ragini Devi (1972), Ashoke Chatterjee (1979), Mohan Khokar (1979), Sunil Kothari (ed) (1979), Leela Samson (1987), and many others. Some concentrate on one form or a particular dancer and her genre, while others survey the array of genres deemed classical, with occasional reference to "creative dance" or contemporary styles, such as those of Uday Shankar and Ram Gopal.

18 My forthcoming paper, "Towards Authenticity: Uday Shankar's first Company

of Hindu Dancers and Musicians," in David Waterhouse (ed.) *Dance of India* (Toronto: University of Toronto South Asia Centre, forthcoming) addresses the difficulty in assertions of "authenticity" in dance and by dancers of oriental and Indian dance.

19 Efforts to insist that "classical" Indian dance must have a *shastric* (textual) basis, deriving from the preoccupation of some Bharata Natyam connoisseurs and dancers with their genre's hegemonic destiny, have now induced a few defenders of Kathak's classicality to promote classical *mudras* and text-based rules as the ancient and appropriate basis for their genre (Prabha Marathe, personal communication, April 29, 1995).

20 In her recent article, "Ruth St. Denis and India's Dance Renaissance," Uttara Asha Coorlawala notes that the 1926 Denishawn Dance Company tour in India "rekindled interest and pride in India's now flourishing dance forms" (1992: 123) through St. Denis's "nonauthentic impressions of Indian dance" (ibid.: 124), presented to huge popular audiences in India's cities.

21 The replacing of vague assertions of oriental dance with expert knowledge of regional dance forms is exemplified by Beryl de Zoete, favorite pupil of Dalcroze, trained in ballet in London and a world traveler, who wrote about dancing in India, Bali, and Ceylon. Her works include *Dance and Drama in Bali* (London: Faber & Faber, 1938), *The Other Mind* (London: Gollancz, 1953) and *Dance and Magic Drama in Ceylon* (London: Faber & Faber, 1957).

22 The issue of transformation and compartmentalization of caste and class memberships in the pre-independence period is beyond the scope of this article. However, the creation of a "public," the interest in status in a British system, albeit colonial, and the use of caste to promote such status are topics which must be considered in the history of Indian classical dance.

23 See my discussion of this process for Uday Shankar in my "Performance As Translation: Uday Shankar in the West" (1987).

24 Sanskritization is a term created by Indian anthropologist M. N. Srinivas to describe efforts by individuals or, more frequently, caste groups, to raise their status on a purity scale by adopting customs and rules of higher castes, such as vegetarianism, feeding of Brahmins on ceremonial occasions, fasting, ritual bathing, and text-based Hindu rites.

25 There was, at this time in India, no idea of a "modern Indian dance," and certainly this description was never applied to Shankarstyle.

26 For a description of the construction of government patronage for the performing (and other) arts after India's independence, see my "Who Should Speak for the Performing Arts? The Case of the Delhi Dancers" (1984).

27 Perhaps the most famous of these next generation male teachers is Kathak guru Birju Maharaj, who inherited his father's and uncles' mantle from Lucknow, and has sustained the Kathak Kendra in New Delhi for several decades, training several generations of Kathak teachers and dancers, who are almost exclusively women. A few other male dancers have continued their hereditary professions, such as Kelucharan Mohapatra, an Odissi guru and artist, while sons of some dancers trained by Shankar have also entered dance and choreography. There are notably fewer male dancers in Bharata Natyam and Odissi, while Kathakali remains a mostly male genre. Because of the ban on *devadasi* dances promulgated in 1947 in Madras, Bharata Natyam dancers tend to be from non-traditional families. No such ruling ever existed for Kathak. Who dances which genre in which region is a topic for further research and study.

28 When Padma Subramanyam gave a performance in New Delhi, based on her findings in her doctoral research on old and forgotten *karana*s, the audience was astounded to find her lifting her leg above her head in some poses. Such movements were considered shocking and perhaps immodest for this pure dance.

29 The evolution of modern North Indian Kathak dance has a somewhat different history, although the relocation of its center to New Delhi in Kathak Kendra (a dance school originally part of Bharatiya Kala Kendra and now government-sponsored through the Sangeet Natak Akademi), legitimized its contemporary innovation and forms through the lineage of the Lucknow and Jaipur masters. The creation of the Bindadin Festival, in honor of these lineages, reorganized Kathak's center by providing an annual national forum for its exponents at Kathak Kendra in New Delhi.

30 Finding a name for Indian dance which is professional but neither folk nor classical has been an issue in writings in India and for presentations abroad. It should not be confused with another new genre, known as "filmidance," which is based on the popular dances that interrupt censored sensuality in Indian films. To call these innovative Indian choreographies "modern" leads to confusion with western modern dance, which is a particular genre arising from a desire to be free of ballet's restrictions. To call it "creative dance" is to deny that all dance is creative; to call it "contemporary" is to merely place it in the here and now. One imaginative solution is "Nava Nritya," or "New Dance," a name taken by a Calcutta choreographer for her works, although it is not clear that other choreographers would accept the epithet.

31 Said's *orientalism* refers to domination or colonial power; but as Gay Morris points out (personal communication), the new Indian choreography may be "more a case of dealing with modernity in an Indian way." Certainly all dance presented away from its own national boundaries must be adapted to local situations and venues; this is as true for Merce Cunningham's company performing in New Delhi as it is for Chandralekha or Mallika Sarabhai performing in the United States. The issues of authenticity and westernization remain, however, when it comes to dancers and choreographers trained in both (western) modern and Indian dance, and group choreographies restaged in balletic blocking for proscenium theaters.

BIBLIOGRAPHY

Ambrose, K. (1950) *Classical Dances and Costumes of India* (with an introduction by Ram Gopal), London: Adam and Charles Black.

Anthology of Indian Dances (and the Arts) (1966) Calcutta: Mani Shankar Jayanti Committee.

Banerji, P. (1942) *Dance of India*, Allahabad: Kitabistan.

Bardhan, G. (ed.) (1992) *Rhythm Incarnate. Tribute to Shanti Bardhan*, New Delhi: Abhinav.

Bharucha, R. (1990) *Theatre & the World: Essays on Performance and Politics of Culture*, Delhi: Manohar.

Bhavnani, E. (1965) *The Dance in India. The Origin and History, Foundations, the Art and Science of the Dance in India – Classical, Folk, and Tribal*, Bombay: Taraporevala's.

Chatterjee, A. (1979) *Dances of the Golden Hall*, New Delhi: Indian Council for Cultural Relations.

Chatterji, U. (1982) *La Danse Hindoue*, Paris: L'Asiatheque.

Coomaraswamy, A. K. ([1924] 1985) *The Dance of Siva: Essays on Indian Art and Culture*, New York: Dover.

Coorlawala, U. A. (1992) "Ruth St. Denis and India's Dance Renaissance," *Dance Chronicle* 15, 2: 123–52.

Copeland, R., and Cohen, M. (eds) (1983), *What is Dance? Readings in Theory and Criticism*, Oxford: Oxford University Press.

Devi, A. (1983) "La decouverte de la danse indienne en Occident", *La Recherche en Danse* 2: 107–11.

Devi, R. (1928) *Nritanjali, An Introduction to Hindu Dancing*, New York: Hari G. Govil for the India Society, and (1962) Calcutta: Susil Gupta.

—— (1972) *Dance Dialects of India*, Delhi: Vikas.

Doshi, S. (ed.) (1989) *Dances of Manipur: The Classical Tradition*, Bombay: MARG Publications.

Erdman, J. L. (1984) "Who Should Speak for the Performing Arts? The Case of the Delhi Dancers," in Lloyd I. Rudolph (ed.) *Cultural Policy in India*, Delhi: Chanakya.

—— (1985) *Patrons and Performers in Rajasthan: The Subtle Tradition*, New Delhi: Chanakya.

—— (1987) "Performance As Translation: Uday Shankar in the West," *The Drama Review* 31, 1: 64–88.

—— (ed.) (1992) *Arts Patronage in India: Methods, Motives and Markets*, New Delhi: Manohar and Columbia, MO: South Asia Publications.

—— (1994) "Performance As Translation II: Uday Shankar, the Europeans, and the Oriental Dance," in *Representations of Modernity in South Asia*, vol. I, Occasional Series, Institute for Culture and Consciousness in South Asia, University of Chicago.

Festival of Oriental Music and the Related Arts (1960) Los Angeles: University of California, Department of Music.

Fuller, L. (republication of 1913 original) *Fifteen Years of a Dancer's Life*, New York: Dance Horizons.

Garafola, L. (1989) *Diaghilev's Ballets Russes*, New York: Oxford University Press.

Gaston, A. (1982) *Siva in Dance, Myth and Iconography*, Delhi: Oxford University Press.

Guha, R. and Spivak, G. C. (eds) (1988) *Selected Subaltern Studies*, New York: Oxford University Press.

Howe, R. W. (1986) *Mata Hari: The True Story*, New York: Dodd, Mead & Company.

Kersenboom-Story, S. (1987) *Nityasumangali. Devadasi Tradition in South India*, Delhi: Motilal Banarsidass.

Khokar, M. (1979) *Traditions of Indian Classical Dance*, Delhi: Clarion Books.

Kliger, G. (1993) *Bharata Natyam in Cultural Perspective*, New Delhi: Manohar.

Kothari, S. (ed.) (1979) *Bharata Natyam: Indian Classical Dance Art*, Bombay: MARG Publications.

Kothari, S. (1989) *Kathak: Indian Classical Dance Art*, New Delhi: Abhinav Publication.

Kothari, S. and Pasricha, A. (1990) *Odissi: Indian Classical Dance Art*, Bombay: MARG Publications.

Marglin, F. A. (1985) *Wives of the God-King. The Rituals of the Devadasis of Puri*, Delhi: Oxford University Press.

Massey, R. and J. (1989) *The Dances of India. A General Survey and Dancers' Guide*, London: Tricolour Books.

Meduri, A. M. (1988) *"Bharatha Natyam* – What Are You?," *Asian Theatre Journal* 5, 1: 1–22.

Misra, S. (1992) *Some Dancers of India*, New Delhi: Harman Publishing House.

Mitter, P. (1978) *Much Maligned Monsters: History of European Reactions to Indian Art*, Oxford: Clarendon Press.

Ragini, S. (1928) *Hindu Dances*, Delhi: Sumit Publications.

Roudanez, L. (1947) *Nyota Inyoka*, Paris: Editions J. Susse.

Said, E. W. (1978) *Orientalism*, New York: Pantheon Books.

Samson, L. (1987) *Rhythm in Joy*, New Delhi: Lustre Press.

Singha, R. and Massey, R. (1967) *Indian Dances: Their History and Growth*, New York: George Braziller.

Sorell, W. (1981) *Dance in Its Time: The Emergence of an Art Form*, Garden City, NY: Anchor/Doubleday.

Srinivasan, A. (1984) "Temple 'Prostitution' and Community Reform: An examination of the ethnographic, historical and textual context of the devadasi of Tamil Nadu, South India," Ph.D. dissertation, Cambridge University, Wolfson College.

Vatsyayan, K. (1968) *Classical Indian Dance in Literature and the Arts*, New Delhi: Sangeet Natak Akademi.

Venkatachalam, G. (ca. 1950) *Dance in India*, Bombay: Nalanda Publications.

17 Balkan Tradition, American Alternative

Dance, Community, and the People of the Pines

June Adler Vail

When you dance *Ličko Kolo* you sense a dozen people's interconnected hands and synchronized steps. The dance begins in silence. To the rhythm of deliberate footfalls, one voice keens and is echoed plaintively by the whole group: "Sing to me, O Falcon, beneath my love's window. She fell asleep; cold was the stone beneath her head. I took away the stone and there I placed my hand." As the dancers follow a curved path, the line expands and contracts, breathing as a single body. The challenge is to adjust your movements to an unspoken common denominator: not to do what "feels right," or dance as brilliantly as possible, but to move in harmony with the group. The ensemble becomes greater than the sum of its parts, a visible embodiment of sensuality and cohesion.

Ličko Kolo is a line dance from the former Yugoslavia's Dalmatian coast and part of the repertory of Borovčani Balkan Dance and Music, a performing group I belonged to from 1978 to 1982.[1] Over time, as a participant and observer, I realized that Borovčani could be interpreted as a community of dancers with its own culture, history, structure, and import. Looking back, the group's staged choreographies and social processes seem to illuminate facets of America's fragmented society in the late seventies and early eighties.

Anthropologists, cultural critics, and dance theorists have carried on lively debates about the relationship between art and society, dance and culture. Should society, or history, be considered as "background" to art (Clark 1984: 250)? Does dancing, as a cultural form, "reflect" social values?

Sociologist Janet Woolf maintains that a mechanistic model of the relationship between cultural forms and social process implied by the word "reflection" is

> ... no longer a notion which theories of representation will allow. Cultural forms, like dance, do not just directly represent the social in some unmediated way. Rather, they *re*-present it in the codes and processes of signification – the language of dance. Moreover, far from reflecting the already-given social world, dance and other cultural forms participate in the production of that world.

(1992: 707)

Similarly, anthropologist Cynthia Novack has articulated dancing's dual process:

> Culture is embodied. A primary means of understanding, knowing, making sense of the world comes through shared conceptions of our bodies and selves and through the movement experience society offers us. Movement constitutes an ever-present reality in which we constantly participate. We perform movement, invent it, interpret it, and reinterpret it, on conscious and unconscious levels. In these actions, we participate in and reinforce culture, and we also create it.
>
> (1990: 8)

Detailed description of specific communities of dancers can document ways in which this mutually constitutive process occurs. Folk dances are often assumed to express the participants' shared identity, reflecting an already defined social world. Anthropologist Clifford Geertz suggests that art "materialize[s] a way of experiencing, bring[s] a particular cast of mind out into the world of objects where men can look at it" (1983: 99). Reciprocally, folk dancing also induces casts of mind and creates ways of experiencing and behaving. We dance the dances, and the dances, in turn, "dance" us.

In this interpretive analysis of Borovčani, my professional interests as a dance critic and researcher intersect with my personal history as a dancer and participant.[2] The justification for writing about a now defunct amateur troupe, at the margins of American culture and the edge of a continent, lies in Borovčani's value as an example of a community of dancers that reinvented Balkan dance and movement for its own purposes, representing an American "cast of mind" and creating its own subculture.

I associate Balkan dancing with an embroidery sampler of Bulgarian patterns I began in 1980 and worked on for more than a year. I now marvel at the tiny cross-stitches, delicate in some designs, dense in others. Red, blue, yellow, olive green, and brown threads dance in intricate, repetitive patterns across the bleached linen. If you turn the sampler over, the reverse of the precise, lively stitching is a mishmash of knots and thread-ends where the bright colors overlap, begin, and end. On the back, the band with the densest pattern is a thick mat of floss, with brown predominant, although on the front brown appears only as minute outline stitches.

The sampler's front and back suggest Borovčani's two interwoven sides: polished, staged performances and casual, rather messy social organization. On the flip-side, tensions surrounded issues of authority and democracy, individual and collective goals, mainstream and counterculture values, professionalism and amateurism, dancing skills and interpersonal relations, and discipline and spontaneity. The fabric of the group tended to unravel into separate strands: long-time members and newer ones, expert dancers and novices, men and women, dancers and musicians. But like the embroidery, the group's intertwined aspects together created colorful, textured, energetic designs.

PERFORMANCE: BALKAN DANCES, AMERICAN ALTERNATIVES

Borovčani's performances often began with a processional dance through the audience and into a space or onto a stage, signaling the continuities between performance and everyday life, and the similarities between performers and viewers. On stage, one musician or dancer would greet the audience and announce three or four dances at a time: she might offer commentaries on the dances' origins, costumes, music, or choreographic details between sets. Before an instrumental interlude or vocal segment a musician would speak briefly about Balkan music or the singers' distinctive open-throat style.

Our musical accompaniment included accordion, fiddles, recorder, and drums (a small and large handmade Macedonian *tupan*). These corresponded fairly accurately to contemporary, if not traditional, Slavic instruments. Instrumental sounds, such as the Bulgarian *gaida* (bagpipe) were mimicked on the accordion, but without any pretense of historical or scholarly authenticity. The musicians learned tunes by imitating records and tapes or playing with other musicians. The accordionist played for all performances and nearly all rehearsals, although she often would have preferred to dance.

Wandering line dances usually skirted the edges of the stage or performance area, close to viewers who often surrounded us on three sides and at the same level. Straight line dances tended to occupy the center of the stage, facing the audience, cutting across on a horizontal plane or moving forward and back, towards and then away from the spectators. Borovčani's stylistic "signature" communicated down-to-earth energy, focused clarity, disciplined dexterity, and responsiveness among the performers and to the audience.

Unison movement is the most powerful stylistic element in Balkan dance, implying solidarity of purpose. Emphatic rhythms and overall group spatial configurations – open and closed circles and lines – also convey a sense of cohesion. Line dancing requires constant body contact: dancers are entwined by hand-, belt-, shoulder-, or waist-holds. The body of the group as a whole reveals important spatial forms. The dancers' individual body shapes are less significant: dancers can be any size, if they are strong and quick-footed.

Balkan rhythms are often complex and irregular: 7/16, 11/15, and 15/16 times are common. Dance phrases do not always coincide exactly with musical phrasing. But most dances reproduce the structure of their musical accompaniment. In performance the dancers sometimes had the sense of being immersed in music and supported, even intoxicated, by its potent rhythms and insistent nasal sonorities.

The musicians placed themselves near the dancers or were enclosed within their circle to communicate visual cues and keep a common tempo: moving musicians and singing dancers. We dancers usually faced the music, and often interacted with the musicians, smiling and calling out to them. They also actively acknowledged remarks from dancers or applause from the audience. Facial expressions, off-hand jokes, and improvised yips or hollers were part of the performance. "Good dancers" could smile, talk with a neighbor, or call out while keeping up with intricate steps and holding proper spacing.

By 1982 the group had accumulated a repertory of over thirty dances, learned entirely through the imitation and repetition of step sequences, taught by a core group of experienced dancers who had mastered them. The repertory was composed principally of dances from Serbia, Croatia, and other provinces of the former Yugoslavia; Bulgaria; and a few East European countries, including Hungary and Poland.[3]

Stylistically, in most Balkan and East European dance the body is held erect but not rigid, and the trunk tends to move as a single unit. The most active parts of the body are the legs and feet, and arms and hands, coordinated with the orientation of the head. Often the upper body rotates contrapposto to the lower. Occasional jumps and hops, leaps, turns, and kneeling movements occur in men's dances, but the basic vocabulary consists of well-grounded, resilient walking and running.

The steps of Balkan dances are named and codified and can be taught relatively efficiently as the minimal units of choreographed sequences. These sequences are learned in sections, usually determined by the structure and rhythm of the music. The sections are then organized into dances or suites, with reiterated refrains or whole sequences repeated twice through. Sometimes a leader spontaneously calls the next section on the spot from among alternative variations. The overall organization of steps into sections, sections into dances, and dances into suites is intimately bound to rhythmic and spatial patterns.

For dramatic effect there are whole body vibrations, heel bounces, quick pas de basque, swooping Yemenite steps, zippy scissors kicks, reel steps, prances with high knees, and military heel clicks. Though most of the step combinations require rhythmic subtlety and intricate footwork, the women's feet are kept carefully close to the ground, and the upper torso is restrained. The men's style is flashier, with low squats and heel slaps, though the actual steps may be the same as the women's. Differences in male and female dance styles portray the male as physically more powerful, aggressive, and airborne, and the female as comparatively modest, stable, earthy.

In Laban Movement Analysis terms, Balkan dances embody direct focus and sudden, forceful, "bound" energy. These movement characteristics can be interpreted as indicating assertiveness, clear thinking, pride, and vitality. The vigorous dances often accelerate from a slow, controlled beginning, growing in speed, complexity, and excitement. The endings of many dances are climactic and exuberant. Our bows were quick, with a running exit, like a circus act, we joked.

One way Borovčani represented "the social" through its codes and processes of signification – its language of dance – was hinted at by a dancer who commented, "Performing brings joy to the audience, but really, I like costumes and being someone else."

The women's costumes were a refinement of the funky peasant aesthetic that prevailed in everyday wardrobes and rehearsal clothing. For performances each of us wore an embroidered white peasant blouse, mid-calf length white cotton skirt with red and black trim, based on Croatian prototypes, white stockings gartered at the knee with red ribbons, Serbian *opanke* (light woven leather shoes with turned-up toes), a woven sash and a green, blue, black, or red flowered challis shawl, usually tied like an apron around the waist. The typical hairstyle was braids, usually pinned up and entwined with red ribbon. The men wore white Croatian shirts (made from a commercial pattern), black pants, red sash, multi-colored hand-knit wool socks, Macedonian *opanke*, and a black vest with red, yellow, and blue piping.

In its costumed references to the world beyond the stage, Borovčani's principal mode of representation was *imitative*, or *metonymic*, to use a literary trope often employed to describe a dance's relationship to worldly events. According to dance theorist Susan Foster, this mode "improves upon, as it replaces, the world to which it refers. The body substitutes for the subject, offering the best version of the subject it can" (1986: 66).

What world was impersonated, what subject improved upon and offered up for scrutiny? Who was the "someone else" one dancer enjoyed becoming? There seemed to be a double, and equivocal, possibility: an exotic "old country" world of modest, marriageable women and strong, energetic men, and simultaneously, an idealized contemporary vision of a homogeneous, egalitarian community "living the good life" in Maine.[4]

The imitative mode "leaves little doubt about the referent" (Foster 1986: 66) and Borovčani theatrically cued the audience to recognize the dancers as a band of exotic yet familiar rustics. In accordance with this category, we also tacitly invited viewers to evaluate how believably we impersonated peasants and how capably we portrayed aspects of our contemporary selves.

Because Borovčani's choreography also displayed virtuoso movement skills, the repertory combined what Foster terms the *reflective* mode with the *imitative*. "Reflective representation makes exclusive reference to the performance of movement itself" (ibid.), and only incidentally to other events in the world. Like the "pure dance" sections of narrative ballets or Indian classical dances, Balkan dancing's *reflective* representation was framed by *imitative* costumes and characteristic Balkan music, but it invited appreciation of the dances' intrinsic physicality and complexity and the performers' charisma and skill.

Finally, in the representation of mutual affection and group cohesion, Borovčani's dances can also be considered *metaphoric*, according to Foster's model. Above all, line and circle dances depicted the quality

Figure 17.1 Members of the Borovčani Balkan Dance and Music group in performance, 1981. (Photo: David Vail)

of harmony, translating shared experience into motion and design. The physical closeness of the dancers, their unison movement and common focus evoked analogies to – family circles? close-knit community? participatory democracy? political alliances? lines of defense? The dancers, although exotically costumed, metaphorically suggested synchrony with one another and their surroundings.

These modes of representation conveyed meanings on different levels simultaneously: traditional Balkan peasantry through colorful costumes and commentaries; virtuosic dance display through exciting energy, unfamiliar rhythms and sonorities; and contemporary community through the dances' inclusive forms, the focus of the performers' gaze and their proximity to the audience.

Borovčani performances seemed to embody the latent utopian tendency in American culture. Unlike indigenous, or professional, Balkan troupes which intentionally represent "the national," the group could more accurately be said to have represented "like-minded, racially homogeneous community" or "back-to-the-land values." As one member put it, "We are authentic Americans dancing in the style of the Balkans."

THE PEOPLE OF THE PINES

As a loosely woven community of dancers and musicians, Borovčani became a Maine institution during its five-year history. The group's most significant behind-the-scenes processes included how members were chosen, how the group structured itself, how it conducted rehearsals and meetings, how it assigned women's and men's responsibilities, what dancing meant as a physical, aesthetic and social activity, and how dancing helped create a culture.

In 1977, the group was christened Borovčani, Serbo-Croatian for "people of the pines." By 1982, when it dispersed, six members remained from the original "clan" of fifteen. Nine had left, and over time nine others had replaced them. Membership fluctuated as some people went back to school, had children, or moved away, but new recruits – several already expert in Balkan dance – always seemed to turn up.

The original group was self-selected, but, after a year, when I joined, the audition process required attendance at weekly rehearsals for a month or two, during which members evaluated a prospect's dancing abilities and social compatibility. The candidate could then ask to be voted in. Voting was usually a formality, since most who stuck it out for the trial period could sense they would be admitted. In five years just one aspirant was actually rejected by vote. Though its dances embodied inclusiveness, Borovčani limited membership to a relatively exclusive few.

The twelve respondents to the questionnaire I administered in 1982 were all white Americans, but within that category there was some diversity in age, education, and occupation. Seven women ranged in age from 24 to 38 and five men from 23 to 37. Nine were single or separated, and three were married – of these, two were parents. The levels of education ranged from college drop-outs (three) to master's degree (two). Seven had an undergraduate B.A. or B.S. degree.

Members included a co-op warehouse worker, a musician, three teachers, a draughtsperson/graduate student, a pharmaceutical salesman, a graphic artist, a carpenter, a greenhouse worker, two odd-jobbers, and one self-styled *bon vivant*. The data records a Quaker, a Catholic convert and seven vegetarians. All had opposed the war in Vietnam, but otherwise we held diverse political views. Most had moved to Maine during the great in-migration of the seventies.

Our mongrel ethnic backgrounds, going back two or more generations, included various combinations of Italian, Scottish, Polish, French, Belgian, English, Lithuanian, German, Lebanese, Dutch, Swedish, Irish, and Swiss, but there was not a Balkan among us. Despite variations in height, weight, and coloring, our physical appearances suggested essential similarities rather than differences.

Most of us actively participated in social, folk, and theater dance forms besides Balkan dancing. Members listed ballroom, boogie, and disco; New England contra dancing, Morris dance, English country dance, international folk dance, and Appalachian clogging; contact improvisation and modern dance. Two dancers played recorder and penny whistle, and one each piano, violin, pipe and tabor, acoustic bass and squeezebox. Three were singers.

It is difficult to characterize Borovčani's internal organization and relationships. There was no single elected, or even informally acknowledged, leader. Most decisions about where or when to perform, and for what fee, were made during lengthy, often disorganized meetings held after weekly practices. Borovčani performed several times a year in Maine and elsewhere in New England – often at arts centers, elderhostels, schools and colleges, resort hotels, weddings, folk clubs, in self-produced concerts, and annually at the Maine Festival.[5] Fees ranged from gratis programs to $350 for roughly an hour's performance. Revenues covered transportation costs to performances and miscellaneous expenses for publicity, costumes, and rent for rehearsal space at a local church. There was no profit or income to individuals.

Despite its collective ethos, Borovčani exhibited some aspects of a meritocracy: those who executed dances best were the ones most likely to lead, when it was necessary. The ability to direct in a non-threatening way was also important. One member commented: "The better dancers or organizers usually take over and make good leaders. Those that can't dance well but try to be leaders just annoy the rest of the group."

Because we were ideologically committed to participatory decision-making and consensual action, meetings sometimes became chaotic. A despot or two usually rose to the occasion. One dancer observed ironically that, "Borovčani is run by temporary dictators who assume command (usually in a fit of pique), only to be softened, modified, and eventually reassimilated by the group. Thus things get done in a truly [?] democratic way."

Still another important structural factor was seniority. Most of the original, and older, members agreed that "leaders seemed to emerge when needed" and that the group "has a loose structure, but a shared sense of values." In spite of "personal differences" and "too much gab and gossip" they felt Borovčani were "dear people." In contrast, several newer, younger members thought there was "little communication," because the group was "a bit scattered," and "too anarchistic." In their view, there was "too much time spent talking and not enough dancing." They would have preferred more efficient, centralized leadership, taken on by senior members.

Rehearsals often demonstrated the dilemma of leaderlessness. Endless joking and teasing, small talk and gossip created a familiar, familial intimacy. We chose a particular dance, performed it, discussed it, repeated parts, then ran the entire dance again. Milled around, drank some water, broke into groups. Finally a weary musician or self-appointed director would loudly call everyone together for another dance.

In preparation for a performance, someone (usually the person who taught the dance) would volunteer constructive criticism and suggest who should perform publicly. Although this was sometimes a source of tension, everyone agreed that the goal was the best possible performance. Dancers themselves often opted out of a particular dance to give others a chance. Line dances were led and called by those who knew or performed them best. By 1982 the repertory's most complex dances were taught and led by one male expert.

Apart from teaching, however, most of Borovčani's off-stage tasks were undertaken by women. Several men in the group cultivated a devil-may-care nonchalance about the details of governance. We women sensed that if we didn't do it, no one would. Ad hoc female committees took on financial decision-making, booking arrangements, publicity, program design and execution, and often choreography and staging for a particular event. But we never called it "artistic direction" or "administration."

Women also sewed costumes, partly of necessity and partly because of pride in "women's work." Departing members passed along skirts or vests, which were collectively owned; but new articles, including the more elaborate men's shirts, were often needed.

The roles of men and women as members of the group diverged from their danced representations. While aspects of male dominance and female submissiveness were dramatized choreographically, most members, men and women, would have insisted that they personally rejected traditional roles.

Whatever individuals' contradictory motivations or behavior, the central focus of the group was dancing. Most members cited the physical discipline and challenge of dancing as their prime reasons for belonging. However, a few mentioned social, spiritual, or aesthetic motives, with comments such as, "I love people, and any activity that brings people together in a holistic and spiritual way is very attractive to me," and, "Dance and music are a necessary part of living – we express cooperatively the love of movement and beauty. I like doing ethnic dance because it is what people have been doing for centuries." Others cited changing considerations: "First, I became a member because I loved the dance and music but also needed to be with people who were like me in some ways. Then, because I mainly needed the people. Now, because I mainly love to dance."

But most saw the group essentially as yet another way to dance:

"I love to dance and Boston is too far away."

"I like to be active, wear costumes, have the chance to really learn a dance – the only way you can get people to work hard to learn something perfectly is if they have performance as a goal."

"I like to dance with good dancers. If the group's level of dancing went down I would probably quit. I also like the people involved and there is an opportunity to socialize."

Even for those who emphasized technical challenges as their motivation, social experiences became integrated with the physical and aesthetic. Dancing with the goal of eventual public display modeled particular patterns of interpersonal relations. Researchers of folk and social dance forms have commented on the "instant community" and "intimate anonymity" that dancing creates in voluntary associations, in contrast to groupings based on long-shared values or primary relationships, such as family, neighborhood, ethnicity, or religion (Abbott 1987: 164–5, Ronström 1992: 259, Hast 1993: 21).

An example of "instant community" is described in Owe Ronström's study of Yugoslav immigrants in Stockholm, Sweden, between 1983 and 1988. Before the civil wars and disintegration of the Yugoslav Republic, dances and parties in Stockholm included Serbs, Croatians, Bosnians and others to learn common dances and define a "Yugoslav" community in an alien setting:

> As they perform, the musicians and dancers ... tune their bodies and minds into communication with each other, with previous performers, and with the other people present in a social relation based on living through several temporal dimensions at the same time. Yet one neither can nor need suppose that the coordination of bodies and minds in time and space leads to the integration of values, experiences, or meaning. This is probably an important explanation for the fact that Serbs, Croats, Macedonians, Montenegrins, Bosnians and Hungarians – people who in other contexts perhaps regard themselves as dissimilar rather then alike – so easily can interact as Yugoslavs in the contexts I have studied.
>
> (Ronström 1992: 259)

As a performing group Borovčani differed in obvious ways from an immigrant association defining itself in relation to a foreign host society. But in both groups Balkan dance created, for a time, a sense of community among dancers without a profound or articulated "integration of values, experiences, and meanings."

Dancing, particularly in unison with others, can structure a confluence of self and situation that corresponds to what Victor Turner calls the shared flow of *communitas*, "the holistic sensation when we act with total involvement, when action and awareness are one (one ceases to flow if one becomes aware that one is doing it)" (1986: 133).

This perception is similar to what Gestalt therapists term "spontaneous engagement," in which emotion, perception and movement are unified. As a "person-in-action," the individual experiences a sensation of actualizing and losing the self at the same time: "there is no sense of oneself or of other things other than one's experience of the situation. The feeling is immediate, concrete and present, and integrally involves perception, muscularity and excitation" (Perls *et al.* 1951: 377).

For some Borovčani members, rehearsing and performing offered this kind of personal liberation and social integration: "When the chemistry is right," one male dancer confided, "the music, dancers, mood and all, it's an ecstatic moment for me. It's experiencing the now."

The sensation of *communitas* was strongest in performance, but also developed at weekly rehearsals, which were closer to "folk dancing" or just folks dancing. We rehearsed year-round, from six to eight on Wednesday evenings in a local church social hall, a large empty room with a hardwood floor. Only two dancers lived in town: the rest came from up to fifty miles away in all directions. Most members were full-time workers for whom the evening trip was a labor of love, especially in winter.

Members described the way dancing felt in vivid terms that help explain this commitment:

> "[Balkan dance is] lots of fun and intense action. Different from any other type of dancing I know."

> "I find Balkan dancing very sexy, stimulating, exciting, and seductive."

> "It's a rich meaty type of dance good for flirting, showing off, working up a sweat – the music is great . . . you can put your soul into it."

> "I think the music creates a big part of the feel. There's a proud feeling that comes with the music and Balkan steps."

> "It's ordered – the steps are very interesting and controlled, not crazy, but balanced – contra dancing is more social, boogie more individual."

> "Balkan is a very primal, yet highly precise and sophisticated form of dance, probably the most of any folk dances."

These comments point out Balkan dancing's physical pleasures, emotional resonances, aesthetic challenges, erotic possibilities, and social constraints. They suggest that dancing participates in the production of social worlds in part by reshaping individual understanding and collective behavior through biological and psychological means. Gratifying dance experiences move us physically and emotionally in particular ways that can influence behavior on and off the dance floor. Kinesthetic memories of Bulgarian line dances, no doubt adrenaline-assisted and neuro-chemically transmitted, arouse for me an intense response: intellectual appreciation, aesthetic satisfaction, physical animation, emotional warmth.[6] Dancing channeled a powerful group energy flow and modeled collective effort.

But despite powerful shared experiences, Balkan dancing was clearly not an integral part of members' ethnic heritage or social worlds. One dancer said dryly, "Sometimes it's very alien. I can tell my ancestors were not Balkan." Although several of us had visited Eastern Europe and the Balkan countries and one was a graduate student in Slavic studies, most knew almost nothing about the origins of the dances and songs we performed. The focus was on learning dances with attention to traditional style, but without scholarly regard for the circumstances that engendered them.

Borovčani reinterpreted the Balkan tradition for American purposes. The goals of the performers suited the spirit of the times and delighted enthusiastic audiences.

In appropriating Balkan dances, Borovčani posed American alternatives: "What if . . . " (the staged representations of happy peasants and communal harmony suggested) bodies could be channels for communication without manipulation or violence? What if individuals could experience elusive feelings of shared identity and fellowship in concerted action: a disciplined, joyous, sensuous and complex sense of belonging?

And, "What if . . . " (the troupe's behind-the-scenes life implied) adult Americans could dance together; share physical closeness and trust (with or without personal entanglements); become exasperated, vent their anger, and reconcile their differences; take turns as leaders and followers; and accommodate one another in the interest of a community greater than the sum of its parts?

"SELL THE HORSE, SELL THE HOUSE: ONLY DANCE"[7]

However, between 1978 and 1982 the country's social and political mood was changing, and while Borovčani "performed" communalism and collaboration, the dominant ideology of the Reagan era celebrated individualism and competition. Following the 1980 election many Maine people, particularly transplants "from away" in their twenties and thirties, either focused on careers or retreated further upcountry.

Within our group, new opportunities and pressures from families and jobs affected individuals' levels of energy and commitment. Obvious rifts opened along old fault lines. While some members pushed for more professionalism, others took a more relaxed attitude. Before the group's final concert, one dancer successfully lobbied for the inclusion of her boyfriend, an inexperienced dancer, and the quality of dancing suffered.

As a performing ensemble on the margins of the dominant culture, Borovčani embodied attitudes characteristic of a particular time and place. We danced small-is-beautiful rural ideals, traditional gender roles, physical discipline, and individuals' strong connections to the group. The dancing had brought "a particular cast of mind out into the world . . . " (Geertz 1983: 99). And the dances had danced us, inducing a cast of mind in members and audiences, suggesting ways of experiencing and behaving that are still with me. Offstage, Borovčani earnestly if untidily enacted egalitarianism, non-commercialism, and collective responsibility.

Unlike a living folk dance tradition on native ground, often integral to maintaining social identities and achieving political goals, Balkan dance in Maine had only a transitory capacity to create a world for its members and communicate with its viewers. By 1982, Borovčani's moment had passed.

To several of us the "public images of sentiment" (ibid.: 82) the group had represented began to seem naive. And contradictions had become apparent: we were an exclusive group performing inclusivity; our public displays of feminine modesty and male charisma belied the organization's realities. Though we imagined ourselves opponents to mainstream values we sometimes catered to mainstream audiences, offering them a slice of feel-good utopianism; and while the choreography signaled a larger solidarity, as a group we lacked purposeful intent beyond perfecting and performing the dances.

This version of Borovčani's story circles back to the dance and song that began it. At the 1982 Maine Festival performance, jazz dancers waited in the wings with a Devo soundtrack, wearing leopardskin leotards and flesh-colored tights, black jazz shoes and little white socks, black lipstick and pointy fifties shades. On stage, we concluded the vocal for *Ličko Kolo*. The dancers held hands and followed the leader, creating staccato rhythms of increasing speed and force with our footfalls. The line snaked in S-curves that doubled back on themselves. In passing, we wordlessly, warmly acknowledged each other. At last, the leader began a circle that coiled into a tight spiral, faster and closer, until there was nowhere to go. We stamped together and stopped, in silence.

NOTES

1 In 1982 I surveyed the Borovčani membership as part of a research project on dance and culture. I also wrote and narrated a half-hour video documentary on the group, broadcast by Maine Public Television.
2 This narrative approach can be loosely categorized as processual analysis, a position in anthropology which "stresses the case history method; it shows how ideas, events, and institutions interact and change through time" (Rosaldo 1989: 92–3).
3 New dances were learned at dance festival workshops, dance camps, or during visits by visiting professionals.
4 *Living the Good Life: How to Live Sanely and Simply in a Troubled World* (1970) by Helen and Scott Nearing of Harborside, Maine, inspired a generation of Maine homesteaders.
5 The Maine Festival, founded in 1977, was conceived as a celebration of Maine arts, crafts, music, performance and folk traditions. It expanded to include nationally and internationally recognized performers.
6 For a book on chemically based kinesthetic, emotional and intellectual response, see *Descartes' Error: Emotion, Reason, and the Human Brain* (1994) by Antonio R. Demasio, New York: G. P. Putnam's Sons.
7 The Serbian song "Ajde Jano" goes: "Come, Jana, dance the Kolo! Sell the horse, sell the house: only dance" (Graetz *et al.* 1977: 6–7).

BIBLIOGRAPHY

Abbott, P. (1987) *Seeking Many Inventions*, Knoxville: University of Tennessee Press.

Blacking, J. (1982) "Movement and Meaning: Dance in Social Anthropological Perspective," *Dance Research Journal* (Spring) 1, 1: 89–99.

Clark, T. J. (1984) *The Painting of Modern Life: Paris in the Art of Manet and His Followers*, London: Thames & Hudson.

DMC Library (1975) *Bulgarian Embroideries*, revised edition, Mulhouse, France: Editions Th. de Dillmont.

Foster, S. L. (1986) *Reading Dancing: Bodies and Subjects in Contemporary American Dance*, Berkeley: University of California Press.

Geertz, C. (1973) *The Interpretation of Cultures*, London: Hutchinson.

—— (1983) *Local Knowledge: Further Essays in Interpretive Anthropology*, New York: Basic Books.

Graetz, A., Buchholz, J., and Peppler, J. (eds) (1977) *The Laduvane Songbook*, Cambridge, MA: Myxomop Publications.

Hast, D. E. (1993) "Performance, Transformation, and Community: Contra Dance in New England," *Dance Research Journal* (Spring) 25, 1: 21–32.

Maine Festival (1982) *Program* (August 6, 7, 8) Brunswick, Maine.

Nearing, H. and Nearing, S. (1987 [1970]) *Living the Good Life: How to Live Sanely and Simply in a Troubled World*, New York: Schocken Books.

Novack, C. (1990) *Sharing the Dance: Contact Improvisation and American Culture*, Madison: University of Wisconsin Press.

—— (1993) "Ballet, Gender and Cultural Power" in H. Thomas (ed.) *Dance, Gender and Culture*, New York: St. Martins Press.

Perls, F., Hefferline, R. F., and Goodman, P. (1951) *Gestalt Therapy*, New York: Dell Publishing.

Ronström, O. (1989) "The Dance Event – A Terminological and Methodological Discussion of the Concept," in L. Torp (ed.) *The Dance Event: A Complex Cultural Phenomenon*, Proceedings from the Fifteenth Symposium of the ITCM Study Group on Ethnochoreology, Copenhagen: ICTM Study Group on Ethnochoreology.

—— (1992) *Att Gestalta ett Ursprung*, Stockholm: Stockholm University, Institutet för folklivsforskning.

Rosaldo, R. (1989) *Culture and Truth: The Remaking of Social Analysis*, Boston: Beacon Press.

Turner, V. (1986) *The Anthropology of Performance*, New York: PAJ Publications (a division of Performing Arts Journal, Inc.)

Wolff, J. (1992) "Excess and Inhibition: Interdisciplinarity in the Study of Art," in L. Grossberg, C. Nelson, and P. Treichler (eds) *Cultural Studies*, New York: Routledge.

18 High Critics/Low Arts

Carol Martin

In the debate over high and low culture, it is well known that modernist critics were antagonistic to low culture, especially in its form as a burgeoning mass culture industry. Conversely, postmodern theorists have maintained that mass culture is not as detrimental to the public psyche as previously thought. Long after postmodern concepts made inroads into other fields, dance critics and scholars continued to take their cues from a modernist point of view, considering only "serious" choreography as their subject. Until recently, dance criticism and scholarship have been theoretically and historically inscribed within the narrow purview of late modernism's formalist concerns. This position translated into critical verification of what many modern and even postmodern choreographers were claiming – that movement was the sole determiner of meaning. All else could be ignored.

The inheritance of this critical and theoretical history has been a mixed blessing. A tremendous amount has been gained from the inquiry into how movement creates meaning and the problems of translating dance meanings into a powerful prose that reverberates with the presence of the moving body. Yet the narrowness of such an investigation has kept dance scholarship running to catch up with the theoretical accomplishments of other fields. Embedded in the predicament are a number of dichotomies of little use: high v. low, art v. life, objective v. subjective, formalist v. utilitarian and/or political, modern v. postmodern. It is not that these categories no longer exist but that continuing to translate the differences within them into a dialectic does little to illuminate historical complexity. Nor does it further contemporary critical thinking. Yet these dialectics are still found defining both subject matter and critical approach.

An example of this was Arlene Croce's refusal to review *Still/Here* (1994) by Bill T. Jones on the grounds that by including the words and images of dying or ill people, Jones put his work beyond the reach of criticism – "literally undiscussable" (Croce 1994/5: 54). The operative assumptions that allowed Croce to reach this conclusion were many: in theater one has to have a choice about who one will be, and those who are sick have no choice; using actual illness in art is tantamount to displaying victimhood and martyrdom and is a menace to critical evaluation as well as to critical discussion. Yet it is also true that none of us chooses our race, our gender, our age, our country of origin. Nor can these characteristics simply be thought of as fixed. Immigration, passing, and gender play are all part of contemporary life. Performance is capable of reconfiguring the social conventions around such constructions. Yet according to Croce, illness should be avoided along with overweight dancers, old dancers, dancers with sickled feet or physical deformities (ibid.: 55). Similarly problematic are "dissed blacks, abused women, or disenfranchised homosexuals" all of whom make victim art (ibid.). Clearly, as a black, gay, HIV-positive choreographer, Jones was a triple threat to Croce's critical criteria. While Croce asserted that the self-righteousness of what she labeled victim art was tantamount to blackmail in the complicity that it summoned from its spectators, I suspect it was actually the dichotomies Croce used to support her critical position that were the problem: art v. life, objective v. subjective, and formalist v. utilitarian. These were most clearly stated in Croce's assertion, "I can't review someone I feel sorry for or hopeless about" (ibid.). Croce contended that the express intentions of Jones's work – to do the ill some good – were not appropriate for dance theater. In the age of AIDS is it really possible or desirable for the performing arts to exclude people who are actually ill?

I did not see *Still/Here*. But as Croce did not see *Still/Here* either, her objections to it were entirely based on the construction of a critical position, not the work itself. Thus it is not the dance that is the subject of my discussion but Croce's critical yardstick, which is indicative of a late modernist sensibility that is inapplicable to postmodern work. Illness, in Croce's construction, is a monolithic condition which can only be represented on stage as such. However, being ill does not prevent one from engaging in the representational play of theater. Consider a letter by Karen Gerald, a member of the *Still/Here* workshop in Iowa City, to Jones about her experience:

> My feeling of remorse then has to do with the fact that I gave an incomplete picture of my life with a chronic illness – all of the tears, but none of the laughter. . . .
>
> That winter had begun with a November that contained twenty-two straight sunless days. I knew that the dreariness weighed heavily on me. What wasn't clear then was the fact that I would never be rid of the FEAR or of the diagnosis. By the end of the winter I realized I walked with a stoop not unlike the days just after surgery. Six months of chemotherapy and the subsequent afternoons spent in bed, did little to improve my posture. The extra pounds I picked up in that year really had tipped the scales and I don't even know what caused it – the drugs, stress, drug-induced menopause, a long winter? So when would I recover this lost physicality? How could I shed this burden? Daily walks

did not do it. I just walked the way I felt, slow and awkward. The exercise classes I took were too difficult for me and reminded me of how labored my movements had become. Finally, at the end of this long winter I thought I just might recover my lost physicality when I had the desire to plant flowers in the spring. I knew that I would recover emotionally when I was able to see the humor in feeling my breast prosthesis pop out of my shirt and end up in a freshly dug hole.

(Gerald 1994)

Gerald's depiction of her illness is the opposite of self-pity: It is, instead, a testimony of transformation – a respectable subject for artistic work. Whether or not Gerald's transformational humor and subsequent healing were incorporated into Jones's work was not the issue. Her representational status as an ill person (she appeared on video) no matter how she chose to portray her illness created critical closure for Croce. Similarly for Jones who in Croce's powerful prose "has taken sanctuary among the unwell" (Croce 1994/5: 60). But as Gerald's letter documents, the representation of actual illness can be as theatrically viable as any other subject. Was it fair to assume that those who have suffered life-threatening illnesses are necessarily in a critically or physically terminal condition?

In all this there was another subject that kindled Croce's diatribe. No matter how provocative her attack on Jones – she called him the John the Baptist of victim art and Arnie Zane, his former lover who died of AIDS in 1988, his Christ – what Croce was really lamenting was the fact that her critical criteria were useless in the face of contemporary works. Her critical approach was cut off (ibid.: 54) by what she called utilitarian art, of which victim art was a subgenre (ibid.: 55). Yet if one is familiar with the complex variety of critical positions among performance scholars and critics, it becomes clear that it was not "the critic" that was threatened but *this* particular critic. Croce's wrath was palpable as she documented Jones's "war on critics, the most vocal portion of the audience" (ibid.: 58). Jones's aggressive undermining of the authority of the critic was understood by Croce as a silence-demanding dictum. Croce admonished Jones for declaring "No back talk" (ibid.). I suspect, however, that she also might have entertained using this censure on certain occasions. What else would one expect?

In response to Jones's plea for those who are ill, Croce entered a plea for the critic, with the awareness that this might make her seem a victim herself. For Croce, the origin of Jones's work was the radicalism of the sixties. In that epoch choreographers' formal concerns did away with the need for interpretation and therefore abolished the necessity of evaluation. The irony is that Jones, who was accused of a continuation of a sixties sensibility, caused Croce to write one of the most enraged and provocative pieces of criticism in years. One cannot help admiring Croce for forcing the issue, even though her piece could have been used as a witness for the prosecution in the NEA hearings.

From Croce's point of view, not only is the critic threatened, but the public who appreciates this "victim art" is suffering from "mass delusion" (1994/5: 54). Cozy complicity, not compassion, is the emotion that generates the audience's patronizing applause (ibid.: 55). The bond, according to Croce, between performer and spectator in work like Jones's and Pina Bausch's is a "mutually manipulative union" (ibid.) which leaves no room for critical observations. And the audience (characterized as a deluded mass with an uncritical and monolithic response) that is most guilty of this critically perfidious affiliation is Brooklyn Academy's Next Wave subscription audience. Clearly, audience is an important consideration. Both choreographer and critic must cultivate their own.

Croce's comments seemed, at times, as cruel and uncensored as anything Jones might have said about critics: "If an artist paints a picture in his own blood, what does it matter if I think it's not a very good picture? If he mixes the blood with Day-Glo colors, who will criticize him? The artist is going to bleed to death, and that's it" (ibid.: 58–9). Given that Jones, who is HIV positive, has a blood-born disease, Croce's image of an artist bleeding to death in a piece provoked by Jones's use of illness was macabre, to say the least. When the fog in the graveyard cleared, Croce appeared too eager to sound the death knell. My point is not that the malice was undeserved, but that it left Croce with too many corpses cluttering her critical project. Perhaps the epitaph she was writing was her own.

To further her position Croce asserted that the crisis in art emerged with the arts bureaucracy, in the form of government and private funding, which privileges socially useful art as opposed to an aesthetically sophisticated and compelling one (ibid.: 56). This proclivity, she said, dated both from the ideological wars that emerged from the sixties and from the proletariat sensibility of the thirties (ibid.). While I would agree that both periods were seminal for American theater and dance, as historical determiners of utilitarian art born out of big-government bureaucracy, they provide evidence that contradicts Croce's argument. What has come to be a salient feature of these two decades is that they advanced *both* political and aesthetic art, which, in fact, were not conceived as diametrically opposed. Nevertheless, the master narrative that has typified modern dance and ballet is one of canonical choreographers with aesthetic agendas. Choreographers with political pursuits have, until recently, been marginalized for a variety of reasons, not the least of which is the narrow spectrum of critical thought. As Ellen Graff noted in her article "Dancing Red: Art and Politics," in the 1950s, in particular, art and politics were thought of as separate spheres (Graff 1995: 1). One of the consequences of this division was that for many years political dance eluded critical and historical reflection.

Croce looks back to the nineteenth century, the real historical source of her critical practice, as a time when art was a vehicle for both the expression and transcendence of the individual spirit. Her nostalgia is for the transformative power of art, provided it is the spirit as distinct from social consciousness that is transformed. "But we have also created an art with no power of transcendence, no way of assuring us that the grandeur of the individual spirit is more worth celebrating than the political clout of the group" (Croce 1994/5: 59). Interesting inconsistencies abound. According to Croce, because nineteenth century artists did not name their illnesses they were able to override disease and death with their art (ibid.: 60). Croce values the individual spirit over the group, as long as it is not so personalized as to have an actual identity. Paradoxically, for critics like Croce, to celebrate the individual spirit is to surmount the self. To surmount the self is to express the universal – one of the worst conceits of western art: it was only western art, according to the nineteenth-century sensibility to which Croce subscribes, that reached the pinnacle of universal expression. The grandeur of the individual cannot be attached to any group, especially not clamorous blacks, women, and homosexuals. It is not that these people cannot make art. But they must do so only as individuals, not as groups or even representatives of groups. As members of groups Croce assumes they have an ideological axe to grind which separates them from an art-for-art's-sake sensibility. That transcendence can include spiritual, social, and political engagement does not occur to Croce. Nor would she even entertain the idea that perhaps transcendence as a measure for art should be reconsidered.

It was the vehemence of Croce's argument that made it so antagonistic. In a letter to the editor published in the *New York Times*, Susan Sontag succinctly summarized what might have been Croce's objection: "That a work of art may appeal to our sympathy but is not validated by the worthiness of this appeal seems so elementary, so obvious, that one might hope the point does not need repeating" (1995: 9). True enough. The confusion Croce rightly deplores, I think, is between art and self-expression. The problem comes when the narcissism of the artist cripples the fashioning of self-expression into art. Yet even if this were the pith of Croce's claim, one cannot excuse the means she used to make her case. She founded her evidence for a lack of aesthetic values and the resulting critical anomie she experienced on the 1960s, illness, blacks, women, and gays. No matter if one agrees that worthy aesthetic inquiries are being lost. Croce's objections were not simply spiritual and aesthetic, they were material and political, as well.

From the modernist perspective of Croce's criticism, art should be transcendent and universal. But as Mark Franko has pointed out in *Dancing Modernism/Performing Politics*, the narrative history of dance has been disabled by a lack of critical distance from the tenets of modernism. One of the consequences of this has been a critical perspective unable to "expose the modernist narrative's omission of politics, mass culture, and sexual difference" (Franko 1995: ix). Modernism does not only indicate stylistic difference in performance, but historical and theoretical attitudes toward the categories of "high" and "low" art. As Andreas Huyssen has pointed out, modernism was defined by the mind-set of machine aesthetics and espousal of progress, as well as by critiques of standardization and alienation (1986: 186). From this perspective, subjectivity carried the stigma of bourgeois ideology (ibid.: 213). The modernist enterprise polarized mass culture and high art and institutionalized high art, in part, as a response to the powerful and ubiquitous mass culture industry.

In the case of dance, ballet and modern dance were institutionalized as integral cultural components of major urban centers and in the academy. A formidable seriousness about the cultural value of dance was sought to counter doubts about the validity of intellectual and artistic pursuits based upon the dancing body. Choreographers and dancers feared the taint of popular culture as did most modern artists. Initially, both critics and choreographers were absorbed in establishing the legitimacy of corporeal expression. The similarity of their concerns generated a complicity in their approaches.

Drawing the line between "high" and "low" art was central to this endeavor. One result was that until recently popular forms of theater and dance have been largely ignored by performance scholars. As popular culture historian Brooks McNamara points out:

> I don't believe I overstate the case very much when I suggest that a quarter of a century ago writing about theatre and dance was hermetically sealed – that the reference points were almost all within the forms themselves. What actor or dancer did this? What company did that? What was the design like? What was the critical reception? . . . Among theatre scholars, for example, there was a conviction that throughout history there had been some sort of performance hierarchy that ranged from "greatest artistic achievement" to charming but basically inconsequential works in the folk and popular idioms.
>
> (1994: xi)

This hierarchy became dramatically apparent to me when I was researching dance marathons. Not only were former marathoners ashamed of their profession (yes, some of them were professionals), but the degraded status of marathons was institutionalized in the attitude of archivists.

The Dance Collection at Lincoln Center, for example, allowed me to freely photograph dance marathon scrapbooks, a liberty that greatly aided my research. This same privilege would not have been offered were the material deemed more valuable. Similarly with the Library of Congress, a stack pass allowed me invaluable and unlimited access to old and crumbling copies of *Billboard* which I carefully copied. It is not that I would like these documents to become less accessible or that I did not appreciate the generosity of librarians at these institutions. Rather, I am simply pointing out that even the documents of high and low culture are treated differently by institutions whose job it is to safeguard cultural/ historical documents and artifacts.

Even if the politics of patronage and archives is implicated, which it usually is, the real culprit for Croce is mass culture. It is mass culture that has spawned mass-produced art devoid of spiritual dimensions (Croce 1994/5: 60). Even worse, this mass-production sensibility often uses the disguise of high art.

In fact, the categories of "high" and "low" have been increasingly blurred as artworks quote, borrow, and appropriate each other. The common designation of this occurrence is "postmodernism." Like modernism, postmodernism is not just an artistic style but a historical designation. Postmodernism is different from modernism in that, as Huyssen claims "it raises the question of cultural tradition and conservation in the most fundamental way as an aesthetic and a political issue" (1986: 216). The tensions that give postmodern art its vernacular vocabulary exist in the realms of "tradition and innovation, conservation and renewal, mass culture and high art" (ibid.). The surge of political postmodern works in which movement is only part of the production of meaning cannot be comprehended via the dialectics that were so useful in modernism.

A consideration of contemporary performance should take into account the fact that "high" art and "low" art are no longer mutually exclusive categories. Nor does much postmodern performance keep a distance from mass culture. Some critics, well before Croce, have argued that "high" culture needs to be protected from the capitalist culture industry with its mass production sensibility. In reality, protection is no longer the issue. A merging of "high" and "low" culture has already occurred. As an example, one could point to the changes that have taken place at the commercially driven magazine for which Croce writes. *The New Yorker*, since the new editorship of Tina Brown, is full of advertisements that push mass culture and highbrow journalism up against one another. The magazine is no longer aimed at New York intelligentsia but at the *hoi polloi*.

As Huyssen observes, the enterprising relationship between "high" art and mass culture is one of the major differences between high modernism and the art and literature that has followed (1986: 194). What is important at this juncture is the development of a criticism that is fully engaged in examining how aesthetic ideas become commercial commodities and sentimental objects. In this vector it is important to examine both the aesthetics and the identity politics that propel contemporary work. It is not the end of criticism but the advent of a new kind of criticism.

Croce is right: In the face of contemporary work, nostalgia for nineteenth century art will make the critic obsolete. The limitations of this critical position *vis-à-vis* contemporary performance have emerged very strongly. In a work such as Jane Comfort's *Faith Healing* (1993), for example, shunning her quotations of mass culture would prevent the critical and historical perspective that enables one to examine the implications of the devices Comfort uses. Comfort's work raises crucial issues. Is the breakdown between "high" and "low" in performance an actual break or merely an appropriation of one form by another? The question is important because it addresses the claim that the values and ideology, if not the techniques of "high" art, especially institutionalized "high" art, describe the status quo while low art subverts, transgresses, and negotiates given norms. A breakdown between "high" and "low" art indicates or even necessitates a tension in cultural values. This tension could be variously interpreted as politically ambiguous, or as complicitous with dominant cultural values, or as contesting controlling values, or perhaps as all of these.

Faith Healing is Comfort's revision of the memory play *The Glass Menagerie* (1944) by Tennessee Williams. The plot is unaltered. Amanda Wingfield (played by Mark Dendy, cross-dressed), long ago deserted by her husband, lives with her crippled daughter, Laura (Nancy Alfaro), and working son, Tom (Scot Willingham). Lost in memories of her own suitors, Amanda cautions her daughter to keep herself pretty for gentlemen callers even though the girl has never had any. In lieu of suitors, Laura is given the option of practicing shorthand and typing at a local school. When Amanda learns that Laura has dropped out, she decides it is time for Tom to bring home a gentleman caller for his sister. Tom succeeds in inviting Jim O'Connor (David Neumann) to dinner only to discover he was Laura's high school crush. After dinner Amanda and Tom excuse themselves to wash the dishes. In their absence Laura loses some of her shyness and becomes quite charming. Jim kisses her but then confesses he is already engaged. For Amanda and Laura the evening is a total failure.

Not only does Comfort translate the plot of *The Glass Menagerie* into dance theater with major portions of Williams's text intact, she also interjects lip-synched scenes from major films situated in such a way to give Tom and Laura's unstated desires a vivid reality. The seething discontent and remote sexuality that fuel Williams's play become in Comfort's production explicit fantasies of sexual exploration and conquest. In the realm of imagination, at least, Tom and Laura escape the narrative constraints of the play and in so doing parody any nostalgia for the conventions of southern gentility and sexuality the play portrays. This parody takes the form of a humorous and seamless interaction between "high" art, as represented by the play, the historical heritage of the modern dance movement vocabulary Comfort uses, and mass culture, as represented by the films Comfort quotes.

In the play and in Comfort's dance, Tom is both the narrator and a character. He presents the action as his personal memory, simultaneously evoking both the past of his character and the present of the narrator. Further disrupting conventions of realism are the screen images, danced throughout Comfort's piece, that Williams originally wrote as stage directions. For example, after Tom in his role as narrator tells the audience how his mother's obsession with a gentleman caller haunted the mood of the house, there is a stage direction for the projection of an image of a young man at the door of a house (Williams 1945: 37). Rather than a literal

Figure 18.1 Faith Healing: Nancy Alfaro as Laura and David Neumann as Jim.
(Photo: Arthur Elgort)

representation of the caller in the play, the image prescribed by Williams is of an archetypal suitor. Thus Amanda's obsession with an actual suitor for Laura is juxtaposed with a fictional archetype. The distance between the archetype and the actual is the measure of Amanda's illusions about Southern gentility.

In Comfort's production, the screen images become exactly that, excerpts from films that portray the urgent but unstated emotions that flicker through the characters' lives. Tom postures as Arnold Schwarzenegger in *Terminator II* in response to his mother's nagging. While duplicating the terminator's posture and in perfect synch with the soundtrack that momentarily blares through the theater, Tom says, "Hasta la vista, baby" to his mother as he prepares to leave. This happens in a flash that simulates the film even as it expresses Tom's subconscious. Although Tom's attitude toward his mother is sanctioned by the authority of the film, the displacement and recognition of the film is also very funny. The humor of the simulation – art imitates mass culture – is underscored by an almost subliminal familiarity with the soundtrack and body postures of the film.

The controlling memory of Tom as the narrator who reflects upon the single incident of a dinner guest is transformed by the filmic fantasies/ scenarios that disrupt the narrative. The ambiance of flashback, memory, and nostalgia is forsaken in favor of the humor of making immediate and apparent the sexuality that gives Williams's devices their pathos. In this way Comfort exposes the conventions that create dramatic tension in *The Glass Menagerie* while she ridicules their protocol. This exposure is furthered by the contrast between the canned soundtrack and the virtuosic immediacy of the acting and dancing of Willingham, Neumann, Alfaro, and Dendy who also contributed their ideas to the making of the work.

Unlike Amanda and Laura, Tom has a life outside the home. The movies and the dance hall across the street tease his fantasies of untamed sexuality. When Amanda asks Tom where he has been his reply is always "the movies." She suspects, however, that he has been doing things of which he should be ashamed. Tom does not have a girl and later in the play we learn that he hangs out in the bathroom stalls at the factory writing poetry. Comfort leaves no doubt about the homoerotic subtext linking Tom (the character most like Williams) to Jim, the friend he asks home to meet Laura. An encounter between the two men quickly turns into the love scene from *Kiss of the Spider Woman*. In a downstage spotlight, Willingham and Neumann take off their shirts. We are confronted with the immediate sexuality of their half-naked bodies in close proximity to one another as they simulate one of the film's most erotic scenes. In Comfort's choreography Tom's homoerotic desires are deftly given their due in a copious archeology of lust. Willingham and Neumann, both beautiful to look at, lip-synch the dialogue spoken by William Hurt and Raoul Julia as Valentine and Malino in *Spider Woman*: "Wait I'm squeezed up against the wall. Let me lift my legs."

Tom may go to the movies to attach shape and form to his desires, but whether he actually realizes these desires or they are just internalized filmic fantasies remains ambiguous. Either way, as Comfort depicts them, Tom's secret sexual longings are no longer mysterious.

Ambiguity marks Comfort's decision to appropriate film scenarios and text. Using film to portray characters' desires can be read as the creation of a conformity of response to the manipulations of mass culture. Film images stand in for the articulation of a character's unique and complex desires. Whatever might have been provocatively uncertain about Tom's late night hours is now given absolute closure with the identification of Tom with *Kiss of the Spider Woman*. This perspective does not explain, however, the effect of watching the dancers/actors lip-synch film fragments while dancing Comfort's choreographic versions of the scenarios. The mastery is in usurping and recirculating what seems monolithic and immovably powerful film images. Comfort's choreography turns on gaining possession of an abstraction – the idealized scenarios of mass culture – and using it for her own purposes. At times, in Comfort's hands, the narrative of Williams's play seems in the service of a series of film fragments. Not only are *Terminator II* and *Kiss of the Spider Woman* quoted but so are *Raiders of the Lost Ark*, *Gone With the Wind*, *Superman*, *The Princess Bride*, and *The Big Easy*. However, all these films have scenarios concerning a certain kind of hero and heroine that allow Comfort to control the subtext of the play.

The enthusiasm *Faith Healing* generated in the audience at New York's PS 122 indicates both a fascination with dismantling the power of mass culture and mourning for what might have replaced it. Tom's speech to Jim in scene six of the text mirrors this sentiment: "People go to the *movies* instead of *moving*! Hollywood characters are supposed to have all the adventures for everybody in America, while everybody in America sits in a dark room and watches them have them" (Williams 1945: 79). The knowing laughter these lines evoked was based on the fact that the opposition of movies and moving clearly does not hold true for the performers of this work. They were able to do what the characters were forbidden from doing: give their ideas and fantasies immediate physical representation.

Both Williams's text and Comfort's choreography address mass culture but in very different ways. Williams's characters are burdened with the stereotypes of southern masculinity and femininity and their inability to articulate their desires. Williams invokes the movies, like the typewriter Laura fails to master, to signify the modern world in which both Amanda and Laura are out of place. In Comfort's revision, however, film is not a mysterious representative of unstated desires or of the modern world. It is the vehicle for dismantling the narrative that controls both Tom and Laura. While Williams situates Tom and Laura in the ambiance of Amanda's memories of lost gentility, Comfort gives them the opportunity to fantasize scenarios of their own. Williams's narrative conventions are interrogated by Comfort's display of Tom and Laura's vivid fantasy life.

This cross-examination is furthered by the fact that Amanda is played by a man. Dendy's dialogue with the character of Amanda is not disguised with makeup or hairstyle. He wears a dress but all the other marks of his masculinity remain visible. What is normalized about motherhood in Williams's play – nagging, overprotection, the loss of active sexuality – is subtly reconfigured by Dendy. Because he does not attempt any particular kind of stylized transformation of his physical self, Dendy is able to present both the character and his commentary on her. Dendy's Amanda creates an aura not of nostalgia but of urgent action. This action becomes inevitably humorous precisely because Amanda is not aware of the explicit fantasies of Tom and Laura to which the audience is privy. Although Comfort keeps Amanda's fantasies bound by the conventions of southern gentility by conflating her with Scarlet O'Hara, Amanda does hold her own in a wonderfully choreographed physical fight with Tom. Dendy's Amanda uses the full strength of her body when fighting with her son. For a moment this mother is neither retiring nor lost in the past, she quite literally enacts her anger with a physical force that matches her son's. The convention of using southern fragility to mask intense sexuality is repudiated by the prowess of Dendy's well-muscled body.

Film is the medium that unites the contemporary audience with a work whose sensibility is over fifty years old. For it is via the film fragments that Comfort opposes the patriarchal structure of sexuality that oppresses the characters in *The Glass Menagerie*. By depicting the characters' lust with re-enacted segments of film and with choreographed sequences, Comfort gives sexuality a graphic reality denied in Williams's play. This is perhaps most significant for Laura. Williams prefers to leave Laura suspended in her world of glass ornaments whereas Comfort has her literally ripping off her clothes.

Laura's desires are revealed in a manner similar to Tom's. The fantasies that the gentleman caller represents for both Amanda and Laura are impossible to realize. Just before Jim arrives, Comfort segues the narrative to a sequence from *Superman*. Laura and Jim enact a scene in the film in which Superman takes Lois Lane for a little spin in the skies. The sexual innocence of the respectable Lois and the supernice superhero culminates in the dancers balancing on two stools to simulate Superman showing Lois the world from his on-high perspective.

The naiveté of this filmic fantasy is subverted when Jim enters. Laura, who in the text has to be persuaded by her mother to open the door, in Comfort's version takes Jim's hand and rubs it all over her body. Tom's comment that Laura is shy becomes completely ironic. Laura's undisclosed sexual desires are graphically revealed. She and Jim simulate copulation in every conceivable position. Comfort makes explicit what Williams only implies. The tension between the text and the meanings it generates and Comfort's revisionist interludes are not resolved. The critical implications of quoting mass culture go well beyond the recirculation of already known imagery. In *Faith Healing*, mass culture provides a critique of the sexual and social conventions of Williams's work. Comfort's appropriation of mass culture does not simply mean complicity with its values. She successfully exploits the critical opportunities in this endeavor. Comfort's directing and choreography are part of a new body of work that marks an important shift away from a suspicious relationship between high art and mass culture to a recirculation of mass culture by high art and of high art by mass culture. The implications of this move and the kinds of critical perspectives it seems able to generate need further artistic and theoretical consideration.

The disintegration of aesthetic dichotomies and boundaries such as "high" and "low" is part of the dissolution of modernism. Modern western society is/was actually and theoretically based on clear distinctions of class, race, ethnicity, nation, language, and religion. The modern aesthetics in which Croce believes were part of modern culture – the culture of clear-cut differentiation. Modern culture, however, has long been eroding. Jones's and Comfort's work represents a different world view that challenges the categories Croce espouses. This is what makes it so unsettling.

Classical Western aesthetics are based on "seeing," on maintaining enough distance between the object of art and the persons viewing that object. In this distance differentiation takes place. This differentiation separates the various parts of the artwork. Seeing the different roles, knowing that the performers, for example, are only playing at or representing the social realities on stage separates the performer from the character. Aesthetics based on seeing lead to a willing "suspension of disbelief" in which the spectator feels with the characters in a provisional and temporary way. Provisional and temporary because part of suspension of disbelief is the certainty that the performers are pretending.

Jones, however, privileges *experience* over *pretense*. Thus the gap narrows between art and life, and, in turn, perhaps between the stage and the spectators. As that distance diminishes, so too do some of the aesthetic rules that are derived from it. In displaying the real, Jones seems to be insisting on a connection between those on one side of the proscenium with those on the other. The subjectivity of the individual is no longer experienced solely in isolation at the theater. It is part of a larger experience that favors participation over viewing. As Jones blurs these distinctions, the authenticity, intentionality, self-centered subjectivity, and personal identity of both the performers and the spectators are thrown open to re-examination.

BIBLIOGRAPHY

Croce, A. (1994/5) "Discussing the Undiscussable," *The New Yorker* (December 26/January 2): 54–60.
Franko, M. (1995) *Dancing Modernism/Performing Politics*, Bloomington: Indiana University Press.

Gerald, K. (1994) letter to Bill T. Jones (March).

Graff, E. (1995) "Dancing Red: Art and Politics," *Studies in Dance History* V: 1.

Huyssen, A. (1986) *After the Great Divide*, Bloomington: Indiana University Press.

McNamara, B. (1994) foreword in C. Martin, *Dance Marathons: Performing American Culture of the 1920s and 1930s*, Jackson: University of Mississippi Press.

Sontag, S. (1995) letter to the *New York Times* (March 5): 5.

Williams, T. (1945) *The Glass Menagerie*, New York: New Directions Publishing.

Index